THE BORDERS OF PUNISHMENT

The Borders of Punishment

Migration, Citizenship, and Social Exclusion

Edited by

KATJA FRANKO AAS

and

MARY BOSWORTH

OXFORD

UNIVERSITY PRESS

OXFORD

UNIVERSITY PRESS

Great Clarendon Street, Oxford, OX2 6DP,
United Kingdom

Oxford University Press is a department of the University of Oxford.
It furthers the University's objective of excellence in research, scholarship,
and education by publishing worldwide. Oxford is a registered trade mark of
Oxford University Press in the UK and in certain other countries

Published in the United States of America by Oxford University Press
198 Madison Avenue, New York, NY 10016, United States of America

British Library Cataloguing in Publication Data
Data available

Library of Congress Control Number: 2013937833

ISBN 978–0–19–966939–4

KFA: For my grandparents, Vida and Iztok
MB: For my daughters, Ella and Sophia

Preface

Katja Franko Aas and Mary Bosworth[1]

Immigration and its control are highly charged topics in contemporary policy and politics. Over the past two decades they have become subjects of extensive scholarly analysis, primarily in fields such as anthropology, sociology, human geography, refugee studies, and human rights law. It is all the more surprising then, that, with some notable exceptions, criminologists have been relatively slow to pay them much attention. The apparent lack of criminological interest is by no means merited by the size of the phenomena and the intensity of the legal, social, and sociological developments in this area. In the United States, for instance, immigration-related prosecutions outnumber all other federal criminal prosecutions, including drugs and weapons prosecutions, while Immigration and Customs Enforcement is now the largest investigative arm of the US Department of Homeland Security (Stumpf, Chapter 3 in this volume). In Europe, rapidly growing foreign populations represent on average 20 per cent of prison inmates, reaching extraordinary highs in countries such as Switzerland (71.4 per cent), Luxembourg (68.8 per cent), Cyprus (58.9 per cent), Greece (57.1 per cent), and Belgium (44.2 per cent).[2] All states have criminalized at least some aspects of immigration, establishing networks of immigration detention centres and extending their powers to deport.

Under these conditions, traditional distinctions between criminal law and immigration law are eroding. Institutions like the police and the prison, previously bound to the nation state, these days extend well beyond its borders. As more foreigners end up in prison and as states pursue more vigorously additional forms of confinement in immigration detention alongside deportation, the distinct justifications of punishment and administrative penalties blur. The book's title, *The Borders of Punishment*, alludes, on the one hand, to the literal activities of border control, and on the other hand, to punishment in its extended sense, where its borders become blurred and merge with various forms of migration control, deprivation of welfare, and social exclusion. Finally, the overlapping nature of those subject to internal and external border controls and minority communities within host countries, reveal the enduringly racialized nature of citizenship and its protections.

[1] This has been a collaborative venture, not just between the editors but also with the contributors. We would therefore like to thank our contributors, each of whom produced a fascinating account at the conference at the Centre for Criminology in the University of Oxford in April 2012, as well as those who helped us in organizing that event and participated in it (in particular, in Oslo: Per Jørgen Ystehde and Julie E. Stuestøl; in Oxford: Ana Aliverti, Steve Allen, Chris Giacomantonio, Sophie Palmer, and Lea Sitkin). Finally, we would like to thank the European Research Council 2010 and 2012-StG, the British Academy, the University of Oslo, and the Law Faculty and Centre for Criminology at the University of Oxford each of whom provided funding for various aspects of this project.

[2] Source: <http://www.prisonstudies.org/info/worldbrief/>.

Such developments solicit in new ways some of the fundamental and enduring questions of criminal justice and criminology: What is punishment? What is crime? What should be the normative and legal foundation for criminalization, for police suspicion, for the exclusion from the community, and for the deprivation of freedom? How, if at all, does popular punitivism shift in relation to foreign citizens? They also raise questions about methodology. Can we understand the prison today, for instance, simply in terms of life within it, when its effect may be felt many continents away? Do qualitative or quantitative techniques developed with citizens in mind, work when applied to foreigners? How might we capture the similarities between criminal justice and migration control while remaining alert to the specific nature of each field and to the vulnerabilities of non-citizens?

These questions animate this volume. In it we seek, with the assistance of colleagues drawn from across the world, to bring migration and borders to the criminological home front. We believe not only that an understanding of criminal justice is essential to explaining practices such as detention and deportation of foreign citizens, but also that mobility and its control are central to any analysis of the criminal justice system. The purpose of this collection is therefore to sketch out a particular sub-field within criminology and criminal justice, the *criminology of mobility*. We do this, not to put up borders to keep people out, but rather to chart an intellectual space and a theoretical tradition within criminology to house scholars dealing with issues of citizenship, race, ethnicity, and immigration control.

In so doing, we seek to extend traditions of criminological theory concerned with membership, matters of social exclusion, and penal power. With some notable exceptions, theoretical work on punishment and criminal justice has not explicitly questioned the national frame of analysis, leaving the discipline with an implicitly static notion of society at its core. As a result, according to Dario Melossi (Chapter 15 in this volume), even when classical theorists such as Marx addressed issues of migration and mobility, these have not been taken into account in further theoretical analyses of punishment.

Matters of mobility are by no means an historic novelty. They have productively inspired sociological and criminological writings in previous periods, including the writings of the Chicago School, the Birmingham Centre for Cultural Studies, postcolonial criminology, and critical race studies. Nonetheless, the present scale of global movements of people, goods, and capital is introducing new dimensions that are radically transforming the contours of society. These developments, generated by globalization, have brought issues of citizenship to the forefront of numerous political and policy debates. As states reflect on such matters, punishment and the criminal justice system have become increasingly important mechanisms for guarding the gates of membership. The criminology of mobility is therefore a study of the contested and precarious nature of membership in a deeply divided global order, and the practices of policing of its (physical and symbolic) boundaries. As such, it relates to the traditional issues of race, gender, and class, which endure as migration pathways often connect to existing inequalities. For some, these developments raise questions about a developing global apartheid (see Bowling, Chapter 16 in this volume).

The challenge for the criminology of mobility lies in making sense of these continuities while also identifying new manifestations of membership, social solidarity, and belonging. The task is partly an empirical one. We simply have little evidence documenting the experiences and effects of migration control. What is it like to be detained indefinitely? How does it feel to face deportation? What are the challenges that mobility poses for police officers, prison guards, policy makers? However, the criminology of mobility seeks to do more than just fill in the gaps. Significant conceptual work also needs to be done. Many recent developments in migration and criminal justice cannot be fully captured and understood by the vocabulary of the past, nor can they be named and described by criminological and criminal justice concepts alone. Terms of art that have been so productive within criminology, such as legitimacy and (in)justice, alongside work on penality and (human) rights, are called into question in a global frame. What is the relevance of borders (conceptual, empirical, identity) for the 'right to have rights' (Arendt 2004; Benhabib 2004)? Who is the subject of rights within a society and what is the relevance of the relationship between citizenship and criminal justice?

The book may be dipped into or read from cover to cover. Hindpal Singh Bhui's introduction and Ben Bowling's concluding remarks synthesize the volume's main arguments, while raising additional questions and issues for future consideration. The chapters in between are clustered around five central questions, which underpin much of criminal justice thinking and research: criminalization, policing, imprisonment, punishment, and social exclusion. Though seemingly familiar, contributors demonstrate how these traditional topics become transformed, taking on a new guise and adopting novel rationalities and modes of existence under conditions of mass mobility.

In the first section, Katja Franko Aas, Lucia Zedner, Juliet Stumpf, and Catherine Dauvergne explore how migration unsettles the traditional anchoring of justice and criminal law in the nation state and citizenship. Mobility, and its control, they argue, introduces new forms of illegality and criminalization, often undermining due process rights established within the criminal law. The chapters outline the multiple points of intersection between criminal law, immigration, and refugee law, as well as the eroding distinctions between internal and external aspects of sovereignty and between the process and punishment. As the traditional moorings of criminalization in (national) criminal law and membership begin to unsettle, a challenge arises of doing justice to non-citizens and those whose membership status is in question. Such developments, these chapters suggest, though typically overlooked by criminal lawyers and criminal justice scholars, require new frames of analysis.

The second section takes up the issue of policing. In it, Sharon Pickering and Leanne Weber, Darshan Vigneswaran, and Maggy Lee critically assess the transnational scope and nature of contemporary policing practices. While acknowledging the relevance of historically established practices of racial and colonial control, the authors demonstrate the salience of new ideas and rationalities in practices apparently designed to produce immobility in the form of closed borders and fortress continents. Termed by Weber and Pickering as 'transversal' logic, contemporary policing transgresses traditional boundaries separating states, between inside and outside the society, and among various policing and administrative domains. In so doing, the police identify who must be immobilized as well as prevent, or in some cases, force movement across boundaries. As Zygmunt Bauman (1998) and others have pointed out (Aas 2007; Weber and Bowling 2008), in a world otherwise marked by transnationality and the freedom of movement, immobility has become a prime form of social exclusion. Under these conditions, the power of the police has shifted and been amplified.

Immobility remains an important theme in the third section of this volume, which considers the imprisonment and detention of foreign citizens. Here, chapters by Mary Bosworth, Emma Kaufman, and Thomas Ugelvik examine the transformation of the 'traditional' prison as well as the growth of special institutions of detention dedicated to the housing of the growing foreign populations. While resembling familiar institutions of confinement, such places, the authors argue, break with or fail to adhere to many of the key assumptions that justify restricting people's liberty. Foreign citizens, are, in short, held to different standards. In prisons and detention centres, states not only mark out a national identity based on exclusion, but reveal the limits of the liberal political ideal of inclusion.

The fourth section explores the corollary of forced immobility: expulsion. The section starts with the particular in a moving account by David Brotherton and Luis Barrios of the traumatic effects of deportation on a group of women and men sent back to the Dominican Republic. Then, while maintaining a focus on specific nation states—the United Kingdom and Sweden—chapters by Matthew Gibney and Vanessa Barker consider more generally the extent to which the established notions of citizenship, democracy, and belonging are being unsettled and transformed through banishment. Through their increasing reliance on deportation, nation states reinforce and redraw the political and legal boundaries of membership, thus raising, in all its complexity, the perennial question of who belongs in the community.

In the final section on the changing nature of social exclusion, Nicolay Johansen's chapter provides a detailed exploration of mechanisms—such as deprivation of welfare and medical aid—used to encourage failed asylum seekers in Norway to leave 'voluntarily'. While fascinated by the apparent novelty and complexity of the phenomena, the final chapter by Dario Melossi brings to our attention the historic antecedents of these developments as well as the persisting salience of the political economy in their formation.

Conclusion

The criminology of mobility introduces new, substantive topics and sites of research as well as transforming old ones with novel empirical and theoretical considerations. The focus of the discipline shifts, on the one hand, to the literal activities of border control, and, on the other hand, to punishment in its extended sense. The criminology of mobility therefore addresses not only issues pertaining to mobility as such (which may seem to be situated at the outskirts of the social), but rather to those phenomena which are at the heart of contemporary debates about membership and social exclusion in our globalized and increasingly diverse societies. As Honig (2001) points out, foreigners—and the discourses about them—do a particular kind of work in terms of the political constitution of the society. Although generally seen as a threat to social unity and stable identity, foreigners—and the growing punitive regimes to which they are subjected—also serve as a conduit for the articulation of new forms of identity and belonging. This book does not aspire to do justice to the enormity of these topics, yet it is, we believe, a productive step on the way towards their understanding.

Drawing the border to the centre of criminological and penological concerns expands the imaginary of justice (Carlen 2008), by including into the discourse of justice new categories of people as well as some so far overlooked institutional arrangements and geographical locations. This is both a normative and an empirical task, since many of the phenomena in this collection have hitherto neither been adequately described nor named. As a result they have also not been regulated or subjected to scrutiny. At the most basic level, statistics on many of the issues considered in this volume are only inadequately kept. To some extent, the lack of evidence is inevitable. We simply cannot know for certain how many undocumented people are present. On the other hand, however, the government itself at times obscures the topic. In the United Kingdom, for instance, the government rarely publishes details about those held in prison under Immigration Act powers. Details about the make-up of the detained population beyond raw figures are also hard to come by. We know very little, in any country, of what happens to those who are removed or deported.

However, the invisibility pertains not only to the national context but also has global dimensions as it often results from the territorial scope of mobility control beyond the borders of the nation state. Several aspects of mobility control addressed in this volume take place outside respective national territories, or are conducted by non-state agents; for example the extra-territorial policing described by Aas and Weber and Pickering, the suffering of the deportees revealed by Brotherton and Barrios, and the practices of the international NGOs reported by Lee. These are by and large not policies and practices that are publically proposed, debated, democratically agreed, and scrutinized by the (national) media. They are often developed in an ad hoc fashion by individual institutional actors or they may arise through international cooperation. Rather than being delineated by the law, they thrive in its shadow or, what Barker aptly terms, 'no man's lands'. These cross-border activities thus also demand a 'de-bordering of national normative frames' (Sassen 2008: 63) and the formation of novel ethical and legal mechanisms of regulation. An expansion and de-bordering of criminology's analytical and imaginative space— one of the central features of the criminology of mobility—is therefore intrinsically connected with the transcendence of disciplinary boundaries and an expansion of normative and legal spaces. Several chapters, albeit with varying degrees of optimism, refer to human rights and the emerging humanitarian discourses as potential means of empowerment as well as an emerging technique of governance.

We consider this set of essays a first step, along with others, in carving out this new part of our discipline. As governments increasingly develop and apply their powers of exclusion, these issues should concern us all.

References

Aas, K.F. (2007) *Globalization and Crime*. London: Sage.

Arendt, H. (2004) *The Origins of Totalitarianism*. New York: Schocken.

Bauman, Z. (1998) *Globalization: The Human Consequences*. Cambridge: Polity Press.

Benhabib, S. (2004) *The Rights of Others: Aliens, Residents, and Citizens*. Cambridge: Cambridge University Press.

Carlen, P. (2008) *Imaginary Penalities*. Cullompton: Willan.

Honig. B. (2001) *Democracy and the Foreigner*. Princeton and Oxford: Princeton University Press.

Sassen, S. (2008) 'Neither Global nor National: Novel Assemblages of Territory, Authority and Rights', *Ethics and Global Politics* 1(1–2): 61.

Weber, L. and Bowling, B. (2008) 'Valiant Beggars and Global Vagabonds: Select, Eject, Immobilize', *Theoretical Criminology* 12(3): 355.

Contents

List of Contributors

Editors

Katja Franko Aas is Professor of Criminology at the University of Oslo. She has published widely in globalization, borders, security, and surveillance of everyday life. She is the author of *Cosmopolitan Justice and Its Discontents* (co-edited with C. Baillet) (Routledge, 2011), *Technologies of Insecurity* (co-edited with H.M. Lomell and H.O. Gundhus) (Routledge-Cavendish, 2009), *Globalization and Crime* (Sage, 2007), and *Sentencing in the Age of Information: From Faust to Macintosh* (Routledge-Cavendish, 2005). She is currently heading an ERC Starter Grant project 'Crime Control in the Borderlands of Europe'.

Mary Bosworth is Reader in Criminology and Fellow of St Cross College at the University of Oxford and, concurrently, Professor of Criminology at Monash University, Australia. She has published widely on race, gender, and citizenship in prisons and immigration detention. Her books include *What is Criminology?* (co-edited with Carolyn Hoyle) (Oxford University Press, 2011), *Explaining US Imprisonment* (Sage, 2010), *Race, Gender and Punishment* (co-edited with Jeanne Flavin) (Rutgers University Press, 2007), *The US Federal Prison System* (Sage, 2002), and *Engendering Resistance* (Ashgate, 1999). She is currently (2012–2017) heading an ERC Starter Grant project 'Subjectivity, Identity and Penal Power: Incarceration in a Global Age'.

Contributors

Vanessa Barker is Associate Professor of Sociology at Stockholm University. Her research and teaching focus on globalization, border control, comparative penal sanctioning, and ethnicity. She is the author of *The Politics of Imprisonment: How the Democratic Process Shapes the Way America Punishes Offenders* (Oxford University Press, 2009) and has published in *Law and Society Review*, *Theoretical Criminology*, *Punishment and Society*, *Law and Social Inquiry*, and *Criminology and Public Policy*. She is currently working on a comparative analysis of global mobility and penal order.

Luis Barrios is a psychologist and a professor at John Jay College of Criminal Justice and a member of PhD faculties in social/personality psychology, Graduate Center-City University of New York. As an Episcopalian priest, Barrios was a missionary in the Dominican Republic for nine years, and in New York City he has been a leader in the city's Latino communities. In 1997, together with Dr David Brotherton, Barrios co-founded the Street Organization Project, which seeks to create dialogues among youth gang members, academic researchers, and community activists. Barrios co-authored *The Almighty Latin King and Queen Nation: Street Politics and the Transformation of a New York City Gang* (Columbia University Press, 2004) with Brotherton. He also co-edited *Gangs and Society: Alternative Perspectives* (with Louis Kontos and Brotherton) (Columbia University Press, 2003).

Hindpal Singh Bhui is an Inspection Team Leader at HM Inspectorate of Prisons where he heads inspection of the immigration detention estate in the United Kingdom. He has led major thematic reviews on Muslim prisoners (2010), foreign national prisoners (2006, 2007) and the quality and impact of immigration detention casework (2012). He was formerly a community probation officer, a prison-based foreign national specialist, and a visiting criminal justice lecturer. He was editor of the *Probation Journal* from 1997 to 2007. He has published a number of articles and chapters on prisons, probation, race issues, and foreign prisoners and, in 2009, an edited book, *Race and Criminal Justice* (Sage).

Ben Bowling is Professor of Criminology and Criminal Justice at King's College London School of Law where he teaches on LLB, LLM, and MA courses. His books include *Stop and Search: Police Power in Global Context* (with Leanne Weber) (Routledge, 2012), *Global Policing* (with James Sheptycki) (Sage 2012), *Policing the Caribbean: Transnational Security Cooperation in Practice* (Oxford University Press, 2010), *Racism, Crime and Justice* (with Coretta Phillips) (Longman, 2002), and *Violent Racism* (Oxford University Press, 1998).

David C. Brotherton is Professor and Co-Chair of Sociology at John Jay College of Criminal Justice and a member of PhD programmes in Criminal Justice, Sociology, and Urban Education at the Graduate Center, The City University of New York. Dr Brotherton has published widely on street gangs, schooling, immigration, and deportation and was named Critical Criminologist of the Year in 2011 by the American Society of Criminology. His recently co-authored or co-edited books include: *How Do They Got Away With It: White Collar Criminals and the Financial Meltdown* (2012); *Banished to the Homeland: Dominican Deportees and Their Stories of Exile* (2011); *Keeping Out The Other: A Critical Introduction to Immigration Control* (2009); *Globalizing the Streets: Cross-Cultural Perspectives on Youth, Marginalization and Resistance* (2008); and *The Almighty Latin King and Queen Nation: Street Politics and the Transformation of a New York City Gang* (2004), all published by Columbia University Press. Dr Brotherton's current projects include a comparative study of the occupy movements in Europe, the development of holistic policing strategies vis-à-vis gangs and organized crime in the European Union, and deportation as state performance in a theatre of cruelty.

Catherine Dauvergne is Professor of Law at the University of British Columbia. From 2002 to 2012 she held the Canada Research Chair in Migration Law. In October 2012, she was named a Fellow of Canada's Pierre Elliot Trudeau Foundation in recognition of her contributions to critical public issues in Canada. Dauvergne's most successful book to date is *Making People Illegal: What Globalization Means for Migration and Law* (Cambridge University Press, 2008). She has also published three other books, and more than 50 scholarly articles and book chapters over the past 15 years. Dauvergne is a lead investigator for nearly $1 million in research funding. Dauvergne teaches immigration and refugee law and does pro bono legal work in these areas.

Matthew J. Gibney is Reader in Politics and Forced Migration at the University of Oxford, Official Fellow of Linacre College, and Deputy Director of the Refugee Studies Centre. He is a political scientist who has published many scholarly articles and books on issues relating to refugees, migration control, and citizenship from the perspectives of normative theory and comparative politics. His books include, which has been translated into Spanish and Italian, *The Political, Social and Historical Contours of Deportation* (with B. Anderson and E. Paoletti) (Springer, 2013), (with R. Hansen) a three-volume encyclopedia, *Immigration and Asylum: From 1900 to the Present* (ABC-Clio, 2005), and *The Ethics and Politics of Asylum* (Cambridge University Press, 2004), *Globalizing Rights* (Oxford University Press, 2003).

He is currently writing a book on the evolution of expulsion power entitled, *Unmaking Membership: Banishment, Denationalization, and Deportation in the Liberal State.*

Nicolay B. Johansen is a post-doctoral researcher at the Institute of Criminology and Sociology of Law, University of Oslo, Norway. He has published in a variety of criminological areas such as drug addiction, social control, violence, and classical sociology, as well as white-collar crime, urban life, and the foundations of social theory.

Emma Kaufman received her BA from Columbia University and her MPhil and DPhil from the University of Oxford, where she was a Marshall and Clarendon Scholar. She was a Guest Scholar at the University of California, San Diego's Center for Comparative Immigration Studies from 2011 to 2012 and now attends Yale Law School. Emma's doctoral research examined the treatment of foreign national prisoners in the British penal estate. She has published on American immigration imprisonment, gender and punishment, and British prison policy.

Maggy Lee is Associate Professor in the Department of Sociology at the University of Hong Kong and Visiting Fellow in the Department of Sociology at the University of Essex, United Kingdom. She is currently working on research projects on British lifestyle migration in Asia (funded by the ESRC/Hong Kong Research Grants Council) and female transnational migrants in Hong Kong (funded by the Hong Kong Research Grants Council). Her recent publications include *Trafficking and Global Crime Control* (Sage, 2011) and *Human Trafficking* (Willan, 2007).

Dario Melossi is Professor of Criminology in the School of Law of the University of Bologna. After having being conferred a law degree at this university, he went on to do a PhD in Sociology at the University of California, Santa Barbara. He was then Assistant and thereafter Associate Professor at the University of California, Davis, from 1986 to 1993. He has published most recently, *Travels of the Criminal Question: Cultural Embeddedness and Diffusion* (with Maximo Sozzo and Richard Sparks) (2011), *Controlling Crime, Controlling Society: Thinking about Crime in Europe and America* (2008), *The State of Social Control: A Sociological Study of Concepts of State and Social Control in the Making of Democracy* (1990), and *The Prison and the Factory: Origins of the Penitentiary System* (with Massimo Pavarini (1981 [1977]). In 2003 he introduced the new Transaction Edition of Georg Rusche and Otto Kirchheimer, *Punishment and Social Structure* (1939). He is one of the most prominent spokespersons for the so-called 'critical criminology' movement. He is the main editor of *Studi sulla questione criminale*, editor-in-chief of *Punishment and Society*, and member of the board of many other professional journals. His current research concerns the processes of construction of deviance and social control within the European Union, especially with regard to migration.

Sharon Pickering is Professor of Criminology at Monash University in Melbourne Australia. Pickering researches irregular border crossing and has written in the areas of refugees and trafficking with a focus on gender and human rights. She is an Australian Research Council Future Fellow on Border Policing and Director of the Border Crossing Observatory (<http://www.borderobservatory.org>). Her books include *Sex Work: Labour Mobility and Sexual Services* (with Maher and Gerard) (Routledge, 2012); *Borders and Crime* (with McCulloch) (2012); *Globalization and Borders: Deaths at the Global Frontier* (with Weber) (2011); *Gender, Borders and Violence* (Springer, 2011); *Sex Trafficking* (Willan, 2009) (with Segrave and Milivojevic) (Springer, 2011) *Counter-Terrorism Policing* (2008); *Borders, Mobilities and Technologies of Control* (2006) (with Weber); and *Refugees and State Crime* (2005).

Juliet P. Stumpf is Professor of Law at Lewis & Clark Law School in Portland, Oregon. Stumpf's research explores the intersection of immigration law with criminal law, constitutional law, civil rights, and employment law. She seeks to illuminate the study of immigration law with interdisciplinary insights from sociology, psychology, criminology, and political science. Representative publications include 'Getting to Work: Why Nobody Cares about E-Verify (and Why They Should)' (2012) 2 UC Irvine L Rev 381; 'Doing Time: Crimmigration Law and the Perils of Haste' (2011) 58 UCLA L Rev 1705; 'States of Confusion: the Rise of State and Local Power over Immigration' (2008) 86 NCL Rev 1557; and 'The Crimmigration Crisis: Immigrants, Crime, and Sovereign Power' (2006) 56 Am UL Rev 367. Before joining the Lewis & Clark Law School faculty in 2005, Professor Stumpf was on the Lawyering Program faculty at the New York University School of Law. She clerked for the Honorable Richard A. Paez on the Ninth Circuit and served as a Senior Trial Attorney in the Civil Rights Division of the US Justice Department. She practised with the law firm of Morrison and Foerster.

Thomas Ugelvik is a post-doctoral research fellow at the Department of Criminology and Sociology of Law at the University of Oslo. He has published articles on different aspects of everyday life in prison, such as food-related resistance, imprisonment as masculinity challenge, and the narrative 'othering' of fellow prisoners common in prisoner culture. He is series co-editor (with Ben Crewe and Yvonne Jewkes) of the book series *Palgrave Studies on Prisons and Penology*. He is currently doing research on foreign prisoners in Norwegian welfare-oriented prisons, and the relationship between the prison and the immigration detention systems.

Darshan Vigneswaran is an Assistant Professor at the Centre for Urban Studies and Department of Political Science, University of Amsterdam and has held research posts at Oxford University, the Max Planck Institute for Religious and Ethnic Diversity, and the University of the Witwatersrand. He is the author of *Territory, Migration and the Evolution of the International System* (Palgrave, 2013) and co-editor of *Slavery, Migration and Contemporary Bondage in Africa* (Africa World Press, 2013). His research interests include political geography, state territoriality, migration, and urban segregation.

Leanne Weber is a Larkins Senior Research Fellow in the School of Political and Social Inquiry at Monash University, specializing in migration policing. She has studied and worked at the Institute of Criminology in Cambridge and the Human Rights Centre at Essex University; held research contracts at the Centre for Criminological Research at Oxford University; and taught criminology at the University of Western Sydney and the University of New South Wales. She is the co-author, with Sharon Pickering, of *Globalization and Borders: Death at the Global Frontier* (Palgrave, 2011) and the author of *Policing Non-Citizens* (forthcoming from Routledge).

Lucia Zedner is Professor of Criminal Justice in the Faculty of Law, Law Fellow at Corpus Christi College, and a member of the Centre for Criminology, University of Oxford. Since 2007 she has also held the position of Conjoint Professor in the Law Faculty at the University of New South Wales, Sydney, where she is a regular visitor. Her most recent publications include *Principles in Criminal Law and Criminal Justice: Essays in Honour of Andrew Ashworth* (co-edited with Julian Roberts) (Oxford University Press, 2012) and *Prevention and the Limits of the Criminal Law* (co-edited with Andrew Ashworth and Patrick Tomlin) (Oxford University Press, 2013).

List of Abbreviations

AFP	Australian Federal Police
ASEAN	Association of Southeast Asian Nations
AusAID	Australian Government Overseas Aid Programme
BID	Bail for Immigration Detainees
CBP	Customs and Border Protection (US)
DCO	detention custody officer
DFID	Department for International Development
DIAC	Department of Immigration and Citizenship (Australia)
EEA	European Economic Area
EFTA	European Free Trade Association
ERC	European Research Council
ESRC	Economic and Social Research Council
EUROSUR	European Border Surveillance System
FATF	The Financial Action Task Force
HMIP	Her Majesty's Inspectorate of Prisons
ICE	Immigration and Customs Enforcement (US)
ICIBI	Independent Chief Inspector of Borders and Immigration
ICMC	International Catholic Migration Commission
IIRIRA	Illegal Immigration Reform and Immigrant Responsibility Act of 1996 (US)
IOM	International Organisation for Migration
IRC	Immigration removal centre
LPR	legal permanent resident
NAO	National Audit Office
NOMS	National Offender Management Service
RAN	Royal Australian Navy
RGC	Research Grants Council of Hong Kong
SIAC	Special Immigration Appeals Commission
STHF	short-term holding facility
TIP Report	Trafficking in Persons Report (US)
UAV	unmanned aerial vehicle
UKBA	UK Border Agency*
UNESCAP	United Nations Economic and Social Commission for Asia and Pacific
UNESCO	United Nations Educational, Scientific and Cultural Organization
UNHCR	United Nations High Commissioner for Refugees
UNIAP	United Nations Inter-Agency Project in Human Trafficking
UNICEF	United Nations Children's Fund
UNIFEM	United Nations Development Fund for Women
USAID	United States Agency for International Development
VEVO	Visa Entitlement Verification On-line (Australia)

* At the end of March 2013, the British Government announced that the UKBA was to be abolished, returning immigration and enforcement services to the Home Office and the direct control of ministers. Chapters in this collection refer to the UKBA, since they were written before the announcement was made.

Introduction: Humanizing Migration Control and Detention

Hindpal Singh Bhui[1]

The collection of essays in this volume draws together accounts of border control practices around the world. The authors reflect on the nature and effect of attempts to regulate and stem the flow of migrants in a rapidly globalizing world and explore the boundaries of a new sub-field of criminology—the criminology of 'mobility'. In this introduction, I discuss some of the main themes from the chapters that follow. I suggest that greater emphasis on empirical work, particularly migrant and detainee narratives, will generate a more reflexive understanding of the dynamics of migration and border control policies, as well as their human costs.

It may appear difficult to reconcile matters of individuality and agency, or migrant and detainee experiences, with a field of study concerned with globalization and world migratory trends. However, the scope of this field is precisely what makes the human experience at its centre so important. The academic literature on mobility and its control has made considerable advances in a short space of time, but it remains highly theoretical and has not connected with policy and practice in the same way as, for example, the increasingly influential 'desistance' literature in the broader criminal justice field (Maruna 2001; McNeill 2006; McNeill and Weaver 2010). The latter has led to a greater emphasis in both academic discourse and criminal justice practice on the importance of 'lived experience'. It has been particularly effective in developing understanding of behaviour and opening up new directions for research. Similar engagement with migrant and detainee experiences, and with border control and detention staff, can moderate the often theoretically complex debates that dominate the criminology of mobility, and make them more meaningful to policy makers. The valuable group of essays in this collection initiates an important conversation, revealing how much more needs to be done in this respect.

Drawing on first-hand accounts, mainly on data derived from inspections of immigration detention centres in the United Kingdom, I develop three themes that

---

[1] This essay is written in a personal capacity and does not necessarily represent the views of HM Chief Inspector of Prisons. I am grateful to Mary Bosworth, Keith Davies, Finola Farrant, Paul Iganski, and David Smith for their comments on an earlier draft.

emerge from this volume: first, the various mechanisms for objectifying migrants and detainees that make the belligerent pursuit of narrow national interest more palatable; second, the brittle legal status afforded to detainees that allows their sense of worth to be undermined, particularly through criminalization alongside a lack of the protections that apply in criminal law; and, third, the importance, despite these realities, of identifying the agency possessed by migrants and detainees, and resisting the temptation to see them as a homogenous block, rather than people with diverse characteristics, needs, and experiences. In so doing, I hope to balance what can too easily become a stultifying and polarizing 'migrant as victim' thesis and bridge the gap between governmental policies and an often severe academic critique that fails to articulate alternatives to the security-dominated response to border management.

Both tasks are critical. It is unsustainable for migration control strategies to remain mired in the narrow security-focused approach documented by many contributions to this volume. Richer countries cannot detain and deport their way out of world migratory trends driven by inequality. Nor can they avoid the fact that current approaches are having some unanticipated and invidious consequences, potentially including the growth of organized transnational crime (Griffin 2009). There is, in short, a need for a more imaginative approach to managing mobility, a theme to which I shall later return.

Objectification in Action

Migrants and asylum seekers are often conflated in the media, in political debate, and in populist rhetoric, with terrorists, criminals, those who are not to be trusted ('bogus'), or the socially unworthy, who place a burden on public services. Such accounts often carry unsubtle racist undertones (Malloch and Stanley 2005; Rudiger 2007; Cooper 2009). In the United States, Cisneros (2008) argues that visual images of immigrants appear as 'pollutants' in news media, collecting like piles of dangerous 'toxic waste' rolling towards the frightened US citizen. Such imagery combines notions of threat with the undeserving irrelevance of Zygmunt Bauman's (2004) 'waste products' of globalization, effectively dehumanizing whole swathes of the community. Andriani Fili's (2013) work on immigration detention in Greece reveals an extreme example of the consequences of such processes. In a space designed for nine people, Athens airport detention centre holds as many as 120 individuals for months at a time. These people are locked in the cells all day, allowed out only to use the toilet. 'At times even this "trip" to the toilet is not allowed due to severe overcrowding or staff inaction', she writes. 'As detention officers put it: "We are not their servants here. They cannot go to the toilet whenever they want. They are too many, so we will take them only when we can"' (Fili 2013: 37).

Inside the cells:

When it is crowded ... the men cannot all lie down and sleep at the same time. ... The effect of absolute control is not lost on the male detainees: 'we are buried alive here. This is like a mass grave ... but we are not animals, we are humans and we have human rights, no?' (Fili 2013: 37)

In Fili's account, detention officers appear to have lost any sense of empathy with detainees, objectifying them beyond recognition. Human Rights Watch (2000) has documented a similar process in Japan, where the vulnerability and abuses experienced by trafficking victims are ignored in the decision to remove them from the country. A Japanese commentator has described detainees as being treated like 'living packages' waiting to be delivered abroad and, in the eyes of the Japanese system, 'not yet human beings'.[2]

These may be extreme examples, but they are not entirely unfamiliar in the United Kingdom. Emma Kaufman examines in Chapter 9 in this volume the reaction, bordering on political panic, to the releases in 2006 of over 1,000 foreign nationals from UK prisons before they were considered for deportation. The lurid media reporting, public angst, and political opportunism that accompanied these events articulated a latent xenophobia otherwise officially illegitimate in tolerant neo-liberal societies. Foreign national prisoners, hitherto considered relatively vulnerable, were recast as a major threat, despite the absence of any evidence that they were any more dangerous than British prisoners (Bhui 2007). The sense of fear and panic even led in some cases to the unlawful detention of British citizens who happened to have been born abroad (HMIP 2007; LDSG 2010).

In one case, a Jamaican man detained after the deportation crisis complained that 'they [ie the government] are generalising all foreign nationals, not treating them as individuals' (HMIP 2007: 16). He had lived in the United Kingdom since childhood, had a history of mental health problems, and had previously been released into the community after serving a sentence for his only offence, importation of drugs. He had a job, was complying fully with both his parole licence and immigration reporting conditions, and had kept health services appointments. His mother suffered from a serious physical illness and his brother was also mentally ill. Despite this, after more than 18 months in the community, he was abruptly returned to prison in 2006. Both prison and probation staff were very concerned about him, rightly as it turns out since he narrowly survived two serious suicide attempts just after his recall to prison. None of his personal circumstances were taken into account in the decision to recall him to prison.

Front line detention staff cannot escape making basic human connections with the people in their care. In contrast, immigration caseworkers, who are relatively junior government officials, generally do not meet the detainees about whom they are making far-reaching decisions. Within the UK's immigration control agencies, it is harder and there is less motivation to see detainees as individuals.

The notion of an overriding group threat has been further reinforced recently by the creation of a new UK Border Force with 'a separate operational command, with

---

[2] Personal communication from Koichi Kodama, a Japanese lawyer and expert on refugee issues, representing the family of a Ghanaian detainee who died during a forced removal. See also <http://www.japantimes.co.jp/text/nn20120228i1.html>.

its own ethos of law enforcement'.[3] It came into being after another political scandal, this time concerning the relaxing of some passport controls to ease long queues, an event that led to a public row between the Home Secretary and the senior civil servant in charge of border controls[4] (Vine 2012). The message conveyed about this event was that there had been a failure to protect the United Kingdom against uncertain risks posed by potentially dangerous foreign nationals. Together, this example and the earlier deportation crisis capture the process described by a number of authors (including Wacquant 1999 and Palidda 2009), in which attempts to enhance state security, including border security and in-group national identity, buttress the notion of 'enemy immigrants' against whom extreme measures become legitimate.

In the United States matters appear to be worse. According to Kil, Menjivar, and Doty (2009) the militarized US/Mexico border has created an environment in which violence has become a legitimate response to undocumented migration. The border is policed not only by state-sanctioned personnel but also by private citizens. This combination of patriotism, vigilantism, and racism amplifies security concerns and suppresses the humanity of those crossing the border clandestinely.[5] The illegal migrant becomes primarily the embodiment of a threat, one that helps to legitimate what in other circumstances would be considered a disproportionate response.

In Europe, the use of technology in border control increasingly associates migration control with the language and hardware of warfare. For example, the European Border Surveillance System (EUROSUR) could involve unmanned air vehicles (UAVs), resonating uncomfortably with the US government's use of unmanned 'drones' in the Afghanistan conflict in particular. This has resulted in an uncertain but probably high number of 'innocents' killed. The United States has itself deployed surveillance drones on the Mexico border since 2011.[6] It is not that any symbolic threshold has been crossed—detention of migrants has until recently taken place mainly during wartime (Wilsher 2012), some borders are already heavily militarized, and the notion of 'Fortress Europe' has been around for a while (Geddes 2000). However, such policies reveal most starkly the tendency to draw migration control discourse closer to the blunt notion of a war on (predominantly) non-white migrants (*people*) rather than the *act* of illegal entry.[7]

---

[3] Home Secretary's statement to the House of Commons, *Hansard*, col 623 (20 February 2012).

[4] See <http://www.guardian.co.uk/uk/2012/mar/16/brodie-clark-border-agency-dispute>.

[5] The 'minutemen' vigilante group was formed in 2005 to patrol the border, and though now officially disbanded, has had loosely affiliated offshoots 'guarding' the border ever since, sometimes with lethal results: see <http://www.dailymail.co.uk/news/article-2127586/Two-killed-men-camouflage-open-truck-suspected-carrying-illegal-immigrants-Arizona.html>.

[6] See, for example, <http://articles.washingtonpost.com/2011-12-21/world/35285176_1_drone-caucus-predator-drone-domestic-drones>.

[7] See also Krasmann's (2007) detailed discussion of Jakobs' concept of 'enemy penology', in which she quotes him as follows: 'Enemies are currently non-persons. To put it bluntly, enemy penology is thus warfare, whether it stays on the leash or is let loose totally' (Jakobs, 2000: 53, in Krasmann 2007: 303).

On a more mundane level, the consequences of UK border control and deportation crises, and the associated dehumanization, are evident in the lack of attention given to individual circumstances in decision-making. In one case a man who had been in detention for 18 months at the time he was interviewed, had a British partner and child. He was increasingly worried and feeling guilty about his child's deteriorating behaviour during his lengthy absence. A review of detention, which should have assessed all relevant personal factors, including family ties, noted simply that 'there is no evidence of close ties with the UK' (HMIP and ICIBI 2012: 26). In Chapter 8 of this volume, Mary Bosworth also shows how women seeking protection may be held to expectations that overlook their experiences of gendered violence. She quotes a Ugandan woman who was reportedly told that she was to be removed because she did not have strong ties to the United Kingdom, was not married, and had no children: 'there are some things I cannot do because of what happened to me.' The suggestion is that she was penalized by the system for being a woman who was subject to sexual violence.

The simple formulation of detention as a tool to achieve deportation hides a multitude of other, less overt functions and meanings of detention, which find expression in the way that immigration control operates, and emerge piecemeal from analysis of official approaches. For example, the UK Border Agency (UKBA) has been especially criticized for failing to take account of the human impact of detainee transfers, seeing foreign nationals as objects about whom decisions—who is to be detained, for how long, and where—are made at a distance (HMIP 2011, 2012; Wilsher 2012). In Chapter 9 of this volume, Kaufman reflects this point when she describes the relocation of foreign nationals to 'hub and spoke' prisons regardless of family or other ties. Another recurring issue is that detainees can be moved frequently around the United Kingdom between detention centres hundreds of miles apart, often in the middle of the night. These moves are for administrative convenience, filling detention spaces and making best use of escort vehicle capacity, with little regard to the emotional and practical impact on detainees who may be moved far away from legal and family support. Exhaustion and disorientation are common outcomes (HMIP 2008, 2010, 2011). Musinguzi (2013: 5) sums up the impact of this practice well:

One of the worst things I experienced … Imagine having to move house every three months and on occasions every other month, and having to almost instantaneously integrate within a new community.

He goes on to describe being moved from London to Scotland and back again within 24 hours, before being told he was about to go to an airport detention room:

I thought it was a bit odd to be driven 12 hours to be issued RDs [removal directions] and then returned to the same centre the next day … I think there are convenient administrative procedures in the systems that are attractive to Border Agency staff but cause absolute untold misery to detainees.

Racialization of Immigration

There is considerable scope for the mobility literature to engage more effectively with racism, a concept that connects strongly with objectification and distancing (see Ben Bowling's concluding Chapter 16 in this volume; also Bosworth, Bowling, and Lee 2007; Bosworth and Kellezi 2013). Debates around the criminality and imprisonment of black people are, to an extent and with some important differences, replicated in the discussion of foreign nationals and crime (Bowling and Philips 2002; Bosworth, Bowling, and Lee 2007; Cooper 2009). Criminological debates since the 1970s and 1980s have explored whether the high rates of recorded crime and imprisonment amongst black people are a result of 'black criminality' or unfair treatment by the criminal justice system. Much of the immigration debate in the United Kingdom has similarly mixed up refugee and asylum issues with criminality and, more perniciously, with terrorism. The United States provides what is perhaps the most extreme example of enthusiasm for racialized detention, which has now 'turned with renewed vigour toward immigrants' (García Hernández 2012: 364). Meanwhile, taking a cross-European perspective, Wacquant (1999: 219) argues that the media and politicians have been 'eager to surf the xenophobic wave that has been sweeping across Europe since the neoliberal turn of the 1980s', and there seems to have been some displacement of racist attitudes to target these groups.

This point is developed by Matthew Gibney in Chapter 12 of this volume, where he discusses how membership status in the United Kingdom has been gradually manipulated in relation to non-white Commonwealth citizens, who have gone from being virtually undeportable to the most likely to be removed from the United Kingdom. Gibney makes a convincing case that immigration legislation is racially driven, a point that was reinforced by the influential 'Parekh Report' into the future of multi-ethnic Britain (2000). Parekh argued that the effect of much immigration legislation was to reinforce in the national psyche the superiority of white people over others, because it applied primarily to non-whites. While the debate about racism based on lines of colour has been usefully complicated in the UK context by Eastern European migration in particular (Smith 2009), the felt distinction between white and non-white foreign nationals is apparent in detainee accounts:

White people are all treated better; if you are white you are recognised as Europeans—so share the culture of officers. (HMIP 2006: 11)

I have been called a dirty foreigner by inmates, and I have observed racist comments to black prisoners. You get treated better as a white foreign national than a black person. (HMIP 2006: 10)

The link between visible difference and immigration enforcement is also illustrated by the persistence of both covert and, in some cases, explicit racial profiling in the policing of immigration law. In Germany, for example, suspected illegal immigrants are targeted on the basis of their racial appearance (Vogel et al 2009; Sitkin 2013), something that may happen in other countries but is not a legitimate policy.

Vogel et al (2009) argue that, as a result, migrants, especially those who are undocumented, are likely to avoid all contact with the German police, even if they are victims or witnesses.

Legal Status, Vulnerability, and Criminalization

A recurrent theme in this volume is how immigration control takes on the language and, in many respects, the spirit of crime control. Such a view, as Dario Melossi points out, overlooks the fact that 'the connection to be established is between deviant behaviour and the condition of lack of documents, not some kind of "personal quality" of undocumented foreigners'. A number of authors argue that the protections of criminal process would improve the legal status of migrants (see in particular the chapters by Barker, Dauvergne, Stumpf, and Zedner, Chapters 13, 4, 3, and 2 respectively in this volume). Lucia Zedner suggests that the centrality of citizenship to the criminal law and punishment 'poses intractable problems for those whose citizenship status is absent'. It is possible, she says, to posit a separate and less favourable criminal law for 'enemies'. Her chapter highlights how, in criminal law, an offence is a wrong against the polity as a whole, not just against the individual victim; this perspective is predicated on certain common values and a shared identity and sense of belonging, to which non-citizens can lay lesser claim.

Zedner also proposes that the core principles of criminal law are often compromised by immigration offences, many of which fail to satisfy the basic requirements of Mill's (1859) harm principle. The incomprehension of detainees of what they may have done to deserve what they see as a severe punishment is a common finding. The following quotations are from detainees in the United Kingdom and Australia respectively:

What sort of law is this? You get 3 month sentence and end up in prison for 3 years.

[I] ran from a war situation and now in a prison. [I] feel confused and disappointed.[8]

It was detention … it was like a prison, only there were men, women and children, all together … instead of being criminals, many of the people in there were the victims … we should not have been there. (Zurek 2004: 37)

Immigration detention is not meant to be punitive. Yet, as Bosworth points out in Chapter 8 of this volume, detainees repeatedly describe it in such terms, finding it equivalent to or worse than imprisonment, with its indefinite nature causing particular anxiety. The impact on detainees with mental health problems can be particularly severe:

My mother was murdered … I find a confined environment is stressful. … I was in prison back in Africa due to my student activities. I feel morbid, depressed … When I get attacks and hallucinations, I can't make out what is real and what isn't. The more I keep it in, the worse it gets. I suffer from violent panic attacks … You become paranoid that the authorities

---

[8] Unpublished quote from research conducted for HMIP and Independent Chief Inspector of Borders and Immigration (ICIBI) (2012).

will harm me ... I sometimes feel that I want to harm myself. ... Sometimes I don't have anyone to speak to ... I can't control my emotions.[9]

The man quoted above, a Kenyan national, was detained for nearly a year following a one-month prison sentence. During that time he was assessed as mentally ill, suffering post-traumatic stress disorder. A psychiatrist and psychologist made repeated recommendations to the UKBA that he should be released to engage with treatment in the community. At one point the psychiatrist wrote that 'he now presents a real risk to his life. Because of his previous traumatic experiences in custody the detention appears particularly harmful to him' (HMIP and ICIBI 2012: 27). Perversely, a letter from UKBA officials to his solicitor used the fact that he had been seen by mental health professionals as a justification for further detention:

With regard to the Doctor's opinions stating your client is not fit for detention and is suicidal ... has been seeing [a] Psychotherapist and. ... a consultant psychiatrist on a regular basis.[10]

A subsequent detention review made no reference at all to the views of the psychiatrist and psychotherapist, and the man was eventually deported. His case is particularly disturbing in the context of four recent judgments against the UKBA establishing that mentally ill people were subject to inhuman and degrading treatment under Article 3 of the European Convention on Human Rights and unlawfully detained.[11] There was little evidence in these cases of the effectiveness of the systems that are supposed to safeguard such vulnerable detainees.

In Chapter 3 of this volume, Juliet Stumpf illustrates the dangers of the lack of due process and the breakdown of protection that comes with placing immigration and criminal law on the same continuum. 'The process', she argues, 'is punishment'. Although her work is conducted in the United States, a similar view emerges in the United Kingdom, where, for example, detainees should receive monthly updates on their cases. Usually, the UKBA complies with this regulation. However, 'updates' routinely provide no new information at all, even though the reasonable assumption (both legal and ethical) in each case of detention should be that officials have actively been working to progress cases. Rather, as one detainee reported to HMIP about his monthly update, 'It repeats the same information, that removal is imminent. They've said that for the last two years'.[12] Worse, the 'updates' may provide information that cannot be understood by detainees, even those who speak English:

I read them because I can understand them but when they start using sections of immigration acts I get lost. They are not in layman's terms. They can be detrimental to my case but I don't understand them. (HMIP and ICIBI 2012: 24)

---

[9] Extended version of quotation summarized in HMIP and ICIBI 2012: 27.

[10] Unpublished quotation from HMIP and ICIBI 2012 relating to case study on pp 27–28.

[11] See HMIP and ICIBI 2012: 13–14, for links to all cases.

[12] Unpublished quotation taken from research done in the course of the thematic review of detention casework undertaken by HMIP and ICIBI (2012).

The punitive nature of the process can also be discerned in how the UKBA sometimes deals with 'non compliance'.[13] If a detainee is thought to be non-compliant with the re-documentation process, a stand-off can develop, where detention is extended, seemingly in the hope that the detainee will relent and provide correct information. In fact, section 35 of the Asylum and Immigration (Treatment of Claimants) Act 2004 allows prosecution of those who fail to comply with the re-documentation process, and a punishment of up to two years in prison and/or a fine. Yet, in the financial year 2009/2010, only six people were charged in England and Wales, all of whom were convicted and imprisoned.[14] In the following year (2010/2011) only eight were found guilty.[15] Prosecution places the burden of proof on the UKBA, which has to prove beyond reasonable doubt that the detainee is not cooperating, and allows disputed cases to be scrutinized by an independent judge. The fact that one-third of appeals against deportation by ex foreign national prisoners are won, mostly on human rights grounds (Vine 2011), suggests that the reticence of the UKBA to take 'non-compliant' detainees to court may be due in large part to a lack of confidence in the strength of decision making.

'Protections' that increase vulnerability

Both Maggy Lee and Nico Johansen, drawing on the work of William Walters (2011), consider in Chapters 7 and 14 respectively the development of a 'humanitarian industry' to manage borders. Both show how such humanitarian intervention can add to victimization of the weakest and poorest. Lee discusses how border management has been strengthened (to some degree unwittingly) through international programmes and actors who are 'in the process, becoming "active subjects" in the contemporary (re)making of borders'. She questions whether the NGOs claiming to help deal with trafficking are effective, noting their sometimes ambiguous relationships with the state. What may seem a secure border to police and NGOs may in fact be a 'space of insecurity' for poorer girls and women, and encourage criminalization and further securitization.

Sharon Pickering and Leanne Weber in Chapter 5 make a related point in their discussion of how the increased involvement of the Australian Federal Police in 'deterring and disrupting' asylum seekers arriving by boat has given the police a more ideological, politicized role. It has had other perverse effects such as creating a

[13] Wilsher (2012: 350) notes the difficulty of defining non-compliance: 'The very concept of "non-compliance" is fraught with uncertainty. There have been successful challenges to such executive assessments in the United States and the United Kingdom. ... Criminal prosecution is preferable because it puts the burden on governments to justify their non-compliance claims before independent forensic examination.'

[14] UKBA response to a freedom of information request from the Northern Refugee Centre dated 3 July 2010. Bail for Immigration Detainee's Travel Document Project's 'Briefing on Co-operation & Removability', February 2012.

[15] Ministry of Justice, Justice Statistics Analytical Services response to a freedom of information request from Bail for Immigration Detainees (BID) November 2011. BID Travel Document Project's 'Briefing on Co-operation & Removability', February 2012.

'symbiotic relationship' between people-smugglers and the police: they argue that the construction of people-smuggling as a criminal and policing problem has diverted attention from considering why people were arriving in Australia to claim asylum and simplified the debate. It has also led to a succession of moves and counter moves by the smugglers and police, while the risks for the victims of smugglers continue to increase. Again, the human impact of policy is relegated in the process. The authors argue that the lived realities of people at the heart of border policing can help 'to mount a sustained critique of the trafficking-as-immigration crime control discourse'.

Exclusion and risk of reoffending

In Chapter 10 Thomas Ugelvik describes how the Norwegian prison service has created separate wings in which to keep foreign prisoners because it is assumed that they will be deported and will not need the range of welfare-oriented services that are otherwise an integral part of imprisonment. A similar trend can be observed in the United Kingdom where, since 2006, a small number of foreign national prisons have existed.[16] They lack a clear strategy or guidance on their mission (HMIP 2012c, 2012d) as a result mainly of the (false) assumption that all foreign nationals will be deported. Although all prisoners are told that they are held in these specialist prisons to speed up their deportation, up to one-third are returned to the community directly from prison, and further substantial but uncertain numbers are released after being transferred to detention centres (HMIP 2012c, 2012d).

For all its faults and contradictions (see Zedner in Chapter 2) the UK's legal framework does not easily allow a desire to exclude to become exclusion. Nonetheless, the underlying assumption that all will be deported creates a damaging narrative, with practical and psychological consequences. Inspected foreign national prisons in the United Kingdom had no accredited programmes to address offending behaviour, and joint prison and probation systems designed to reduce the risk of offending and support prisoners through to release were effectively unavailable. Even if there was very little chance of them being removed from the country, foreign nationals had more limited access to normal avenues of sentence progression and preparation for life outside, such as temporary release (HMIP 2012c, 2012d). Setting aside the fact that many were actually released into the United Kingdom, to remove people, some potentially dangerous, without doing anything to address their offending behaviour is unethical and irresponsible. In a global world, such an approach also makes little sense.

For non-citizens, Zedner points out that reintegration is not considered much of a possibility. She notes the tendency toward social exclusion of non-citizens, who, if

---

[16] The prisons are HMP Canterbury and HMP Bullwood Hall. As of early 2012, a third, larger prison, HMP Huntercombe, also became a foreign national prison. In January 2013, it was announced that Canterbury and Bullwood Hall were to be closed.

they are undocumented or irregular, 'are quickly categorized as objects of distrust by the state, all the more profound because, as outsiders, they *owe no loyalty* to the polity' (emphasis added). With its strict delineation between citizens and non-citizens, such an approach denies the reality of the broader community in which, for example, the non-citizen group includes people who have lived in their country of residence since early childhood, been educated and worked there, paid taxes, and developed deep-rooted political allegiance and social attachments with citizens. That the actual differences in values and outlook of non-citizens as compared to citizens may be slight is not a great revelation, but the dissonance and confusion that can be created for unwanted non-citizens who believe themselves to be a part of the community, with attendant rights, can be considerable, especially when they have absorbed a positive self-portrayal of criminal justice (Winder 2004). As the following detainees put it:

if I commit a crime then, fair enough, I'll take my punishment cause I do something wrong, but I didn't commit a crime and I've been locked up for 21 months for no reason. (GDWG 2012: 10)

The UK has a reputation for compassion for refugees. I see no reason to be put in prison living with criminals. I am not a criminal I've done nothing wrong. (Amnesty International 2005: 30)

Not 'Bare Lives'—Agency, Resistance, and Diversity

A theoretical approach that fails sufficiently to incorporate human experience or to connect with the kind of lived experience outlined above can lead to flawed understanding and undermine progress. There are also dangers in becoming so immersed in the evidence of objectification and systematic disempowerment of migrants and detainees that a damaging parallel process of objectification occurs. Recognizing and engaging with evidence of agency, even among migrants in detention, can help to present a more balanced picture. The alternative is a one-sided and simplistic 'migrant as victim' thesis that is inaccurate, rejects individuality, and does little to persuade governments of the need for change.

When applied to foreigners in detention, Giorgio Agamben's (1998, 2005) much-cited notion of 'bare life' describes a political state, but suggests an empty monochrome existence characterized by misery, lack of self-determination, and irrelevance. In Agamben's formulation, detainees are without rights and have relevance to the system of justice only in so far as it relates to the process of exclusion. The notion of 'bare life' has genuine explanatory power, but the dramatic nature of the insights it offers is perhaps too seductive (see Johansen's Chapter 14). 'Homo sacer' is a vivid way to conceptualize the unwanted foreigner and is appealing precisely because it expresses so strongly the human illegitimacy imposed on the individual in detention. However, such abject pessimism oversimplifies people's experiences, undermining the critical utility of the concept.

Johansen provides a detailed critique of 'homo sacer' in order to refute the notion that rejected asylum seekers are 'abandoned'. He argues that they are rather excluded *into* the 'funnel of expulsion', albeit that they are 'made into objects' amenable to this particular form of governance. His paper encourages a more accurate and respectful view of people who are frequently disempowered, distressed, and victimized, but rarely helpless. There can be joy as well as distress in the deportation experience, and some deportees may be happy to leave (HMIP 2012b). Detainees may also experience a kind of deferred power, a strength of purpose and identity that emanates from the clarificatory and defining experiences of incarceration. On his release, Kizza Musinguzi (2013: 6) describes a determined attempt to obtain a stake in the society of which he was now a more accepted part, though still without permanent status. What he describes is essentially a rejection of the mentality that the dramatic conceptual lines of homo sacer can induce:

The next day after my release I registered on the electoral register and have voted in every election ever since. A legacy law that allows Commonwealth citizens to exercise their right to vote in local elections in the UK enabled me to. Just imagine if every Commonwealth asylum seeker exercised this right?

This is not a man without power or identity, a helpless victim of an unequal and dangerous world. Ellermann (2009) also stresses agency in her discussion of migrants who destroy their identity documents to evade state control, what she calls the 'reverse state of exception'. She questions Agamben's premise that legal status is the basis for individual rights, and considers how illegal migrants may resist expulsion and reject legal identity by destroying their identity documents. This demonstrates not only agency but also the dilemma for states attempting legitimately to manage migration.[17]

On the basis of research that involved a degree of immersion into the life of immigration detention centres, in Chapter 8 Bosworth also takes a more complex view of detention. While the emotional and physical brutality of detention is strongly reflected in her work, she finds that detention centres are 'marked by resistance and creativity', and implies that they are places where real lives are lived out in all their messy complexity, including moments of power and agency. This approach takes the detention centre's occupants from categories to individuals. The opposite mindset can unwittingly reinforce the objectification of detainees.

In this spirit, it is useful to note the diversity in the detained population. Foreign nationals in detention centres have much in common and feel considerable solidarity with each other—as evidenced by the remarkably high level of cooperation and harmony that is reported in UK detention inspection reports.[18] The picture is similar among foreign national prisons (Bhui 2004). However, while there is a certain camaraderie developed from shared experience and stress, this should not obscure what Bosworth refers to as the 'hyper-diversity' of immigration detention centres (see also Bosworth and Kellezi 2013). Use of broad categories when

---

[17] Few people argue that uncontrolled migration is currently a realistic short-term option given the probable severe socio-economic and environmental consequences.

[18] See <http://www.justice.gov.uk/publications/inspectorate-reports/hmi-prisons/immigration-removal-centres>.

discussing people's lives can mask the views of those subsumed under the broad umbrella classifications, leading to misleading assumptions about 'hidden' populations (Garland, Spalek, and Chakraborti 2006). There is no single foreign detainee experience any more than there is a 'black' or 'female' experience, and foreign prisoners in England and Wales currently come from 170 countries, with the vast array of cultures that entails.

A thematic review of foreign prisoners in England and Wales (HMIP 2006)[19] identified a range of common problems and needs that justify attention to foreign nationals as a distinct category while also demonstrating the importance of developing a more sophisticated understanding of the multiple factors that impacted on their experiences. Different forms of prejudice and discrimination emanated from static and dynamic characteristics such as skin colour, nationality, language skills, and residency, to define the prison experience for foreign nationals, and in many cases to intensify negative experiences. For example, foreign nationals who were also black tended to report a broader range of negative experiences of imprisonment than white foreign nationals. Similarly, Muslim foreign nationals were more negative than non-Muslim foreign nationals, and residency outside of the United Kingdom emerged as the single most influential predictor of problems. UK-resident foreign nationals were almost three times more likely to have English as a main language (40 per cent as opposed to 15 per cent), which appeared to act as a protective factor. Some felt that Europeans were treated better than non-Europeans, 'Third world country versus rich European country, your treatment is different. Seen as economic migrants' (HMIP 2006: 11). Meanwhile, women were particularly likely to report difficulties with family contact, reflecting the greater likelihood of their being the primary carers for children. There is then a need to reflect this diversity in future research, for example through drawing on the concept of intersectionality (Crenshaw 1989). Farrant (2009) usefully does this to analyse the ways in which gender, race, class, nationality, and other forms of identity, in different contexts, can help to understand the multi-faceted experiences of foreign national women in prison.

Conclusion—A More Positive Vision

In this introduction, I have suggested that research and policy around border control and detention reveal contradictions between the inevitability of migration and the distress of migrants on the one hand, and the effectiveness of official responses on the other. States and state actors manage this dissonance through a process of administrative, physical, and emotional distancing in a context of weak legal safeguards. I have selected some themes and ideas from the chapters that follow to illustrate how the discussions of theory, politics, and history connect to the lived experience of people subject to detention in particular. My assumption is

[19] The review was based on research in 10 prisons and data from 6,000 prisoner questionnaires.

that the reductionist and distancing approach regularly applied to foreign nationals crossing borders can be addressed through counter-narrative and a promotion of the voices and experiences of migrants and detainees themselves.

This is not a theory without supporting evidence in the UK context: the changing approach to child detention in the United Kingdom reflects what can happen when the human impact of detention is brought home to governments and its legitimacy is questioned as a result. The practice of detaining families had been described by the British deputy prime minister as a 'moral outrage' and followed a long campaign to end child detention, which provided plenty of evidence over a long period of the distress experienced by children (BID 2011; Bhui 2013). The government did not abandon the policy of child detention altogether, but established an 'exceptional' new children's centre (HMIP 2012a) with an open and non-institutional design. A children's charity plays a central role in running the facility, and, crucially, families can be held for no more than a week, undermining the previous assumption in the United Kingdom that for immigration control to be effective it must include the possibility of indefinite detention. These are significant reforms that demonstrate how the damage to individuals caused by migration control processes can be mitigated if the will is there. These changes should also force an official articulation of the essential moral difference between administrative detention of children and adults, given that there is at least as much evidence of distress and the negative impact of current approaches to detention on adults (HMIP and ICIBI 2012), and no real evidence that indefinite detention leads to better immigration control.

Fear of migration and migrants lies at the root of many of the negative trends highlighted in this book. One way forward is to create a more hopeful narrative, predicated on the value of individual liberty and human worth, such as that outlined by Casey (2010), who argues that open borders should be a long-term policy aspiration even if they are hard to achieve in the short term. This would constitute a considerable paradigm shift and would require abandoning immigration as an 'electoral bully pulpit' (Casey 2010: 43). As spending on border control has had a minimal impact on irregular migration rates, he argues that ultimately the '"decriminalisation" of immigration is the only answer to irregular immigration' (Casey 2010: 43). Such a view implies a conceptual shift away from the bonds between citizens and nation states and towards a more complex view of responsibilities between interdependent states, and between citizens and the international community of citizens—a very different and reinterpreted form of social contract.

References

Agamben, G. (2005) *State of Exception*. Chicago: University of Chicago Press.

Agamben, G (1998) *Homo Sacer: Sovereign Power and Bare Life*. Stanford, California: Stanford University Press.

Amnesty International (2005) *Seeking Asylum is Not a Crime: Detention of People Who Have Sought Asylum*. London: Amnesty International.

Bail for Immigration Detainees (BID) (2011) *Last Resort of First Resort? Immigration Detention of Children in the UK*. London: BID.

Bauman, Z. (2004) *Wasted Lives: Modernity and Its Outcasts*. Cambridge: Polity Press.

Bhui, H.S. (2013) 'The Changing Approach to Child Detention and Its Implications for Immigration Detention in the UK', *Prison Service Journal* 205.

Bhui, H.S. (2007) 'Alien Experience: Foreign National Prisoners after the Deportation Crisis', *Probation Journal: The Journal of Community and Criminal Justice* 54(4): 368.

Bhui, H.S. (2004) *Developing Effective Policy and Practice for Work with Foreign National Prisoners*. London: Prison Reform Trust.

Bosworth, M. and Kellezi, B. (2013) 'Citizenship and Belonging in a Women's Immigration Detention Centre', in C. Phillips and C. Webster (eds), *New Directions in Race, Ethnicity and Crime*. London: Routledge.

Bosworth, M., Bowling, B., and Lee, M. (2007) 'Globalization, Ethnicity and Racism: An Introduction', *Theoretical Criminology* 12(3): 263.

Bowling, B. and Phillips, C. (2002) *Race, Crime and Justice*. Harlow: Longman.

Casey, J.P. (2010) 'Open Borders: Absurd Chimera or Inevitable Future Policy?', *International Migration* 48(5): 14.

Cisneros, J.D. (2008) 'Immigrant Communities: The Metaphor of "Immigrant as Pollutant" in Media Representations of Immigration', *Rhetoric and Public Affairs* 11(4): 569.

Cooper, C. (2009) 'Asylum Seekers, Refugees and Criminal Justice', in H.S. Bhui (ed), *Race and Criminal Justice*. London: Sage.

Crenshaw, K.W. (1989) 'Demarginalizing the Intersection of Race and Sex: A Black Feminist Critique of Antidiscrimination Doctrine, Feminist Theory and Antiracist Politics', *The University of Chicago Legal Forum*: 139–167.

Ellermann, A. (2009) *Undocumented Migrants and Resistance in the State of Exception, University of British Colombia*. <http://www.unc.edu/euce/eusa2009/papers/ellermann_02G.pdf>.

Farrant, F. (2009) 'Gender, "Race" and the Criminal Justice Process', in H.S. Bhui, *Race and Criminal Justice*. London: Sage.

Fili, A. (2013) 'The Maze of Immigration Detention in Greece: A Case Study of the Athens Airport Detention Facility', *Prison Service Journal* 205, January 2013.

García Hernández, C.C. (2012) 'The Perverse Logic of Immigration Detention: Unraveling the Rationality of Imprisoning Immigrants Based on Markers of Race and Class Otherness', *Colombia Journal of Race and Law* 1(3): 353.

Garland, J., Spalek, B., and Chakraborti, N. (2006) 'Hearing Lost Voices: Issues in Researching "Hidden" Minority Ethnic Communities', *British Journal of Criminology* 46(3): 423.

Gatwick Detainee Welfare Group (GDWG) (2012) *A Prison in Mind: The Mental Health Implications of Detention in Brook House Immigration Removal Centre*. London: GDWG.

Geddes A. (2000) *Immigration and European Integration, Towards Fortress Europe?* (1st edn) Manchester: Manchester University Press.

Griffin, C.E. (2009) 'Deportation and Reintegration in the Caribbean and Latin America: Addressing the Development-security Paradox', in W.F. Mcdonald (ed), *Immigration, Crime and Justice (Sociology of Crime Law and Deviance, Volume 13)*. Bingley: Emerald Group Publishing Limited.

HMIP and ICIBI (Independent Chief Inspector of Borders and Immigration) (2012) *The Effectiveness and Impact of Immigration Detention Casework. A Joint Thematic Review by HM Inspectorate of Prisons and the Independent Chief Inspector of Borders and Immigration*. London: HMIP.

HMIP (2012) *Annual Report.* London: HMIP.

HMIP (2012a) *Report on an Unannounced Full Inspection of Cedars Pre-departure Accommodation, 30 April–25 May 2012.* London: HMIP.

HMIP (2012b) *Detainees under Escort: Inspection of Escort and Removals to Afghanistan, 25–26 June 2012.* London: HMIP.

HMIP (2012c) *Report on an Announced Inspection of HMP Canterbury, 16–20 July.* London: HMIP.

HMIP (2012d) *Report of an Announced Inspection of HMP Bullwood Hall, 3–6 September.* London: HMIP.

HMIP (2011) *Annual Report.* London: HMIP.

HMIP (2010) *Annual Report.* London: HMIP.

HMIP (2008) *Report on an Announced Inspection of Dungavel Immigration Removal Centre.* London: HMIP.

HMIP (2007) *Foreign National Prisoners: A Follow Up Report.* London. Home Office.

HMIP (2006) *Foreign National Prisoners: A Thematic Review.* London. Home Office.

Human Rights Watch (2000) *Owed Justice: Thai Women Trafficked into Debt Bondage in Japan.* New York: HRW.

Jakobs, G. (2000) 'Das Selbverstaendnis der Strafrechtswissenschaft vor den Herausforderungen der Gegenwart', in A. Eser, W. Hassemer, and B. Burkhardt (eds), *Die deutsche Strafrechtswissenschaft vor der Jahrtausendwende: Rueckbesinnung und Ausblick.* Muenchen: Beck.

Kil, S.H., Menjívar, C., and Doty, R.L. (2009) 'Securing Borders: Patriotism, Vigilantism and the Brutalization of the US American Public', in W.F. Mcdonald (ed), *Immigration, Crime and Justice (Sociology of Crime Law and Deviance, Volume 13).* Bingley: Emerald Group Publishing Limited.

Krasmann, S. (2007) 'The Enemy on the Border: Critique of a Programme in Favour of a Preventive State', *Punishment and Society* 9(3): 301.

London Detainee Support Group (2010) *No Return, No Release, No Reason. Challenging Indefinite Detention.* London: LDSG.

Malloch, M. and Stanley, E. (2005) 'The Detention of Asylum Seekers in the UK: Representing Risk, Managing the Dangerous', *Punishment and Society* 7(1): 53.

Maruna, S. (2001) *'Making Good': How Ex-convicts Reform and Build Their Lives.* Washington: American Psychological Association.

McNeill, F. (2006) 'A Desistance Paradigm for Offender Management', *Criminology and Criminal Justice* 6: 39.

McNeill, F. and Weaver, B. (2010) 'Travelling Hopefully: Desistance Research and Probation Practice', in J. Brayford, F. Cowe, and J. Deering (eds), *What Else Works? Creative Work with Offenders.* London: Willan Publishing.

Mill, J.S. (1859/1979) *On Liberty.* Harmondsworth, Middlesex: Penguin.

Musinguzi, K. (2013) '45991', *Prison Service Journal* 205, January 2013.

Palidda, S. (2009) 'The Criminalization and Victimization of Immigrants: A Critical Perspective', in W.F. Mcdonald (ed), *Immigration, Crime and Justice (Sociology of Crime Law and Deviance, Volume 13).* Bingley: Emerald Group Publishing Limited.

Parekh, B. (2000) (The Parekh Report) *The Future of Multi-Ethnic Britain.* London: Profile Books.

Rudiger, A. (2007) *Prisoners of Terrorism? The Impact of Anti-terrorism Measures on Refugees and Asylum Seekers in Britain.* London: Refugee Council.

Sitkin, L. (2013) '"The Right to Walk the Streets": Looking for Illegal Migration on the Streets and Stations of the UK and Germany', *Prison Service Journal* 205, January 2013.

Smith, D. (2009) 'Key Concepts and Theories about "Race"', in H.S. Bhui (ed), *Race and Criminal Justice*. London: Sage.

Vine, J. (2012) *An Investigation into Border Security Checks*. London: Independent Chief Inspector of Borders and Immigration.

Vine, J. (2011) *A Thematic Inspection of How the UK Border Agency Manages Foreign National Prisoners*. London: Independent Chief Inspector of Borders and Immigration.

Vogel, D., McDonald, W.F., Jordan, B., Düvell, F., Kovacheva, V., and Vollmer, B. (2009) 'Police Cooperation in Internal Enforcement of Immigration Control: Learning from International Comparison', in W.F. Mcdonald (ed), *Immigration, Crime and Justice (Sociology of Crime Law and Deviance, Volume 13)*. Bingley: Emerald Group Publishing Limited.

Wacquant, L. (1999) '"Suitable Enemies": Foreigners and Immigrants in the Prisons of Europe', *Punishment and Society* 1(2): 215.

Walters, W. (2011) 'Foucault and Frontiers: Notes on the Birth of the Humanitarian Border', in U. Bröckling, S. Krasmann, and T. Lemke (eds), *Governmentality: Current Issues and Future Challenges*. New York: Routledge.

Wilsher, D. (2012) *Immigration Detention*. Cambridge: Cambridge University Press.

Winder, R. (2004) *Bloody Foreigners: The Story of Immigration to Britain*. London: Abacus.

Zurek, Y. (2004) 'The Experiences of Women in Australian Immigration Detention Centres', *Forced Migration Review* 20, May 2004.

PART I

CRIMINALIZATION

1

The Ordered and the Bordered Society: Migration Control, Citizenship, and the Northern Penal State

Katja Franko Aas[1]

Introduction

Any analysis of punishment is intrinsically connected to the issue of the state as the main agent of criminalization. Most accounts of punishment concentrate on the 'internal organs' of the state: its mechanisms of social control, the agents and processes behind the criminalization process, the legal and philosophical rationalities, the penalties and their institutional make-up. In those cases where attention has been turned outwards, across the border, and into the international domain, scholars have been predominantly interested in international criminal law, human rights, and transitional justice. The intention of this chapter is to look closer into this established partition between the domestic and the international in the studies of criminalization. Its objective is to bring the global into the domestic and vice versa, in order to situate what may appear as 'internal punishment' within the broader sphere of global geopolitical relations.

The main argument of the chapter is that contemporary practices of migration control disrupt traditional frames of understanding within criminal law and criminology. First, they demand a de-privileging of the national as the self-evident scale of enquiry. An essential aspect of the globalizing condition has been its destabilizing qualities (Sassen 2008). National and local no longer appear as fixed categories but are shot through with transnational elements and marked by hybridity and movement. When entering the field of crime control, migration destabilizes some of the central categories and building blocks of the national penal domain.[2] This chapter

[1] I am very grateful to Mary Bosworth, Sverre Flaatten, Lill Scherdin, and Leanne Weber for their insightful comments and to the European Research Council (StG 2010) for the financial support. Many thanks also to Helene I. Gundhus, Nicolay B. Johansen, Sigmund B. Mohn, Kjersti R. Strømnes, and Thomas Ugelvik for stimulating weekly discussions on the topics discussed in the chapter.

[2] The usual usage of the term 'penal' refers to a number of activities and practices of the state 'relating to, or involving punishment, penalties, or punitive institutions' (<http://www.merriam-webster.com>).

maps this process of destabilization and de-composition of the national as it pertains to the functioning of the (traditionally domestic) field of punishment and crime control. By doing so, the chapter is also an invitation to reflection on questions of *scale* when it comes to issues of criminalization and crime control. Scalar narratives and classifications can, as Moore (2008: 214) points out, 'constrain or enable certain ways of seeing, thinking and acting'. This chapter suggests that the 'ontological privilege' (Held 2010) accorded to the national within studies of modern penality constrains critical analysis under conditions of intensified global mobility. For most of modernity the national frame has been and still is the natural 'category of practice' of domestic criminal justice systems, underpinning the imagery of homogenous, territorially bounded nation-states. The national order of things thus passes as the normal or natural order of things (Koshravi 2010: 2). However, while the national frame may seem to be a natural category of practice, this chapter suggests that the reification of the national scale as a 'category of analysis' (Moore 2008) can be a block against insight and prevent us from capturing the variety of processes and transformations taking place inside the national or beyond it.

The second disruption proposed in this chapter relates to *space* rather than scale. The chapter makes an argument for the importance of spatialization and geopolitical context as a key to understanding criminalization under conditions of globalization. By situating contemporary crime control within a broader context of international relations I show how global inequalities are inscribed into (domestic) crime control and criminalization patterns and how they in turn reinforce and reify these inequalities. The 'disruptions' created by transnational mobility offer a unique insight into the transformations of penality under conditions of globalization. They challenge us critically to re-examine the existing conceptual maps and vocabulary of the criminological landscape. By taking the border as our vantage point, this chapter aims to disassemble the existing topology in a conceptual and territorial sense, uncovering elements of the penal outside the traditional criminal justice institutions and beyond the confines of the Northern nation state. Borders and control of mobility enable us to examine two related aspects of the state and its sovereignty, which are, nevertheless, seldom seen together: its defence from outside intrusion (ie the defence of the border) and its internal consolidation and control (the traditional function of crime control and punishment). By doing so, this chapter asks: what are the social functions of punishment and criminal justice in a globalizing world?

The terms 'penal' and 'penal state' shall not be used to denote a particularly punitive nature of state practices and, as we shall see later, the argument will be made that the meaning of 'penal' becomes transformed to encompass novel phenomena and practices with punitive elements, which are (institutionally and conceptually) placed outside of the traditional domain of punishment, crime control, and criminal law.

The Ordered and the Bordered Society: The Novel Assemblages

Sovereignty is, as Wendy Brown (2010: 52) observes, 'a peculiar border concept'. Its meaning denotes both supremacy and autonomy; understood as the state's capability of being 'a decisive power of rule and as freedom from occupation by another' (Brown 2010: 52). These two meanings and functions have traditionally belonged to the separate spheres of internal and external security. The role of criminal law and policing has been to preserve the internal security, to establish the sovereign's supremacy and the moral order of the society, in short to create a well-*ordered* and disciplined society (Foucault 1977; Simon 2007). The sphere of external security, on the other hand, has traditionally been governed by military security and international relations, as well as border security and immigration law, whose task has been to preserve the state's territorial integrity and autonomy. Traditionally, border control seeks to maintain clear boundaries between the inside and the outside of the state—the maintenance of a *bordered* society.

Although inhabiting separate domains, border issues and crime control possess some essential similarities. They share the language of protection and security and, as Juliet Stumpf (2006) observes, both criminal and immigration law traditionally act as 'gatekeepers of membership', defining the terms of social inclusion and exclusion. Questions about who belongs, and what kind of rights they deserve, are embedded in penal sanctions as well as in decisions to expel and deny entry. As the intensification of globalization in the past decades has destabilized the established boundaries between internal and external security, between policing and soldiering, and between the domains of immigration and criminal law, the distinction between the two aspects of sovereignty has become increasingly unclear (Andreas and Price 2001; Stumpf 2006; Bigo and Walker 2007). A central argument of this chapter is that the growing mobility and the influx of non-citizens into the territorial domain of the nation state is producing fragmentation and to some extent dissolving the (national) penal domain by mixing elements of the 'internal' and the 'external', thus creating novel configurations of the penal. Exemplified by the growing foreign populations in European prisons and crime statistics, and various policing strategies directed at non-citizens, (domestic) punishment is becoming increasingly internationalized, taking on the symbolic and practical functions of border control. The project of creating an 'ordered society' through penological intervention has thus become increasingly intertwined with the control of the border and the project of creating a 'bordered society'.

According to Sassen (2008), globalization processes lead to 'novel assemblages of territory, authority and rights'. While one may justifiably question the novelty of the phenomenon—after all, several contributions in this volume and elsewhere (see, *inter alia*, Gibney in Chapter 12 and Ugelvik in Chapter 10 of this volume; Melossi 2003) testify to its long historic roots—the concept of the assemblage offers a productive insight into the current transformations of the penal domain. Stemming from Deleuze and Guattari's classic *A Thousand Plateaus*, the strength of this concept lies in its connotations of instability and difference, and the productive qualities of the two (Marcus and Saka 2006). It introduces 'a radical notion of multiplicity into phenomena which we traditionally approach as being discretely bounded, structured and stable' (Haggerty and Ericson 2000: 608), which is how national criminal justice systems have traditionally been perceived and conceived. Sassen (2008) thus outlines a movement from 'centripetal nation-state articulation'—where one entity, the nation state, aggregates most of territory, authority, and rights—to a 'centrifugal multiplication of specialized assemblages', which unsettle existing scalar and normative arrangements. As a concept, an assemblage 'makes it easier to think about disparate elements with contingent and emergent roles but which ultimately work together' (Lippert and Pyykkönen 2012: 1). It may therefore be usefully employed to pull together the disparate forms of control, which although heterogeneous, have varied degrees of 'borderliness'[3] and punitiveness inscribed in them.

How the two elements—'the bordered' and 'the ordered'—come to be put together varies, revealing the complexity of existing control practices, populations, and actors involved in them, and demands concrete empirical investigation. Their juxtaposition can at times form an uneasy allegiance and may even 'feel wrong' for the actors involved (see Bosworth, Kaufman, this volume). Nor does the assemblage of the 'bordered' and the 'ordered' need to imply their merger and melting (as the concept of 'crimmigration' is at times understood), but rather demands an examination of their constitution in different institutional, national, and historical configurations. Analytically, one of the main advantages of the global assemblage is precisely its concreteness, partiality, and situatedness. As Ong and Collier (2004: 12) argue:

An assemblage is the product of multiple determinations that are not reducible to a single logic. The temporality of an assemblage is emergent. It does not always involve new forms, but forms that are shifting, in formation, or at stake. As a composite concept, the term 'global assemblage' suggests inherent tensions: global implies broadly encompassing, seamless, and mobile; assemblage implies heterogeneous, contingent, unstable, partial, and situated.

Several observers have noted the recent proliferation or 'implosion' (Squire 2011: 2) of border controls and ID checks within the national territories of Western states, captured in the popular phrase that 'the border is everywhere' (Feeley and Simon 1994; Lyon 2005; *Policing & Society* 2011). While the practices may be conceived first and foremost as administrative, their practical application is, depending on the context, often the responsibility of the police force, which may employ a more or less clear crime-fighting modus. Although administrative in principle, they may be intertwined with various crime-fighting objectives (trafficking in drugs and human beings, counterfeit documents, terrorism, and organized crime), thus revealing

---

[3] The term 'borderliness' (coined by Sarah Green) emerged as a concept during the development of the EastBordNet project. Its meaning denotes 'what gives something or somewhere the sense of being a border' and refers to border as a *quality* rather than as an object, and more as ongoing activity rather than a fixed 'thing'. See <http://wiki.manchester.ac.uk/eastbordnet/index.php/Borderliness>.

various degrees and configurations of the punitive.[4] In these contexts, it may be more productive to speak of these measures as *punitive* rather than punishment, in order to free them from the conceptual constraints imposed by the existing notions of punishment within the traditional (national) criminal justice institutional arrangements which, by comparison, seem to have a relatively 'clear' character in terms of their institutional and legal bases and a clearer sense of purpose. As shown by several chapters in this volume, contemporary penal measures vary according to the extent of immigration-related objectives inscribed in them. In some cases, such as the deportation of foreign offenders, the penal and the bordered are so enmeshed and achieve a level of hybridity which makes it pertinent to ask whether we are witnessing qualitatively distinct forms of control, which might be, paraphrasing Stumpf (2006), described as 'crimmigration control'. In other cases, traditional penal technologies, when faced with populations of non-citizens and denizens, gain an additional, sharper, exclusionary edge (Ugelvik 2012). In the latter, the defence of the border is essentially transforming the parameters and the moral climate of national, particularly European, penal systems.

What is important at this point is that the element of border control seems to direct traditional penal technologies not only towards various degrees of social control and exclusion, but ultimately towards expulsion from the national territory. Getting unwanted individuals out may thus take priority over punishing them for wrongdoing. Returns have in recent years become an independent and increasingly important measure of performance. Although expulsion can be seen as a sub-variety of social exclusion, it has several distinct elements. While sharing long-term exclusionary traits with such measures as life imprisonment and long-term incapacitation, expulsion differs from more customary penal measures in its lack of concern about reintegration to society. Its objective is precisely to banish or ex-capacitate rather than to incapacitate (Westfeldt 2008; Ugelvik 2012; and see Johansen, Chapter 14 in this volume). Whether an administrative 'removal' or a more punitive 'deportation', its rationality is ban-optic rather than the disciplinary panopticism and biopolitical objectives characteristic of modern penality (Bigo 2006; Aas 2011a). The biopolitical and disciplinary forms of penal control, although displaying great national and historic variety, are nevertheless primarily based on scientific and moral rather than territorial exclusion. They are *internally* directed, aiming to control populations occupying the state territory (Schinkel 2010). Biopolitics is, as Foucault (2004: 247) put it, the 'power to make live', hence the concern with health and the centrality of the narrative of reform and rehabilitation. Expulsion, on the other hand, is characterized by a different logic, which comes closer to Agamben's notion of zoepolitics and which sees the ban as the original political relation (Agamben 1998; Schinkel 2010; Aas 2011a). Here,

---

[4] Oslo Police, for example, created in 2009 a special task force against the open drug scene consisting of ordinary police officers and immigration police. Of the 737 individuals arrested in 2010, 122 were charged with violation of the Immigration Act, 28 with violation of the Penal Code, and criminal court proceedings were initiated against 17 (for the remaining 214 no charges were considered justified). Source: Oslo politidistrikt: 'Felles innsats mot åpne rusmiljøer—statusrapport pr. 31.12.10'.

the sovereign power is marked by the 'production of bare life' and by the ability to expel life from the sphere of legal protection. Rather than multiplying its productivity, banoptic power creates the conditions of precariousness of life, evident in the withdrawal of health care services (Johansen, Chapter 14 in this volume) and in the harrowing numbers of border deaths (Weber and Pickering 2011).

What is of further interest at this point is that the act of expelling is directed towards another geographic locality. It is *externally* directed towards persons outside the state territory. This external dimension is vital for understanding the changing role of contemporary penality and reveals another essential quality of global assemblages: bringing distant locations into interaction with the national and local. In what follows, this chapter argues that by striving for expulsion the criminal justice domain not only becomes internally fragmented (ie taking in elements of border control), but also enters the external sphere of international relations. By entering the matrix of geopolitical relations, penal technologies lose their internal character and become (even when used domestically) marked by their (northern) geopolitical origin.

The Northern Penal State and the Global Prohibition Regimes

An essential counterpart to the implosion of control, outlined above, has been an 'explosion of control' (Squire 2011: 2)—a progressive diffusion of border policing and crime control practices into the domain external to the nation state. To achieve the objectives of internal ('crimmigration') control the Northern state has, particularly over the past two decades, progressively expanded its control activities into the international domain, externalizing its 'domestic' control functions and exporting a migration control agenda (Mitsilegas 2010; Weber and Pickering 2011; Pickering and Weber, Lee, Chapters 5 and 7 respectively in this volume). The trend is evident in the growing size and complexity of deportation regimes (Brotherton and Barrios 2009; De Genova and Peutz 2010). In recent years, one of the fastest growing activities of the European external border control agency, Frontex, has been the organization of chartered return flights to countries such as Serbia, Nigeria, Kosovo, The Democratic Republic of the Congo, Iraq, etc. These flights pool resources of Schengen states and offer assistance in returning to the global South various types of unwanted mobility, including irregular migrants, foreign citizens who have committed criminal offences, and rejected asylum seekers.

These charter flights act primarily in the interest of the Northern states organizing them. Many Southern societies greatly depend on the remittances from their citizens abroad, and several observers have pointed out the detrimental effects that particularly the return of 'criminal aliens' has on the returnees and on their countries of origin (Weber and Bowling 2008; Brotherton and Barrios 2009). The flights are nevertheless supported by an elaborate political and legal regime in which many Southern states are more or less active participants. Taking the European Union as an example, we can see that it has been particularly effective in using the stick and carrot approach in exporting its migration control agenda and co-opting its Southern and Eastern neighbours into doing its policing jobs, effectively creating 'law enforcement buffer zones' (Andreas and Nadelmann 2006: 15). Frontex, for example, seeks to 'constantly develop reliable and effective network of partnerships at the operational level with the relevant authorities of non-EU states'.[5] Frontex has thus been exporting not only unwanted aliens but also border control training standards and surveillance equipment, while simultaneously expanding the geographical scope of its own activities and de facto extra-territorializing the European border (Aas 2011b; Gammeltoft-Hansen 2011).[6] However, the EU's burden-shifting strategies are by no means an anomaly and share several traits and objectives with the Australian Pacific Solution and the American Caribbean Solution (Mitsilegas 2010; Weber and Pickering 2011). There has been, as Mitsilegas (2010: 39) observes, a 'convergence between models of extraterritorial immigration control globally'. Moreover, Frontex activities should be seen as part of a broader set of political and legal strategies and strategic partnerships which have put 'co-operation against illegal migration' firmly on the EU's international agenda and at the centre of its development and aid strategies.

Evidently, geopolitics matters, in migration control, as well as in crime control. Although the state is usually the main agent of criminalization, it is important to acknowledge that states are not the same and that their interests depend on their geopolitical position. Some states are more sovereign than others (Dauvergne 2008: 172). Several historic and contemporary accounts of the internationalization of crime control have pointed out that what is illegal, and how it is policed, often depends on the political interests of certain states, most notably the United States and Western Europe (Andreas and Nadelmann 2006). This variation has been particularly evident in the international efforts to combat drug trafficking and sexual slavery: '[T]he models, methods, and priorities of international crime control are substantially determined and exported by the most powerful states in the international system' (Andreas and Nadelmann 2006: 10). A similar situation exists in the illegalization and policing of migration. Spatialization is, as Coutin (2005: 6) observes, 'the key to both criminalization and to challenging how criminality is defined'. It offers an opportunity to explore and embrace the geographical and political situatedness of law. Extra-territorial border controls and the outsourcing of asylum are, according to Gammeltoft-Hansen (2011), an example of doing 'politics through law', where governments strategically seek to shift or deconstruct legal responsibilities otherwise owed by reference to law itself.

One of the main arguments of this chapter is that the objectives of migration control are formative of novel contours of criminalization, punitiveness, and the state—the Northern penal state—which is crucially defined by its geopolitical position. The Northern state has been creating an elaborate legal regime that criminalizes certain forms of movement, effectively rendering large proportions of the world's population 'illegal' (Dauvergne 2008). While the control regimes are driven by the interests of the Northern (migration importing) states, the people

---

5 See <http://frontex.europa.eu/partners/third-countries>.

6 As of March 2012, Frontex had concluded working arrangements with the authorities of 16 countries and was in various stages of negotiations with the authorities of a further nine countries (see <http://frontex.europa.eu/partners/third-countries>). Several aspects of this cooperation, particularly those concerning Libya, have been heavily criticized for prioritizing border control objectives at the expense of human rights (Aas 2011b).

affected by them are primarily citizens of the global South.[7] The regimes consist not only of legal regulation, but also of an assemblage of mechanisms of policing, enforcement, and social exclusion related to the illegalization—the mechanisms which are becoming increasingly transnational in their nature. Moreover, as the dynamics of criminalization under conditions of globalization becomes increasingly international, the internationalization also includes the creation of globally meaningful labels of crime and deviance. As Dauvergne (2008: 18) observes:

[A]s 'illegal' emerges as a globally meaningful identity label, the characteristics of all those nations against which this other is imagined also tend to merge. The line between having and not having can no longer be easily conceived as fitting around the border of *a* nation and must instead fit around the border of *all* prosperous nations, creating a global understanding of 'insiders' and 'outsiders'.

In other words, while traditionally class interests have been seen, particularly by Marxist scholars, as a driver behind state criminalization policies, when it comes to migration, the process still seems to be related to social inequality; however, the inequality is now globalized.

The 'illegality' of migration follows a similar, although not identical, trajectory to other forms of international criminalization, where new laws and prohibition regimes are not simply a response to a stable category (ie crime), but rather depend on the activities of powerful states and actors who have the capacity to redefine certain cross-border activities once considered 'normal' and condemn them as 'deviant' (Andreas and Nadelmann 2006: 7). This understanding builds on a conception of law as grounded, geographically and geopolitically contextual, rather than universal, abstract, and immutable. In it, illegality is not 'a relatively fixed property or status that a given individual holds', but rather:

a condition that any given individual can flit in and out of depending on the relation between his and her movements and activities and the movements and activities of national, international and/or transnational agencies. (Squire 2011: 7)

It may seem self-evident that 'illegality' is contested. However, it deserves further examination because it is precisely through the official state production of illegality (rather than irregularity) that the intertwining of border control and crime control is being played out.

From Deviant States to Deviant Citizens: Global Hierarchies of Citizenship

An illegal immigrant is, in Elspeth Guild's terms (2009: 15), 'someone in respect of whose presence of the territory the state has passed a law making mere existence

---

[7] Although the distinction between the 'mobility exporting' and mobility importing/restricting countries reflects approximately the global north–south division, this is not absolute and can also be seen within countries, for example in the former Yugoslavia, Italy, or the EU itself (the case of Roma).

a criminal offence'. While the prerogative to decide the right of entry into the country is one of the essential traits of any sovereign state, it is applied selectivity. What this means on the individual level is that the accident of being born in the global South becomes a legal handicap for the citizens of these countries, particularly the disadvantaged ones (Dauvergne 2008: 17; Aliverti 2012). This handicap stems from the assumption that there are different categories of states: those whose citizens' mobility is desirable (and is in fact something to be attracted, as tourists, students, and professionals), and those states who are literally black-listed.

The 'illegality' of migration is not simply an effect of transgressing immigration law, but denotes a more pervasive and insidious connection between migration, crime, and insecurity. As Dauvergne (2008: 16) puts it, 'The predominance of the term "illegal" also underscores a shift in perception regarding the moral worthiness of these migrants'. Despite heavy criticism, the concept of 'illegality' has in recent years had a profound impact on the nature of the political and legal thinking about migration. Punishing the 'deviant immigrant' (Melossi 2003) sends potent symbolic political signals even if, as Aliverti (2012) argues in the UK context, few immigration-related offences are prosecuted. The progressive securitization of migration (Huysmans 2006) has legitimated a complex process of exclusionary practices, in which the 'various forms of security provide an organizing principle around which territorial and social inclusion and exclusion are drawn' (Guild 2009: 190). On a global level, this approach has created a finely meshed gradation of states according to the security risk presented by their migration, or what might be termed their 'deviance'. Looking at the European Union, this gradation has, according to Guild (2009: 188–189), produced the following 'typology of European inclusion and exclusion':

1. The citizen of the state in Europe.

2. The citizen of the European Union who is not the national of the state where he or she is living (expulsion and exclusion possible only on the grounds of public policy, public security, and public health).

3. The citizen of the European Union who is temporarily excluded (time-limited restrictions for some nationals of the 2004–2007 EU enlargement).

4. Swiss, Norwegian, and Icelandic nationals.

5. Turkish workers in the European Union.

6. Third-country nationals with a long-term residence (who enjoy protection against expulsion equivalent to that of the migrant citizens of the European Union).

7. Third-country national whose country of nationality is on the EU's visa white-list (eg US nationals).

8. Third-country nationals whose country of nationality is on the EU's visa black-list but with which the European Union has a visa facilitation agreement (eg Russia).

9. Third-country nationals whose country of nationality is on the EU visa black-list and with which there is no visa facilitation agreement (eg China); there is a presumption that these persons pose a security risk and must obtain a visa.

10. Third-country nationals whose country of nationality is on the EU visa black-list and whose country has been specified in the EU visa rules as a country of specific security concern by at least one Member State.

Such hierarchies of national exclusion are based on a pre-established racialized, and colonial, ranking. It is this global hierarchy that determines the levels of protection and rights nationally, including the various degrees of protection that individuals may have against expulsion. While there may be national differences, most countries follow the norms of affluence, cultural and political affinity, security, and, what is vital for the purpose of this chapter, the norm of cooperation with crime and immigration control objectives of the Northern state. Failure to cooperate is directly felt by the citizens of the 'deviant state'. Citizens of 'black-listed' countries (points 8, 9, and 10 above) are collectively described as a potential security risk of some kind (illegal migration, criminality, political violence, depending on the state to which he or she belongs). Such risk can be neutralized, however, by visa facilitation if these countries offer the European Union a security reassurance in the form of a readmission agreement, offering to accept their citizens when they are expelled (Guild 2009: 190).

We are here witnessing a constitution of two qualitatively different positions of statehood: the *deviant state* (which may be cooperative or non-cooperative) and the *Northern penal state*, which is defined by its objectives and capacity to export its 'crimmigration control' agenda. This tendency to evaluate a state's capacity to govern crime according to its ability to respond to issues on the international crime control agenda is neither new nor unusual. Think of the US-sponsored war on drugs, the Financial Action Task Force (FATF), and the US State Department's rankings of countries according to their money laundering and anti-trafficking efforts (Andreas and Nadelmann 2006). What is of particular importance, however, is that in the case of migration control, the deviance of the state has direct consequences for the individual citizens of the 'deviant state'. For example, in its yearly *Risk Analysis* Frontex creates 'Top Ten nationalities' rankings, which are the lists of countries whose citizens have the highest probability of illegal stay, refusal of entry, applications for asylum, using false documents, etc.[8] Other examples can be found in the domestic patterns of control, in which deviance of the state 'rubs off', triggering suspicion of the Northern state, and is thus producing deviant identities of its citizens. Untrustworthy states produce untrustworthy identities. This is most obviously happening through the increased focus on ID documents and identification (*Policing & Society* 2011). 'Ascertaining the correct identity of the individual, and in particular the foreigner, is increasingly accepted as a security issue' (Guild 2009: 121) and is resulting in extensive practices of searching for documents aimed

---

[8] Source: <http://www.frontex.europa.eu/assets/Attachments_News/ara_2011_for_public_release.pdf>.

at connecting the national identity to the subject (Weber 2011). While identification has, since its inception, been a vital preoccupation of the modern state (Cole
2001), it is receiving intensified focus under the contemporary conditions of
globalization and mass mobility.

The rise of the ubiquitous ID—the biometric ID card and passport, the 'enhanced' driving licence, DNA databases, fingerprinting and iris scans, and the related
databases—are thus 'identification efforts aimed at making citizens more "legible"
within the "embrace" of the state' (Lyon 2009: 22). However, while these measures
may be ubiquitous in the West, creating what some fear to be a climate of general
surveillance and raising privacy concerns, they have markedly different effects on the
citizens of the global North and the global South (Aas 2011a). When it comes to the
latter, their lack of 'legibility' and of a trustworthy identity is treated as a criminal
matter with progressively intrusive measures (Aliverti 2012). For example, the
Norwegian government has recently lowered the threshold of evidence for imprisonment in cases of false identity, doubts about identity, or perceived lack of cooperation
with the authorities in establishing identity. Moreover, due to the changed EU
legislation (Directive 2008/118/EC on common standards and procedures in
Member States for returning illegally staying third-country nationals), the maximum
length of imprisonment[9] in these cases has now been extended to 18 months (Bø,
forthcoming). Individuals can thus be imprisoned for not providing documents, or
for providing inadequate ones, and the duration of imprisonment may be longer if
the individual's state of origin is not cooperative, which means that it may in fact
be longest for individuals originating from war-torn countries without functioning state bureaucracies. In these cases the deviance of an individual, his or her
perceived security risk, stems from the 'deviance' of the state and its inability to
comply with the identification demands of the more powerful states. In the
immediate aftermath of 9/11, the United States was able to export its security
agenda and, due to its geopolitical supremacy, imposed biometric passports on the
rest of the world despite at times fervent protests of European countries with
higher data protection standards. It should be also noted that it is no coincidence
that biometrics is establishing itself as the preferred answer to the challenges of
identification. Such technology enables the Northern state to identify foreign
citizens without having to rely on foreign documents; the state can create its own
regime of knowledge, whereby the foreign body, rather than the foreign state or
the foreign citizen, becomes the main source of truth (Aas 2006, 2011a).

What we are witnessing in the examples above is a more general pattern of, on
the one hand, Northern legal production and creation of standards of conduct and
governance, and on the other hand, Southern compliance and the import of
standards in exchange for trading and mobility benefits, development funds,
promises of potential EU membership, etc. It is important to keep in mind that
this is not a one-way process. As Comaroff and Comaroff (2006) astutely observe,

---

[9] The proposition uses the term 'imprisonment'; however, this may in practice mean a closed
detention centre or a traditional prison. In Italy, these institutions are aptly named 'Identification and
Expulsion Centres' ('I Centri di Identificazione ed Espulsione').

when the West is trying to impose its legal order on the chaotic nature of the post-colony, a form of resistance and a resource of the disadvantaged is 'counterfeiting modernity' (producing fakes, false credentials, and illusions). Counterfeit documents are one of several deviant industries which have developed due to the Northern states' intensified regulatory efforts. They are, however, part of a broader spectrum of illicit activities, which Gilman et al term 'deviant globalization', whose essence 'is "regulatory arbitrage"—that is, taking advantage of the differences in rules and enforcement practices across jurisdictions in order to make a profit' (2011: 16). Illicit migratory industries, such as human trafficking and smuggling and other forms of illicit facilitation, are thus a source of income as well as a form of 'survival entrepreneurship' and innovation for those without access to legitimate market opportunities.

For citizens of the global South, deviant immigration, like other forms of deviant globalization, 'is both a powerful engine of wealth creation and a symbol of their exclusion and abjection' (Gilman et al 2011: 4). The fortified borders and strict mobility regimes are thus an immense source of vulnerability and create conditions of precariousness of life. However, the very logic of prohibition also empowers the adaptive strategies of deviant entrepreneurs for whom 'every prohibition is a business opportunity', thus creating illicit economies, which can potentially offer a ticket out of poverty for individuals, families, and entire communities. For this reason, the participants themselves may not see these activities through the lens of crime and victimization, and may eschew the categories of the criminal and the victim. Moreover, as several observers have pointed out, 'deviant supply is driven by deviant demand' (Gilman et al 2011: 16). What Calavita (2005) aptly calls the 'economics of *alterité*' has been very beneficial to the economies of particularly Southern European countries, but has also reinforced the migrants' otherness, increasing their fragility as well as deepening their legal and social exclusion. The deviant migration that the elaborate transnational order of actors and regulations is trying to suppress is thus in many ways a product of its own making, driven by global inequality, and the economic opportunities opened by prohibitions and the demand for illicit services.

'This is a Full Country': The Bordered Penality and Citizenship in a Limited World

The point of the discussion so far has not just been to reiterate the divisions between the global North and South, or what Bauman (1998) famously termed 'tourists' and 'vagabonds'. The discursive, legal, and political coupling of migration and crime is creating a specific dynamic of social exclusion within the territorial space of the Northern state, which to some extent defies the classic divisions between the North and South, West and the rest, inside and outside of society. Where the North lies is a relative question. And it is precisely at the point where the lines of exclusion become blurred and do not simply function as border-lines, but are breaking down the 'inside', that we can begin to see the productive role played by the mechanisms of crime control. The special functional and discursive role played by crime and security is not only structuring the hierarchies of states and their citizens, but is also breaking down and fragmenting the 'domestic' field of citizenship (Zedner 2010; Aas 2011a).

Practices such as deportation are essentially related to the termination of citizenship privileges that individuals may have enjoyed previously on a given territory. Stumpf (2006: 30) thus describes lawful residence as 'probationary membership'—a legal status that can be revoked through criminal law. Using Simon's (2007) term, we might say that crimmigration control practices are 'governing citizenship through crime' (see also Bosworth and Guild 2008). Similarly, I have shown elsewhere how European surveillance systems are offering various dis/advantages to groups of supra- and sub-citizens, which destabilize the traditional notion of universal citizenship rights (Aas 2011a). The disassemblage of the national penal domain, in other words, also unsettles the notion of citizenship and leads to the fragmentation of the established penal narratives and legal regimes. This observation is in line with Ong's (2006) claim that globalization and neo-liberalism are producing mutations in the established practices of citizenship and sovereignty driven by the logic of exception. Ong (2006: 5) sees exceptionalism at work not only when individuals are stripped of their legal protections, but 'conceptualize[s] the exception more broadly, as an extraordinary departure in policy that can be deployed to include as well as to exclude'. The discourse about the deviant immigrant (the 'crimmigrant') is thus directed both at non-citizens, denizens, and full citizens of foreign origin, who may find their citizenship status questioned through various control practices, such as intensified surveillance, stop and search, and even more so through the political discourse. Also the 'flawed' citizenships status of these groups often comes close to being 'probationary citizenship', which, although developed in respect of immigrants, 'is extended to all those whose standing as full citizens is in doubt' (Zedner 2010: 379). Consequently, the crimmigration control policies are directed not only towards the exclusion of undesirable non-citizens but also 'seep into domestic crime control' (Zedner 2010: 381).

While the general normative framework, at least in the European context, still operates according to the basic premise and ambition of eventual inclusion, through various biopolitical, moral, and disciplinary interventions, this is no longer the case for those whose citizenship status is in question. Depending on the seriousness of his or her offences, the level of his or her denizenship, and the 'deviance' of his or her state of origin, the 'crimmigrant' is subjected to the various combinations of moral and territorial exclusion, of punitiveness and border control. The concerns of the ordered society (about justice, physical and mental health, education and work training, etc) are here combined with, or overridden by, the concerns of the bordered society (with banishment and territorial exclusion, or simply with 'getting them out'). Aliverti (2012) thus points out that, when it comes to immigration-related offences, criminal law, while clearly playing a moral and symbolic function, is in practice auxiliary to expulsion and to be used when removal is not possible.

What the 'ordered' and the 'bordered' have in common, however, are concerns with membership and belonging (Stumpf 2006). Like punishment, borders, as Brown

(2010) points out, produce political subjectivity, identity, morality, and goodness; they do not just bound but *invent* the societies they delimit. Borders are 'deeply rooted in collective identifications and the assumption of a common sense of belonging' (Balibar 2010). The former French president Sarkozy, for example, stated in 2012 that a crackdown by the authorities on radical Islamists 'will allow us to expel from our national territory a certain number of people who have no reason to be here'.[10] The answer to why expulsion, rather than (domestic) punishment, often is the preferred political solution is to be found in the intensified struggles over who has the right to belong to the national, who has a legitimate 'reason to be here'. Bordered penality is thus part of a broader trend of 'rebordering' of political and territorial space (Andreas and Biersteker 2003; Brown 2010). In a deeply stratified global order, citizenship is a privilege, and crime control is seen as one of the most legitimate reasons for border maintenance and thereby social exclusion. It transforms issues of global privilege and scarcity of resources into questions of morality and the maintenance of the moral order. Criminality thereby becomes a conduit for establishing the right of belonging in a world marked by intensified struggles over citizenship and belonging. These struggles are, as Peter Geschiere (2009) suggests, increasingly articulated through claims about autochthony, about creating special links with the local, or, quite literally, 'to be born from the soil' (Geschiere 2009: 2). While this may be essentially a primordial form of belonging, it is, as Geschiere points out, also a very contemporary and global one that is undergoing a powerful renaissance in many parts of the world, not only the West. In an ironic reversal of history, we can see that while previous global conquests of space were symbolized by the planting of national flags in faraway and undiscovered places, we are witnessing, in the present wave of globalization, the symbolic planting of flags in the midst of the local community.

These struggles of belonging are grounded in a conceptualization of the world as not only geographically bordered but, more importantly, limited in terms of wealth and resources. 'This is a full country' and 'The Netherlands is full' were frequently repeated slogans of the Dutch populist politician Pim Fortuyn, who achieved a remarkable popularity through his anti-immigration stance. The claims of autochthony and the struggles for exclusion, therefore, ultimately need to be situated in the context of global inequality and the intensified 'attempts to reserve the benefits of the welfare state for those who really belong' (Ceuppens and Geschiere 2005: 397). By making crime into a marker of cultural otherness and non-belonging, the punitive and the bordered begin to mesh and to complement each other.

Conclusion

Through the complex intertwining of the national and the global, the practices of creating ordered and bordered societies are ultimately a result of global inequality and the ability of the Northern state to turn this inequality into a question of illegality.

[10] See <http://m.bbc.co.uk/news/world-europe-17607155>.

Paradoxically, contemporary penality is, simultaneously, more nationalized and bordered, as well as globalized and interconnected with the rest of the world. These dialectics of dividedness and connection are nowhere more visible than in the conflicted, yet increasingly salient presence of the humanitarian discourse and human rights principles, which are, although in different ways and degrees, influencing both state authorities and various NGOs working in the field. The humanitarianization of borders (Walters 2010) is an understudied and under-communicated aspect, which seems to some extent to represent a corrective to the punitive and exclusionary impulses, just as rehabilitation and welfarism do (or used to do) on the domestic level. Although excluded from belonging to the national, humanitarianism is based on awareness that the immigrant belongs to the larger sphere of global humanity and is thus deserving of human rights. Humanitarianism is creating a space where immigrant life is not simply passive and excluded, but also enveloped in a discourse of rights (Guild 2009). Nor is it, as often drawn from Agamben, completely bare, but rather comes closer to being barely bearable. It is a form of what Walters (2010: 145) terms minimalist biopolitics, which is '[h]olding together in an uneasy alliance a politics of alienation with a politics of care, and a tactic of abjection and one of reception' (see also Johansen, Chapter 14 in this volume).

The humanitarian element is yet another testimony of the diversity and com-plexity of the global (penal) assemblages and their irreducibility to a single logic of exclusion. The diverse and complex nature of the assemblages makes it analytically challenging to map the diverse networks of national and transnational actors, technologies, and rationalities of governance (bio- and zoepolitical, humanitarian, nationalist, etc). It also makes it difficult to disassemble and disentangle the 'punitive' from the 'bordered', the sovereign from the regulatory, and, ultimately, also the humanitarian from the exclusionary. The diverse and varied nature of the border is also reflected in the varied, and often contradictory, nature of its legal regulation: the lawlessness of the frontiers and the seeming absence of the state stand in contrast to the spaces of intense state surveillance and almost Kafkaesque bureaucratic regulation. The dynamics of the law's presence and absence is evident in the growing discursive and symbolic presence of human rights and their simultaneous elusiveness and the inability of the majority of migrants to access them. We are therefore dealing not only with borders, but also frontiers, marked by the shifting terrain between legality and illegality—the 'no-man's-lands', alluded to by Barker (Chapter 13 in this volume). They are the 'zones of not yet—not yet mapped, not yet regulated' (Tsing 2005: 28).

The globalizing processes are producing what Sassen (2008: 67) terms 'third spaces' which 'are not exclusively national or global but are assemblages of elements of each'. They are a result of denationalizing dynamics which are disaggregating the unitary character of the nation state. The bordered penality, discussed in this chapter, brings to our attention what might be termed the 'scalar disconnect' within much of criminal justice studies: a disconnect between the (self-)understanding of criminal justice as bounded, territorially coherent, and citizenship and jurisdic-tion based, and what is increasingly its scale of existence, which is multi-scalar, spatially fragmented, with overlapping sovereignties and diverse citizenship regimes. It is therefore of particular importance that criminological scholarship should distinguish between what Moore (2008: 203) terms scale as a category of *practice* and scale as a category of *analysis*. By treating the national as the essential and natural entity of analysis, we could be in danger of uncritically adopting 'a social category employed in the practice of sociospatial politics as a central theoretical tool'. The reification of the national within criminological scholarship has produced several blind spots, for example the oversight of detention centres within prison studies (Bosworth, Chapter 8 in this volume) and the lack of attention paid to the penal regimes directed at non-citizens.

The disconnected spaces and individuals may find themselves territorially included but analytically and normatively excluded from the national political space. The disconnected spaces may also escape the national through the extra-territorial activities of the agents of the Northern state. The disassembling of unitary nation-state framings presents not only an analytical challenge, but has profound normative implications that await thorough analysis. Here, criminology needs to rise to the challenge outlined by cosmopolitan theorists, such as Held (2010: 36–37), who point out the disjuncture between the traditional, territorially bounded conception of democracy and political power and the new and changing forms of political capacity. The mechanisms of penal governance outlined in this chapter bring to our attention that the distinctions between internal and external, domestic and foreign are no longer clear-cut. Nor is there correspondence between state power, citizenship, and territory. Several recent decisions of the European Court of Human Rights[11] point to the gradual expansion of the European legal space beyond its territorial borders, and to the severing of the traditional ties between jurisdiction, territory, citizenship, and rights. On a similar note, this chapter can be read as an invitation to criminal justice scholarship to follow and to transcend its traditional scalar and spatial imaginaries.

References

Aas, K.F. (2011a) '"Crimmigrant" Bodies and Bona Fide Travelers: Surveillance, Citizenship and Global Governance', *Theoretical Criminology* 15(3): 331.

Aas, K.F. (2011b) 'A Borderless World? Cosmopolitanism, Borders and Frontiers', in C.M. Bailliet and Katja Franko Aas (eds), *Cosmopolitan Justice and Its Discontents*. London: Routledge.

Aas, K.F. (2006) <http://cmc.sagepub.com/content/vol2/issue2/> 'The Body Does Not Lie; Identity, Risk and Trust in Technoculture', *Crime, Media, Culture* 2(2) 143.

Agamben, G. (1998) *Homo Sacer: Sovereign Power and Bare Life*. Stanford, California: Stanford University Press.

---

[11] According to the ECHR judgment *Hirsii Jamaa v Italy* of 23 February 2012, Italy violated the European Convention of Human Rights by exposing the migrants to the risk of ill-treatment in Libya and to being repatriated to Somalia/Eritrea.

Aliverti, A. (2012) 'Making Home Safe? The Role of Criminal Law and Punishment in British Immigration Controls'. PhD Thesis.

Andreas, P. and Biersteker, T.J. (eds) (2003) *The Rebordering of North America: Integration and Exclusion in a New Security Context*. New York: Routledge.

Andreas, P. and Nadelmann, N. (2006) *Policing the Globe: Criminalization and Crime Control in International Relations*. Oxford: Oxford University Press.

Andreas, P. and Price, R. (2001) 'From War Fighting to Crime Fighting: Transforming the American National Security State', *International Studies Review* 3: 31.

Balibar, E. (2010) 'At the Borders of Citizenship: A Democracy in Translation?', *European Journal of Social Theory* 13(3): 315.

Bauman, Z. (1998) *Globalization: The Human Consequences*. Cambridge: Polity Press.

Bigo, D. (2006) 'Security, Exception, Ban and Surveillance', in D. Lyon (ed), *Theorizing Surveillance: The Panopticon and Beyond*. Cullompton: Willan Publishing.

Bigo, D. and Walker R.B.J. (2007) 'Political Sociology and the Problem of the International', *Millennium: Journal of International Studies* 35(3): 725.

Bosworth, M. and Guild, M. (2008) 'Governing through Migration Control: Security and Citizenship in Britain', *The British Journal of Criminology* 48: 703.

Brotherton, D.C. and Barrios, M. (2009) 'Displacement and Stigma: The Social-psychological Crisis of the Deportee', *Crime, Media, Culture* 5(1): 29.

Brown, W. (2010) *Walled States, Waning Sovereignty*. New York: Zone Books.

Calavita, K. (2005) *Immigrants at the Margins: Law, Race, and Exclusion in Southern Europe*. New York: Cambridge University Press.

Ceuppens, B. and Geschiere, P. (2005) 'Autochtony: Local or Global? New Modes in the Struggle over Citizenship and Belonging in Africa and Europe', *Annual Review of Anthropology*, 34: 385.

Cole, S. (2001) *Suspect Identities: A History of Fingerprinting and Criminal Identification*. Cambridge, MA: Harvard University Press.

Comaroff, J.L. and Comaroff, J. (2006) 'Law and Disorder in the Postcolony: An Introduction', in Jean Comaroff and John L. Comaroff (eds), *Law and Disorder in the Postcolony*. Chicago and London: The University of Chicago Press.

Coutin, S.B. (2005) 'Contesting Criminality: Illegal Immigration and the Spatialization of Legality', *Theoretical Criminology* 9(1): 5.

Dauvergne, C. (2008) *Making People Illegal: What Globalization Means for Migration and Law*. Cambridge: Cambridge University Press.

De Genova, N. and Peutz, N. (2010) *The Deportation Regime: Sovereignty, Space, and the Freedom of Movement*. Durham & London: Duke University Press.

Feeley, M. and Simon, J. (1994) 'Actuarial Justice: The Emerging New Criminal Law', in D. Nelken (ed), *The Futures of Criminology*. London: Sage.

Foucault, M. (1977) *Discipline and Punish; The Birth of the Prison*, Translated by Alan Sheridan. New York: Vinatge Books.

Foucault, M. (2004) *Society Must be Defended*. London: Penguin Books.

Gammeltoft-Hansen, T. (2011) *Access to Asylum: International Refugee Law and the Globalisation of Migration Control*. Cambridge: Cambridge University Press.

Geschiere, P. (2009) *The Perils of Belonging: Autochtony, Citizenship and Exclusion in Africa and Europe*. Chicago: The University of Chicago Press.

Gilman, N., Goldhammer, J., and Weber, S. (2011) *Deviant Globalization: Black Market Economy in the 21st Century*. New York and London: Continuum.

Guild, E. (2009) *Security and Migration in the 21st Century*. Cambridge: Polity Press.

Haggerty, K.D. and Ericson, R.V. (2000) 'The Surveillant Assemblage', *The British Journal of Sociology* 51(4) 605.

Held, D. (2010) *Cosmopolitanism: Ideals and Realities*. Cambridge: Polity Press.

Huysmans, J. (2006) *The Politics of Insecurity: Fear, Migration and Asylum in the EU*. London and New York: Routledge.

Koshravi, S. (2010) *'Illegal' Traveller: An Auto-Ethnography of Borders*. Basingstoke: Palgrave Macmillan.

Lippert, R. and Pyykkönen, M. (2012) 'Introduction: Immigration, Governmentality, and Integration Assemblages', *Nordic Journal of Migration Research* 2(1): 1.

Lyon, D. (2009) *Identifying Citizens: ID Cards as Surveillance*. Cambridge: Polity Press.

Lyon, D. (2005) 'The Border is Everywhere: ID Cards, Surveillance, and the Other', in E. Zureik and M. Salter (eds), *Global Surveillance and Policing: Borders, Security, Identity*. Cullompton: Willan Publishing.

Marcus, G.E. and Saka, E. (2006) 'Assemblage', *Theory, Culture and Society* 23(2–3): 101.

Melossi, D. (2003) '"In a Peaceful Life": Migration and the Crime of Modernity in Europe/Italy', *Punishment and Society* 5(4): 371.

Mitsilegas, V. (2010) 'Extraterritorial Immigration Control in the 21st Century: The Individual and the State Transformed', in B. Ryan and V. Mitsilegas (eds), *Extraterritorial Immigration Control: Legal Challenges*. Leiden and Boston: Martinus Nijhoff Publishers.

Moore, A. (2008) 'Rethinking Scale as a Geographical Category: From Analysis to Practice', *Progress in Human Geography* 32(2): 203.

Ong, A. (2006) *Neoliberalism as Exception: Mutations in Citizenship and Sovereignty*. Durham and London: Duke University Press.

Ong, A. and Collier, S.J. (eds) (2005) *Global Assemblages. Technology, Politics and Ethics as Anthropological Problems*. Malden, Oxford, Victoria: Blackwell Publishing.

Policing and Society (2011) Special issue: Stop and search in a global context, L. Weber and B. Bowling (eds) 21(4).

Sassen, S. (2008) 'Neither Global nor National: Novel Assemblages of Territory, Authority and Rights', *Ethics and Global Politics* 1: 61.

Schinkel, W. (2010) 'From Zoepolitics to Biopolitics: Citizenship and the Construction of "Society"', *European Journal of Social Theory* 13(2): 155.

Simon, J. (2007) *Governing through Crime: How the War on Crime Transformed American Democracy and Created a Culture of Fear*. Oxford: Oxford University Press.

Squire, V. (2011) 'The Contested Politics of Mobility: Politicising Mobility, Mobilizing Politics', in V. Squire (ed), *The Contested Politics of Mobility: Borderzones and Irregularity*. Abingdon: Routledge.

Stumpf, J.P. (2006) 'The Crimmigration Crisis: Immigrants, Crime, & Sovereign Power' *Bepress Legal Series*. Working Paper 1635; <http://law.bepress.com/expresso/eps/1635>.

Tsing, A.L. (2005) *Friction: An Ethnography of Global Connection*. Princeton and Oxford: Princeton University Press.

Ugelvik, T. (2012) 'Imprisoned on the Border: Subjects and Objects of the State in Two Norwegian Prisons', in S. Ugelvik and B. Hudson (eds), *Justice and Security in the 21st Century: Risks, Rights and the Rule of Law*. London: Routledge.

Walters, W. (2010) 'Foucault and Frontiers: Notes on the Birth of the Humanitarian Border', in U. Bröckling, S. Krasmann, and T. Lemke (eds), *Governmentality: Current Issues and Future Challenges*. New York and Abingdon: Routledge.

Weber, L. (2011) '"It Sounds Like You Shouldn't be Here": Immigration Checks on the Streets of Sydney', *Policing and Society* 21(4): 456.

Weber, L. and Bowling, B. (2008) 'Valiant Beggars and Global Vagabonds: Select, Eject, Immobilize', *Theoretical Criminology* 12(3): 355.

Weber, L. and Pickering, S. (2011) *Globalization and Borders: Death at the Global Frontier.* Basingstoke: Palgrave Macmillan.

Westfelt, L. (2008) *Migration som straff? Utvisning på grund av brott 1973–2003 med fokus på flykningskydd.* Stockolm: Kriminologiska Institutionens avhandlingsserie.

Zedner, L. (2010) 'Security, the State, and the Citizen: the Changing Architecture of Crime Control', *New Criminal Law Review* 13(2): 379.

2

Is the Criminal Law Only for Citizens?
A Problem at the Borders of Punishment

Lucia Zedner[1]

It is a shame and bad taste to be an alien, and it is no use pretending otherwise. There is no way out of it. A criminal may improve and become a decent member of society. A foreigner cannot improve. Once a foreigner, always a foreigner. There is no way out for him.[2]

Introduction

Crimes of mobility, the policing of borders, and the carceral institutions of immigration detention and deportation are all relatively new objects of criminological enquiry. A developing convergence between criminology, migration, and refugee studies refocuses attention away from the study of domestic crime to borders and beyond, to examine the ways in which unlawful immigrants are policed long before they step on domestic soil. Scholars interested in the policing of borders are, perhaps predictably, chiefly interested in what happens at those borders and in the institutions of border control, wherever they are physically located (Aas 2012). This chapter suggests that understanding the borders of punishment might profit from closer attention to internal questions about the constitutional structures of the criminal law, its authority, and its scope. We need to address the question of border, in other words, from the inside out.

Competing accounts of what grounds the criminal law and what justifies punishment attach different weight to the importance of relations between state and citizen and to lateral relations among citizens—of which more anon. But they hold in common the view that citizenship is central in explaining the obligations

[1] I am grateful to Ambrose Lee for his research assistance; to Katja Franko Aas, Andrew Ashworth, Antony Duff, Rajeev Gundur, and Malcolm Thorburn for commenting on earlier drafts; and to the AHRC for supporting the 'Preventive Justice' project (ID: AH/H015655/1), out of which this chapter arises.
[2] Mikes 1946: 8. This gem of a book was given to my father, a *Kindertransport* child, on the occasion of his naturalization—of which process Mikes wryly observes, 'before you are admitted to British citizenship you are not even considered a natural human being' (Mikes 1946: 82).

that individuals owe under the criminal law and in justifying the censure and sanction of those who transgress its norms.[3] Citizenship is also said to ground the obligations that the state owes to the accused, and it has been deployed very effectively to articulate a parsimonious account of the limits of justified punishment (Duff 2010a). This is all well and good if one is a citizen in receipt of the protections and party to the reciprocal obligations that attach to being a legal resident of one's country. But the grounding of criminal law and punishment in the person of the citizen leaves unanswered large questions about the ambiguous status of those who are not, or not yet, or no longer, legal citizens.[4]

This chapter examines the place of the citizen in differing conceptions of the criminal law, and explores the implications for those who are not citizens. It goes on to examine contemporary debates in criminal law theory about the 'problem' of the non-citizen. These range between, at best, treating the non-citizen as a guest to whom hospitality is owed, to, at worst, treating him or her as a non-member of the legal community, an untrustworthy figure to whom lesser obligations are owed. The chapter will suggest that the difficulties entailed by these accounts reveal the hazards of predicating the obligations of criminal law upon citizenship. Important too are changes in the architecture of offences and in criminal procedure. The trend toward status offences and recourse to civil-criminal hybrid preventive orders, designed to restrain and monitor those deemed untrustworthy, also has adverse implications for responses to the non-citizen.

Notwithstanding the fact that the criminal law is conventionally predicated on the figure of the citizen, the criminalization of the non-citizen for breaches of immigration laws proceeds apace. Aliverti reports that while 70 immigration offences were passed in the UK from 1905 to 1996, 84 new immigration offences were created from 1997 to 2010 in six Acts passed by the Labour government. The Immigration and Asylum Act 1999 alone created 35 new immigration-related offences, including deception intended to circumvent immigration enforcement actions; false or dishonest representation by asylum claimants; failure by a sponsor to maintain claimants; and offences relating to the enforcement of discipline inside removal centres. The Nationality, Immigration and Asylum Act 2002 added further offences, including assisting unlawful immigration to a Member State by a non-EU citizen; helping an asylum seeker to enter the United Kingdom 'knowingly and for gain'; and assisting entry to the United Kingdom in breach of a deportation or exclusion order. Further offences were added by the Asylum and Immigration Act 2004 (which made failure to produce a passport and failure to

---

[3] Beyond the scope of this chapter is the question of how far this conception of the criminal law is challenged by the development of international policing and arrest provisions, international extradition, and international criminal law. The establishment of the International Criminal Court raises further questions about the normative community to which international criminal law is addressed and what grounds its authority.

[4] To speak of legal citizens leaves open a further ambiguity about the standing, duties of, and obligations owed to those who are de facto citizens but who do not enjoy that legal status—but that is beyond the scope of this chapter. See further Norrie 2009. An extended analysis of the varieties of citizenship is to be found in the classic work of Marshall 1950.

cooperate with deportation or removal procedures without a reasonable excuse crimes), as well as by the UK Border Agency Act 2007 and the Borders, Citizenship and Immigration Act 2009 (Aliverti 2012a; Aliverti 2012b). The phenomenon of 'crimmigration' has rightly attracted scholarly attention and concern.[5] Less attention has been paid to the fact that many immigration offences fail to satisfy basic principles of criminal law. This failure, and our acceptance of it, demands explanation. In seeking to explain these trends, the chapter will examine the tenets of *Feindstrafrecht*—a criminal law for enemies distinct from *Bürgerstrafrecht*, the criminal law only for citizens. According to Jakobs, *Feindstrafrecht* applies to those to whom the normal protections of the criminal law and criminal procedure do not and should not apply. This chapter will explore heated debates in Germany and elsewhere about the claims of *Feindstrafrecht*. It will suggest that the possibility of positing a separate, less favourable 'law for enemies' derives directly from the fact that the criminal law is predicated upon citizenship, since it is this that opens the way to differential, less favourable treatment of non-citizens. In short, this chapter will suggest that the centrality of citizenship to the criminal law and punishment poses intractable problems for those whose citizenship status is absent, in doubt, or irregular and makes it possible to conceive of *Feindstrafrecht*, with all the adverse consequences that this entails. The chapter concludes by suggesting some possible ways out of this impasse.

1. Criminal Law as Public Law

Domestic criminal law is an inherently bounded entity defined by reference to the collective interests it serves. It is a truism that what distinguishes the criminal law from tort actions between private parties is the public character of criminal wrongdoing. A wrong is identified as criminal because it is deemed a public wrong: that is to say it is 'a wrong against the polity as a whole, not just against the individual victim' (Duff 2007: 141). The idea of public wrong rests on the assumption that we have obligations to our fellow citizens that are transgressed by those forms of wrongdoing which go beyond personal injury to violate or threaten values that underpin the polity. It also requires that members of the public share a sufficient commitment to a set of common values (whatever they may be and even if there is disagreement about the values themselves) to ground a criminal law that articulates their boundaries. What those values are need not detain us here; the important point is rather that the definition of crime as a public wrong relies upon a notion of the public as a self-defined and finite entity. Duff argues that 'the "public" character of crime is therefore an implication, rather than a ground, of its criminalizable character: the reasons that justify its criminalisation are the very reasons why it is "public"' (Duff 2007: 142). In short, the public nature of criminal

---

[5] Stumpf 2007; Stumpf 2008: 1587–1600; Legomsky 2007. For a more historically grounded account, see Aliverti 2012a.

wrongdoing is built upon the idea of a polity that enjoys enough commonality to be able to specify its collective values and to enforce them.

The idea of crime as public wrong is central not only to the definition of offences but also to the 'public interest test' that must be satisfied if prosecution is to proceed. Only transgressions of public values—those held to be sufficiently important to the self-definition of the polity to require public condemnation of their breach—are prosecutable. In English law, for example, the Code for Crown Prosecutors requires the prosecutor to consider whether it is in the public interest to bring a prosecution or whether 'there are public interest factors tending against prosecution which outweigh those tending in favour'.[6] In Thorburn's view, the public interest decision derives from the fact that the criminal law is a branch of public law and officials acting upon it exercise public powers on behalf of the citizenry in the collective interest. He argues that state officials can therefore 'make a legitimate claim to be acting on behalf of us all' (Thorburn 2011: 42). However, the 'us' in 'us all' is not a universal 'us' but a bounded 'us'. The 'public' in both the public wrong requirement for criminalization and the public interest test for prosecution and the 'us' on behalf of whom the criminal law censures wrongdoing and sanctions wrongdoers is a restricted population of those who are citizens. To the extent that citizenship and the idea of the public underwrite the definition of what is a crime and what is prosecutable under domestic law, the criminal law is bordered, its territory is defined, and its audience limited to those who belong to that collective public, for and to whom it speaks.

2. State, Citizen, and the Authority of the Criminal Law

Just as the scope of domestic criminal law is bounded, so too are the bases of its authority. Competing accounts of the authority of the criminal law go to the very definition of the state, its powers, and its relationship to citizens. This is the stuff of jurisprudence and political theory, upon which sophisticated treatises have been elaborated and debated.[7] What follows is a brief and necessarily simplified overview of the two main camps of thought: liberalism and communitarianism (on which, see Mulhall and Swift 1996).

A classic liberal conception of the relationship between state and citizen focuses upon the obligations citizens owe to the state and the state owes to its citizens. The citizen's obligation to obey the law is explained variously by reference to tacit consent to its authority; ideas of benefit or gratitude to the state for the protection and services it provides; reciprocity or fair play to other citizens; or the consequentialist ground that, absent obedience to law, chaos or return to a Hobbesian state of nature would result. Even in respect of those crimes that do not tend toward disorder, the grounds for obligation are found in the desirability of coordination

---

[6] CPS 2010: 10 at <http://www.cps.gov.uk/publications/docs/code2010english.pdf>.
   See discussion in Ashworth and Redmayne 2010: 204–206.
[7] For helpful introductions, see Knowles 2010; Swift 2006.

and efficiency (for example, laws determining on which side of the road to drive). It is these collective values that underpin much *male prohibita* criminal law. The historically dominant account of the state as a sovereign who issues commands loyally obeyed by obedient subjects has been overlaid by liberal democratic accounts of the relationship between state and citizen as based upon mutual agreement or contract. Variant theories of political authority share as a common core the idea that citizens consent to state authority in return for which the state undertakes 'to prevent people from mistreating others, and to safeguard good order and the basic means by which citizens can live good lives' (Ashworth and Zedner 2011: 280).[8] Questions about the nature and extent of state authority, the measure of liberty to be sacrificed in return for protection, and the scope of the public sphere are answered differently in different accounts of liberalism. Citizenship appears in many accounts, underpinning the idea that moral norms derive their force from a contract between state and citizen or among citizens in respect of the state.[9]

By contrast, and at the risk of further oversimplification, communitarianism questions the atomistic account of individual autonomy and the hierarchical relations between citizen and state suggested by liberalism. Communitarians place greater emphasis upon the relational links among citizens and upon their membership of community. They see obligations under the criminal law as being vested in the bonds of community; the values upheld by the criminal law as being those held in common; and its ability to communicate censure as being dependent on a linguistic and normative commonality (Duff 2001: 131). Communitarianism, too, is territorially bounded, though the borders are context specific to whatever community is at issue, whether familial, professional, local, or national. Antony Duff has developed a sophisticated communicative account of the criminal law and punishment which derives from communitarian thinking and which addresses people as citizens (Duff 2010a; Duff 2011). He distinguishes between citizens and subjects, arguing that 'if people are to be bound by the law as citizens, rather than merely as subjects, their law must be a "common" law ... It must be addressed to them by the community, as members of that community' (Duff 1998b: 256). The role of citizenship in Duff's account is important because it is the citizen *to whom* the criminal law speaks, it is the community of citizens *by whom* the defendant is called to account, and it is the community *in answer to whom* the offender owes penance for breaching the criminal law. Authorship of the criminal law derives from the political community of citizens in a liberal democracy through their elected representatives. Its norms are those norms held in common by that community—it is this that makes 'the criminal law, a common law' (Duff 2007: 50). And its

---

[8] For further discussion, see 'Contractarianism' and 'Contractualism' in the *Stanford Encylopedia of Philosophy* at <http://plato.stanford.edu/entries/contractarianism/> and <http://plato.stanford.edu/entries/contractualism/>.

[9] For an overview of this literature, see 'Citizenship' at <http://plato.stanford.edu/entries/citizenship/>.

For an alternate view, grounded in ideas of autonomy, which does not distinguish between citizen and foreigner in the same way, see Blake 2001. Also important is the substantial literature on liberal cosmopolitanism.

addressee is the citizen who is made answerable (or, one might say, responsible) to fellow citizens for breach of those norms.

So important is this communitarian ideal to Duff's thinking that he is led to conclude that 'if we do not live in what can count as political communities, the legitimacy of criminal law is radically undermined, as is much else about the state' (Duff 2011: 141). Criminal law for communitarians like Duff is, therefore, a civic enterprise: it is based upon prior associative obligations, breaches of which are subject to criminalization. These associative obligations are owed not out of gratitude or consent to the authority of the state but by virtue of 'our shared membership of the polity' (Duff 2011: 140). Membership of a community and common bonds under-pin mutual obligations and posit a horizontal basis for the authority of the criminal law that is distinct (though how distinct might be debated) from a hierarchical model of state sovereignty. There is, however, a latent sting in the communitarian tail: namely its treatment of those who do not belong; who as the stranger, the alien, or the excluded, stand outside the bonds of membership and commonality.[10] Nor is there any guarantee that all those who enjoy citizenship will enjoy fair and equal treatment. Duff recognizes that 'communities can be, and all too often are, oppres-sive, illiberal, and unjust. They can also ... be in various ways *exclusionary*: they can exclude from full membership or participation groups or individuals whom they (mis)perceive as alien, inferior, or "other"' (Duff 1998b: 257; Zedner 2010).

3. The Territory of the Criminal Law and the Problem of the Outsider

Sparse and inadequate as these sketches of liberal and communitarian accounts of citizenship are, they suffice to establish that in so far as the criminal law is predicated upon citizenship this sets sharp bounds to its remit. As Gibney has observed, 'citizenship is inherently exclusive. To define a state's citizenry is simultaneously to define who is not a citizen' (Gibney 2006: 2). Although 'by far the most common way for non-citizenship (or alienage) to be generated is through *boundary crossing*: moving out of a state in which one holds formal membership (nationality) into another sovereign state' (Gibney 2006: 3), citizenship may also be revoked, withdrawn, or lost through fundamental changes in the nature of the state (for example civil war, revolution, or the introduction of discriminatory citizenship-stripping regimes such as Nazism). Gibney (2006) observes that members of other groups, though they are formally citizens, may nonetheless be treated as second-class or 'stunted' citizens as a result of gender, ethnic, religious, or economic discrimination. It follows that attaching the protections of the criminal law to full citizenship and legal standing has the effect of limiting its scope and availability to those who do not belong or whose membership is in doubt. I have addressed the problem of the bounded nature of the criminal law elsewhere, arguing that:

---

[10] To be clear this is an issue to which Duff attends directly and upon which he has much of interest to say, not least in Duff 1998a; Duff 1998b; Duff 2011: 141–148.

insistence that all those subject to the criminal law must be citizens in the sense of being full members of the political community does not acknowledge that even to speak of community is, of necessity, to acknowledge its boundaries. A model of the criminal law predicated upon the idea of community presumes a bounded civic entity to which most will belong but from which, if community is to mean anything, some must by definition be excluded. (Zedner 2010: 400)

In what follows, I explore further how the criminal law should address those who as non-citizens stand beyond its borders, as well as those deemed second-class or stunted citizens whose enjoyment of its legal protections is limited by their subordinate standing.

The problem of boundaries and exclusion is not confined to communitarian accounts of the criminal law. The problem is no less pressing under liberalism, as Blake observes:

Liberalism has difficulty with the fact of state borders. Liberals are, on the one hand, committed to moral equality, so that the simple fact of humanity is sufficient to motivate a demand for equal concern and respect. Liberal principles, on the other hand, are traditionally applied only within the context of the territorial state, which seems to place an arbitrary limit on the range within which liberal guarantees will apply. (Blake 2001: 257)

In both classical accounts of the power of the sovereign command over its subjects and in contractarian accounts of relations between state and citizens, the scope of domestic criminal law is also clearly bounded. It extends only to the borders of the sovereign realm or the limits of the nation state—the so-called 'principle of territoriality' (Duff 2007: 44; Aas 2011: 135).[11] The territorial aspect of domestic criminal law draws its authority not from its geographical limits but from the normative significance of the relations (sovereign/subject, contractarian, communitarian) that bind those within its borders. And it is this that creates the particular problem of the outsider.

Duff is alive to the territoriality of the domestic criminal law and the problem of the non-citizen. He advances an appealing, but not unproblematic, response to the problem by suggesting that we should think of non-citizens as temporary residents, as visitors, or, better still, as our guests. To posit non-citizens as guests presupposes that we assume the role of hosts and, with it, all the obligations of hospitality. It follows that not only should we treat our guests decently, with 'respect and concern', but, says Duff, we should afford them no less protection and support than we offer to full members of our community (Duff 2011: 141). In turn, this ethic of hospitality imposes reciprocal obligations upon those who come as guests to abide by our rules, if for no other reason than 'respect for the local values and attitudes' (Duff 2011: 142). Where the conduct of visitors is wrongful, whether or

---

[11] Duff acknowledges that in the case of serious and wide-reaching wrongs the demands of justice require that domestic courts recognize the standing of the courts of other jurisdictions and of an international court, like the International Criminal Court, whose authority derives not from the nexus of community but which acts in the name of humanity, as a moral (though not a political) community (Duff 2010b: 596). Human rights law and international criminal law are increasingly important in this regard.

not it would be a wrong elsewhere, it becomes *our* business by virtue of the fact that it is committed on our territory and the rightful object, therefore, of our attention as a polity.

Duff's account offers a more decent, civilized approach to the problem of the outsider and responds to important questions, which might otherwise appear to be without answer, about how the criminal law should speak to non-citizens. But it is more sanguine about the role of respect and concern in a civilized polity than seems consistent with what might realistically be expected of modern states in an era of mass migration that is said to test hospitality to its limits. It presupposes that the polity is indeed civilized or at least capable of civility, that we are willing to treat all who visit as our guests and extend to them our hospitality as hosts. The idea of hospitality might plausibly apply to those who come as tourists, visitors, or temporary residents, but in practice it is strained in the case of those who enter as long-term economic migrants, asylum seekers, or refugees. The antagonistic, often exclusionary, and at times xenophobic tenor of contemporary immigration politics stands in direction tension with the idea of hospitality (Fekete and Webber 2009). It is further undermined by the fact that governments increasingly impose penalties upon hosts such as transportation companies, employers, and landlords for failing to uphold immigration laws.[12] The result is that far from acting as hosts, these groups are co-opted into the role of law enforcement agents, obliged to report undocumented entrants to the authorities if they are to avoid penalties themselves (see Pickering and Weber, Chapter 5 in this volume).

Political realism aside, the concept of hospitality might be thought to set up a dependent relationship between host and guest. If hospitality, concern, or protection is not to be a matter of largesse on which the welfare of the guest depends, then we need a more developed normative conception of what hospitality entails and what duties it places upon the host. More problematic are the obligations placed upon non-citizens as guests, which seem too closely akin to the obligations owed by subjects to the sovereign to fit well with modern liberal democratic accounts of the criminal law.

Since non-citizens are by definition not citizens, it may be argued that there is nothing wrong or inconsistent with them being treated as such. But in so far as we have independent concerns about treating people who are bound by law as subjects, then to regard non-citizens as *subject* to law is problematic. To do so brings all the dangers of addressing non-citizen defendants not as members of a normative community but as subjects upon whom legal obligations are imposed despite the fact that, as non-citizens, they have no right to share in the authorship or amendment of our common norms and they enjoy reduced protections under our laws. Inasmuch as the criminal law is predicated upon the reciprocity of citizenship, a criminal law that is addressed to non-citizens as guests also raises questions about our standing, as hosts, to call non-citizens to account. Duff observes that 'unless a

[12] So, for example, the Immigration, Asylum and Nationality Act 2006 introduced financial penalties for knowingly employing adults who are subject to immigration control (Aliverti 2012a: 90–93).

person is addressed ... by the law of a community of which he is a member, he cannot be bound by that law as a citizen' (Duff 1998b: 257), yet this leaves open the question of how and upon what basis the non-citizen is then bound.

In a time of mass migration, refugees, asylum seekers, and illegal immigrants are more often perceived, at best, as uninvited guests, at worst as threatening intruders. The public's willingness to trust those whose provenance is unknown or whose values and world view may differ radically from their own makes the extension of hospitality appear to many as an act of altruism too far. As Waldron observes in respect of foreign nationals suspected of involvement in terrorism, all too often ' "the individual" in question is not really thought of as a member of the community at all: he is an alien, a foreigner' (Waldron 2010: 35).

4. Some Hazards of Criminal Law at the Border

All this begins to explain why we have difficulty in addressing the non-citizen as a full member of our community and why, in practice, we may find it problematic to extend the hospitality owed to a guest. It does not follow, however, that the non-citizen should be treated with hostility. So the increasing trend toward exclusion and expulsion, made manifest in the growth of immigration offences, the extraordinary increase in foreign national prisoners, and in deportation of non-citizens, requires explanation (Bosworth 2008; Bosworth 2011; Bosworth and Kaufman 2011). The bounded nature of domestic criminal law is made toxic by an exclusionary turn in contemporary penal politics that is prone to identify 'monsters and aliens', not only on our borders but also in our midst (Hudson 2006: 237). The antisocial youth, the sex offender, and the would-be terrorist, through their proclivities or conduct, are seen to have breached civic trust and, in so doing, to have placed themselves outside civil society. As such, they are deemed to be legitimate objects of monitoring, restraint, or even exile (Zedner 2010: 389). Non-citizens, as outsiders par excellence, are objects of suspicion to be stopped, searched, and interrogated even before they reach the border. Those whose ethnicity, appearance, or documentation fails to provide countervailing reassurance are liable to be turned back, detained, or criminalized.

The tendency to social exclusion, which draws bright lines between 'them' and 'us', is a topic much discussed in criminological literature[13] but its focus has, until recently, been principally upon the drivers, practices, and consequences of exclusion within society. The implications of these trends for the ways in which we think about those who were never members of our society, and for whom *re*integration is not a possibility, merit further attention (though see Hudson 2006: 237–241). They raise questions about how far the valorization of community and the tendency toward social exclusion bleeds into our treatment of the non-citizen. As Hudson observes, 'The other figure at the borders of community is the *alien*.

---

[13] See, for example, Simon 1998; Young 1999; Garland 2001: 131–137.

Unlike monsters, the alien is a figure we have not yet judged ... The alien is not-yet-classified, the *undecided* who has yet to persuade that she is friend not foe' (Hudson 2006: 239).

The role of trust is particularly relevant here. Ramsay has identified, as an important characteristic of contemporary penal politics, the emphasis placed upon the vulnerability of citizens, the consequent popular demand for reassurance, and the intolerance of those who by virtue of their conduct fail to reassure (Ramsay 2009; Ramsay 2010: 724). Ramsay's chief object of inquiry is the antisocial offender, but his analysis extends no less plausibly (one might say even more plausibly) to the serial sex offender, to the would-be terrorist, or persistent offender whose conduct places their fidelity to the criminal law in question. Ohana invites us to consider the role of trust and distrust in our construction of offenders who, by breaching the norms of the criminal law, are deemed to fail in fulfilment of their duties as loyal citizens and who, in so doing, disappoint 'the expectations of fellow members of the polity' (Ohana 2010: 724). Whereas these offenders have, through their conduct, provided positive grounds for distrust, the outsider has yet to prove his or her trustworthiness. While trust can be established relatively easily by those in receipt of the requisite papers, bank balance, and bona fide travel plans, undocumented or irregular aliens are quickly categorized as objects of distrust by the state, all the more profound because, as outsiders, they owe no loyalty to the polity.[14]

These questions of trust and distrust lie at the heart of a heated contemporary debate in European legal scholarship[15] prompted by the work of the German criminal law scholar Günther Jakobs, who infamously developed the concept of *Feindstrafrecht* (enemy criminal law) (Jakobs 1985). *Feindstrafrecht* is advocated by Jakobs as a distinct branch of criminal law distinguishable from the norms of criminal law for citizens (*Bürgerstrafrecht*) so as to preserve the integrity of that law by providing grounds for departing from its fundamental precepts and principled constraints. *Feindstrafrecht* is directed principally at the disloyal citizen who by dint of persistent and unrepentant offending is deemed to foreclose the possibility of his or her reintegration into society and restoration to full citizenship. It thus promises security for loyal citizens against those deemed dangerous or irredeemably defiant. Trenchant criticisms have been mounted at the assumptions underpinning Jakobs' account: namely that it levers the claims of public security to justify overly extensive preventive measures; that it strait-jackets the borders of the citizens' criminal law by confining its audience to supposedly 'loyal' citizens; and that, by privileging communitarian values and group identity, it exacerbates the exclusionary turn of contemporary penal politics (Ohana 2010: 729–730). As Ohana observes, 'the logic of *Feindstrafrecht* ... marks actors who cannot be trusted to abide by the law on their own and subjects them to special restrictions for the sake of protecting the

---

[14] Although of course employers and the economy as a whole rely heavily on undocumented workers. Indeed, economists argue that modern labour markets create a structural demand for unskilled immigrant labour to do low-paid, undesirable jobs that citizens will not fill.

[15] See, for example, the discussion in Gomez-Jara Diez 2008; Heinrich 2009: 96; Ohana 2010: 727–730.

public' (Ohana 2010: 741). This implication has not been overlooked by the Far Right in Germany who seized upon Jakobs' ideas to argue that foreigners, who were in fact non-citizens, should be treated differently to German citizens 'on the grounds that their lack of affiliation to the nation posed a grave threat to Germany and justified their classification as "criminal enemies"' (Fekete and Webber 2009: 5).

For all the criticism fairly levelled at Jakobs' theory as a normative account of the criminal law, there remains explanatory value in his identification of the precepts and attributes of *Feindstrafrecht* to illuminate key attributes of contemporary penal politics. Its explanatory value extends beyond our treatment of those who can be deemed to have demonstrated their disloyalty by dint of their conduct (and thus rendered themselves outsiders or enemies), to our responses to those who are deemed untrustworthy by virtue of their status *as* outsiders. Furthermore, attributes, positively condoned by Jakobs as central precepts of *Feindstrafrecht*, correspond to parallel trends in the contemporary overextension of criminalization to immigration. Both seek to punish pre-emptively to prevent harms before they occur; both license the imposition of disproportionate sanctions, indefinite detention, or even exile in the name of security; and both license departure from the fundamental procedural protections of the criminal law on the grounds that those outside citizenship do not deserve such protection. These trends can be observed in the criminalization of immigration. Criminal liability is extended back in time to encompass inchoate and even pre-inchoate liability, for example criminalizing at the point of departure or before the border is even attained (Aas 2012). New laws expand participatory liability for crimes of association, for example in respect of illegal immigration and trafficking. And criminal liability is attached to what were once regulatory requirements of immigration law but which are now recast as criminal offences.[16]

5. The Criminalization of Immigration and the Limits of the Criminal Law

This leads to our final observations on the status of immigration offence within criminal law and some worrying aspects of those offences that transgress the legitimate limits of criminal liability. Much has been written on the trend toward criminalizing breaches of immigration law (eg Stumpf 2007; Chacon 2009). Less has been said about the ways in which that trend results in the creation of offences that breach fundamental principles of the criminal law (though see Stumpf, Chapter 3 in this volume). A full treatment of this question is beyond the scope

---

[16] Although the criminalization of immigration in Britain can be traced back to the early nineteenth century, it was expanded considerably under the Labour government. See discussion in Aliverti 2012a: 85, 102, 103; Aliverti 2012b.

of this chapter,[17] yet it can be argued that core principles of the criminal law are imperilled by many immigration offences.

First, a basic requirement of the criminal law is fair warning. Although ignorance of the law is no defence and visitors to a country are bound by the laws of land, it could be said that the creation of immigration offences risks breaching the requirement of fair warning, that people should be given adequate notice of any legal requirement, so that they can reasonably adjust their conduct to accord with it. Notices now proliferate in the crowded arrivals halls of major airports which, in lengthy, minute script, enumerate just some of the many immigration offences. Whether this suffices to satisfy the requirements of fair warning merits further consideration, especially given the difficulty, to which any traveller will attest, of ensuring that one accords with the minutiae of local immigration requirements.

A second objection is that many immigration offences lack a sufficient culpability requirement or are offences of strict liability. Indeed, one of the classic cases of strict liability is the immigration case of *Larsonneur* (1933) in which a French woman was found guilty of no more than being 'an alien' illegally landed, through no fault of her own, on English soil.[18] Many modern immigration offences render would-be immigrants or refugees liable for serious offences in respect of which liability is satisfied by limited knowledge requirements or by strict liability alone. For example, one of the most commonly prosecuted of immigration offences is section 2 of the Asylum and Immigration Act 2004, the strict liability offence of failure to produce a passport (Aliverti 2012a: 103).

The third and perhaps most important objection is that it is questionable whether immigration offences satisfy the basic requirements of JS Mill's harm principle, namely that 'that the only purpose for which power can rightfully be exercised over any member of a civilised community, against his will, is to prevent harm to others' (Mill 1859/1979: 68). A necessary condition of criminalization is that some non-trivial harm is risked or caused by the offender (Simester and von Hirsch 2011: Ch 3; Ashworth and Zedner 2012). Yet in respect of many immigration offences it is unclear what the harm, or putative harm, is. Given that most immigration offences are crimes of strict liability, neither can it be said that they impose a wrongfulness criterion. Taken together these lapses raise profound questions about the justifiability of criminalizing illegalities by immigrants where these do not meet the basic precepts of criminalization.

The question remains why we are so willing to depart from adherence to ordinary principles of criminalization in respect of immigration. Enough has been said about the centrality of citizenship to suggest that our understanding of the criminal law derives its authority from and addresses itself to citizens. This provides a licence for the standards applied to non-citizens to be reduced, compromised, or dispensed with altogether. In theory, if not always in practice, citizens in a democratic polity share the privileges of a fundamental right to be presumed

---

[17] Such a treatment is proposed by my Italian colleague Alessandro Spena, University of Palermo (personal communication).

[18] *R v Larsonneur* (1933) 24 Cr App R 74.

free from harmful intentions; they enjoy common authorship, through an elected legislature, of the criminal law; and they benefit from the security of due process protections from unwarranted state interference in their lives. By contrast the non-citizen is more often a figure of mistrust and, in many respects, offered lesser protections. In so far as criminalization rests on the idea that citizens are responsible agents responsive to reasons and that those reasons are ones the individual can fairly be expected to understand by dint of his or her shared membership of law's community, the very basis for criminal responsibility is attenuated in the case of the non-citizen. Perhaps we should not be surprised, therefore, by the apparent readiness to erode ordinary standards in respect of those to whom no such civic trust is owed and whose very membership of the polity is denied or in doubt.

6. Concluding Thoughts

This chapter has explored the contention that we cannot understand the borders of punishment, still less what is happening at the borders of states, unless we attend first to internal questions about the scope, authority, and territory of domestic criminal law. It has examined the centrality of the citizen as the subject to whom the criminal law speaks, and has examined the importance of law's community in constituting the normative authority by whom the citizen is called to account. In so doing it has suggested that the non-citizen, as an outsider, poses particular problems for the criminal law and especially for policing of immigration. The chapter has identified important lapses in adherence to basic principles of criminalization in respect of immigration offences and has suggested that failure to observe these principles derives in no small part from the subordinate standing accorded to non-citizens.

All this leaves unanswered questions about the grounds upon which the protections of criminal justice might be extended to those who are not citizens. This chapter has raised some doubts about the ethics of hospitality and has probed the plausibility of the idea that non-citizens be treated as our guests. It has questioned the idea of basing our penal practices upon our capacity for empathy, our ability to embrace difference, or our acceptance of the stranger at our gate. As has been made clear, present practice suggests a worrying tendency to regard non-citizens as untrustworthy and unworthy, therefore, of the full protections ordinarily accorded by the criminal law to citizens. Whether working towards a cosmopolitan conception of community grounded in our common humanity would have any greater chance of changing attitudes in the medium term remains open to question.

The plight of the non-citizen is not a matter of easy resolution. What follows are no more than tentative avenues of enquiry that seek to address the problems identified in this chapter. One approach might be to question whether we should allow citizenship to do so much work in our thinking about responsible agency and the role of the criminal law. Given the evident hazards entailed in predicating our criminal law upon citizenship, might we do better to explore how far ideas of autonomy and of responsibility that underpin the ways in which we address and respond to citizens can be extended to non-citizens?[19] Another possible way of overcoming the citizen/non-citizen binary is the idea of 'denizenship' (Hammar 1990). Denizenship recognizes the hybrid status of those with long-standing or permanent residence who possess many legal and social rights but lack full political citizenship. Also important is the argument that citizenship should not be a predicate for basic rights and that in a liberal democracy the protections of the criminal law, criminal process and just punishment apply to all irrespective of citizenship. As Cole insists, 'basic protections of liberty ... are not, and should not be, deemed privileges or rights of citizenship' (Cole 2003; Cole 2007; see also discussion in Zedner 2010: 392–393). An important feature of human rights law is that it provides safeguards for persons by virtue of their status as humans and out of respect for humanity, regardless of whether or not they are citizens. Article 6 ECHR rights to a fair trial, for example, apply equally to the foreigner and to the stateless person and Article 3 shields immigrants from being deported to countries where they face torture, or inhuman or degrading treatment.

The dangers posed by the evident willingness of governments to resort to criminalization at the border raises further questions about how best to delimit the phenomenon of 'crimmigration'. A first step might be to require that immigration offences satisfy basic principles of criminalization and, where they do not, to mark those offences as suitable candidates for decriminalization. Only by comprehensive review of existing offences and careful pre-legislative scrutiny of proposed offences might the over-readiness to criminalize breaches of immigration law be forestalled. So doing would serve to check the exercise of the police power over non-citizens by limiting immigration offences to those that are fairly labelled, clearly wrongful, and entail harms of a sufficient gravity to merit criminalization. A second step would be to scrutinize more closely the coercive and otherwise burdensome qualities of immigration measures and practices outside the criminal law. Proceedings in civil or hybrid civil-criminal channels are an increasingly common feature of contemporary crime control, attractive to the authorities because they sidestep the requirements of the criminal process (Zedner 2007; Stumpf, Chapter 3 in this volume). Yet, where civil procedures impose burdens akin to punishment, they are clearly detrimental precisely because they deny criminal process protections to those who are subject to them (Ashworth and Zedner 2010). Where proceedings and measures result in burdens of a severity comparable to punishment—immigration detention springs to mind as an obvious example—the process protections and standard of proof should surely be akin to those applied in criminal proceedings (Ashworth and Zedner 2010: 75).

This latter step may overcome the dilution of procedural protections inherent in many aspects of border policing and immigration, not least in the workings of the UK Special Immigration Appeals Commission (SIAC), an appeal court in which

[19] See, for example, the discussions in Lee 2011 and Aas 2011. An alternate account of an 'impartial liberalism' might allow that responsible agency is grounded in the 'autonomous agency of us all' and so is equally applicable to non-citizens (Blake 2001: 259).

the controversial office of the special advocate was first introduced.[20] The use of the special advocate is much criticized because it flouts the right of the individual to know the case against him or her—a basic principle that applies in criminal but no longer, it would seem, in civil hearings.[21] In similar vein, Bosworth's detailed empirical studies of immigration detention suggest that the bigger problem is not so much that detention centres look like prisons but that they do not. The absence of rights, adequate legal protections, and legal representation are all salient features of a dismal regime that leaves detainees in a legal limbo that can last for months or even years (Bosworth 2012). Looking beyond criminal or civil law labels to focus on the potential severity of the consequences of proceedings is an established way of importing appropriate due process protections such as an adequate standard of proof.[22] It might be extended to ensure access to legal advice, guarantees of legal representation, and fair and open hearings in civil proceedings just as in criminal ones. In place of profiling, often on dubious religious and racial grounds, and the adoption of targeted and discriminatory practices by immigration officials, we might insist upon the uniform application of the law and on fair and equal treatment. In place of protracted detention in the no-man's-land of the immigration detention or deportation centre, we might seek to ensure that detention is time-limited and that, as a minimum, conditions approximate to the standards laid down in international prison rules. Perhaps this importation of standards and protections relies upon an idealized account of the criminal law and process, but it does suggest some powerful reasons why we should be slow to conclude that the criminal law is only for citizens.

References

Aas, K.F. (2012) '(In)security-at-a-distance: Rescaling Justice, Risk and Warfare in a Transnational Age', *Global Crime* 13(4) 235.

Aas, K.F. (2011) 'A Borderless World? Cosmopolitanism, Borders and Frontiers', in C. Bailliet and K.F. Aas (eds), *Cosmopolitan Justice and its Discontents*. London: Routledge.

Aliverti, A. (2012a) 'Making Home Safe? The Role of Criminal Law and Punishment in British Immigration Controls'. Oxford DPhil Thesis.

Aliverti, A. (2012b) 'Making People Criminal. The Role of the Criminal Law in Immigration', *Theoretical Criminology* 16(4): 417.

---

[20] See <http://www.justice.gov.uk/tribunals/special-immigration-appeals-commission> and <http://www.official-documents.gov.uk/document/cm81/8194/8194.pdf>.

For critical commentary, see Kavanagh 2010; Tomkins 2011. Special advocates are lawyers with security clearance to view secret or closed documents from the intelligence services but who are not permitted to speak to suspects once they have seen this material.

[21] The proposal in the Justice and Security Bill (2013) to extend the role of special advocates to wider civil proceedings is hugely controversial, which only highlights the fact that it was not seen to be similarly problematic when introduced in respect of immigration appeals by non-citizens. See Cabinet Office 2011 at <http://www.official-documents.gov.uk/document/cm81/8194/8194.pdf>.

[22] *Engel v Netherlands* (1976) 1 EHRR 647; *Clingham v Royal Borough of Kensington and Chelsea*; *R (on behalf of McCann) v Crown Court of Manchester* [2003] 1 AC 787.

Ashworth, A. and Redmayne, M. (2010) *The Criminal Process*. (4th edn) Oxford: Oxford University Press.

Ashworth, A. and Zedner, L. (2012) 'Prevention and Criminalization: Justifications and Limits', *New Criminal Law Review* 15(4) 542.

Ashworth, A. and Zedner, L. (2011) 'Just Prevention and the Limits of the Criminal Law', in R.A. Duff and S.P. Green (eds), *Philosophical Foundations of the Criminal Law*. Oxford: Oxford University Press.

Ashworth, A. and Zedner, L. (2010) 'Preventive Orders: A Problem of Under-criminalization?', in R.A. Duff et al (eds), *The Boundaries of the Criminal Law*. Oxford: Oxford University Press.

Blake, M. (2001) 'Distributive Justice, State Coercion, and Autonomy', *Philosophy and Public Affairs* 30(3): 257.

Bosworth, M. (2012) 'Deportation and Immigration Detention: Globalising the Sociology of Punishment', *Theoretical Criminology* 16(2) 123.

Bosworth, M. (2011) 'Deporting Foreign National Prisoners in England and Wales', *Citizenship Studies* 15: 583.

Bosworth, M. (2008) 'Border Control and the Limits of the Sovereign State', *Social and Legal Studies* 17(2): 199.

Bosworth, M. and Kaufman, E. (2011) 'Foreigners in a Carceral Age: Immigration and Imprisonment in the U.S.', *Stanford Law and Policy Review* 22: 101.

Cabinet Office (2011) *Justice and Security Green Paper* Cm 8194. London: HMSO.

Chacon, J.M. (2009) 'Managing Migration through Crime', *Columbia Law Review* 109: 135.

Cole, D. (2007) 'Against Citizenship as a Predicate for Basic Rights', *Fordham Law Review* 75: 2541.

Cole, D. (2003) *Enemy Aliens: Double Standards and Constitutional Freedoms in the War on Terrorism*. New York: The New Press.

Crown Prosecution Service (CPS) (2010) *Code for Crown Prosecutors*.

Duff, R.A. (2011) 'Responsibility, Citizenship and Criminal Law', in R.A. Duff and S.P. Green (eds), *The Philosophical Foundations of the Criminal Law*. Oxford: Oxford University Press.

Duff, R.A. (2010a) 'A Criminal Law for Citizens', *Theoretical Criminology* 14(3): 293.

Duff, R.A. (2010b) 'Authority and Responsibility in International Criminal Law', in S. Besson and J. Tasioulas (eds), *Philosophy of International Law*. Oxford: Oxford University Press.

Duff, R.A. (2007) *Answering for Crime: Responsibility and Liability in the Criminal Law*. Oxford: Hart Publishing.

Duff, R.A. (1998a) 'Dangerousness and Citizenship', in A. Ashworth and M. Wasik (eds), *Fundamentals of Sentencing Theory*. Oxford: Clarendon.

Duff, R.A. (1998b) 'Inclusion and Exclusion: Citizens, Subjects and Outlaws', *Current Legal Problems* 51: 241.

Fekete, L. and Webber, F. (2009) 'Foreign Nationals, Enemy Penology and the Criminal Justice System', *European Race Bulletin* 69: 2.

Garland, D. (2001) *The Culture of Control: Crime and Social Order in Contemporary Society*. Oxford: Oxford University Press.

Gibney, M.J. (2006) *Who Should be Included? Non-citizens, Conflict and the Constitution of the Citizenry CRISE Working Paper No.17*. Oxford: CRISE, Queen Elizabeth House.

Gomez-Jara Diez, C. (2008) 'Enemy Combatants versus Enemy Criminal Law', *New Criminal Law Review* 11(4): 529.

Hammarberg, T. (1990) *Democracy and the Nation State: Aliens, Denizens and Citizens in a World of International Migration*. Avebury: Aldershot.

Heinrich, B. (2009) 'Die Grenzen des Strafrechts bei der Gefahrprävention', *Zeitschrift für die gesamte Strafrechtswissenshaft* 121(1): 96.

Hudson, B. (2006) 'Punishing Monsters, Judging Aliens: Justice at the Borders of Community', *Australian and New Zealand Journal of Criminology* 39(2): 232.

Jakobs, G. (1985) 'Kriminalisierung im Vorfeld einer Rechtsgutsverletzung', *Zeitschrift für die Gesamte Strafrechtswissenschaft* 97(4): 751.

Kavanagh, A. (2010) 'Special Advocates, Control Orders and the Right to a Fair Trial', *Modern Law Review* 63(5): 836.

Knowles, D. (2011) *Political Obligation: A Critical Introduction*. Abingdon: Routledge.

Lee, A. (2011) 'Co-national and Cosmopolitan Obligations towards Foreigners', *Politics* 31(3): 159.

Legomsky, S.H. (2007) 'The New Path of Immigration Law: Asymmetric Incorporation of Criminal Justice Norms', *Washington and Lee Law Review* 64: 469.

Marshall, T.H. (1950) *Citizenship and Social Class and Other Essays*. Cambridge: Cambridge University Press.

Mikes, G. (1946) *How to be an Alien*. London: Wingate.

Mill, J.S. (1859/1979) *On Liberty*. Harmondsworth, Middlesex: Penguin.

Mulhall, S. and Swift, A. (1996) *Liberals and Communitarians*. Oxford: Blackwell.

Norrie, A. (2009) 'Citizenship, Authoritarianism and the Changing Shape of the Criminal Law', in B. McSherry, A. Norrie, and S. Bronitt (eds), *Regulating Deviance: The Redirection of Criminalisation and the Futures of Criminal Law*. Oxford: Hart Publishing.

Ohana, D. (2010) 'Trust, Distrust and Reassurance: Diversion and Preventive Orders through the Prism of *Feindstrafrecht*', *Modern Law Review* 73(5): 721.

Ramsay, P. (2010) 'Overcriminalization as Vulnerable Citizenship', *New Criminal Law Review* 13(2): 262.

Ramsay, P. (2009) 'The Theory of Vulnerable Autonomy and the Legitimacy of Civil Preventative Orders', in B. McSherry, A. Norrie, and S. Bronitt (eds), *Regulating Deviance: The Redirection of Criminalisation and the Futures of Criminal Law*. Oxford: Hart Publishing.

Simester, A. and Von Hirsch, A. (2011) *Crimes, Harms and Wrongs: On the Principles of Criminalization*. Oxford: Hart Publishing.

Simon, J. (1998) 'Managing the Monstrous. Sex Offenders and the New Penology', *Psychology, Public Policy and Law* 3: 452.

Stumpf, J. (2008) 'States of Confusion: The Rise of State and Local Power over Immigration', *New Criminal Law Review* 86: 1557.

Stumpf, J. (2007) 'The Crimmigration Crisis: Immigrants, Crime and Sovereign Power', *Lewis & Clark Law School Legal Research Paper Series* Paper No 2007–2: 1.

Swift, A. (2006) *Political Philosophy: A Beginner's Guide for Students and Politicians*. London: Polity Press.

Thorburn, M. (2011) 'Criminal Law as Public Law', in R.A. Duff and S.P. Green (eds), *Philosophical Foundations of Criminal Law*. Oxford: Oxford University Press.

Tomkins, A. (2011) 'National Security and the Due Process of Law', *Current Legal Problems* 64(1): 215.

Waldron, J. (2010) *Torture, Terror and Trade-Offs: Philosophy for the White House*. Oxford: Oxford University Press.

Young, J. (1999) *The Exclusive Society: Social Exclusion, Crime and Difference in Late Modernity*. London: Sage.

Zedner, L. (2010) 'Security, the State and the Citizen: The Changing Architecture of Crime Control', *New Criminal Law Review* 13(2): 379.

Zedner, L. (2007) 'Seeking Security by Eroding Rights: The Side-Stepping of Due Process', in B. Goold and L. Lazarus (eds), *Security and Human Rights*. Oxford: Hart Publishing.

3

The Process is the Punishment in Crimmigration Law

Juliet P. Stumpf[1]

Introduction

In May 2008, federal immigration agents raided a chicken-packing plant in Postville, Iowa. The agents arrested over 300 assembly line workers. The raid was the product of cooperation between federal, state, and local law-enforcement agencies, including US Immigration and Customs Enforcement (ICE) and the federal prosecutor for the area. Dozens of federal agents swarmed the plant and questioned and arrested those suspected of immigration violations. They herded the arrested workers into white vans and transported them to a nearby cattle fairground that ICE had converted into a temporary detention centre (Duara et al 2008; Saulny 2008; Moyers 2009).

Rather than taking the arrestees to the local criminal court, which lacked the physical space needed to process that number of defendants, the government set up a temporary criminal court in the fairgrounds. Federal judges relocated to the courtroom to process the cases. The judges convicted and sentenced all of the employees within four days, handing out five-month sentences to most for using false documents to obtain work and convicting a handful of others for re-entering the United States without authorization. The plea agreements required the non-citizens to waive the right to appear before an immigration judge and to agree to deportation (Moyers 2009: 675–676).

The uniformity of the sentences was due to the prosecutor's office generating nearly identical plea agreements offering the five-month jail time and rejecting bids for a more lenient sentence. Prosecutors told defence counsel that if their clients refused to take the plea and chose to go to trial, they would face a charge of aggravated identity theft carrying a minimum two-year sentence. Choosing to go to

[1] Professor of Law, Lewis & Clark Law School. For invaluable comments and discussions I am indebted to Katja Franko Aas, Mary Bosworth, Mary Holland, Hiroshi Motomura, David Nelken, Jenny Roberts, Dirk van Zyl Smit, Lucia Zedner, participants at the University of Oxford's conference on Borders of Punishment: Criminal Justice, Citizenship and Social Exclusion, and commentators at the Works-in-Progress session of the 2012 Immigration Law Teachers Conference. Angie Ferrer contributed excellent research assistance. Special thanks to Eric, Liam, and Kai.

trial would also have prolonged the clients' detention well beyond the five months the prosecutor offered. Because the workers' primary concern was to secure work to provide for their families, even those with strong immigration cases were willing to agree to a plea that mandated deportation. The plea offered the certainty of quicker release and the avoidance of formal proceedings. The vast majority of the workers took the deal (Camayd-Freixas 2008).

Some workers spoke up, asking for immediate deportation instead of the insistence on incarceration. In the strength of their assertion that they were not criminals, the workers drew a defining line between the implications of being accused of a crime and the non-criminal nature of deportation for unlawful presence. They resisted being the object of public expression of criminality.

From the government's perspective, that sentiment aligned with its approach. Federal prosecutors stated that the Postville raid was a way of deterring unauthorized employment and migration using criminal process and punishment. If undocumented employees experienced the sentence as sufficiently unpleasant, some would decide that seeking work in the United States was not worth risking the ordeal of the criminal process and the resulting sanction.

The Postville events commanded intense media attention. The case was newsworthy not because of the sentences, which were relatively short, nor the charges, which were minor. In Postville, authorities transformed an employment-related immigration violation into a criminal transgression worthy of a massive sting operation, a special tribunal, and a parade of shackled immigrants undergoing mass processing of plea agreements in a facility otherwise used as a cattle showground (Camayd-Freixas 2008; Duara et al 2008; Hsu 2008; Saulny 2008; Schulte et al 2008).

In other words, it was the nature of the process that made the event noteworthy. The authorities leading the Postville raid relocated the criminal justice system, tailoring the traditional shape of pre-trial processes to fit a population of non-citizen defendants. The spectacle that this process enacted became a form of symbolic politics (Newburn and Jones 2007), directed beyond mere deterrence of border violations to express to the populace at large that unauthorized non-citizens were criminals. Targeting a largely Latino, low-wage workforce engaged and affirmed a widespread perception of that group as undocumented immigrants. These procedural choices sent a strong message that undocumented employees belonged in the criminal justice system and deserved criminal sentences.

The Postville raid unearthed the practical, social, and psychological consequences of combining the criminal justice and deportation systems and of issuing sanctions with elements from both. This chapter will evaluate whether the interaction between criminal and immigration law, or 'crimmigration' law, is transforming these related processes into punishment. Crimmigration law is a developing trend toward integrating the criminal justice and immigration systems. This integration tends to generate more severe outcomes, limit procedural protections, and encourage enforcement and adjudication processes that segregate non-citizens. The crystallization of crimmigration process as a sanction sets it apart from the formal penalties of criminal law and deportation.

Can a process function as punishment? Authorities may use the processes of the criminal justice system and deportation proceedings in order to sanction non-citizens for their status or in ways that non-citizens uniquely experience as indistinguishable from formal punishment. Crimmigration processes become punishment either when they create a punitive experience for non-citizens, as with immigration detention, or when they take the place of formal punishment, such as when the purpose of a police arrest is to channel a non-citizen into a deportation track.

Part I of this chapter examines how the rise of crimmigration law complicates the question whether deportation constitutes criminal punishment in US law (Markowitz 2011). It traces the ongoing evolution of crimmigration law in the United States, sketching the interactions between immigration law, criminal law, enforcement strategies, and politics.

Part II draws on Malcolm Feeley's work on the punitive nature of criminal process to analyse how crimmigration law has extended and complicated the processes of prosecuting and deporting non-citizens (Feeley 1979). It evaluates whether the processes that implement crimmigration law function to punish people on the basis of their status as non-citizens, becoming part of the penalty exacted by the state. The chapter will illustrate that crimmigration legitimizes greater expenditures of state power to control the liberty of the non-citizen using criminal and immigration enforcement tools. Both immigration and criminal justice actors cherry-pick processes from immigration law (such as detention), and from criminal law (such as police arrest), to fulfil official goals. Crimmigration law goes a step further, using mass prosecution of non-citizens, segregation from ordinary criminal law practices, expedited procedures, and uncertain and indefinite pre-trial and immigration detention policies to construct a separate and unique set of processes that segregate and penalize non-citizens in ways that are distinct from both the criminal justice system and removal proceedings.

The chapter concludes by reflecting on the relationship between the process of crimmigration and the contours of punishment. It identifies two critical markers that signal when the processes of crimmigration law may shade over into punishment: when the motives of the authorities enacting and enforcing the criminalizing process are to exact a sanction, and when the non-citizen commonly experiences the process as punitive.

I. Crimmigration Law and the Punishment Debate

Over the past several decades, criminal law and immigration law have developed a complex set of processes that point toward two formal substantive outcomes: the criminal sentence and deportation (Stumpf 2006; Legomsky 2007; Chacón 2009). Assessing whether these crimmigration processes can operate as punishment requires a map of those processes. This section will sketch the contours of crimmigration law and the current state of the law governing whether crimmigration outcomes qualify as punishment under US constitutional law.

Crimmigration law is an umbrella term for two loosely connected and overlapping legal trends (Stumpf 2013). Scholars have begun documenting and analysing these trends in Europe and Canada as well as the United States (Mitsilegas 2003; Pakes 2004, 2013; Aas 2011; Bosworth 2011; Pacella 2011; van der Leun and van der Woude 2011; Guia et al 2013). The first is the expansion of criminal grounds for deportation combined with a drastic reduction in the avenues for relief from deportation. In the United States, the criminal justice system has become a direct pathway to deportation. The proliferation of crime-based deportation grounds has directly impacted lawful permanent residents of the United States, who are vulnerable to few other bases for removal. A lawful permanent resident with an applicable conviction now has a much narrower chance of avoiding deportation (Demleitner 2002; Legomsky 2007: 482–485; Brown 2011).

Two further developments have exacerbated this effect. First, legislation making some criminal deportation grounds retroactive meant that old convictions became subject to the later expansion of crime-based deportation grounds. As a result, those convictions unexpectedly came to carry the greater—and later—sanction of expulsion from the non-citizen's community. Second, the inadmissibility grounds similarly expanded to include more minor crimes so that lawful permanent residents returning to their homes in the United States found themselves in the same legal position as if they were initial applicants for admission. Under the expanded inadmissibility grounds, lawful permanent residents have been denied readmission.[2]

The second crimmigration trend is the regulation of migration through immigration-related criminal grounds such as unlawful re-entry, newer crimes such as fraudulent marriage for immigration purposes, or crimes that by their nature involve non-citizens, such as human smuggling or harbouring unlawfully present migrants (Stumpf 2006; Chacón 2009). One of the rationales for criminalizing migration was to heighten the punishment for unauthorized border crossing. Criminalization was in part a reaction to a practice disparagingly referred to as 'catch and release' in which immigration enforcement officers apprehended non-citizens crossing unlawfully, initiated the removal process by serving them with a notice ordering them to appear for an immigration hearing at a future date, and then released them within US territory (US Immigration and Customs Enforcement 2010; Morton 2011).[3] This approach resulted in a minimum of process and avoided detention. However, it came under fire when detractors asserted that the practice gave non-citizens a free pass to enter the United States and that

---

[2] See Immigration and Nationality Act § 237(a), 8 USC § 1227(a) (2006) (listing deportability grounds); INA § 212(a), 8 USC § 1182(a) (2006) (providing grounds for inadmissibility).

[3] See Memorandum from John Morton, Director of US Immigration and Customs Enforcement, to All ICE Employees 2 (2 March 2011) <http://www.ice.gov/doclib/news/releases/2011/110302 washingtondc.pdf> (setting a priority 'to avoid a return to the prior practice commonly and historically referred to as "catch and release"'); ICE Strategic Plan: FY 2010–2014, US Immigration and Customs Enforcement 6 <http://www.ice.gov/doclib/news/library/reports/strategic-plan/strategic-plan-2010. pdf> (confirming that '[t]he Department of Homeland Security has worked diligently to phase out a practice known as "catch and release". Now, newly arriving aliens who do not successfully evade detection are apprehended, detained and removed as appropriate by law').

immigration officials failed to keep track of those released (US Immigration and Customs Enforcement 2010; Morton 2011).

This second form of crimmigration law entails an increased emphasis on crimes that only non-citizens can commit, such as unlawful entry or re-entry. Although many of these acts have long constituted crimes, the US government traditionally enforced them solely through deportation rather than prefacing deportation with a criminal prosecution and sentence. In contrast to the expansion of crime-based deportability grounds, this second trend of criminalizing unauthorized movement across the border targets a different group of non-citizens: unlawfully present migrants and those who associate with them (Stumpf 2013: 15–16).

The impact in the United States of this second trend has been twofold. First, unlawfully present non-citizens are much more likely to acquire a criminal record. Along certain stretches of the US border with Mexico, the federal government instituted an enforcement plan called Operation Streamline under which government officials criminally prosecute almost all unlawful border crossers prior to removing them. Non-citizens exit the United States with a criminal conviction and a bar to re-entering the United States for a prescribed span of years.

Second, conceiving of border crossing as a crime rather than a civil violation changed the nature of the government institutions charged with regulating migration. In the United States, immigration enforcement officials now constitute the largest armed law-enforcement body in the federal government. There are more federal criminal prosecutions of immigration-related offences than of drugs or weapons crimes (US Customs and Border Protection 2005; TRAC 2012).[4]

This crimmigration trend has also inspired the participation of non-federal criminal justice actors (Stumpf 2008). State and local law-enforcement authorities in many areas have taken it on themselves to enforce federal immigration law. State legislatures, notably those in Alabama and Arizona, have passed laws that criminalize unlawful presence in the United States and permit or require police to question or arrest non-citizens suspected of violating federal immigration law. Some of these laws place others in the position of immigration regulators, requiring school officials to establish registers of schoolchildren with unlawfully present parents or prohibiting landlords from renting to unlawfully present non-citizens on pain of criminal sanction. Legal challenges to these laws continue to play out in US courts with mixed results.[5]

---

[4] The US Customs and Border Protection (CBP) advertises itself as the 'largest law enforcement organization in the nation' <http://www.cbp.gov/xp/cgov/about>. As of September 2012, prosecution for immigration-related matters represented 54.9% of the total number of federal prosecutions during the year, whereas drug-related and weapons crimes represented 16% and 4.6%, respectively. Transactional Records Access Clearinghouse (TRAC), *Prosecutions for 2012* <http://tracfed.syr.edu/results/9x205123f48012.html>.

[5] The US Supreme Court struck down sections of Arizona's Support our Law Enforcement and Safe Neighborhoods Act (SB 1070), 2010 Ariz Sess Laws, ch 113, as amended by Act of 30 April 2010, 2010 Ariz Sess Laws, ch 211 (codified in scattered sections of Ariz Rev Stat Ann (West, Westlaw through Second Regular Session of the Fiftieth Legislature (2012))). *Arizona v United States* 132 SCt 2492 (2012); see also 689 F3d 1132 (9th Cir 2012). Alabama's Beason-Hammon Alabama Taxpayer and Citizen Protection Act (HB 56), 2011 Ala Acts 535 (codified at Ala Code §§ 31-13-1–31-13-30

The closer connection between criminal and immigration law enforcement feeds a growing perception that immigration violations are on the same continuum as traditional crimes. Other aspects of crimmigration law add to that understanding, such as the expanding use of immigration detention to ensure that non-citizens attend their deportation proceedings or that they submit to removal.[6] Similarly, the multiplying of state laws requiring or allowing state law-enforcement officers to make immigration-related stops and arrests enacts that perception, often turning a federal civil violation into a state criminal offence (Stumpf 2008; Chin et al 2010). As David Brotherton and Luis Barrios (2011) illustrate elsewhere and in this volume with respect to Dominican deportees, the heavy reliance on detention and mass deportations have impacted both individuals and communities. These impacts follow lines of nationality, class, and race.

As the connections between immigration and criminal law have grown more elaborate, a longstanding debate has revived, one with deep roots in legal history, over whether deportation is sufficiently close to criminal punishment to trigger the constitutional protections of criminal law. These protections include, among others, the right to legal representation at government expense, protections against self-incrimination, double jeopardy and retroactive punishment, and proportionality-based restrictions on excessive or cruel and unusual punishment.

US courts have classified only one of the two outcomes of crimmigration law as punishment meriting criminal constitutional protections. While a criminal sentence resulting from a trial or plea agreement constitutes formal punishment calling for criminal procedural protections, deportation does not. In place of the multi-faceted constitutional protections of criminal law, less robust due process protection and subconstitutional rules govern deportation proceedings, setting few limits on the severity of removal from the country.

Scholars and advocates have argued that if the processes and strategies of immigration control share so many elements with criminal law as to be almost indistinguishable from it, the result of those processes—deportation—should be treated as if it were a criminal punishment (Kanstroom 2000; Markowitz 2008).[7] In 2010, the US Supreme Court in *Padilla v Kentucky* affirmed its longstanding conclusion that deportation proceedings were civil and not criminal.[8] It acknowledged, however, the close connection between immigration and criminal law.

(West, Westlaw, through End of the 2012 Regular and 1st Special Sessions)) has been challenged in *United States v Alabama* 813 FSupp2d 1282 (ND Ala 2011), aff'd in part, rev'd in part, dismissed in part, 691 F3d 1269 (11th Cir 2012).

[6] Kalhan (2010) (analysing the convergence of criminal enforcement and immigration control in the context of immigration detention); Noferi (2012) (evaluating the effects of the expansion of mandatory detention in the US).

[7] See Kanstroom (2000) ('It is time to recognize that deportation of legal permanent residents for criminal and other post-entry conduct is punishment. If it must be done, then it must be done with specific, substantive constitutional protections'); Markowitz (2008: 289, 291) (arguing that while exclusion from entry is a civil proceeding, expulsion of a lawful permanent resident is a criminal proceeding in which the non-citizen should enjoy 'the full panoply of criminal procedural protections guaranteed by the Constitution').

[8] *Padilla v Kentucky*, 130 SCt 1473, 1481–1482 (2010).

The Court emphasized that deportation constitutes a severe penalty for non-citizens with roots in the United States, and that when deportation was a clear consequence of a criminal conviction, it triggered the constitutional right to effective assistance of counsel. In *Padilla*, recognition of the growing intersection between criminal and immigration law inspired the Supreme Court to strengthen procedural protections for non-citizens.

In sum, the criminal sentence and the deportation order, which are the central substantive outcomes of crimmigration law, differ in how they restrict the liberty of the non-citizen. They stand on opposite sides of the constitutional divide between civil and criminal law. They have in common, however, the government power to impose by force a substantial deprivation of liberty on the non-citizen. The question this chapter takes up is whether the processes that surround and determine these outcomes, and not just the outcomes themselves, can constitute a form of punishment.

II. The Procedural Landscape of Crimmigration: When Does Process Become Punitive?

Examining whether crimmigration processes can operate as punishment begins with an inquiry into whether a process can impose punishment in the first place. Malcolm Feeley's pioneering work on process as punishment in the field of criminal law offers to deepen our understanding of crimmigration law (Feeley 1979). Feeley posited that, at least in the lower criminal court, the power to sanction is distributed beyond the judge to many non-judicial actors with a role in the criminal justice process. Sanctions in the criminal justice system, he found, were not confined to the sentence at the end of the process but appeared at junctures throughout the process. These included pre-trial detention and arrest, as well as the elemental unpleasantness of the criminal procedural experience (Feeley 1979).

Feeley's taxonomy of how criminal process can become punishment provides the beginnings of a similar taxonomy for crimmigration law. First, the process becomes the punishment when the costs of contesting the criminal charges become higher than the cost of pleading guilty. This cost can be financial, but can also manifest in time, anxiety, and interruptions to work or family obligations.

Second, procedural elements can take the place of traditional criminal punishment. For example, pre-trial detention takes the place of the criminal sentence when it is longer than the sentence or when the population in pre-trial detention is significantly higher than those jailed post-trial. Third, the process becomes like punishment when authorities use procedural elements such as arrest or detention for the purpose of imposing a negative experience on an individual, independent of its function as a step toward prosecution for the crime (Feeley 1979: 205–206, 235).

Crimmigration law's unique procedural architecture contributes to its potential for punitiveness in two additional ways. The interplay between the criminal and deportation adjudication systems relegates one system to a procedural stepping stone to the outcome of the other. Also, crimmigration law creates procedural stratifications within the criminal justice system that set non-citizens apart from citizens. The next sections will analyse these five earmarks.

1. Costs of procedure ordain outcomes

When the burdens the process imposes determine the decisions people make about whether to accept deportation, plead guilty, or agree to a sentence, the lines between the process and the outcome blur. In crimmigration law, the experience of arrest and detention imposes heavy costs, especially in combination with elongation of the procedural precursors to adjudication. The experience of the criminal or deportation process can also contribute to making the costs of the process comparable to or greater than the cost of the ultimate outcome. Especially for non-citizens who arrived relatively recently in the United States, being thrust into a foreign criminal justice system can be particularly unsettling and may outstrip the formal sanction that follows that process.

Any arrest for a criminal or immigration offence brings individuals into contact with law-enforcement officers exercising one of their greatest powers. For low-level offences, the confrontational nature of that interaction and the role of arrest as the gateway to the rest of the criminal or deportation process alone may surpass the formal sanction in terms of time, uncertainty, and unpleasantness (Feeley 1979: 199–201; Motomura 2011).[9]

Pre-trial detention similarly puts pressure on non-citizens. Defendants facing minor criminal charges may accede to a plea agreement on the prosecutor's terms because the cost of contesting the charges is often higher than taking the plea. Non-citizens arrested on deportation grounds may agree to deportation if, like the Postville defendants, immediate release would allow them to care for children or find new work. That will especially hold true if the longer term consequences, such as ineligibility for later lawful entry, are distant.

Elongation of the process plays an important role. Choosing to contest the criminal or deportation charges can prolong pre-trial custody and immigration detention. It can impose costs such as loss of work or childcare time, attorneys' fees for those not represented by a public defender, and the stress and aggravation that comes with being submerged in the procedural gamut of criminal litigation. From the point of deciding to contest the charges to the day of the actual trial, criminal defendants often experience a series of pre-trial hearings, delays, and reschedulings. Upon reaching their 'day in court', they are relegated to the role of minor players in the courtroom (Feeley 1979: 154–158). Immigration proceedings lack the motivating stick of a speedy trial requirement or constitutional bail rights, so for many, overflowing dockets and detention mandates result in long waits in detention for deportation hearings.

---

[9] See Motomura (2011) (explaining that the decision whether to arrest often determines the outcome of crime-based immigration cases).

2. Procedural elements take the place of traditional criminal punishment

The procedural components of crimmigration may substitute for formal punishment, especially for minor offences. In the United States, non-citizens may choose to avoid or at least minimize the negative experience of the criminal justice process through a negotiated conviction. A guilty plea may be attractive if the agreement avoids incarceration and the defendant is unaware of or incapable of evaluating the risk of later consequences. Those consequences, however, may include deportation, limitations based on sex offender status, or other penalties following from the conviction or removal order (Chin 2011; Roberts 2011a).[10] When low-level offenders do not serve jail time, the procedural consequence takes the place of any formal criminal sanction.

Non-citizens arrested on suspicion of criminal conduct are often detained first as part of the criminal pre-trial process and then on the request of US immigration authorities who issue an immigration 'detainer'. Immigration detainers have regularly led to judges denying bail for detained non-citizens, increasing the length and uncertainty of their detention. Non-citizens also find themselves transferred to federal immigration detention, either after the state authorities decline to prosecute the criminal charge or when federal immigration authorities begin deportation proceedings before the end of the state or local criminal prosecution. As a result, a non-citizen's detention can either be longer than the outcome of the criminal sentence, especially for low-level crimes, or it can completely take the place of the criminal sentence (Eagly 2010).[11]

3. Non-judicial actors more active than judges in imposing procedural burdens

As in Postville, actors such as police and prosecutors can be more influential than judges as arbiters of criminal and immigration sanctions. Especially in the lower courts where prosecution of minor crimes and misdemeanours take place, pre-trial processes governed by non-judicial actors determine who is punished. The threat of deportation, combined with the expansion of deportable offences and migration-related crimes, have imbued both police and prosecutors with greater powers over non-citizens in the criminal justice system.

In crimmigration law, the expansion of criminal laws has granted police much greater discretion to decide who will enter the criminal adjudicatory system. As criminal law has come to prohibit a wider swath of conduct, police have gained

---

[10] See Roberts (2011a) (illustrating how a defendant's knowledge of certain consequences influences the rationality of a decision to plead guilty); see also Chin (2011) (discussing the importance of defence counsel's role in advising clients about potential collateral consequences to guilty pleas).

[11] See Eagly (2010) (noting that because of immigration detainers, the defendants in the Postville raid would have spent a longer time in pre-trial detention than they would serve in prison by entering a guilty plea).

greater leeway to decide whom to stop or arrest. Police may arrest individuals with no intention that prosecution will follow, as when an arrest is made to break off tension between two groups. An arrest may be a courtesy to immigration agents, a substitute for federal immigration enforcement, or intended as a form of punishment that post-arrest immigration detention can exacerbate (Feeley 1979: 46; Motomura 2011; Gaynor 2012; Pettersson and Hermann 2012).[12] When arrest takes on a life of its own, independent of its role as a procedural step toward prosecution, it becomes a means of penalizing the arrested non-citizen.

Criminalization, then, expanded the discretion of law-enforcement officers to impose layers of process on non-citizens suspected of unlawful migration. Police now have discretion to decide which non-citizens pass through the criminal justice system prior to deportation rather than proceeding directly to removal. Since arrest has become a gateway to removal, it is often the discretion to decide who will be deported and who may remain (Motomura 2011).

Meanwhile, prosecutors exercise control over the shape of the criminal procedure gauntlet. Their charging decisions and plea negotiations can determine whether a non-citizen becomes deportable. Especially in misdemeanour cases, plea bargains are the most common avenue to concluding a criminal case (Motivans 2011; Roberts 2011b).[13] A prosecutor's decision about which crimes to charge and what sentence to seek in a criminal justice proceeding becomes the basis for determining whether the non-citizen has committed a deportable offence. For example, when a prosecutor decides to charge a non-citizen with possession of a marijuana joint with intent to sell instead of the lesser charge of possession of the joint, that choice, translated into a verdict or plea agreement, renders the non-citizen deportable.

As a result, prosecutors' discretion to decide whom to release, what to charge, and how to structure a plea offer plays a larger role in whether and how a defendant will be punished than the judicial power to set a sentence after a guilty verdict.

Finally, defence counsel and bondsmen also influence the weight of procedural burdens. These actors have parts to play in determining the length of pre-trial detention, the shape of the plea agreement, and how long the criminal adjudicatory process will last (Feeley 1979: 209–215).

In sum, the criminalization of migration has changed who imposes the formal sanction. Legislative expansion of criminal grounds had the effect of creating greater police discretion to impose formal criminal punishment as well as expulsion from the United States. Police and prosecutorial discretion means that law-enforcement officers and prosecutors decide which non-citizens received criminal punishment in addition to deportation, rather than deportation alone.

---

[12] See Motomura (2011: 1847): 'State and local jurisdictions and officers that see immigration enforcement as part of their law enforcement duties will be especially inclined to view civil removal as a tangible result that makes the arrest worthwhile'. See also Gaynor (2012) (describing a class-action lawsuit against Sheriff Joe Arpaio of Maricopa County, Arizona, alleging pretextual stops singling out Latinos suspected of being in the US unlawfully).

[13] According to the US Department of Justice Bureau of Justice Statistics, guilty pleas represented 97% of convictions in US district courts in 2009. See Motivans (2011). See also Roberts (2011b) (observing that 'the vast majority of misdemeanor convictions come after a guilty plea').

4. Criminal prosecution and adjudication of deportation as procedural precursors for each other

The greater interaction between the criminal justice system and deportation processes has meant that one serves as a procedural stepping stone to the other. The shift from using only deportation as the main response to unauthorized border crossing to a heavy emphasis on criminalization meant that non-citizens experienced heightened sanctions from the conviction but also from the exposure to the procedural gauntlet that the combined systems represent. The criminal conviction does not replace deportation; it precedes it or occurs nearly simultaneously.

Secure Communities, a federal immigration enforcement initiative, represents one of the most intricate ways in which criminal investigative tools are tied together with immigration enforcement. Secure Communities piggybacks on police arrests of non-citizens suspected of committing crimes, using criminal investigative tools to identify unauthorized non-citizens for deportation. When non-citizens are booked at the police station, their identifying information is matched to immigration records in the federal database. If that search reveals an immigration violation, the immigration agency may ask the police department to detain the non-citizen, usually in the police lockup, until the federal agents can take custody of the non-citizen and initiate removal proceedings (Chacón 2010; US Immigration and Customs Enforcement nd). As a result, an arrest for a traffic violation or on suspicion of driving under the influence could result in a federal request to detain the arrestee for immigration proceedings and ultimately deportation (Motomura 2011; US Immigration and Customs Enforcement nd).

In sum, every criminal arrest becomes a potential deportation case. The shift to prosecuting migration-related conduct transformed the role of the criminal justice system from a means toward the end of adjudicating criminal punishment to a mere procedural step in the deportation system.

5. Segregation of non-citizen defendants

Crimmigration law has carved out both formal and functional spaces in which non-citizens are segregated from citizens in the criminal justice system. Formally, the US criminal justice system treats citizens and non-citizens alike, at least in the adjudication of traditional crimes such as theft where migration is not at issue. A growing body of laws and practices, however, create impacts that run contrary to traditional criminal justice principles. First, they impose different or heavier sanctions on non-citizens and establish procedures applied only to non-citizens. Second, they fail to distinguish between non-citizens as individuals, treating them instead as an undifferentiated mass.

The still-evolving legal frameworks that set non-citizens apart from citizens through both formal law and functional practice result from the incongruence of applying to non-citizens a criminal justice system grounded in conceptions of citizenship, as Lucia Zedner (Chapter 2 in this volume) points out. Zedner illustrates that competing justifications for a criminal justice system that empowers the government to punish tend to centralize citizenship.

Citizenship explains both the obligations individuals owe to the state and the obligations the state owes to the accused, such as procedural protections and the guarantee of a fair trial. The classic liberal and communitarian schools of thought on the authority of criminal law both rely on citizenship. The liberal camp conceives of the relationship between state and individual as grounded on a hierarchical social contract in which citizens consent to cede some liberty to the state in exchange for protection and the maintenance of order, among other things. The communitarian approach, in contrast, locates the source of authority of the criminal law in the relational bonds among citizens. The obligations those bonds place on members of the community, and the state's authority to censure, are grounded in a 'linguistic and normative commonality' associated with citizenship (Zedner, Chapter 2 in this volume).

Zedner notes that both the liberty-restraining power of the state and the limits on that power become ambiguous in the absence of legal citizenship. When the theoretical justifications for the exercise of state power to punish are based on citizenship, the justification for recognizing rights and protections for non-citizen defendants weakens. This weakness manifests in the US criminal justice and immigration systems in ways that single out and exclude non-citizens.

Unauthorized border crossing has long been a criminal violation in the United States, but it was traditionally addressed through a non-criminal deportation proceeding. Process leading to deportation was often minimal. Border patrol agents sometimes effected deportation of Mexican nationals after unlawful entry by turning them around and ushering them across the border (Kanstroom 2007).

Since then, more federal prosecution of these acts as crimes and more intense immigration enforcement has resulted in heightened deportation counts and enforcement operations, such as Operation Streamline, that target specific areas of the border. States like Arizona and Alabama have passed laws criminalizing the same conduct that federal immigration law prohibits or surpassing the federal prohibitions by criminalizing a non-citizen's unauthorized presence within the state. These laws have created a new procedural channel to state-imposed punishment. Non-citizens prosecuted under these laws still face possible deportation proceedings and federal criminal prosecution for the same conduct (Chin et al 2010: 50; Chin and Miller 2011).[14]

Crimes related to unlawful presence in the United States are in a category of their own. In contrast to traditional criminal violations which target conduct, migration crimes are unique in requiring as an element the status of being a non-citizen without federal immigration authorization. In other words, it is not conduct but

---

[14] See Chin et al (2010: 50) (noting that 'S.B. 1070 creates or amends four sections of the Arizona Revised Statutes, which impose criminal liability based on undocumented presence in the United States'); Chin and Miller (2011: 251, 253) (exploring the 'mirror-image theory [which] proposes that states can help carry out federal immigration policy by enacting and enforcing state laws that mirror federal statutes').

rather a person's citizenship status that defines the violation of criminal law. The same conduct, committed by a US citizen (or a lawfully present non-citizen), would not constitute a crime.

Shifting from a civil to a criminal response to unlawful presence and unlawful entry places two different burdens on non-citizens caught up in the process. The first is a straightforward heightening of the sanction for unlawful border crossing. In addition to deportation, the government imposes a criminal conviction and sentence for these acts. Added to that is the expressive power of the conviction in labelling the conduct a crime and its perpetrator a criminal (Garland 2001).

Moreover, for lawful permanent residents, imposing deportation on top of the criminal sentence seems to have little purpose other than to exacerbate the punishment for the conviction. This is especially true for criminal deportation grounds that apply retroactively, rendering removable lawful permanent residents who had reason to believe, upon serving their sentences, that the state had exhausted its power to punish for that crime.

Mass arrest and prosecution processes for migration-related crimes impose unique burdens on non-citizens. Arrests for the crimes of unlawful entry or re-entry, administrative arrests for working without authorization, and criminal arrests for using false or fraudulent documents are undertaken on a mass scale. These mass proceedings can result from workplace or neighbourhood raids or human-smuggling apprehensions.

Mass criminal prosecution of non-citizens for migration-related offences sends a singular message (Newburn and Jones 2007). In Postville, the mass roundup and processing of the convictions communicated that the employees were so distinct from other criminal defendants that they warranted special procedures. The operation diverted the non-citizens from the low-level criminal court that was the usual venue for criminal defendants accused of equivalent crimes (Preston 2008a; Preston 2008b). Using a force of immigration enforcement agents and police, a fleet of white transport vans, and rented fairground space to detain and process the large groups of arrested migrants marked them as too numerous, too poised for flight, the situation too unique for the ordinary workings of the criminal court.

While acting upon differences between the Postville prosecution and the everyday low-level criminal case, the prosecutors recognized none of the differences that existed between the employees. They approached the group of employees as a featureless throng suited to a common process and a common sanction. The workers were too much like criminals for mere deportation, but too much like each other in their foreignness and their alleged immigration-related crimes for individual processing in the criminal court. Both perceptions were necessary to justify a mass, fast-tracked process that foreclosed immigration relief and separated the workers physically and procedurally from ordinary criminal court and immigration proceedings. At the same time, the process played out on the national stage, telling a political narrative about waves of unauthorized migrants that only exceptional innovations in criminal and immigration procedures could thwart.

As the process proceeded, however, distinctions between the non-citizens emerged. Some of these distinctions seemed inconsequential but had major legal impacts, such as higher sanctions imposed on employees who unknowingly had used a Social Security number that belonged to a real person rather than being merely false. Other distinctions between the employees may have been significant in a deportation proceeding but not in criminal law, such as whether the non-citizens had US family members or other US ties. Because the non-citizens waived via the criminal process the right to raise these US ties in an immigration proceeding, they remained personally consequential and yet legally unrecognized.

The theatrical nature of the Postville proceeding—from the fleet of white vans holding throngs of arrestees, to the transformation of a cattle showground into a temporary detention centre, to the ephemeral courtroom constructed with black curtains through which prosecutors paraded the shackled defendants—illustrates a way in which crimmigration at times operates as a form of symbolic politics.[15] Crimmigration exercises significant symbolic power. The commingling of criminal law and immigration law suffuses the process in both legal arenas with elements of lawlessness and foreignness. The Postville operation told a compelling political narrative with the public as the audience. The volume of arrested migrants promised to stoke submerged fears of a mass influx of aliens unchecked by porous borders and permeating the innermost regions of the United States. This unique threat required a distinct form of justice.

The Postville operation made a public splash, but it was not unprecedented. Along stretches of the south-west border with Mexico, immigration enforcement authorities have cooperated with prosecutors to arrest, detain, and convict for unlawful entry or unlawful re-entry almost every non-citizen caught crossing the border without authorization (US Customs and Border Protection 2005; Eagly 2010: 1328–1330). Operation Streamline was intended to increase the costs to non-citizens of unlawful border crossing by imposing both a criminal and an immigration consequence, adding a conviction and sentence to the deportation sanction.

The streamlined process, however, itself became a sanction. As in Postville, Operation Streamline employed a fast-track process that required mass processing of the arrested non-citizens. US judges handling Streamline cases accepted plea agreements from as many as 80 non-citizen defendants at one time, asking them as a group to confirm the knowing and voluntary waiver of their constitutional rights. The expeditious proceeding and the treatment of the defendants as an indistinct group guilty of the same crime suggested that, in the eyes of the law, these defendants both differed from ordinary criminal defendants yet remained functionally identical to one another, lacking the individual circumstances that could lead to distinct formal outcomes.

There is another way in which the experience of the criminal justice system is unique for non-citizens. Criminalizing acts of migration is changing the nature of the lower criminal court proceeding by raising the stakes of pre-trial processes. Plea bargaining has become more than a step toward a conviction and criminal sanction.

---

[15] Newburn and Jones (2007: 236) (describing the notion of a 'policy narrative' as an element of symbolic politics).

It has become a gateway to expulsion from the country. A plea agreement may contain an explicit provision requiring the defendant non-citizen to depart the country after completing any other term of the plea agreement, or deportation may be implicit—an unexpected consequence of an agreement to plead guilty to a crime for which conviction requires removal.

Under *Padilla*, many non-citizens became entitled to their defence counsel's advice about the immigration consequences of a guilty plea. That advice had the potential to change the stakes of taking the plea deal. It put pressure on non-citizens invested in continued US residence to take their chances at trial rather than agreeing to a conviction that would almost certainly render them deportable. After *Padilla*, non-citizens were more likely to learn of the consequences of conviction at a time when they could choose whether to take the immediate plea or extend the process by rejecting it and going to trial.

In sum, the punishment for crossing the border without authorization is the piling on of process. In place of the former civil deportation scheme, criminalizing unlawful border crossing meant that non-citizens were exposed to an entirely different legal system, and one that often treated them more harshly than other criminal defendants accused of similar crimes.

6. Bars to re-entry

There is a final procedural innovation addressing the question whether the process of US crimmigration law takes form as a punishment. Many unlawfully present migrants incur still another layer of process when they encounter statutory bars to re-entering the United States after deportation. In 1996, US legislation established a bar to re-entering the country for 10 years or more for non-citizens who had stayed in the United States for a long time without permission, or who had left the United States under a removal order or re-entered the United States after the government had removed them.[16] The removal order that triggers the bar to re-entry can result from a plea agreement to a charge of unlawful entry or re-entry (Eagly 2010: 1328–1329; INA § 212(a)(9)).[17]

These bars to re-entry arise as a result of extended unlawful presence, a prior deportation, or a criminal conviction. They come into play, however, only when non-citizens seek to return to the United States lawfully, usually based on marriage or work or other ties to US residents or employers.

The result is a procedural marathon. After the arrest, criminal prosecution, and deportation, the non-citizen encounters a new and lengthy process, a barrier composed of time, of deliberate delay woven into the process of lawfully re-entering

---

[16] Illegal Immigration Reform and Immigrant Responsibility Act (IIRIRA), Pub L No 104-208, Div C, § 301(b), 110 Stat 3009-575–3009-578 (1996) (codified at 8 USC § 1182(a)(9) (2006)) (establishing a 10-year bar to re-entering the United States for, eg, non-citizens who had departed after the issuance of a removal order or who were unlawfully present for more than a year).

[17] See 8 USC § 1182(a)(9) (2006) (barring subsequent re-entry of any non-citizen convicted of an 'aggravated felony').

the country. The only way to avoid that process is by initiating another process: seeking a waiver of the bar to re-entry.

III. Burdens versus Punishment

The intermingling of immigration and criminal law has expanded and complicated the processes that government actors and others use to regulate non-citizens. Whether these processes impose the kind of burden that rises to the equivalence of criminal punishment is an ongoing debate. The opacity of the proceedings, segregation from the normal criminal justice system, mass processing, and obstacles to later lawful entry that result from the interlocking complexities of crimmigration law lead us to question whether the processes of crimmigration have generated a form of punishment uniquely imposed on non-citizens.

Crimmigration pushes the boundaries of the legal space circumscribing punishment. Criminal sentences and deportation deprive individuals of liberty, but so do the procedural steps leading up to or supplanting those outcomes. The intersection of criminal and immigration law has significantly extended the government processes that lead to removal determinations and expanded the contact between law enforcement and migrants. Crimmigration law has reached beyond legislative changes in substantive law to enact procedural changes and enforcement strategies with major consequences for non-citizens. This set of sanctions is more functional than formal, experienced as a sanction and often exacerbated by the bewildering subjection to an unfamiliar legal system. Moreover, as with Feeley's low-level criminal defendants, this punitive procedural experience is visited on both the innocent and the guilty.

As a result, non-citizens may experience the process through which the government determines whether it will impose a criminal or immigration sanction as so similar to the criminal sentence or deportation, as detention is to post-trial incarceration, as to amount to punishment. In addition, the government system or actor may intend to impose an experience—a deprivation of liberty like an arrest or detention—as a way to sanction individuals for their conduct or status. When the government seeks to impose a penalty through crimmigration law, or non-citizens widely experience as punitive the procedural web that crimmigration has woven, the process has become the punishment.

References

Aas, K.F. (2011) ' "Crimmigrant" Bodies and Bona Fide Travelers: Surveillance, Citizenship and Global Governance', *Theoretical Criminology* 15: 331.

Bosworth, M. (2011) 'Deportation, Detention and Foreign-National Prisoners in England and Wales', *Citizenship Studies* 15: 583.

Brotherton, D.C. and Barrios, L. (2011) *The Social Bulimia of Forced Repatriation: A Case Study of Dominican Deportees.* New York: Columbia University Press.

Brown, D.K. (2011) 'Why Padilla Doesn't Matter (Much)', *UCLA Law Review* 58: 1393.

Camayd-Freixas, E. (2008) 'Interpreting after the Largest ICE Raid in U.S. History: A Personal Account', *New York Times* <http://graphics8.nytimes.com/packages/pdf/national/20080711IMMIG.pdf>.

Chacón, J.M. (2010) 'A Diversion of Attention? Immigration Courts and the Adjudication of Fourth and Fifth Amendment Rights', *Duke Law Journal* 59: 1563.

Chacón, J.M. (2009) 'Managing Migration through Crime', *Columbia Law Review Sidebar* 109: 135.

Chin, G.J. (2011) 'Making Padilla Practical: Defense Counsel and Collateral Consequences at Guilty Plea', *Howard Law Journal* 54: 675.

Chin, G.J. and Miller, M.L. (2011) 'The Unconstitutionality of State Regulation of Immigration through Criminal Law', *Duke Law Journal* 61: 251.

Chin, G.J. et al (2010) 'A Legal Labyrinth: Issues Raised by Arizona Senate Bill 1070', *Georgetown Immigration Law Journal* 25: 47.

Demleitner, N.V. (2002) 'Immigration Threats and Rewards: Effective Law Enforcement Tools in the "War" on Terrorism?', *Emory Law Journal* 51: 1059.

Duara, N. et al (2008) 'ID Fraud Claims Bring State's Largest Raid', *Des Moines Register*, A1 <http://www.desmoinesregister.com/article/20080513/NEWS/805130408/ID-fraud-claims-bring-state-s-largest-raid>.

Eagly, I.V. (2010) 'Prosecuting Immigration', *Northwestern University Law Review* 104: 1281.

Feeley, M.M. (1979) *The Process is the Punishment*. New York: Russell Sage Foundation.

Garland, D. (2001) *The Culture of Control: Crime and Social Order in Contemporary Society*. Illinois: University of Chicago Press.

Gaynor, T. (2012) ' "America's Toughest" Sheriff on Trial over Discrimination Claims', *Reuters* <http://www.reuters.com/article/2012/07/20/us-usa-arizona-sheriff-idUSBRE86J03920120720>.

Guia, M.J. et al (2013) *Social Control and Justice: Crimmigration in the Age of Fear*. The Hague: Eleven International Publishing.

Hsu, S.S. (2008) 'Immigration Raid Jars a Small Town', *Washington Post* <http://www.washingtonpost.com/wp-dyn/content/article/2008/05/17/AR2008051702474.html>.

Kalhan, A. (2010) Rethinking Immigration Detention, *Columbia Law Review Sidebar* 110: 42.

Kanstroom, D. (2007) *Deportation Nation*. New York, London: Harvard University Press.

Kanstroom, D. (2000) 'Deportation, Social Control, and Punishment: Some Thoughts about Why Hard Laws Make Bad Cases', *Harvard Law Review* 113: 1889.

Legomsky, S.H. (2007) 'The New Path of Immigration Law: Asymmetric Incorporation of Criminal Justice Norms', *Washington and Lee Law Review* 64: 469.

Markowitz, P.L. (2011) 'Deportation is Different', *University of Pennsylvania Journal of Constitutional Law* 13: 1299.

Markowitz, P.L. (2008) 'Straddling the Civil-Criminal Divide: A Bifurcated Approach to Understanding the Nature of Immigration Removal Proceedings', *Harvard Civil Rights-Civil Liberties Law Review* 43: 289.

Mitsilegas, V. et al (2003) *The European Union and Internal Security: Guardian of the People?* New York: Palgrave Macmillan.

Morton, J. (2011) *Memorandum to all ICE Employees*, US Immigration and Customs Enforcement <http://www.ice.gov/doclib/news/releases/2011/110302washingtondc.pdf>.

Motivans, M. (2011) *Federal Justice Statistics 2009*. US Department of Justice <http://bjs.ojp.usdoj.gov/content/pub/pdf/fjs09.pdf>.

Motomura, H. (2011) 'The Discretion That Matters: Federal Immigration Enforcement, State and Local Arrests, and the Civil–Criminal Line', *UCLA Law Review* 58: 1819.

Moyers, P.R. (2009) 'Butchering Statutes: The Postville Raid and the Misinterpretation of Federal Criminal Law', *Seattle University Law Review* 32: 651.

Newburn, T. and Jones, T. (2007) 'Symbolising Crime Control: Reflections on Zero Tolerance', *Theoretical Criminology* 11: 221.

Noferi, M. (2012) 'Cascading Constitutional Deprivation: The Right to Appointed Counsel for Mandatorily Detained Immigrants Pending Deportation Proceedings', *Michigan Journal of Race and Law* 18: 63.

Pacella, J.M. (2011) 'Welcoming the Unwanted: Italy's Response to the Immigration Phenomenon and European Union Involvement', *Georgetown Immigration Law Journal* 25: 341.

Pakes, F. (2004) 'The Politics of Discontent: The Emergence of a New Criminal Justice Discourse in the Netherlands', *Howard Journal of Criminal Justice* 43: 284.

Pakes, F. (ed.) (2013) *Globalisation and the Challenge to Criminology*. New York: Routledge.

Pettersson, E. and Hermann, W. (2012) 'Arizona Judge Told Sheriff to Blame for Latinos' Abuse', *Bloomberg Business Week* <http://www.businessweek.com/news/2012-07-19/arizona-sheriff-arpaio-goes-to-trial-over-immigration-crackdown>.

Preston, J. (2008a) 'Immigrants' Speedy Trials after Raid Become Issue', *New York Times* <http://www.nytimes.com/2008/08/09/us/09immig.html>.

Preston, J. (2008b) 'An Interpreter Speaking up for Migrants', *New York Times* <http://www.nytimes.com/2008/07/11/us/11immig.html>.

Roberts, J. (2011a) 'Proving Prejudice Post-Padilla', *Howard Law Journal* 54: 693.

Roberts, J. (2011b) 'Why Misdemeanors Matter: Defining Effective Advocacy in the Lower Criminal Courts', *UC Davis Law Review* 45: 277.

Saulny, S. (2008) 'Hundreds are Arrested in U.S. Sweep of Meat Plant', *New York Times* <http://www.nytimes.com/2008/05/13/us/13immig.html>.

Schulte, G. et al (2008) 'Town of 2,273 Wonders: What Happens to Us Now?', *Des Moines Register* <http://www.desmoinesregister.com/apps/pbcs.dll/article?AID=/20080514/NEWS/805140371/-1>.

Stumpf, J.P. (2013) 'The Two Profiles of Crimmigration Law: Criminal Deportation and Illegal Migration', in F. Pakes (ed), *Globalisation and the Challenge to Criminology*. New York: Routledge.

Stumpf, J.P. (2008) 'States of Confusion: The Rise of State and Local Power over Immigration', *North Carolina Law Review* 86: 1557.

Stumpf, J.P. (2006) 'The Crimmigration Crisis: Immigrants, Crime, and Sovereign Power', *American University Law Review* 56: 367.

Transactional Records Access Clearinghouse, Syracuse University (TRAC) (2012) *Prosecutions for 2012* <http://tracfed.syr.edu/results/9x205123f48012.html>.

US Customs and Border Protection (2005) *DHS Launches 'Operation Streamline II'* (Press Release) <http://www.cbp.gov/archived/xp/cgov/newsroom/news_releases/archives/2005_press_releases/122005/12162005.xml.html>.

US Customs and Border Protection (nd) *About CBP* <http://www.cbp.gov/xp/cgov/about>.

US Immigration and Customs Enforcement (2010) *ICE Strategic Plan: FY 2010–2014* <http://www.ice.gov/doclib/news/library/reports/strategic-plan/strategic-plan-2010.pdf>.

US Immigration and Customs Enforcement (nd) *Secure Communities* <http://www.ice.gov/secure_communities>.

van der Leun, J. and van der Woude, M.A.H. (2011) 'Ethnic Profiling in the Netherlands? A Reflection on Expanding Preventive Powers, Ethnic Profiling and a Changing Social and Political Context', *Policing and Society* 21: 444.

4

The Troublesome Intersections of Refugee Law and Criminal Law

Catherine Dauvergne[1]

Not so very long ago, most refugee scholars seeking the areas of overlap between refugee law and criminal law would have turned first to the ways in which criminal law may function as a mechanism of persecution and thus, in combination with other factors, become part of the reason that an individual requires protection as a refugee. The ensuing analysis would then consider whether the criminal provision in question was a 'law of general application' or, alternatively, whether it had a discriminatory purpose, or was applied in a discriminatory fashion. A body of judicial opinion has developed around these questions, as well as a moderate amount of scholarly commentary (Hathaway 1991: 169–179; Goodwin-Gill and McAdam 2007: 102–104). At this point in time, however, I mention this 'old' intersection of refugee law and criminal law solely for the purpose of excluding it. Perhaps, in light of this chapter's title, this original overlap should be called the 'un-troublesome' intersection of refugee law and criminal law.

Instead, in this chapter I trace out the consequences of the recent expansion of criminal law *within* refugee law. This chapter's project is a logical corollary of the criminalization of asylum seeking itself, which I have addressed before (Dauvergne 2008). At its simplest, my assertion that asylum is being criminalized is made out by the myriad evidence of prosperous Western states seeking to limit access to their borders to those who would seek asylum, and, for those who do make it across the border, to make the process as difficult as possible within (or even beyond) the law. Criminalization of asylum seeking has been in train since the 1990s and is apparent in provisions such as safe third country agreements, carrier sanctions, visa requirements, safe country of origin requirements, restricted access to welfare state benefits, and the imposition of 'eligibility' provisions as a precondition of access to domestic asylum systems. It is also deeply intertwined with many of the phenomena analysed elsewhere in this volume, most importantly the marked rise

[1] I am grateful for research assistance from Fathima Cader, Daphne Chu, and Brendan Naef. I also acknowledge the support of the Social Sciences and Humanities Research Council of Canada for funding my project 'An International Human Rights Audit: Is the Charter Failing Non-citizens in Canada?', of which this chapter forms one part.

in the use of detention for those seeking asylum and the discursive rise of the 'illegal' migrant. All state moves to restrict border access and thereby to 'criminalize immigration' bite most sharply at the asylum end of the immigration continuum for two reasons. First, because asylum seekers have few options, the 'incentives' that discourage their movement must by definition be harsher than the persecutory conditions they face at home. Second, because a successful asylum claim defeats the sovereign aspiration of the closed border, it is always in the foreground of policy makers' concerns. The Australian instance explored by Pickering and Weber in Chapter 5 is almost exclusively an asylum story, and the migration flows from the global South that Aas theorizes in Chapter 1 are also increasingly comprised almost wholly of asylum seekers. It is also vital to foreground that as contemporary asylum flows are predominantly from the global South, issues surrounding asylum are deeply racialized.

My argument in this chapter is about criminalization *within* refugee law. It focuses on the jurisprudence of refugee law, and in this way differs from my earlier work on how asylum is criminalized. The linkage between these two perspectives is my assessment that an increasingly hostile public and political discourse towards refugees and asylum seekers has penetrated the doctrine of refugee law itself. Misguided concern about the criminality of refugees has led to a much greater ambit for criminal law within refugee jurisprudence. This infusion of criminal concern pulls against the originary human rights focus of refugee law. It sits uneasily with the established interpretive principles for refugee law because the central logic of criminal law differs so greatly from that of refugee law. The reach of criminal law within refugee jurisprudence is particularly harmful to the rights interests of asylum seekers because it is unconstrained by the 'rights of the accused' context.

As a final introductory point, it is a significant capitulation for any refugee scholar to write about refugee law in a volume devoted to defining a criminology of immigration. Refugee movements are not a form of immigration, and are even a contested terrain within the ambit of 'forced migration' (Hathaway 2007: 349). The definitional core of the international refugee law regime requires that refugees are neither considered nor treated as migrants. Refugee law is the sole legal constraint on state sovereignty in regard to people entering territory. But the separation of refugee law and migration law is hard to maintain and is resisted by states seeking greater control over refugee movements. It is also resisted by individuals turning to asylum as a route toward secure immigration status at a time when states are increasingly restricting migration opportunities, especially for poor people with limited labour market skills. For all of these reasons, refugee law scholars, and refugee advocates, find themselves writing about immigration criminology: a position of deep retreat. And so it is with some reluctance that I turn to the troublesome intersections of refugee law and criminal law, buoyed by the rich intellectual terrain of the workshop that led to this volume, and by the strengthen of both the criminal law and the advocacy of criminologists.

There are three 'troublesome intersections' in this chapter. The first is the place of criminal law within refugee exclusions. The second is the dissonance created by the clash between the criminal standard of proof and the refugee law standard of proof. The third is the irony of extraditing refugees. I will develop each of these arguments in turn, devoting the greatest attention to the extradition analysis, because it is in this setting that troublesome intersection is displayed most acutely. To conclude, I return to consider how these developments affect the 'un-troublesome' analysis of criminal law as a potential source of persecution, and thus in the refugee law setting, of an entitlement to protection. This final point illustrates the flow of these consequences into the heart of refugee law.

Criminal Law and Refugee Exclusions

In 2011, Asha Kaushal and I published the results of our analysis of 11 years of Canadian refugee exclusion decisions (Kaushal and Dauvergne 2011). Individuals can be excluded from refugee protection if they are found to be undeserving in any of three ways: because of involvement in internationally defined crime (war crimes, crimes against humanity, or crimes against peace), because of serious non-political crimes, or because of activities contrary to the purposes of the United Nations.[2] Of course, some acts will fall into all three categories at once. Our study sought to trace the influence of contemporary concerns about terrorism on these provisions. In the process we identified two trends that are vital in tracing the influence of criminal law within refugee jurisprudence.

The first is that the growth of international criminal law has been transported into refugee law.[3] As the reach of international criminal law has grown, and as this development has been generally applauded (see Lee (2002) and Schabas (2001)), this growth is translated almost directly into interpretation of the refugee law exclusion provisions. This adaptation is certainly by design. The drafters of the Convention deliberately left space to accommodate an anticipated comprehensive statement of international crimes (Grahl-Madsen 1966: 276). This impetus is supported by the interpretive guidelines of the United Nations High Commissioner for Refugees (UNHCR), which reference the expansion of international criminal texts (UNHCR 1992: para 150). The result of this twinning, however, is beyond what could have been contemplated at the time the Convention was drafted. Despite the general growth of international criminal law and applause for it, convictions remain few and far between. The pursuit of justice in the

---

[2] United Nations Convention Relating to the Status of Refugees, 28 July 1951, 189 UNTS 150 ('Refugee Convention'), Art 1F states: 'The provisions of this Convention shall not apply to any person with respect to whom there are serious reasons for considering that: (a) he has committed a crime against peace, a war crime, or a crime against humanity, as defined in the international instruments drawn up to make provision in respect of such crimes; (b) he has committed a serious non-political crime outside the country of refuge prior to his admission to that country as a refugee; (c) he has been guilty of acts contrary to the purposes and principles of the United Nations.'

[3] Our data was all Canadian, but a 'spot check' approach to leading cases elsewhere showed this was a generalizable trend.

international realm is notoriously slow and resource intensive.[4] This reflects, at least in part, the seriousness of international criminal responsibility and the extensive procedural protections. A persistent debate in international criminal law occurs around the question of who should be prosecuted, because it is well known that only a select few individuals—among many potential guilty parties—will ever be brought to justice in an international setting (Schabas 2001; Mills 2012). Within refugee law, however, these constraints do not apply. Any growth in the framework of international criminal responsibility expands exponentially the areas of exclusion within refugee law. There is no need for the formalities of charge, accusation, or defence. And thus, as international criminal law matures, it may be time to revisit the automatic linking of refugee exclusion and international criminal law.

The second trend we observed is that the idea of a 'political crime' has shrunk considerably. This shrinkage is vital to the operation of refugee exclusions because the second category of exclusion is the commission of serious *non-political* crimes. There is an irony here, as there was in regard to international criminal law. It has been a hard-fought battle to wrest refugee law away from the overt politicization of its Cold War roots (Fitzpatrick and Pauw 1992: 751). And thus the shrinking of overtly 'political' considerations within refugee law doctrine ought generally to be applauded. But in the area of exclusions, the diminution of the political equates with the contraction of protection. The principal way this has happened has been by pressing the idea that some crimes are so serious that they will not be considered political even if they have an explicit political objective. This is a jurisprudential sleight of hand. The issue is not that the acts in question fail to meet established standards for what constitutes a political crime. Rather, the concern is that some individuals have committed crimes so serious that we do not want to accord them refugee protection, regardless of the political character of those crimes (Goodwin-Gill and McAdam 2007: 116–123).[5] There is a refreshing transparency to the way this is set out in this jurisprudence, but it is nonetheless disturbing.[6] It is a direct contradiction of both the 'plain reading' and the 'object and purpose' of the Refugee Convention provision.

Of all the battles in the war on refugee protection, most refugee advocates recognize that asylum for those who have committed serious criminal acts is potentially the least winnable, and maybe even the least worth winning. With so many issues on the refugee advocacy agenda at present, it is unlikely that sustained work will be focused on maintaining an appropriately broad definition of 'political crime'. In the exclusion realm, advocacy efforts have instead focused on issues such

---

[4] For example, the International Criminal Court, which commenced operations in 2002, has so far launched 16 prosecutions and issued 20 warrants. There has been one conviction to date (September 2012). The annual budget of the Court is €108,800,000 (see <http://www.icc-cpi.int/iccdocs/asp_docs/ASP11/ICC-ASP-11-5-ENG-CBF18-Report.pdf>).

[5] Not surprisingly, these standards are highly malleable. But this is a 'known quantity' type of problem, rather than a new development.

[6] For a recent Canadian example, see the decision of the Immigration and Refugee Board in M96-04265.

as the expansion of 'war crimes', the use of secret evidence, and the doctrinal creep of complicity principles.[7]

Both the expansion of international criminal doctrine and the contraction of the 'political' category of crime alter the framework of refugee law. The exclusion criteria are the point of formal intersection between refugee law and criminal law, and each of these shifts troubles that intersection. As exclusions become increasingly important in refugee law (in part driven by the criminalization of asylum at a political level) this has grown to be the key site of overt doctrinal intertwining of refugee law and criminal law. But most refugee advocates would probably be prepared to live with or even support the jurisprudential dissonance these trends create. It is increasingly, incessantly, apparent that political support for the international asylum regime is fragile and that its supporters must be certain to demonstrate that refugee law does not protect criminals. This political reality acts to constrain critique in significant ways. However, what moves the concern about these trends beyond the theoretical is how they interact with the standard of proof issues, to which I now turn.

Asylum Seekers as Suspects: No Evidence, No Burden

In shorthand terms, the issue is this: criminal law has the highest standard of proof in our legal system and refugee law has the lowest. They do not mix well.

The clash of individual and state at the heart of the criminal law, the extent of state power in the criminal context, and the importance of the liberty interest of the individual have combined to develop strong procedural protections for the accused under criminal law. There are myriad skirmishes about whether these protections achieve their objectives, how this tradition has been eroded, and whose interests it serves. At a rhetorical level this is a firmly anchored feature of criminal law. Much stands behind the idea that a crime must be proven 'beyond a reasonable doubt'. The theoretical and jurisdictional dissonance that results from moving the criminal law paradigm away from its traditional object/subject—the citizen—is explored in Lucia Zedner's contribution to this volume (Chapter 2). The disconnect between standards of proof in refugee law and criminal law illustrates Zedner's broader theoretical point that criminal law can presently be observed as dangerously bifurcated between a variety applied to citizens and one applied to 'others' of various sorts.

While refugee law does not have the same long tradition as criminal law, its low standard of proof is equally integral to its logic. The central inquiry in a refugee determination is future looking—what will happen if a person is returned to his previous home?[8] Typically, there is no evidence presented to the decision maker

---

[7] See as examples, *Ezokola v Canada (Citizenship and Immigration)* 2011 FCA 224, [2011] 3 FCR 417 (SCC granted leave); ruling of the CJEU in Joined Cases C-57/09 and 101/09 *Bundesrepublik Deutschland v B and D* [2010] ECR I-000; Bond (2012); Saul (2004).

[8] See Refugee Convention, Art 1A: 'For the purposes of the present Convention, the term "refugee" shall apply to any person who: ... (2) ... owing to well-founded fear of being persecuted for reasons of race, religion, nationality, membership of a particular social group or political opinion, is outside the country of his nationality and is unable or, owing to such fear, is unwilling to avail himself of the protection of that country'.

beyond the individual's own account and a variety of 'country information' generated by governments and NGOs. These features of refugee determination have combined to establish a central proof standard that is alternately expressed as 'a serious possibility', a 'real chance', and 'less than a balance of probabilities'[9] and to jettison rules of evidence. Both these features are justified because of the advantages they provide for the individual concerned (Dauvergne and Millbank 2003). But when the issue is exclusion and criminality, these advantages are turned on their head. The standard of proof for criminal activity in the exclusion context is higher, expressed in the Convention itself as 'serious reasons for considering', but this is still a long way from the criminal burden of proof beyond reasonable doubt.[10] This low standard, combined with relaxed evidentiary rules, means that individuals suspected of criminal activity may be excluded in circumstances that could not possibly lead to a criminal conviction.

In this regard, the issue is that criminal law principles have not been sufficiently intertwined with refugee law. The aspects of the criminal law that aim specifically at protecting individual rights are precisely the features that have *not* been creeping into refugee law. Because of this, exclusion from refugee protection is emerging as an alternative to prosecution.[11] Allegations which would not reach criminal law standards become the basis for withdrawing protection from refoulement. This is immensely important because refugee protection is surrogate protection, available to those whose home states are unwilling, or unable, to protect them. Withdrawing this subsidiary, and lesser, level of human rights protection leaves individuals with almost nothing by way of rights protection. The strong protection for the rights of the accused within criminal law is justified by the prospect of loss of liberty that follows conviction. The consequences of a failure of refugee protection are similarly serious: those whom refugee law does not protect can be returned to states that will not protect them from the most serious human rights abuses. Refugee law begins from the premise that without a right to remain *somewhere* other rights protections will not be meaningful. This linkage to a right to 'remain'—the central commitment of refugee law—points us towards deportation, and the historical trajectory that Gibney traces in Chapter 12.

And thus, this second troublesome intersection of refugee law and criminal law also presents an irony: those who risk being pushed out of the realm of human rights altogether have fewer rights protections than those facing a limited term loss of liberty. What sustains this doctrinal dissonance is, again, the politicized criminalization of asylum. Faced with a rhetoric suggesting that many asylum seekers are criminals, punitive action against the entire group appears justifiable. As the trope

---

[9] *Canada (Attorney General) v Ward* [1993] 2 SCR 689; *Chan v Minister for Immigration and Ethnic Affairs* [1989] HCA 62, 169 CLR 379; *R v Secretary of State for the Home Department ex p Sivakumaran et al* [1988] 1 AC 958, HL.

[10] See notes from UNHCR Lisbon Roundtable Meeting of Experts, Summary Conclusions, 2001 May.

[11] This trade-off parallels that between deportation and prosecution, which Juliet Stumpf explores in this volume (Chapter 3).

of the bogus refugee is deployed politically, rhetoric emerges which obscures the irony of this intersection between criminal law and refugee law. Criminal law presumes innocence and develops a rights framework that reflects this: refugee law increasingly presumes guilt. In the matter of extradition, these conflicting presumptions have the potential to collide most sharply.

Extraditing Refugees

The third intertwining of criminal law and refugee law is the question of extraditing refugees. The possibility that a refugee may be extradited has been advanced significantly in Canada by the recent paired rulings of the Supreme Court of Canada in *Nemeth* and *Gavrila*.[12] While each of these cases must be tallied as a 'win' in that the two extradition orders were found to have been made incorrectly, the principles followed depart from the framework of the Refugee Convention and reshape the intersection of refugee law and criminal law at this juncture, at least in Canada.

To unpack this assertion, one must begin with the Refugee Convention. In simplest terms, it ought to be close to impossible to extradite a refugee to her country of nationality or former habitual residence, because it is on the basis of a serious risk of being persecuted there that refugee status was accorded in the first place.[13] The potential criminality of refugees and asylum seekers was clearly contemplated by the drafters of the Convention. They sought to ensure that refugee status would not become a cloak to protect criminals (Hathaway 1991: 22).[14] In the security climate of the early twenty-first century, this objective is more important than ever in ensuring support for the refugee regime. The Convention addresses potential extradition requests in two ways. First, through the exclusion clauses discussed above, especially Article 1F(b), which concerns serious non-political crimes prior to obtaining refugee status. Second, the possibility of an extradition request is confronted in Article 33, the non-refoulement provision, which forms the core of the Convention.[15]

Article 33 is the more important of these provisions, as an extradition request is most likely to arise once refugee status is granted. It reads in full:

1. No Contracting State shall expel or return ('refouler') a refugee in any manner whatsoever to the frontiers of territories where his life or freedom would be threatened on account of his race, religion, nationality, membership of a particular social group or political opinion.

2. The benefit of the present provision may not, however, be claimed by a refugee whom there are reasonable grounds for regarding as a danger to the security of the country in

---

[12] *Nemeth v Canada* [2010] 3 SCR 281; *Gavrila v Canada* [2010] SCR 342.

[13] It is, of course, a different question when an extradition request comes from another state.

[14] The 'serious non-political crime' exclusion provision was tailored to ensure this.

[15] Article 32, which was referenced in the *Nemeth* ruling (fn 12), deals with expulsion and thus is not directly relevant to questions of extradition (eg it contemplates those being expelled needing to find admission somewhere else).

which he is, or who, having been convicted by a final judgment of a particularly serious crime, constitutes a danger to the community of that country.

A plain reading of this provision tells us two things: first that a refugee must not be returned 'in any manner whatsoever', obviously including extradition; and, second, that this protection will not be extended to those who are a danger to the security or, following a conviction, a danger to the community of the country of refuge. Plainly, the permissible reasons for returning a refugee are not linked to a request for extradition. The danger exceptions may coincide with an extradition request, but in many instances would not. Article 33 establishes that refugees cannot be refouled (and, hence, extradited) because of criminal activity in a general sense. Only some types of criminal convictions ('particularly serious crimes') where the person is also found to be a 'danger' to the community will result in withdrawal of protection against refoulement. Furthermore, a crime for which extradition is sought cannot be the basis of withdrawing the protection of Article 33 unless the facts surrounding that crime are such that they constitute a risk to the security of the country *of refuge*.

The Article 33 exceptions (security risk or danger following a conviction) mean that the threshold for withdrawing protection from non-refoulement is higher than that for denying refugee status in the first place under Article 1F. Article 33 also means that under some limited circumstances, states are permitted to refoule refugees. It is not necessary to remove a person's refugee status prior to returning her to a risk of persecution if the Article 33(2) conditions are met.

An important addition to understanding the relationship of criminality to the Convention's non-refoulement provisions is to appreciate that, under the Convention, refugee status need not be considered permanent. Article 1C lists the circumstances in which refugee status will cease either because the conditions in one's home country have changed or because one has found protection elsewhere. In addition, most states have developed the practice of allowing for refugee status to be stripped from an individual if it is discovered after the fact that she could have been excluded from protection under Article 1F at the time the original status determination was made, or if, subsequent to being accorded status, she becomes involved in international criminal activity or acts contrary to the purposes of the United Nations.[16] The Convention does not specifically address cancellation of refugee status, but it is common practice, and is accepted in UNHCR guidance (UNHCR 1992: para 117). This means that someone who has refugee status may stop having it, and that this cancellation—unlike the Article 33 non-refoulement provisions—may be linked to criminal activity.

Despite these features of the Convention text and the established practice that demonstrate that refugee status need not be permanent, it is also evident in the text that refugee status was not intended to be fleeting or ephemeral. The heft of the rights enumerated in the Convention suggests a long-term settlement in the

---

[16] As defined in Arts 1F(a) and 1F(c). Exclusion under Art 1F(b)—serious non-political crimes—is limited to actions prior to admission to the country of refuge.

country of refuge. The provisions include, among others, rights to wage-earning employment and self-employment (Articles 17 and 18), to a range of welfare state entitlements (Articles 20–24), and to travel documents (Article 28). Most tellingly, Article 34 requires that states 'shall as far as possible facilitate the assimilation and naturalization of refugees.'

The Refugee Convention, in sum, provides that individuals may be extradited to their home states to face prosecution for serious non-political crimes committed prior to obtaining refugee status. In the case of criminal activities committed after having this status, extradition would not be possible unless the narrow Article 33 exceptions are met. To this basic framework, there are two less common provisos. The first is that if the request comes from a third state, the question of refoulement arises without the backdrop of a risk of persecution which has already been determined; and, second, is that if the request relates to a crime which is not covered in Article 1F(b), but is instead within the scope of Article 1F(a) or 1F(c), then the timing of the offence is not a bar to extradition.

All of this boils down to two questions for refugees in the extradition context. First: is refugee status ever secure? Second: will an extradition request become a trigger for removing refugee status? The Supreme Court of Canada's answer to these questions in *Nemeth* and in *Gavrila*[17] means that refugee status is increasingly insecure.

Both Nemeth and Gavrila had obtained refugee protection in Canada because of their risk of being persecuted as ethnic Roma in their respective home countries, Hungary and Romania. Nemeth (along with his wife and co-accused) had become a law-abiding permanent resident in Canada. His experience in Hungary included a series of violent crimes committed against him. Gavrila had not been able to become a permanent resident in Canada because of a series of criminal convictions (all property crimes) in Canada. In each case, the country of nationality sought extradition on the basis of low-level fraud offences (sums of less than $5,000 were involved in both instances) committed prior to departure from the home country, and included in Gavrila's case a conviction *in absentia*.

There was nothing in either case that could come close to triggering the Article 33 exceptions to protection from non-refoulement. Nor was the criminal activity alleged anywhere near the standard of exclusion in Article 1F(b). Refugee Convention jurisprudence does not treat a low-level property crime as a 'serious non-political offence' (Hathaway 1991: 221–225; Goodwin-Gill and McAdam 2007: 176–184). To its great discredit, the Court continued to treat this as a possibility throughout its reasoning, largely on the basis that under Canadian immigration law this offence could possibly be categorized as 'serious' for the purposes of a uniquely Canadian inadmissibility finding.[18] Finally, no evidence had been presented that

---

[17] See fn 12.

[18] It is not likely on the facts of the charge in *Nemeth* that the offence would have a Canadian equivalent that would bring it into the 'serious crime' category. The Court, however, did not interrogate this point but instead relied on the Minister's finding that the crime was 'serious' in immigration terms (para 7 of the judgment). In *Gavrila* there was even less analysis.

refugee status had ceased. For all of these reasons, the Refugee Convention would appear to provide a full and complete answer for the *Nemeth* and *Gavrila* facts: refuse the extradition request. Indeed, this is the straightforward approach taken by the High Court of England and Wales in a case that is remarkably similar: *Ostroleka Second Criminal Division (A Polish Judicial Authority) v Dytlow*.[19] I will return to *Dytlow* after considering the Supreme Court of Canada's reasoning.

The overarching problem with the decision is its failure to apply the Refugee Convention. While international law provides a complete response to the facts in both cases, the Supreme Court of Canada engaged in an extensive analysis, primarily of domestic provisions, and in the end established four problematic principles: (i) extradition law provides a complete answer to the question and incorporates/overtakes both international refugee law and domestic immigration law; (ii) the question of whether someone is a refugee will always be reinvestigated by the Minister when considering extradition; (iii) the standard of 'serious criminality' in domestic immigration law may be absorbed into the Article 1F exclusion considerations;[20] and (iv) a person's refugee status (or claim to such status) is only relevant in the final phase of extradition considerations, in which the Minister of Justice decides whether to exercise discretion to surrender an individual (when the judicial phase is already clearly made out). These four principles combine to trouble the intersection of refugee law and criminal law immensely.

The Court's analysis began by locating the relevant non-refoulement provision in the Refugee Convention. Moving beyond this, however, the Court found that while the domestic immigration legislation is the principal way in which the Convention is implemented in Canada, in the case of extradition law, the domestic extradition statute provides a complete answer to international obligations.[21] Elevating the domestic statute in this way is problematic because the provision in Canada's Extradition Act does not match up well with the definition of a refugee at international law.[22] In particular, the Extradition Act provision does not use a risk of 'persecution' as its standard, is concerned solely with state action and not with

---

[19] [2009] EWHC 1009 (Admin).

[20] This problem parallels that in the UK, as identified by the Joint House of Commons/House of Lords Committee on Human Rights 2004: 14–15.

[21] At para 35 Justice Cromwell, writing for the unanimous court, states: 'The presumption that legislation implements Canada's international obligations is rebuttable. If the provisions are unambiguous, they must be given effect [internal citations omitted]. As I have discussed at length earlier, s. 115 does not address removal by extradition and so its clear meaning must be given effect. Moreover, I do not accept that this interpretation of s. 115 results in Canadian domestic law failing to respect its *non-refoulement* obligations under the Refugee Convention. *My view is that those obligations in the context of extradition are fully satisfied by a correct interpretation and application of s. 44 of the EA, as I will explain in the next section of my reasons.*' (emphasis added)

[22] Extradition Act, SC 1999, c 18, s 44. Section 44 reads: '(1) The Minister shall refuse to make a surrender order if the Minister is satisfied that (a) the surrender would be unjust or oppressive having regard to all the relevant circumstances; or (b) the request for extradition is made for the purpose of prosecuting or punishing the person by reason of their race, religion, nationality, ethnic origin, language, color, political opinion, sex, sexual orientation, age, mental or physical disability or status or that the person's position may be prejudiced for any of those reasons. (2) The Minister may refuse to make a surrender order if the Minister is satisfied that the conduct in respect of which the request for extradition is made is punishable by death under the laws that apply to the extradition partner.'

risks that might be posed by non-state actors, lists grounds of risk which do not match that in the Refugee Convention,[23] and incorporates what is almost certainly a more difficult 'nexus' standard for an individual to meet.[24] For all of these reasons, the Canadian Extradition Act offers less protection than the Refugee Convention. Finding that the domestic law provides a complete reflection of Canada's non-refoulement obligations is not only incorrect at present but also ensures that refugees in Canada are cut off from developments in rights protection at the international level.[25]

The second principle in *Nemeth* also departs from the standard of protection in the Refugee Convention, primarily by removing any sense of security from refugee status. In this instance as well, the Court begins with a straightforward review of the Refugee Convention and notes that 'there should be no burden on a person who has refugee status to persuade the Minister that the conditions which led to the conferral of refugee protection have not changed'.[26] Justice Cromwell then proceeds to review the Article 1C cessation provisions, following on to Article 1F. It is here that his reasoning departs from the Convention:

> Apart from changed circumstances, the Refugee Convention also has exclusion clauses (Article 1F) which may be invoked after refugee status has been granted to demonstrate that the person was not, in fact, entitled to refugee protection. ... As these exclusions relate to the entitlement of a person to refugee status, they will also be relevant to determining entitlement to *non-refoulement* protection. For the purposes of *non-refoulement* protection under the Refugee Convention, it is co-extensive with the entitlement to refugee protection.[27]

With this reasoning, the Court treats the exclusion provisions as parallel to the cessation provisions, and introduces the idea that with every extradition request, the inquiry of entitlement to refugee status begins again. This cuts against the formula of Article 33, and exposes refugees to additional scrutiny. Keeping in mind the limited circumstances in which a refugee might be stripped of that status and consequently extradited, the requirement that entitlement be re-examined ought not to be routine. It should be limited explicitly to circumstances where the details of the extradition request raise a prima facie exclusion issue. The facts in these two cases did not.

The third principle in the *Nemeth* reasoning followed closely from the second. As discussed above, in examining the question of whether there are reasonable grounds that a refugee has committed a 'serious non-political crime', the Minister had made reference to the domestic standard in regard to 'seriousness'. The Court stops just short

---

[23] There is no 'particular social group' provision, the criterion which has been the focus of sustained growth in refugee jurisprudence over the past 10 years.

[24] The Extradition Act provision states that the extradition request be denied if it is made 'for the purpose of'. For a detailed discussion of 'nexus' in refugee law, see 'The Michigan Guidelines on Nexus to a Convention Ground' (2002).

[25] This is a common aspect of the contemporary Canadian approach to international human rights. See Dauvergne 2013.

[26] *Nemeth* (fn 12), para 106.   [27] *Nemeth* (fn 12), para 108.

of approving this standard, which would greatly increase the areas of exclusion in comparison with international jurisprudence on Article 1F.[28] It does state, however, that 'it seems that Parliament, in the IRPA [domestic immigration statute], has decided two issues about how the Refugee Convention should be implemented in Canada. The first is that a crime punishable by at least 10 years imprisonment constitutes a "serious non-political crime" within the meaning of Article 1F'.[29] The Court does not comment on whether this implementation formula is consistent with the Refugee Convention, and, indeed, having decided that domestic law governs, such a conclusion is not strictly necessary. But there is a strong implication that this formula is correct, despite the fact that it does not align with international jurisprudence for two significant reasons.[30] First, it considers only how an offence is written on the books, and does not examine the facts of the offence (UNHCR 1992: para 157); and, second, it concludes that any serious crime cannot be political.

The final principle deployed in *Nemeth* may in fact be the most telling. It is the requirement that when there is a request to extradite a refugee, the potential protection promised by the non-refoulement provision (as translated, imperfectly, into the Extradition Act) arises as a final consideration.[31] That is, all the work of assessing the evidence and the offence, as well as the terms of the particular extradition treaty, is completed before asking the basic question about the effect of refugee protection. Furthermore, this question is to be addressed solely by the Minister. This approach ensures that the Minister will be presented only with cases where, 'but for' refugee status,[32] there is no bar to extradition; the prima facie case is already made out. This raises the stakes against a refugee enormously, and puts basic refugee determination in political and non-expert hands.

Despite the extensive reasons in *Nemeth*, there is one key idea that did not make its way into the decision: the role of the 'exception' provisions in Article 33(2). Article 33(2) is the only provision in the Refugee Convention that addresses when a refugee may be extradited. It is cited in the ruling, but is not discussed in any detail,

---

[28] *Nemeth* (fn 12), para 108; see discussion at paras 119–123. At para 119 Justice Cromwell writes: '[t]hese comments make clear, in my view, that the Minister did not decide whether the serious crime exception applied to the appellants.'

[29] *Nemeh* (fn 12), para 120.

[30] In the companion case *Gavrila* (fn 12), para 12, Justice Cromwell writes: 'I should add that the Minister did not base his decision to surrender on, and appears not to have addressed, whether the appellant was no longer entitled to refugee (and therefore *non-refoulement*) protection by virtue of the serious non-political crimes exception under Article 1F(b) of the *Convention Relating to the Status of Refugees*, Can. T.S. 1969 No. 6 or of his extensive criminal conduct in Canada. While not the subject of argument in this Court, it seems clear from the record that the extradition offence would constitute serious criminality for the purposes of the *IRPA* and it is open to the Minister to consider the possible application of Article 1F(b) of the *Convention Relating to the Status of Refugees* in deciding whether the appellant is entitled to refugee protection.'

[31] See para 112: 'In my view, when the Minister acting under the *EA* is in effect determining that refugee protection (and thus *non-refoulement* protection under the Refugee Convention) of a person sought is excluded or is no longer required by virtue of a change of circumstances in the requesting country, he must be satisfied on the balance of probabilities that the person sought is no longer entitled to refugee status in Canada.'

[32] Or other concerns that would be captured by the 'not-quite-refugee' wording of s 44.

presumably because it is not applicable to these facts.[33] This point was crucial to the succinct and correct reasoning in *Dytlow*.[34] A decision that declines to address this factor is deeply deficient. It is worse that it comes from the Supreme Court of Canada, which has been a leader in developing internationally authoritative interpretations of the Convention.

The ruling in *Dytlow* was made by the High Court of England and Wales in 2009. The facts were strikingly similar to the Canadian cases. Two brothers, Polish nationals of Roma ethnicity, were sought under a European arrest warrant in connection with a 'low value robbery' committed prior to their departure from Poland and successful claim for refugee status in England. The judge at first instance had discharged the respondents on the basis of a potential breach of the European Convention on Human Rights, but, before the High Court, Lord Justice Keane found that the appropriate reason to deny extradition was the brothers' refugee status. The domestic extradition statute differs somewhat from the Canadian one, in that it makes direct reference to the Refugee Convention, but its effect ought to be the same given the Supreme Court of Canada's ruling that Canadian extradition law upholds the Convention's provisions. Lord Justice Keane focused on the Article 33(2) exceptions to protection, and concluded that they would be of 'limited application'.[35] Concluding on this point he stated: '[t]o sum up the legal position so far, it appears to me that once refugee status has been granted to a person, and so long as it persists, that person cannot be extradited to his country of nationality, of whose protection he, by definition, cannot avail himself.'[36] Lord Justice Keane then turned to consider the possibility of revoking or reconsidering the refugee status itself and concluded that this is a very serious step which ought not to be 'undertaken lightly'[37] and, if required at all, should be left to the specialist tribunal, with appropriate appeal rights.[38] Furthermore, he turned directly to the question of whether an extradition proceeding ought to be adjourned to revisit the question of refugee status, and held that this should be rare and must not be triggered merely by an extradition request.[39] Summing up his reasoning, the judge stated: 'To order the extradition of a person or persons enjoying refugee status in this country would ... amount to an abuse of process.'[40] This judgment, therefore, differs from that of the Canadian court on each of the steps in the reasoning.

---

[33] Article 33 is cited in full at para 20.

[34] *Ostroleka Second Criminal Division (A Polish Judicial Authority) v Dytlow* [2009] EWHC 1009 (Admin).

[35] *Dytlow* (fn 34), paras 14–15. This conclusion relies in part on UK domestic law. In this regard, UK and Canadian domestic law are almost identical.

[36] *Dytlow* (fn 34), para 16.

[37] *Dytlow* (fn 34), para 22.

[38] *Dytlow* (fn 34), para 24.

[39] *Dytlow* (fn 34), para 26. He stated: 'an adjournment so that a defendant's refugee status can be reconsidered is not something which would be appropriate as a matter of routine merely because extradition is being sought of the refugee to his home country.'

[40] *Dytlow* (fn 34), para 31.

Conclusions

The *Dytlow* judgment demonstrates that it is at least possible that the Supreme Court of Canada is out of step with others at this particular intersection of refugee law and criminal law. This would certainly be a good thing. On a plain reading of the Refugee Convention, the question of extraditing refugees ought to be so exceptional as almost never to arise. The fact that it now does so with some frequency (at least in Canada) is a measure of the insertion of criminal law into refugee law. Indeed, the extradition analysis in some ways swallows up both of my earlier points: the expansion of exclusion and the problems of proof. The politics of refugee extradition, however, are increasingly a feature of ensuring support for this imperilled regime overall. This politics is transparent on the face of the UNHCR's guidance note on extradition, which begins by outlining the importance of extradition in the fight against terrorism (UNHCR 2008: 4–5). In the Supreme Court of Canada's analysis, the political nature of this dilemma is underlined by putting the question of refugee protection directly in political hands through the guise of extradition—neatly undoing three decades of work to *de*-politicize this determination. The *Nemeth* decision also takes us directly back to my starting point: the *old* way that criminal law and refugee protection intersected. All of these men were granted protection because their home states were unable or unwilling to protect them from being persecuted. It is well established that prosecution under ordinary criminal law may be pursued in such a harsh and discriminatory fashion that it becomes persecution. Nowhere in the decisions is the question of *why* states that were found to be unwilling to protect their nationals are now seeking from afar to prosecute them for low-level crimes addressed. This was formerly the nub of the matter. Extradition—especially as formulated by the Supreme Court of Canada—neatly makes this question vanish.

This brief glimpse at shifts within refugee jurisprudence shows that criminalization is occurring within the intricacies of refugee law doctrine. It is not only the case that in recent decades asylum itself is being made 'illegal'. Even for the reduced numbers who manage to access asylum systems of prosperous Western states, criminality looms large in the assessments that are made within those systems. As asylum systems face increasing political pressures, an ability to demonstrate that the systems themselves are 'tough on crime' becomes an important advocacy piece in their maintenance. For all of these reasons, interrogating the troublesome intersections of refugee law and criminal law is a vital part of the new criminology of immigration.

References

Bond, J. (2012) 'Excluding Justice: The Dangerous Intersection between Refugee Claims, Criminal Law, and "Guilty" Asylum Seekers', *International Journal of Refugee Law* 24(1): 1.

Dauvergne, C. (2013) 'How the *Charter* Has Failed Non-Citizens in Canada—Reviewing Thirty Years of Supreme Court of Canada Jurisprudence', *McGill Law Journal* 58: 1.

Dauvergne, C. (2008) *Making People Illegal: What Globalization Means for Migration and Law*. Cambridge, New York: Cambridge University Press.

Dauvergne, C. and Millbank, J. (2003) 'Burdened By Proof: How the Australian Refugee Review Tribunal Has Failed Lesbian and Gay Asylum Seekers', *Federal Law Review* 31: 299.

Fitzpatrick, J. and Pauw, R. (1992) 'Foreign Policy, Asylum and Discretion', *Williamette Law Review* 28: 751.

Goodwin-Gill, G.S. and McAdam, J. (2007) *The Refugee in International Law*. Oxford, Toronto: Oxford University Press.

Grahl-Madsen, A. (1966) *The Status of Refugees in International Law*, Volume I—Refugee Character. Leyden: A.W. Sijthoff.

Hathaway, J.C. (2007) 'Forced Migration Studies: Could We Agree Just to Date', *Journal of Refugee Studies* 20(3): 349.

Hathaway, J.C. (1991) *The Law of Refugee Status*. Toronto: Butterworth.

Joint House of Commons/House of Lords Committee on Human Rights (2004) *The Nationality, Immigration and Asylum Act 2002 (Specification of Particularly Serious Crimes) Order*, HL Paper 190, HC 1212.

Kaushal, A. and Dauvergne, C. (2011) 'The Growing Culture of Exclusion: Trends in Canadian Refugee Exclusions', *International Journal of Refugee Law* 23(1): 54.

Lee, R.S. (2002) 'An Assessment of the ICC Statute', *Fordham International Law Journal*, 25(3): 750.

Mills, K. (2012) 'Bashir Is Dividing Us: Africa and the International Criminal Court', *Human Rts Q* 34(2) 404.

Saul, B. (2004) 'Exclusion of Suspected Terrorists from Asylum: Trends in International and European Refugee Law' IIIS (July).

Schabas, W.A. (2001) 'The International Criminal Court at Ten', *Criminal Law Forum* 22: 493.

The Michigan Guidelines on Nexus to a Convention Ground (2002) *Michigan Journal of International Law* 23: 211.

UN High Commissioner for Refugees (2008) *Guidance Note on Extradition and International Refugee Protection*, April <http://www.unhcr.org/refworld/docid/481ec7d92.html>.

UN High Commissioner for Refugees (2001) Lisbon Roundtable Meeting of Experts, Summary Conclusions, May.

UN High Commissioner for Refugees (1992) *Handbook on Procedures and Criteria for Determining Refugee Status under the 1951 Convention and the 1967 Protocol Relating to the Status of Refugees*, HCR/IP/Eng/Rev 1.

PART II

POLICING

5

Policing Transversal Borders

Sharon Pickering and Leanne Weber

In this chapter we discuss how traditional policing agencies are being shaped by the political emphasis on border control, consider whether immigration authorities are becoming more police-like, and identify how other government and non-government agencies are being brought into a migration policing role. We do so by focusing on Australia, a nation which has expended significant political, material, and ideological efforts on crafting an expansive border policing regime over the past 15 years.

Border Policing and Transversal Borders

Border control can be regarded as the heart of the regulatory effort to sustain national sovereignty (Sassen 1996). Historically, states have sought to construct their sovereignty as fixed, spatially and temporally. These fixed borders have often been unquestioned in view of the 'inescapable fact' that international state borders 'all have territory, they all *are* territory' (Donnan and Wilson 1999: 44, original emphasis). However, border policing increasingly requires activities that are both *beyond* territory and operate *within* physical borders. This decoupling from territory fundamentally changes the nature of that policing, and in turn the nature of the border. While we might argue about which is cause and which effect, it is reasonable to conclude that they are mutually constitutive. As Pratt (2005: 185) reminds us: 'The border is an ongoing accomplishment, yet the processes by which it is continually produced are erased by its apparent self-evidence.' It is through acts of policing that the juridical border is 'performed' by both state and non-state actors (Wonders 2006).

Conceptualizing borders in terms of statecraft transforms a criminological analysis of border policing from an understanding of the border as fixed to understanding it as dispersed to multiple 'sites of enforcement' (Weber and Bowling 2004; Weber 2006), a process in which policing plays a critical role (Pickering 2004). In considering the policing of multiple borders we seek to apply the idea of transversality. In so doing we take up the work of Soguk and Whitehall (1999) who argue that prior to identifying the multiple boundaries, frontiers, and borders that overlay one another there is a condition of transversality which does not occupy a space easily locatable within this complex, geographical environment. Rather, a state of transversality exists prior to conventional sovereign boundaries 'that enable[s] political inclusions, exclusions and cultural separations across peoples and places' (Soguk and Whitehall 1999: 675). Soguk and Whitehall argue that the transversal is defined both for and by migrants and their movements. Their analysis does not start with the state in order to explore the transversal, but with transversal subjects—the migrants and their crossings. Consequently, studies in this tradition have used the voices of migrants to disrupt official accounts of sovereignty and borders. Applying these ideas about transversality to the internal border shifts the focus away from physical border crossings and towards ethnographic accounts of lives lived in states of illegality (Núněz and Heyman 2007; Fan 2008); the role of migrants as active self-definers, seeking to cross fluid legal boundaries that demarcate zones of differential entitlement (Coutin 2005; Schuster 2005); and the often exclusionary responses of extant populations, as described by Khosravi (2010: 75): 'After crossing many physical, national borders, I found myself facing other kinds of border ... those in the minds of people.'

We argue here that conditions of transversality are not only produced by migrants and their movements, but also by those seeking to police borders. Transversal borders, in other words, are performed by a range of people—openly and officially, or tacitly and unofficially—who may seek to reinforce, transgress, or transcend the juridical border. Inasmuch as the transversal histories of migrants challenge the notion of a sovereign essence it is possible to imagine a policing function both central to, but floating apart from, the state, able to invest in a cross-border, de-territorialized existence which is unbounded in many respects by temporal or geographic constraint. One of us has made this argument elsewhere in relation to the Australian Federal Police (Pickering 2004). The intersection of the many practices of border policing brings into being what we call transversal policing. The Latin definition of *transversus*, which translates as 'lying across', has been applied in medical and other settings to connote a more active process of 'cutting across' an axis, so that the resulting incision or structure is situated at right angles to the original frame of reference. Transversal border policing practices which run, conceptually, at right angles across established borders open up spaces of governance which are ripe for colonization.

While processes of geographical transversality influence *where* border control functions are performed, changes in governance characteristic of globalizing, neoliberal states are bringing about a dispersal of authority across networks or chains of actors (Garland 1996) which affects *who* performs these state-defining functions (Weber and Bowling 2004). This shifts the boundaries of existing government agencies, creates spaces for new private and commercial actors, and redefines the state through border policing processes that are both embodied (through performances by state and non-state actors) and informated (through information exchange that creates an invisible, virtual border). In this chapter we consider how transversality brings new actors into the border policing realm as novel spaces of governance are made available for exploitation by entrepreneurs. At the same time, other agencies resist imposed changes to their established roles. We conclude that transversal policing is an active and entrepreneurial practice which generates deep contradictions and paradoxes for the agencies involved as it cuts across established norms and practices.

In the remainder of the chapter we will consider how Australian immigration authorities have become more police-like under pressure to secure borders; argue that Australian police are increasingly occupied in migration policing roles; and demonstrate that other government and non-government agencies are being drawn into wider migration policing networks. In each context we consider border policing developments at both the external and internal borders.

Proposition 1: Immigration Authorities are Becoming More Police-like

The external border: scientifically managing migration—policing, prediction, pre-emption

The convergence of policing and immigration functions can increasingly be viewed in the use of pre-emptive border control measures by immigration authorities— that is, their efforts to police out undesired persons prior to their arrival in Australia. Pre-emption is concerned with predicting and preventing acts before they occur. Primarily this is occurring through the desire to achieve certainty in an increasingly 'scientific' approach to managing migration through the use of predictive analytics that share common features with crime science, in particular the use of crime mapping by police agencies, models of intelligence-led policing, and the use of biometrics (Wilson 2006). The *politics* of border control can be neutralized and made objective, on the one hand, by translating border politics into problems to be scientifically known and solved and, on the other hand, are rendered banal as calculated risks to be managed. 'Scientific' management—the massing of data and its analysis—are the functions that animate both the transversal border policing space and the frontiers of information-driven policing more generally. It has been argued that the emergence of intelligence-led policing is 'the most significant and profound paradigm change in modern policing' (Ratcliffe 2008: 88). Biopolitics and what Bigo (2002) calls the 'governmentality of unease' (characterized by practices of exceptionalism and acts of profiling and containing foreigners) in the form of immigration-as-policing activities occur prior to and apart from the border. This governmentality of unease produces a border function on/in the individual bodies/lives of those perceived as having a threatening intent. Governing mobilities, Amoore has argued in the US context, means that 'the management of the border. … is more appropriately understood as a matter of biopolitics, as a mobile regulatory site through which people's everyday lives can be made amenable to intervention and management' (2006: 337).

Border policing is a core function of the Department of Immigration and Citizenship (DIAC) in Australia. Currently, the DIAC describes its external policing role as 'promoting visa integrity'. Australia operates a total visa system. It is the prevention aspect of 'promoting visa integrity' that primarily occurs at the external border—that is at the many points prior to arrival in Australia where Australian authorities seek to deter and deflect unwanted travellers. Similar to the pre-emptive and intelligence functions of security and policing agencies (see Zedner 2007; McCulloch and Pickering 2009), the DIAC maintains an offshore network of border intelligence officers, migration intelligence officers, and airport liaison officers to undertake these tasks. The DIAC approaches prevention as 'intent management' which is defined as 'a high level use of information management and predictive analysis [in which] DIAC aims to, in a virtual sense, "extend the borders" by identifying and managing high risk travellers before they get to Australia' (McCairns 2011).

This seemingly Orwellian desire to manage intent requires a range of elaborate and systematized processes to manage large populations of *potential* and *actual* travellers, only some of whom may seek 'migration outcomes' within Australia. It is to assess and respond to undesired travellers to pre-empt and prevent any potential claim on Australia's protection obligations or other contravention of migration arrangements (including anticipated post-arrival compliance breaches). Pre-emptive border control has much in common with pre-emptive policing endeavours (Weber 2006; Wilson and Weber 2008) and pre-crime models (Zedner 2007) which seek to identify and respond to crime before it is committed, particularly crimes related to national security concerns.

The DIAC describes its 'layered' approach to intent management as follows: 'The process starts even before the person books a ticket or lodges an application for a visa to enter Australia' (McCairns 2011). This places intent management as an outermost rim in border policing—one that occurs temporally well before the usual preparatory actions associated with travel (for example buying a ticket or applying for a visa) and physically well before any border crossing. Those who are 'intent managed' are policed out of the licit market in the movement of people. Those who are not intent managed out of the system are then streamed into policing categories by immigration, described by the DIAC as 'risk tiering':

The client's details are assessed against a set of risk ratings. Key objective of risk tiering is to be able to predict high and low risk clients based on historical patterns. Aligning processing effort to client risk levels. Depending on the risk rating, visa applications will be streamed to a particular processing queue: streamlined, standard, high rigour. (McCairns 2011)

Even when a person successfully satisfies the conditions for issuing a visa, a second layer of border policing is undertaken by immigration authorities using predictive modelling to identify risky travellers. These analytics (see Table 1) are routinely changed and updated; however, they always work to filter the most risky aspects of a traveller which include suspect personal attributes (country of birth, citizenship) and suspect authorities (airline, post-granting the visa, point of arrival).

Predictive modelling is operationalized through the 'risk scoring' of all air arrivals. This has two key phases. The first is entirely automated risk scoring based on predictive modelling, detailed above. This identifies persons who will be subject to a second stage of checking by an analyst at the airport of arrival 30 minutes after a traveller has checked in at the airport of embarkation. This analysis,

Table 1 'Risk Profile'—Attributes of interest

Attributes	Values
Previous entries made	<0.5
Visa subclass at the time of movement	159, 416, 418, 422, 427, 428, 570, 572, 573, 773
Birth Country	Belgium, Ecuador, Egypt, Fiji, France, FYR Macedonia, HKSAR of the PRC, Hungary, India, Rep of Ireland, Israel, Jordan, Kenya, Kuwait, Macau, Pakistan, Philippines, Portugal, Qatar, Seychelles, Slovakia, Slovenia, Sri Lanka, Timor-Leste, Tonga, Turkey, USSR, United Arab Emirates
Airlines	Bl (Royal Brunei Airlines), Cl (China Airlines), CX (Cathay Pacific), DJ (Pacific Blue), EK (Emirates), FJ (Air Pacific), GF (Gulf Air), MH (Malaysian Airlines), MK (Air Mauritius), OS (Austrian Airlines), TR (Tiger Airlines), UA (United Airlines), VN (Vietnam Airlines)
Citizenship at the time of movement	Canada, Egypt, France, Kenya, Macau, Pakistan, Portugal, Qatar, Russian Federation, United Kingdom
DIAC post-granting the visa for the movement	Central Office, Darwin, Dubai, Hong Kong, London, Melbourne, Moscow, Southport, Washington
Port of Arrival	Adelaide, Eagle Farm (Brisbane), Perth
PID Percentile Score	<67.5

Source: McCairns (2011).

witnessed during a period of ethnographic research by one of the authors,[1] is undertaken at great speed and seeks to identify and discount any data anomalies—such as data from different systems containing misspellings and being incorrectly matched. Just as risk profiles are used to direct police resources to crime hot spots and repeat offenders (Ratcliffe 2008), risk tiering is used to reduce the list of persons of interest for immigration authorities so that they can be subject to more intensive scrutiny upon arrival, or in some circumstances be prevented from boarding the plane.

The internal border: DIAC compliance—from a 'well oiled' to a 'well targeted' removal machine

Australia's commitment to exercising total visa control continues after arrival in the country. Since the late 1980s Australia's comprehensive visa system has been systematically enforced within its territory, underpinned by comprehensive entry and exit controls. According to a senior DIAC official interviewed by one of the authors:[2] 'I can say this with some confidence ... there's virtually no one in

---

[1] Part of the fieldwork currently being undertaken for her future fellowship by Sharon Pickering on Border Policing: Gender, Security and Human Rights.

[2] Migration Policing project, funded by Australian Research Council Discovery Project grant DP0774554, Leanne Weber sole Chief Investigator.

Australia that either wasn't born here or that this Department … doesn't have a record of in some way' (Interview 45, Canberra DIAC).

The immigration enforcement system has been described as a 'well oiled machine', operating with minimal intervention by human decision makers and with scant external oversight (Nicholls 2007: 149). Under section 14 of the Migration Act 1958, any non-citizen who is not in possession of a valid visa is liable to detention and deportation. The DIAC maintains a relatively small contingent of specialist compliance officers who exercise police-like powers under the Migration Act to enter and search premises (sections 251, 257); question, arrest, and detain (sections 188, 189); and require disclosure of information held by other agencies in relation to suspected unlawful non-citizens (section 18). While these officers are empowered to use force if necessary in the conduct of identification inquiries (section 261AE) and in order to gain lawful entry (section 268CH) they are not armed or trained in the use of force. DIAC Compliance therefore relies heavily on police to provide security during 'high risk' operations in which it is anticipated that resistance may be encountered. As explained by a senior DIAC official: 'It's not unusual with some of these more difficult ones to bring in their Tactical Unit to assist us, and sometimes they will assist by providing a monitoring policeman to escort a person overseas as well … we don't like our staff going into any situations where they don't have any weapons to protect themselves' (Interview 42, Canberra DIAC).

The DIAC removal machine had been operating at peak efficiency until about 2003 (see Figure 1)[3] when a series of revelations about the detention and deportation of Australian citizens forced a temporary slowdown.

The Palmer Inquiry, which examined one of the many unlawful detentions from this era, concluded that the Department operated with a 'blind trust in systems and processes that, on any reasonable assessment, had failed' (Palmer 2005: 162).

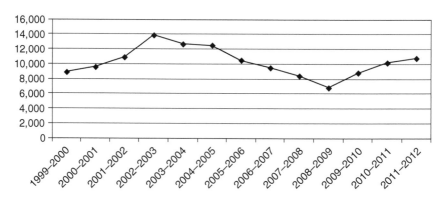

Fig. 1 Removals from Australia

Source: DIAC Annual Reports 2000–2012.

---

[3] Figures include assisted, monitored, and supervised (involuntary) departures; deportations of permanent residents due to criminal convictions may not be included.

DIAC Compliance had relied heavily on police for 'referrals' of suspected unlawful non-citizens. Incredibly, senior officials now admit they 'weren't being critical enough when presented with information from the police' and 'would take their word for it without doing anything more than perfunctory checks' to confirm an individual's legal status (Interview 47, Canberra DIAC). The Inquiry noted the rapid increase in the number of illegal entrants dealt with by the Department which resulted in policy, procedures, and enabling structures being 'developed in tandem and on the run' (Palmer 2005: 164). In other words, immigration authorities were shown to be severely unprepared for the onerous tasks that had been thrust upon them by the law and politics of border control. Significant organizational reforms were instigated in the 'post-Palmer' era, including massive investments in new information technologies, but removals began to rise again from 2009 as political pressure to control borders was once again ramped up. It seems, after all, that the post-Palmer reforms were not intended to reduce the number of removals, but rather to soften the way in which the Department was seen to be achieving its politically determined objectives.

Does this recent history suggest that immigration compliance functions are becoming more police-like? The answer, in part, depends on which model of policing is used as a comparator. Immigration officials interviewed by one of the authors routinely resisted descriptions of their work as 'policing' or even 'enforcement', preferring instead the bureaucratic language of 'compliance' and 'status resolution'. However, the police-like quality of the powers exercised by immigration compliance officers was clearly apparent to the Palmer Inquiry: DIMIA officers are authorized to exercise exceptional, even extraordinary, powers. That they should be permitted and expected to do so without adequate training, without proper management and oversight, with poor information systems, and with no genuine quality assurance and constraints on the exercise of these powers is of concern. (Palmer 2005: ix) On the other hand, the Inquiry noted an obsession amongst immigration officers with rigid and uncritical adherence to departmental processes. This is a characteristic often associated with a bureaucratic mindset, while police are more usually described as focusing on getting results, rather than the processes that produce them.

Despite these differences in organizational culture, there are some significant respects in which recent changes within the DIAC do mirror developments in contemporary policing, such as the increasing reliance on intelligence-led and risk-based approaches described in the previous section. The DIAC removal machine could perhaps be better characterized in the post-Palmer era as aspiring to be 'well targeted' rather than 'well oiled'. DIAC compliance operations are guided by a priorities matrix that explicitly determines low and high priority categories of work as directed by the Immigration Minister. High risk and mandatory work includes the prevention and detection of systematic immigration fraud, 'character' deportations following criminal convictions, and all referrals from police of suspected unlawful non-citizens. These priorities necessitate an ever closer liaison with law-enforcement agencies than previously. Tackling identity fraud has emerged as a particular priority, evidenced by the development of a DIAC Identity Branch, and the building of close connections with CrimTrac—an organization described in the DIAC's latest annual report as 'the Australian Government agency established to provide national information sharing to support law enforcement agencies' (DIAC 2011). By its own admission then, this organizational repositioning places the DIAC compliance function firmly within the domain of law enforcement.

Proposition 2: Police are Getting More Involved in Immigration Enforcement

The external border: people-smuggling and the Australian Federal Police

The Australian Federal Police (AFP) have primary responsibility for investigating criminal offences against Commonwealth laws (leaving state crime legislation to respective state police forces). In the mid- to late 1990s the AFP had little or no regard for border policing in relation to irregular border crossing generally or people smuggling specifically. How quickly people-smuggling was constructed as a policing concern for the AFP has ramifications for understanding how police have become more involved in immigration control. The role of the AFP in combating people-smuggling had the intention of deterring and disrupting people from claiming asylum by travelling to Australia by boat. However, its impact on the policing institution is equally far reaching.

The application of Commonwealth law enforcement to the complex area of forced migration significantly altered the way sovereignty/borders and policing/security featured in the public imagination. The role of the AFP in combating people smuggling had a fourfold effect: the heightened politicization/ideological work of the policing function; an uncontained expansion of policing territory; the development of a symbiotic relationship between people-smugglers and policing agents; and the absorption of federal policing into the security apparatus.

The first impact for policing was the heightened level of ideological work undertaken by the AFP and in turn its increased politicization. The AFP constructed the problem of people-smuggling as a *policing problem*. This had repercussions for both asylum seekers and the law-enforcement apparatus. This was an important symbolic change for the role of policing in relation to the construction of the state, its borders, and the location and nature of threats. In the mid-1990s people-smuggling rated only a passing mention in official AFP documentation. By 2000 AFP public documentation was replete with references to the criminal threat of people-smuggling, yet at the same time the policing tactics used to respond to the problem became increasingly imprecise in relation to being 'off-shore' and concerned with 'disruption'. The ideological importance was clear in the common-sense assumption that arriving by boat in Australia without authorization was a matter of criminality and necessitated police action aimed at prevention (its prosecution proving to be a much thornier and less desirable policing outcome). This omitted considering *why* people were coming to Australia and the impact of preventing people from claiming asylum under international law. To have done so would require more complex policing engagement with forced migration than simply a deterrence and disruption model.

At the same time the national profile of the AFP was accelerating, especially following 9/11, where they were the lead Australian counterterrorism agency. As a result the Commissioner of the AFP maintained a high public profile, and media interventions were frequently about issues that were crafted as matters of national security (for a detailed discussion, see Pickering 2004). The symbolic import of combating people-smuggling contributed further to the political resources of the federal agency and was most clearly demonstrated in the closeness of the AFP to the federal government in the high octane politics of 'deciding who should come to Australia and the circumstances in which they come' (Prime Minister John Howard, 6 December 2001).

Second, the focus on people-smuggling was used to justify a range of imprecise activities that collectively developed an uncontained expansion of policing territory. It required the AFP to operate in geographical spaces beyond Australia where the legislative framework governing their actions was often regarded as partial (Pickering 2004). For example, serious allegations were made that the AFP contracted third parties to undertake disruption activities including disabling asylum seeker boats. The AFP increased their international network of overseas liaison officers as well as other offshore personnel to work in partnership with other agencies—the precise nature and remit of such collaboration constrained to publically unavailable memoranda of understanding.

This fore-grounded the third significant impact on policing: policing entered into what others have described as a symbiotic relationship between people-smugglers and policing agents (Andreas 2000). That is, the policing of people-smuggling became part of an unending series of manoeuvres between smuggling agents and policing agents involving increased police activity, changing tactics by people-smugglers, and escalating risks for those using their services. For example, the use of third parties contracted by the AFP to undertake activities in Indonesia came in for significant media and parliamentary questioning. An Opposition senator alleged that the AFP had contracted an individual known to be involved in the sabotage of boats leaving Indonesia for Australia: 'At no stage do I want to break or will I break the protocols in relation to operational matters involving ASIS or the AFP, but those protocols were not meant as a direct or an indirect licence to kill' (Faulkner 2002).

Fourth, the focus on people-smuggling contributed to the absorption of federal policing into the national security apparatus and expanded its resources. Combating people-smuggling was not only a policing problem but was represented by the AFP as a national security problem that required significant material investment: 'There is no greater imperative, therefore, in ensuring the security and integrity of Australia than to maintain law enforcement on the same plane of importance and relative capability to the nation's defence forces' (AFP Annual Report 1998–1999).

The internal border: New South Wales Police—'getting rid' of problem people

Unlike the United States, where recent steps to involve local police in immigration enforcement have provoked major controversy (Provine and Sanchez 2011), and in contrast to Britain, where police have been involved in immigration enforcement somewhat sporadically and sometimes reluctantly (Weber and Bowling 2004), Australian police are deeply embedded in the enforcement of immigration controls. State and federal police are 'designated officers' under the Migration Act 1958, which means that they are legally mandated to exercise all the powers of an immigration officer. In practice, police limit their exercise of Migration Act powers to section 188, which authorizes them to question suspected non-citizens about their immigration status, and section 189, which requires them to take suspected 'unlawful non citizens' into custody. Research by one of the authors has established that New South Wales police conduct opportunistic immigration checks in the context of traffic stops and proactive street-level policing; make behind-the-scenes checks during criminal investigations; take part in joint operations with the DIAC and other agencies in which the detection of unlawful non-citizens is a possible outcome; assist immigration officers in the execution of 'high risk' search or arrest warrants; and provide escort services for forced departures when off duty (Weber 2011).

In a survey of 371 operational officers conducted in 2008–2009 virtually all (96 per cent) identified the enforcement of immigration law as being important to their job (Weber 2012). On the other hand, it was clear from interviews that while rank-and-file police identified with their migration policing role, the detection of unlawful non-citizens was far from being an organizational priority: 'It's not, as I say, promoted, it's not stressed that we need to rigorously enforce the immigration laws. I'd suggest it's more a by-product of our day-to-day operational activities' (Interview 23, NSW Police Local Area Commander). Immigration powers were seen as a useful tool in the pursuit of the traditional policing goals of criminal prosecution and order maintenance. Checking immigration status could assist with the confirmation of identity during street stops, so that warrants could then be checked or on-the-spot fines issued to the correct name and address. Immigration checks were also used in criminal investigations where they could yield evidence about the whereabouts of suspects, or open up alternative avenues to 'get rid' of individuals who were found to be unlawfully present where the criminal matter was considered minor or difficult to prosecute.

Operational police who took part in the survey were asked whether they thought that the time they spent on immigration enforcement had increased, decreased, or stayed the same during their time with the NSW Police. While the most common answer was that it was about the same, officers with more than 20 years' experience were by far the most likely to say it had increased—54 per cent compared with 12.5 per cent of officers with less than five years' policing experience. Senior officers suggested in interviews that, while migration policing was still far from an operational priority for NSW Police, increased training by the DIAC in Migration Act powers and the development of mechanisms for inter-agency data exchange were beginning to raise the profile of immigration enforcement:

I think it is becoming more prevalent. I think people are more aware of the vast range of things open to them. I think police are more aware of immigration offences. I think people are more aware of visa violations, all of which are federal law; however, they may well have a huge impact on state policing. (Interview 40, NSW Police HQ)

One of the 'vast range of things' open to police is to refer lawfully present non-citizens with criminal records to the DIAC for possible visa cancellation under section 501 of the Migration Act. Interviews with DIAC liaison officers posted within NSW Police suggested that awareness of this possibility was growing: 'I think that most police officers are very aware of the 501 cancellation power, and they are very quick to call and … ask about the possibility of a visa being cancelled' (Interview 51, Sydney DIAC). While this entrepreneurial strategy aligns with government priorities for the removal of 'high risk' individuals, it appears to be driven by relatively independent operational policing objectives.

Because of the longstanding involvement of Australian police in the enforcement of immigration law, it may seem difficult to mount an argument that the role of police has been distorted by the rising political emphasis on migration controls. However, discussions with senior police revealed submerged concerns about the public relations impact of these activities. The most outspoken commander, responsible for a very culturally diverse area, observed that 'immigration officials should perhaps be doing a lot of that stuff themselves. But it is left to the police to do because there is an image problem associated with chasing Johnny through five blocks of units and crash tackling Johnny to the floor' (Interview 6, NSW Police Local Area Commander). In fact, following the death in Sydney of Seong Ho Kang, who ran from DIAC compliance officers during a workplace raid in 2004 and was struck by a taxi, the DIAC appears to be knowingly passing responsibility for the use of force onto police:

It is our department's policy that we do not pursue people and part of the reason for that is if a person is running they tend to run somewhat blindly and we don't want to chase them into a situation of danger … So for example we won't chase—the police generally may. (Interview 47, Canberra DIAC)

Proposition 3: Other Agencies are Being Drawn into Migration Policing Networks

The external border: the Royal Australian Navy and Australian Customs

There has been heated political debate about irregular maritime arrivals in Australia. An often overlooked aspect of this debate is the nature and roles of unrelated agencies being drawn into migration policing networks. In this instance we are concerned with the ways national security agencies are increasingly being tasked with 'migration management' functions that intersect in complex ways with programs of interdiction and rescue. Border protection is a key plank in national security efforts. The Royal Australian Navy (RAN) and Australian Customs have been drawn into the immigration policing function of border protection. This has consequences for their perceived role and in their relationship with the executive and the 'exceptional' politics of border protection.

National security on the edges of the territorial nation state is the typical remit of the RAN; however, its role in the politicization of irregular arrivals/asylum seekers has seen it drawn into the migration field with unwanted and unintended consequences. In October 2001 HMAS *Adelaide* intercepted an Indonesian fishing boat north of Christmas Island as part of Operation Relex aimed at deterring irregular maritime arrivals. When the 223 passengers were disembarked on Christmas Island a report emerged of a conversation between the Commander of HMAS *Adelaide* and Brigadier Mike Silverstone that a child had been thrown overboard. Prime Minister John Howard and senior ministers seized on this information and released to the media a photograph allegedly showing children being thrown overboard. Photographs had been taken by Navy personnel showing the rescue of asylum seekers and Navy personnel caring for asylum seekers on board, including dressing them in Navy overalls. The photographs showed a very humanitarian aspect of their work and were obviously taken with pride in a job well done. These photographs were transmitted to the Executive whereby the captions were removed, and photographs were selected and misused to represent children being thrown overboard. Within days the Navy made clear that no children had been thrown overboard but were in the water because their boat was sinking. By this time, however, this maritime incident (or 'children overboard affair' as it came to be known) was receiving unprecedented national coverage and was used as a lightning rod to rally anti-refugee sentiment.

The Senate Inquiry convened to investigate the matter found that the government failed to alter the public record when information contravening the initial report came to light and that the Minister of Defence had misled the public. However, one of the ongoing reverberations was the assessment of the incident as unnecessarily politicizing the role of the Navy in relation to intercepting asylum seekers. Of concern was the executive direction to the Navy not to speak publically about the issue during the 2001 Federal Election campaign when anti-asylum seeker sentiment was at a peak. In the month following the incident, a psychiatrist who had been recently tasked to a Navy vessel wrote an open letter to the *Sydney Morning Herald* concerned at the impact of deterrence operations on Navy personnel. He said:

These actions are ineffective in deterring people in coming to Australia and merely serve to harass, frighten and demoralise people who are already weak, vulnerable and desperate ... It is my expert opinion, as a senior consultant psychiatrist to the Royal Australian Navy, that they are highly likely to be harmful to the psychological health and moral development of all [RAN] members involved ... Nearly everyone I spoke to that was involved in these operations knew that what they were doing was wrong. (Leys 2001)

Australian Customs manage the 'security and integrity' of Australia's borders. The maritime environment for their migration concern stems from their patrol of Australia's 36,000 km coastline and the Australian Exclusive Economic Zone. In 2008 the Australian Customs service was renamed the Australian Customs and Border Protection Service. This move was said to be:

[in] response to the resurgent threat to our borders of maritime people smuggling. The enhanced Australian Customs and Border Protection Service is set to meet the complex

border security challenges of the future by providing unified control and direction, and a single point of accountability. (Customs and Border Protection 2012)

The new arrangements expanded the role of Customs and absorbed a number of functions and resources from the Department of Immigration and Citizenship including 'analysing and coordinating the gathering of intelligence, coordinating surveillance and on-water response, and engaging internationally to deter maritime people smugglers' (Customs and Border Protection 2012).

What are not clearly articulated are the daily realities of this expanded border control function. In other research we have undertaken this lead role in border protection has meant that maritime enforcement officers operating Customs boats off the Australian north-west coast are expected to perform new and unanticipated roles. This creates tensions between enforcement and rescue responsibilities and managing intercepted populations on board Customs vessels—populations that have often been traumatized and are in the midst of highly stressful, forced migration, including interactions with people-smugglers. Primarily, however, the concern with drawing Customs into this realm is with the politicization of their function and role in this field as compared with the historically less ambiguous tasks centred on the importation of drugs and illegal firearms:

And they're actually taking it to another level now, where we're just solely doing immigration. Because where I've been, we've been solely doing immigration, whereas we were doing fisheries and what not before, but now they were not really trained in what they actually want us to do. (Interview 18 with Customs official, Darwin)

The key issue with the migration function of Customs (and border protection) in the maritime zone is the complication of the humanitarian aspect of intercepting and protecting asylum seekers. While Customs have always been concerned with the movement of people and goods across borders, they have not historically had a role in relation to the management of those forced to cross borders for reasons of persecution and triggering Australia's international protection obligations under the Refugee Convention. Both Customs and the RAN are agencies reluctantly involved in responding to refugees in the maritime environment and stand in some contrast to the more institutional entrepreneurial activity of the AFP.

The internal border: migration policing networks—'making life difficult' for unlawful non-citizens

Supposedly voluntary presentations accounted for 82 per cent of unlawful non-citizens located by the DIAC in the financial year 2011 (DIAC 2011). However, this statistic conceals a labyrinth of monitoring and status checking that can be the catalyst for many of these 'voluntary' contacts. This statement from a senior DIAC manager indicates that multi-agency strategies intended to 'make life difficult' for unlawful non-citizens, while not directly under DIAC control, are being consciously incorporated into the Department's immigration compliance strategy:

Already someone that's overstayed and disappeared and has no entitlements and Medicare benefits or ... any form of social security benefit or anything like that, so they're very dependent on employment ... We're shifting where our resources apply and also we're ... we're looking to these other ways of ... making life difficult for people ... so that they come in and see us. (Interview 45, DIAC Canberra)

Agencies that participate in these 'structural' migration policing projects are recruited through a variety of incentivization schemes, ranging from statutory requirements on service providers to check immigration status before providing benefits or services; government funding arrangements that require proof of legal status in order to recover costs for the provision of services; to the threat of legal sanctions against business owners who employ individuals who lack legal entitlements to work or remain in the country. The effect is to create an invisible and seemingly ubiquitous internal border. It is beyond the scope of this chapter to outline the role and motivation of all of these migration policing partners (see Weber et al, forthcoming). In this section we concentrate solely on the recruitment of private employers to migration policing roles.

   Australian employers have been co-opted into policing the internal border through education and the threat of punishment. Criminal sanctions were introduced in 2007, accompanied by employer awareness training by the DIAC and the introduction of the VEVO (Visa Entitlement Verification On-line) system that can be used by registered employers to check the immigration status of prospective employees. The number of VEVO checks made by employers increased rapidly from 245,000 in 2007–2008 to nearly 600,000 in 2008–2009 (DIAC 2009: 123) and rose to over one million checks by 2010–2011 (DIAC 2011: 167). In addition to the obligation on employers to deny employment to undocumented workers, enquiries to the VEVO system leave a record that provides intelligence to the DIAC. The DIAC Compliance Office in Sydney has a specialist team within the Business Compliance unit that works proactively with industry in an educative role and identifies non-compliant employers who may be liable to prosecution, usually after one or more warning notices. DIAC managers believe that this preventative work has paid significant dividends in terms of preventing illegal working in targeted industries:

Virtually throughout Australia now most of the taxi licensing authorities are doing immigration checks ... so using those sort of methods have had a quite high ... quite a good return. ... To get the security guard's license in New South Wales you know they must conduct an immigration check and that's been very effective ... from our point of view, that industry's been completely virtually tidied up. (Interview 45, DIAC Canberra)

Despite the reported impact of these efforts, the Australian government introduced new legislation in 2011 to toughen the employer sanction regime, in response to a review of existing sanctions. The review concluded that the number of illegal workers in Australia had been growing since around 1998 and that existing sanctions and educational efforts had not been effective (Howells 2011). The new legislation included strict liability civil penalties to supplement existing criminal sanctions (which are likely to be reserved for systematic breaches), new powers to gather evidence, and the extension of liability to a wider range of employers, agents, and contractors. A stronger deterrent was considered necessary for the protection of workers and the integrity of the labour market, but was also identified as an important symbolic function linked to the internal performance of Australian sovereignty: 'The absence of an effective deterrent against the employment of non-citizens who do not have permission to work is an abrogation of Australian sovereignty and a contradiction of the otherwise orderly pattern of migration and the refugee and humanitarian relief programs' (Howells 2011: 12). Responsible employers are therefore expected to align themselves with principles of good governance and become incorporated into the administrative state.

The Ministerial press release announcing the new laws asserted the government's commitment to 'get tough on dodgy employers' in order to 'punish those who wilfully exploit foreign workers' (Bowen 2011). This formulation assumes that the employment of undocumented non-citizens is necessarily exploitative. Moreover, although the DIAC's compliance and enforcement effort in relation to illicit working is said to be directed towards exploitative employers, the continued emphasis on removing unlawful workers is apparent. The Howells review noted that one of the main reasons for the failure to prosecute employers under the 2007 criminal provisions was that illegally employed workers who were likely to be needed as witnesses were often removed before criminal prosecutions could be pursued. As for possible detrimental impacts on employers and bona fide employees, Howells reasoned that the burden on employers of additional regulation was proportionate to the gains to be made in national security and protection of the labour market; and observed that workers who are Australian citizens 'will need to shoulder their part of the inconvenience by being prepared to obtain adequate forms of identification for employment' (Howells, 2011: 15). The slow expansion of employer sanctions appears to be encroaching, seemingly unnoticed, not only on relations between employers and employees, but also on the freedoms enjoyed by citizens.

Conclusion

In the case of Australia significant political, material, and ideological efforts have been spent on crafting an expansive border policing regime over the past 15 years. The result is a series of convergences between historically distinct law-enforcement agencies and the recruitment of a range of commercial entities, service providers, and private actors into a migration policing role. In this chapter we have analysed these developments in terms of geographical transversality which stretches the physical border both inwards and outwards, and institutional transversality in which border policing practices, whether new or familiar, imposed or actively pursued, cut across existing organizational norms.

We have argued that transversal border policing is an active and entrepreneurial space which can generate deep paradoxes for the agencies involved. Immigration authorities have increasingly adopted new policing strategies in the mobilization of pre-crime-type frameworks in the intent management of potentially risky travellers and have developed risk-based compliance mechanisms which mirror in some respects the tactics of intelligence-led policing. Police are increasingly becoming involved in immigration activities including novel 'high policing' functions like people-smuggling as well as more traditional 'low policing' activities through the use of immigration powers to expedite control over troublesome populations. Agencies not traditionally involved in policing or immigration control have also become enmeshed in migration-related matters, including the Navy and Customs which operate in a hybrid space in which interdiction and humanitarian objectives intertwine in relation to intercepting asylum seekers between Australia and Indonesia. Within Australian territory, a range of public and private actors have been recruited into migration policing networks, sometimes motivated by their own organizational interests, but in other cases compelled by responsibilizing regimes such as employer awareness programmes accompanied by criminal sanctions.

Some migration policing agencies have proven to be willing entrepreneurs, while others are reluctant to move into the new spaces created for the governance of borders. These patterns are consistent with O'Malley's suggestion of a '*politically driven* decentring of the state' under neo-liberalism (O'Malley 1997), which promotes the management of public agencies along 'enterprise lines' and the deployment of incentives and disincentives to responsibilize less willing partners and recruit wider sections of the community into governmental agendas. Individually these changes have created significant opportunities for the expansion of social control by individual agencies but have also presented occasions for compromise and contradiction for the remit of the agencies and the everyday experience of individuals with operational responsibilities. Collectively they support an argument that policing mobility is an inherently creative and performative practice that cuts across traditional conceptions of borders and produces a range of transversal practices. The policing of multiple borders creates increasingly distinct, transversal places where the deeply political function of exclusion is driving significant social, legal, and governmental change.

References

Amoore, L. (2006) 'Biometric Borders: Governing Mobilities in the War on Terror', *Political Geography* 25(3): 336.

Andreas, P. (2000) *Border Games: Policing the US–Mexico divide*. Ithaca: Cornell University Press.

Australian Federal Police, *Annual Report 1998–1999* <http://www.afp.gov.au/media-centre/publications/annual-reports/afp.aspx>.

Bowen, C. MP (2011) 'New laws to get tough on hiring illegal workers', 12 December, Press Release by Minister for Immigration and Citizenship, Canberra <http://www.minister.immi.gov.au/media/cb/2011/cb181163.htm>.

Bigo, D. (2002) Security and Immigration: Toward a Critique of the Governmentality of Unease, *Alternatives* 27: 63.

Coutin, S.B. (2005) 'Contesting Criminality: Illegal immigration and the Spatialization of Legality', *Theoretical Criminology* 9(1): 5.

Customs and Border Protection (2012) 'About Customs and Border Protection' <http://www.customs.gov.au>.

DIAC (2011) *Department of Immigration and Citizenship Annual Report 2010–11*. Commonwealth of Australia: Canberra.

DIAC (2009) *Department of Immigration and Citizenship Annual Report*. Canberra.

Donnan, H. and Wilson, T. (1999) *Borders: Frontiers of Identity, Nation and State*. Oxford: Berg Publishers.

Fan, M.D. (2008) 'When Deterrence and Death Mitigation Fall Short: Fantasy and Fetishes as Gap Fillers in Border Regulation', *Law and Society Review* 42(4): 701.

Faulkner, J. (2002) Question time, Australian Senate, *Hansard*, 25 September.

Garland, D. (1996) 'The Limits of the Sovereign State: Strategies of Crime Control in Contemporary Society', *British Journal of Criminology* 36(4): 445.

Howells, S. (2011) 'Report of the 2010 Review of the *Migration Amendment (Employer Sanctions) Act* 2007'. Commonwealth of Australia: Canberra.

Khosravi, S. (2010) *'Illegal Traveller': An Auto-ethnography of Borders*. London: Palgrave.

Leys, N. (2001) 'Demoralised Sailors to Dump Navy Says Analyst', *Sydney Morning Herald*, 8 November.

McCairns, G. (2011) 'Serious and Organised Crime: Promoting Visa Integrity—DIACs response to the commission of serious migration offences', Department of Immigration and Citizenship <http://www.aic.gov.au/events/.../2010/~/media/.../2010...mccairns.pdf>.

McCulloch, J. and Pickering, S. (2009) 'Pre-Crime and Counter-Terrorism', *British Journal of Criminology* 49(5): 628.

Nicholls, G. (2007) *Deported: A History of Forced Departures from Australia*. Sydney: University of New South Wales Press.

Núñez, G. and Heyman, J. (2007) 'Entrapment Processes and Immigrant Communities in a Time of Heightened Border Vigilance', *Human Organisation* 66(4): 3544.

O'Malley, P. (1997) 'Policing, Politics and Postmodernity', *Social and Legal Studies* 6(3): 363.

Palmer, M.J. (2005) 'Inquiry into the Circumstances of the Immigration Detention of Cornelia Rau', Report, July 2005, Commonwealth of Australia <http://www.immi.gov.au/media/publications/pdf/palmer-report.pdf>.

Pickering, S. (2004) 'The Production of Sovereignty and the Rise of Transversal Policing: People-smuggling and Federal Policing', *ANZ Journal of Criminology* 37(3): 362.

Pratt, A. (2005) *Securing Borders: Detention and Deportation in Canada*. Vancouver: UBC Press.

Provine, M. and Sanchez, G. (2011) 'Suspecting Immigrants: Exploring Links between Racialized Anxieties and Expanded Police Powers in Arizona', *Policing and Society* 21(4): 468.

Ratcliffe, J. (2008) *Intelligence-Led Policing*. Uffculme: Willan Publishing.

Schuster, L. (2005) 'The Continuing Mobility of Migrants in Italy: Shifting between Places and Statuses', *Journal of Ethnic and Migration Studies* 31(4): 757.

Sassen, S. (1996) *Sovereignty in an Age of Globalisation*. New York: Columbia University Press.

Soguk, N. and Whitehall, G. (1999) 'Wandering Grounds: Transversality, Identity, Territoriality, and Movement', *Millennium: Journal of International Studies* 28(3): 675.

Weber, L. (2012) 'Policing a World in Motion', in S. Pickering and J. McCulloch (eds), *Borders and Transnational Crime: Pre-crime, Mobility and Serious Harm in an Age of Globalization*. London: Palgrave.

Weber, L. (2011) '"It Sounds Like They Shouldn't be Here": Immigration Checks on the Streets of Sydney', *Policing and Society* 21(4): 456.

Weber, L. (2006) 'The Shifting Frontiers of Migration Control', in S. Pickering and L. Weber (eds), *Borders, Mobility and Technologies of Control*. Dordrecht: Springer.

Weber, L. and Bowling, B. (2004) 'Policing Migration: A Framework for Investigating the Regulation of Global Mobility', *Policing and Society* 14(3): 195.

Weber, L., Wilson, A., and Wise, J. (2013, forthcoming) 'Cops and Dobbers: A Nodal Cartography of Onshore Migration Policing in New South Wales', *ANZ Journal of Criminology*.

Wilson, D. (2006) 'Biometrics, Borders and the Ideal Suspect', in S. Pickering and L. Weber (eds), *Borders, Mobility and Technologies of Control*. Dordrecht: Springer.

Wilson, D. and Weber, L. (2008) 'Surveillance, Risk and Pre-emption on the Australian Border', *Surveillance and Society* 5(2): 124 (Special Issue on Smart Borders and Enclosures).

Wonders, N. (2006) 'Global Flows, Semi-Permeable Borders and New Channels of Inequality', in S. Pickering and L. Weber (eds), *Borders, Mobility and Technologies of Control*. Dordrecht: Springer.

Zedner, L. (2007) 'Pre-Crime and Post-Criminology?', *Theoretical Criminology* 11(2): 261.

6

Making Mobility a Problem: How South African Officials Criminalize Migration

Darshan Vigneswaran

Introduction

Controls on human mobility are a central feature of the modern criminal justice system. Officers of the law commonly regard evidence of vagrancy, trespass, protest, or flight as grounds for suspicion of criminal intent. The territorial manipulation and management of mobility—whether this takes the form of neighbourhood patrols, roadblocks, building raids, or CCTV surveillance—is a fundamental strategic objective and operational ideal of policing strategy (Herbert 1997). Finally, and most obviously, a central goal of the modern prison system has been to restrict the mobility of criminal perpetrators. Since the relationship between criminal justice and mobility is enduring and multi-faceted, any evidence that *international* migrants—people who move across borders—are increasingly targeted as suspects within criminal justice systems should not come as a surprise. The 'criminalization of migration' is not an outgrowth, logical extension, or particularly harsh variant of restrictive immigration policies. Rather, these developments ought to be studied as the reintegration of two parallel judicial systems (immigration and criminal) that have both problematized human mobility but have each been formulated to address different variants of this phenomenon: cross-border mobility and internal or domestic mobility. Human mobility is a fluid and indeterminate process and it has always been difficult to suggest that persons who cross an international border are necessarily engaging in an altogether different type of movement from those who do not. Nonetheless, the institutions which states have developed to regulate and control human mobility have been built upon the premise that this distinction is fundamental and warrants very different types of state intervention. Given this, my aim in this chapter is to trace how these two institutional structures are being conceptually and procedurally synthesized in everyday law-enforcement practices in such a way that specific categories of mobile person become objects of criminal suspicion and/or concern.

Indeed, even this more refined characterization of my research aims may be a slight overstatement in so far as there has always been an abiding connection between the development of the criminal justice system and the formulation of immigration policy and law (Walters 2010). For example, if we look, as many have, to the origins of our contemporary notions of sovereignty, citizenship, and statehood in the Italian city-state of the Renaissance period, we see that early notions of criminal justice were developed through the practice of banishing violent offenders from the capital (Starn 1982). In that context, the criminalization of private violence and the more general control of human mobility went hand in hand (Vigneswaran 2007). Alternatively, we might look to the British Empire and its use of a policy of transportation as a mode of punishment in the eighteenth and nineteenth centuries. In that context, policies regarding migration and settlement were strongly linked to a parallel effort to generate practical and sufficiently harsh sanctions for an over-burdened criminal justice system. Finally, we may choose to look to the development of the criminal justice system in places like apartheid South Africa. The Apartheid regime did not establish distinctions between criminal and immigration law or their respective enforcement and penal policies because the government was fundamentally opposed to unregulated mobility in all its forms, but particularly the mobility of the country's black, Indian, and 'coloured' populations. Instead, one of the core regulatory aims of apartheid was to render the mobility of black people into white areas as the primary source of criminal threat and primary target of anti-crime policing (Brewer 1994; Vigneswaran 2011).

These examples suggest that the separation between immigration and criminal law, as two different legal and institutional mechanisms for regulating and controlling mobility, is a very specific historical outcome that may only make sense within a limited range of political and institutional settings rather than a general condition that applies across all political systems for all times. The moment that we begin to move beyond the traditional set of cases which we conventionally use as meters of encompassing historical trends, namely the small set of advanced states of late twentieth-century and early twenty-first-century Europe and North America, the idea that immigration law is something that can be meaningfully 'criminalized' begins to lose purchase. As we expand our analytical view, backwards in time and outwards across space, we begin to recognize that immigration law has regularly been deeply wedded to the criminal law and its characteristic means of surveillance, investigation, punishment, and redress. The question then becomes one of determining what forms of mobility are being criminalized in particular times and places; and how.

In contemporary South Africa, it is sometimes difficult to detect any separation between the criminal justice and immigration enforcement systems. Whereas theorists of migration policy who work in the comparatively liberal legal traditions of Europe and North America may be interested in the manner in which certain aspects of migration policy and law have become progressively criminalized, their South African counterparts may confront the opposite problem: social scientists, lawyers, and practitioners have struggled to define the contours of a realm of migration control policy and practice which accepts the core principle that a violation of the immigration code constitutes an administrative—as opposed to a criminal—offence.

This claim should not be taken as a suggestion that there has been no significant constitutional and legislative change in South Africa over the past two decades— and that apartheid-style movement controls live on in their fullness of spirit. The process of political transformation, which began in the late 1980s and culminated in the transition to democracy in the mid-1990s, has largely eliminated apartheid's segregation laws—including the Group Areas Act (n. 41 of 1950)—as well as its immigration laws—specifically the Aliens Control Act (n. 95 of 1991)[1]—which explicitly criminalized migration offences. Since then, South Africa has begun to follow global immigration policy norms, defining the enforcement of criminal and immigration laws as the separate responsibilities of two different departments of state. The armed South African Police Service (SAPS) is now responsible for fighting crime, while the unarmed officials of the Department of Home Affairs deal with immigration. Perhaps more importantly, and in an apparent reaction against the racist intent and authoritarian disposition of the former regime, the rights of mobile people are now protected by a variety of constitutional and statutory provisions. For example, section 22 of the new Constitution of the Republic of South Africa (n. 108 of 1996) recognizes that '*everyone* has the right to freedom of movement', pointedly not limiting this freedom by making it an exclusive right of citizens. In addition to this broad commitment to migrant rights, the Immigration Act (n. 13 of 2002) establishes important jurisdictional boundaries between the immigration enforcement and criminal justice systems. For example, police officers are specifically prevented from making determinations about the immigration status of a suspected illegal foreigner and, in order to ensure the separation of penal and immigration detention systems, suspected illegal foreigners can only be detained in cells designed to hold other criminal offenders for limited periods of time.

Despite significant reforms, South African laws provide for custodial sentences— and not merely detention awaiting deportation—for most immigration offences. Hence, for the most basic offence of remaining in the country after one's permit has expired, a foreign national can be detained in prison for a period of up to two years (section 49(1)(a)), regardless of whether or not he or she has committed any other offence. More serious offences attract higher penalties. Only a small number of contraventions of immigration law—including acts like voluntary departure with an expired permit or failure on the part of transport operators to ensure that travellers possess adequate travel documents—are specifically defined as 'administrative offences' which attract only pecuniary penalties (section 50). On this basis, one could easily argue that South African immigration laws continue to define informal cross-border migration as a criminal offence.

We can begin to develop a better understanding of the true meaning of these legal categorizations by examining how they are enforced in practice. South African

---

[1] This Act was a synthesis of a range of immigration laws passed during the apartheid era.

law provides individual officials with a great deal of discretion to determine how the law is enforced and enforcement outcomes vary widely depending on the training and disposition of local level officials who are responsible for deciding whether or not foreign migrants will be treated 'as if' they were criminal offenders. Take, for example, the issue of custodial sentencing. In general, when police officers assume custody of a person who does not possess valid documentation and has not committed any non-immigration offences, they seek to transfer the detainee to the Department of Home Affairs (DHA). The DHA then confirms the person's status and, if it has sufficient reason to believe that he or she does not have authorization to remain in the country, initiate deportation procedures. However, since the law provides considerable discretion for officials to impose harsher penalties, in many cases the transfer of custody is substantially delayed. For example, in 2008 the Johannesburg Central Police Station began adopting its own policy towards suspected 'illegal foreigners', charging them with immigration offences and requesting the local magistrate to hand down a three-month prison sentence. The station commander, frustrated by the fact that many foreign nation-als had returned to South Africa soon after being deported to their countries of origin, had adopted this policy as a strategy of deterrence, which presumably would ensure that migrants would now know not to return to his precinct. This new policy did not stem from any national immigration policy or even correspond with the formal position of his own police commissioner who, earlier in the same year, had issued a circular to all provincial commanders to deprioritize immigration policing and concentrate SAPS resources on identified 'priority' crimes: murder, assault, vehicle theft, etc.

This case is illustrative of a broader trend that can be observed across the South African bureaucracy but which is particularly strong within the South African police. Officials act on their own initiative to utilize some of the harsher criminal sanctions within immigration law (Vigneswaran et al 2010). Of course, officials do not only use the available legal framework to police and punish foreign nationals. South African police officers are equally infamous for using immigration laws as a pretext for extorting migrants for bribes (Vigneswaran 2011). These characteristics of South Africa's policing system stem less from more recent evolutions in migra-tion law or policy and more from institutional hangovers—older apartheid traditions of policing and law enforcement which run deep in the bureaucracy.

Understanding the unique way in which officials behave towards mobile persons requires some understanding of this historical legacy. Over the course of the twentieth century, the South African police had followed a markedly different developmental trajectory to their counterparts in other parts of the world. The institutional evolution of the police was marked by the progressive reduction or stagnation of the police's capacity to detect, investigate, and prosecute 'serious' crimes such as murder and theft, and the ongoing augmentation of their ability to enforce movement controls and the other administrative laws of apartheid (Brewer 1994). Indeed, the concepts of 'crime' and 'crime prevention' were progressively absorbed by the logic and purpose of 'separateness'. Apartheid was seen as a means of protecting the white minority from the threat posed by the co-presence of black people. So, policing resources were heavily concentrated in white areas, where the detection and removal of unauthorized black persons was equated with the successful prevention of criminal activity. In this context, everyday policing practice commonly consisted of the efforts of beat police officers to detect persons who were 'out of place' or lacked formal authorization to be in particular areas at certain times and to arrest these persons and remove them back to their 'own areas', 'homelands', or countries of origin. In some respects, the contemporary policing of immigration merely represents the adaptation of this vast regime of movement control to deal with a new population. As influx control laws were abandoned and South African nationals were amnestied from movement controls, foreign migrants became the new focus for the police, who applied the same modes of surveillance, interrogation, and enforcement to compile huge numbers of immigration arrests.

I have written on this historical legacy in some depth elsewhere (Vigneswaran 2008, 2011; Vigneswaran et al 2010) and instead want to use the remaining space in this chapter to develop more broadly relevant theoretical formulations on the relationship between policing and mobility. More specifically, I want to examine how the police comprehend and interpret the relationship between crime and mobility and how these understandings acquire new dimensions as the policing of internal mobility becomes more deeply wedded to the policing of various forms of cross-border movement: of people, goods, and ideas.

In South Africa, the linkages between criminality and international migration have not been established solely through the application of 'domestic' anti-crime and policing agendas to 'foreign' nationals. Rather, these developments have occurred across a broader range of policing activities as South Africa—following decades of international isolation—has been progressively absorbed into an international regime that increasingly posits cross-border mobility as a distinct criminal threat. While this agenda has its roots in organizations like INTERPOL and an international policing movement that has a long history, its recent momentum stems from the passage of the United Nations Convention against Transnational Organized Crime (Resolution 55/25 of 2000) and its protocols on human trafficking and smuggling. Much has been written on the international formulation of these laws and initiatives, and some attention paid to the manner in which they shape border control policies by immigration departments, customs agencies, and the armed forces. However, we know comparatively little about the way this regime and related initiatives shape or interact with the everyday policing of mobility within national borders. Does the new raft of legislation on human trafficking impact on the way that ordinary police officers deal with individual sex workers on their beat and, if so, how? Does international cooperation filter down to the way precinct commanders deal with the local nodes of transnational criminal networks, and to what effect? Does the increasing attention to the development of standards of policing regarding a wide variety of mobile goods, services, and ideas have spillover effects for the way local officials understand and police human mobility?

In part, answering these questions involves understanding the reasons why global policing regimes condition, influence, and dictate local law-enforcement practices. Such effects could be the result of the development of a broad consensus around international criminal law, or a consequence of the fact that international cooperation is an efficient way of dealing with enforcement problems in an increasingly globalized world, or a reflection of the distribution of power in the international system. As an example of the latter dynamic, in other work I have argued that the relative power imbalances between, on the one hand, powerful states and international organizations, and, on the other, policy makers in Africa, has meant that international organizations seeking to impose international norms, treaties, and institutions concerning human trafficking, drugs, and intellectual property have been able to significantly shape or determine the way domestic or local actors in Africa respond to issues like informal migration and human trafficking (Landau and Vigneswaran 2007; Vigneswaran 2013, forthcoming). In this piece, I extend this point by examining the specific mechanisms through which such similar power imbalances frame local policing strategy.

While acknowledging this 'top-down' process, I also want to look at the problem from the 'bottom up'. The capacity of international actors to influence outcomes in South Africa is only one side of the relationship between global agendas and local practices. The manner in which local officials invoke global and transnational policies and agendas in order to support, buttress, or legitimate forms of enforcement practice, which may have little to do with the primary purposes and intentions of the international agendas themselves, is equally important. Here, I am not simply emphasizing the 'agency' or autonomy of local officials. Rather, I am referring to the fact that this autonomy is commonly expressed in enforcement practices which significantly subvert, re-orient, and, fundamentally redirect policing initiatives that may appear on the surface to be functional outgrowths of global enforcement agenda, but in practice turn out to be something quite different.

The Praxis of Mobility Policing

We can begin to better understand how human mobility becomes the object of criminal suspicion if we first recognize that the default position for state officials is not necessarily one of antagonism to mobility. Human mobility is not a phenomenon that most law-enforcement officials can reasonably or practicably deem to be threatening or problematic—even if they are specifically charged with monitoring and regulating human movements. Allow me to develop this point by way of illustration. Let us take what is perhaps the classic and most recognizable image of law enforcement on the African continent: the road block. To the casual observer—particularly if that observer is in the unfortunate position of being an impatient motorist seeking to get past—the police officer or customs official manning a road block appears to be a means of strategically preventing human movement. He or she slows down traffic, obstructs people who are trying to get where they want to go, and appears to take the mere presence of a driver on the motorway as grounds for suspicion. However, when you observe an officer at a road block over an extended period of time, you soon come to realize that he or she is not in fact categorically opposed to, or interested in preventing, mobility, but rather with the somewhat more subtle art of detecting and defining a specific type or range of mobility which constitutes, in his or her mind, evidence of a criminal act. For example, a police officer will be familiar with a series of visual cues as grounds for concluding that the driver of an approaching vehicle is inebriated: excessively slow speed, poor steering, etc. The art of policing here is in 'reading' a whole range of mobile acts—the officer at the roadblock is caught in a constant swirl of human mobility—in order to isolate the 'mobile criminal element'.

In cases like these, of a hypothetical traffic offender at a road block, the issue of whether the population under surveillance is mobile is not in dispute. The officer can see the movement of actors with his or her own eyes. The task of reading mobility becomes less self-evident and more inferred as we move from an act of policing a transport route to examples of law enforcement in other sites. Take, for example, the border guard who is responsible for checking the passes of incoming passengers at an international airport. Here, the guard may not have witnessed the arrival of the flight in question but may infer that anyone presenting themselves at the immigration desk has flown across an international border. The guard may then move on to determine whether or not the form of mobility was an authorized one. Here, the forms of evidence that an official uses to decide whether a person's movement contains elements of criminality may in fact have little to do with the act of mobility itself. Criminality is instead inferred from the articles in a suspect's possession or from documentation on his or her person. This example points us back to the fact that the act of mobility itself is often not the object of suspicion or the focus of an official's gaze. The more important issue is rather the form of mobility an official can read into the person's appearance, possessions, and behaviour. As we move from direct to indirect forms of investigating mobility, the official becomes engaged in a more interpretative exercise: not simply seeking to see criminal behaviour, but creating a plausible narrative of a potential crime.

This process of reading mobility becomes more indirect and imaginative when we move completely outside transport systems, ports, and channels. Here, the very act of moving cannot immediately be imputed from the context of the interaction between the official and the civilian. For example, how does a police officer begin to develop a tale of mobility which might form the grounds for suspicion of an immigration offence when the officer confronts an unknown civilian in his or her home, far away from any border? In this context, mobility can only be inferred from a range of more indirect forms of 'evidence'—the individual's story, nationality, speech, dress, documents, etc, which may be used as proxies for the act of movement itself. The crucial issue here is that—unlike the case of the airport immigration officials—there are no reasonable grounds at this point for assuming that a person has crossed a border, other than what the officer has been trained or conditioned to infer from these various artefacts, symbols, and cues.

The most common and widely discussed manner in which officials conduct this type of criminal investigation is through ethnic or racial profiling. 'Profiling' refers to 'situations in which race or ethnicity functions as an indicator of criminal propensity, typically by law enforcement officers in the context of a traffic stop' (Batton and Kaldeck 2004: 30). This form of policing has been intensively studied in the context of US race relations (for a useful review, see Engel et al 2002) but also forms a part of the way in which we have theorized the development of anti-immigration policies over the last few decades. Here, the central argument is that many states have come to perceive members of migrant groups as responsible for certain forms of criminal activity. Drawing from this basic assumption, government officials have focused their anti-crime policing practices on particular minority groups, often leading to systematic harassment, persecution, and cases of wrongful imprisonment. While this sort of profiling comes in many different forms, perhaps the most widely publicized version in current discourse is the profiling of Muslims, and Muslim youths in particular, as suspects in anti-terrorism investigations.

In arguing that profiling is a form of 'investigating mobility' I am attempting to distance myself from the claim that profiling is *merely* a form of prejudice. Police officers commonly target minority groups as criminal suspects because they hold racist, ethno-centric, or chauvinistic attitudes towards these groups, or (misguided) beliefs that these groups are particularly prone to criminal activity. In other instances, law-enforcement officials simply desire to victimize and antagonize minorities whom they see as less deserving of rights than themselves. While simple prejudice of this sort no doubt accounts for a significant portion of profiling activity, to suggest that all forms of profiling can be reduced to *mere* prejudice would be to neglect the manner in which law-enforcement officials rationalize and justify profiling as a practice, and why it remains such a highly regarded practice within many police services. When asked to explain why they target minority groups, the South African law-enforcement officials we spoke to tended to offer a relatively cautious set of arguments which accounted for migrant groups' criminal motivations as a plausible and understandable outcome of their history of mobility.

Echoing familiar stereotypes of migrant groups, police officers might reflect on the very different conditions in other African countries—including the lower level of development, higher level of organized violence, and greater incidence of institutionalized corruption—and use these to explain why migrants are more prone to commit crimes. Alternatively, they might reflect on the fact that migrants are less vested in South Africa and therefore more willing to flaunt its legal system. Finally, they might consider the considerable responsibilities of foreign migrants to support families and businesses in their country of origin and suggest that this might drive certain groups to extreme forms of wealth accumulation. In each of these ways, law-enforcement officials in South Africa move beyond the simplistic prejudices that involve equating foreign populations with criminality and develop a more nuanced story of how mobility leads certain migrant groups to adopt specific forms of criminal activity. In recognizing this connection between profiling and mobility, I do not want to suggest that law-enforcement officials necessarily develop accurate portraits of the criminal motivations and propensities of subgroups or that the act of profiling helps them to effectively detect, prevent, and prosecute criminal activity. Instead, I merely want to show how, in the act of profiling, police officers develop and draw upon a narrative about mobility which they believe constitutes an accurate account of the pre-history of a crime.

Profiling is one amongst several ways in which law-enforcement officials develop 'narratives of criminalized mobility'. In the next section I examine two different examples where I have observed this practice in operation in South Africa. The first case discusses how South African officials have been trained to implement human trafficking legislation. In that example, even though migrants are conceived as victims, international mobility has been made central to the way officials investigate and respond to criminal forms of labour exploitation. The second case discusses South African efforts to implement intellectual property law. This discussion shows how migration and mobility laws constitute a 'fall-back' or 'default' position which officials deploy when confronted with forms of crime that they are poorly equipped to control.

Training Officials to See Migration as a Crime: The Case of Human Trafficking

The policing of human trafficking (hereafter trafficking) provides us with a useful example of how officials are often taught to 'read' signs of mobility as evidence of criminality. By way of background, over the past two decades, a variety of lobby groups have joined forces to develop a powerful campaign against international trafficking. While this campaign has ostensibly taken aim at a broad range of exploitative labour practices, the main result of this collective effort has been to create a consensus that a variety of interventions are necessary to protect underprivileged young women who are trafficked across borders for the purposes of sexual exploitation. Leaving aside the trafficking agenda's inherent gender, ageist, and prohibitionist biases for the moment, advocacy around this issue has played a powerful role, side by side with the international campaign against human smuggling, in constituting cross-border mobility as a key marker of crime itself. This critique has been developed previously in work highlighting the way the trafficking regime creates highly stylized representations of criminal victimization, and thereby lends support to control-oriented policies which not only work against the aspirations, interests, and livelihoods of many female migrants, particularly those in the sex industry (Agustín 2007; Dozema 2010) but may increase the vulnerability of migrants generally to would-be traffickers (Hathaway 2008) while failing significantly to assist in the detection, capture, and prosecution of the latter (Berman 2003). These critiques have tended to focus on macro-level phenomena, including transnational advocacy campaigns, international institutions and state policies, international agreements and treaties, and public discourse. As a consequence, while they have been able to draw broad linkages between anti-trafficking and immigration control policies, they have not been able to tell us whether law-enforcement officials construct mobility as an object of criminal suspicion, and, if so, how. So the critics cannot tell us whether new policies are influencing practice. In this discussion, I attempt to build on these macro-critiques by drilling down into the everyday practice of criminal justice systems. Here, I want to find out how this global agenda is transforming the way migration and human mobility are regulated, and to what extent the broad trends and macro-phenomena identified by other authors might practically re-shape the opportunity structures for female migrants in particular and mobile people more generally.

In order to understand how anti-trafficking advocates have encouraged officials to view specific types of mobility as criminal, we first need to examine the degree to which mobility constitutes a core element of the crime of trafficking. Article 3 of the Palermo Protocol defines trafficking as the 'recruitment, transportation, transfer, harbouring *or* receipt of persons' for the purpose of exploitation. While the 'transportation' element necessarily implies an act of mobility, the other elements of the crime need not. Under this definition, a perpetrator may have recruited a victim over the phone and transferred or received possession of a victim while he or she remains in a single place of confinement. Hence, according to this definition, a person may be considered as having been a victim of trafficking without ever leaving his or her place of origin and clearly without having moved to another country. While the protocol on trafficking, which is part of the Convention against Transnational Organised Crime, clearly contemplates a scenario in which the perpetrators at least intend to traffic victims across borders, and where physical distance forms a key part of the context that allows the exploitation to take place, migration is not a *sine qua non* of the crime of trafficking, but rather a component of the crime which is commonly noted and emphasized in public discourse and advocacy surrounding the issue.

In countries like South Africa, this understanding of trafficking as a crime which does not necessarily entail the victim's movement is important because it means that the laws on trafficking can more closely reflect and address a social reality in which: (a) perpetrators of severe labour exploitation commonly originate from and live in the same communities as their victims—particularly in the farming and domestic workplace settings; and (b) very few victims of international trafficking have been uncovered, either by law-enforcement agencies or systematic research processes (for example Gould and Fick 2008). Here, the remarkable inability of the International Organization for Migration (IOM)'s Southern African Counter Trafficking and Assistance Programme to uncover significant numbers of victims is instructive. Despite an extensive publicity, hotline, training, and research agenda, the programme only provided assistance to approximately 306 victims across the Southern African region between January 2004 and January 2010. In recognition of the possibility that a large portion of trafficking victims in South Africa may in fact be South Africans, the Government of South Africa's Prevention and Combating of Human Trafficking Bill (B7—2010) specifically removes the requirement of cross-border movement from its definition of the crime of trafficking.

Despite this deliberate legislative initiative to reframe the trafficking initiative around 'domestic' concerns, the international organizations who have partnered with the South African government to assist in the implementation of its trafficking legislation have tended to undermine this 'non-kinetic' understanding of trafficking in their governmental capacity-building programmes. In particular, they have explicitly presented international migrants as the *primary*, if not sole, victims of trafficking crimes, and have trained domestic officials in this doctrine. A good example of this type of influence can be found in the training protocols prepared by the IOM for delivery to the officials of the DHA. These protocols draw on a set of standard training materials that the IOM has utilized in a wide variety of other national settings, but has adapted to suit the peculiarities of domestic law and enforcement contexts. The protocols are designed to be delivered by an IOM official or trained educator to small groups of mid-ranking 'teacher trainers' within each department. These 'teacher-trainers' are then expected to return to their respective places of work and hand on their newly acquired knowledge to a wider body of officials.

The training materials contain detailed descriptions of the international and domestic laws on trafficking and of the nature of the phenomenon of trafficking in South Africa and internationally. They regularly reiterate the fact that the overarching purpose of anti-trafficking law is to criminalize perpetrators and not victims and that trafficking may occur in a variety of local economic sectors (for example agriculture, domestic work, and the sex industry). However, the step-by-step guides which they provide to the officials about how to initiate and conduct a trafficking investigation consistently reinforce the notion that the mobility of victims across borders is the fundamental element of the crime of trafficking.[2]

The training materials achieve this outcome in two steps. First, the documents construct the individual victim as the sole object of criminal 'analysis'. The protocols envisage an investigative scenario in which the only form of evidence of a criminal act that the official in question has at his or her disposal is the appearance and testimony of a potential victim. The protocols make no reference to the wider range of evidence that might lead an official to become suspicious that a trafficking offence has occurred—whether this evidence is observational (for example encountering signs of trafficking while conducting an inspection of a workplace), interactional (interrogating potential perpetrators of trafficking), or documentary (tip-offs and intelligence received from community sources, media, etc) in nature. Instead, the protocols assume that the only course of events which might plausibly lead an official to begin a trafficking investigation consists of an interpersonal 'encounter' between the official and a potential victim.

The training manual then explains to the official how he or she might interrogate the potential victim in order to acquire information that might lead to an investigation and/or to the provision of victim support. While the protocols mention the possibility of inviting a victim to lay charges, they do not deal with the manner in which the official should go about collecting the evidence, and initiating the appropriate administrative procedures, for a viable case of trafficking in court. While this victim-oriented approach is in some ways merely a reflection of the IOM's mandate to protect migrant populations, it is important to note that it also involves a significant deprioritization of a variety of other

---

[2] This is crucial because, while frontline officers rarely remember the broad principles or legal frameworks provided in such generic training manuals, they tend to be more directly interested in the sections which offer practical instruction on how to handle cases and workflow.

cross-border relationships and forms of mobility that often constitute a part of a trafficking offence: specifically, international financial transactions, the movement of illicit goods in barter for trafficked persons, and, of course, the illegal movements of traffickers themselves. The individual migrant victim is presented as the sole means through which the official can obtain evidence of a trafficking crime.

Having assumed this context of a hypothetical meeting between an official and a potential victim, the training materials then lay out a plan for an observation and interrogation session that is designed to ascertain whether the individual in question is indeed a victim of a trafficking offence. Again, despite the fact that there is nothing in the South African legislation which says that an individual must have moved in order to be a victim of trafficking, the materials provide a working definition which makes migration an essential component of the crime:

For an incident to be identified as a case of Human Trafficking, it must contain 3 elements. Was the person recruited by fraudulent means? Was the person then transported to a distant location? And finally, is there evidence to suggest that the person was exploited in another region or the country of destination?[3]

The materials then outline an interrogation and analytical procedure that is primarily focused on determining whether the person's migration history suggests that he or she has been a victim of a trafficking offence. The majority of the evaluative 'benchmarks' contained in this procedure would become nonsensical if applied to an individual who had not crossed a border. For example, the officials are encouraged to use the person's passport validity as an indicator that a trafficking offence may have occurred. The questions about the recruitment phase focus on how an individual was encouraged or coerced to leave his or her country of origin. The questions on transportation focus on whether the individual was transported across borders illegally and how; whether he or she is in possession of valid documents; and whether he or she spent time in a third country en route to South Africa. The questions about exploitation focus on the work the person has been doing since arriving in South Africa and how long after arriving in South Africa the person began this work. None of these benchmarks are presented as essential elements of a trafficking crime. However, each stylized representation of trafficking's 'general' characteristics ties the crime of trafficking itself more closely into an international migration narrative. As this migration story takes centre stage, other potential variants of the crime recede into the background. In particular, the interrogation protocols do not encourage the interviewer to ask questions that might be crucial in developing a case against perpetrators of trafficking offences, such as questions about the traffickers themselves, their modus operandi, or other victims and their whereabouts.

By representing the victim as the sole analytical object of a trafficking investigation, and presenting this individual's international migration story as the primary

---

[3] No doubt, this is merely just a clumsy failure to adapt a boilerplate training manual to a new legal environment. Nonetheless, the insistence on mobility as a core component of trafficking is revealing of the IOM's broader failure to contemplate other forms of relevant exploitation and abuse.

form of evidence to be used in the construction of a criminal case, the teaching materials criminalize mobility in a particular way. They present the victim's act of international migration as the primary component of a criminal enterprise. In the interrogation model, the hypothetical official is encouraged to ignore the actual exploitation of the individual and the relevant signs of such exploitation, including emotional distress or physical harm. Instead, the officials are taught to focus their attention on the act of reconstructing the individual's migration story in a way that will allow them to detect whether the characteristic 'markers' of trafficking (unrealistic recruitment offers, illegal entry, immediate engagement in the sex work industry) are present. In the process, migration itself, and particularly that of poor women, becomes the main object of investigative concern.

This act of objectification might have some broader rationale if it were presented in such a way that linked the purported victim back to a process of investigation of a criminal trafficking enterprise. However, the teaching materials do not provide the officials with the relevant tools to conduct further investigations or interventions. So, while the Palermo Protocol was crafted with the explicit purpose of aiding in the detection and prosecution of transnational organized criminal networks, these materials do not suggest that officials should busy themselves with detecting and responding to the criminal conspiracies which entrap and exploit international migrants, but with looking for a broad category of persons who constitute likely victims: international migrants without documents.

Using Human Mobility to Make Property Tangible

As I suggested earlier, this habit of criminalizing mobility is not simply taught or imposed in a top-down fashion by global agencies concerned with migration dynamics and problems. It is also a form of practical knowledge—a way of doing—to which law-enforcement officials are particularly accustomed and which they deploy when they deal with a range of enforcement problems. In some respects, South African police officials resort to laws concerning human mobility as a 'default' response to a range of crimes that they are unable to effectively control. A good example of this dynamic can be found in the way in which the police in Johannesburg have sought to crack down on the street trade in counterfeit music and films.

In inner-city Johannesburg, there is a thriving trade for copies of popular CDs and DVDs. An informal network of men and a few women of various nationalities run the trade. Some traders simply walk the streets with a few CDs or DVDs in their hands touting for prospective customers. Others work out of their apartments selling discs to regular customers. However, the most noticeable traders are those that have set up stalls on busy sidewalks, around train and taxi stations, and near large shopping centres. While the occasional stall might be set up on an ad hoc basis, and in isolation, there are several CD/DVD 'markets' across the city which attract most custom and most attention from the police.

Over the last few years the Johannesburg Central, Hillbrow, and Jeppe police stations have conducted regular raids on these markets. While individual patrol officers often conduct their own inspections and arrests, the raids generally involve coordinated and planned surprise attacks on the markets, involving 10 to 20 officers and several support vehicles. The raiding officers generally seize the property on display, destroy and/or confiscate the tables and goods, and arrest the suspected traders. In addition to police raids, a number of civilian groups conduct their own raids on the markets. For example, groups of unarmed civilian 'street patrollers' have, in addition to targeting suspected drug dealers on inner-city corners, taken to raiding the CD and DVD stalls and confiscating their goods. A few different artist collectives, made up of a range of local musicians, promoters, and producers, have occasionally followed suit.

These raids significantly disturb the traders' business. In the lead-up to the 2010 Football World Cup the South African government came under considerable pressure from FIFA and representatives of the recording industry to ensure that counterfeit sporting goods and entertainment material would not be sold in and around the venues. As a direct outcome, police in the inner city of Johannesburg began raiding the stalls so frequently that many stall owners abandoned the markets and adopted more discreet and less effective distribution strategies. Clearly, this was an act of policing performance designed to appease an international audience. However, curiously none of the raids that occurred during the period when we were conducting research yielded convictions relating specifically to piracy or any attendant claims for damages or restitution of the intellectual property concerned. Instead, arrested traders tended to be charged and in a very few cases sentenced to fines for violating city bye-laws (for erecting structures on the sidewalk without a licence, or loitering) and for immigration offences. Perhaps more importantly, the police did not appear concerned to use the raids to cultivate informants or generate evidence which could be used to prosecute those responsible for producing the illegal copies. This was not an assault on the counterfeit supply chain.

In the absence of a concerted investigative and enforcement strategy the outcome was predictable. In the aftermath of the World Cup, and as the political impetus for anti-piracy efforts waned, so too did the raids. The market stalls began to reappear on the city streets, selling the same goods and—we assume—drawing upon a similar set of supply networks.

The raids on the street traders reveal how officials use laws on mobility to respond to complex law-enforcement problems. In this instance, officials deployed laws defining what constitutes a legal form of occupying public space and a right to travel to and remain in a country in order to police a crime which they were poorly equipped to effectively control. This point starts with the recognition that intellectual property crimes are a particularly intractable problem. While anti-piracy campaigners have tried their best, by way of analogy, to encourage us to think of film and music piracy as simple acts of theft, piracy is in fact a far more complex type of crime. Unlike other infringements on property rights, the criminal component of the act of piracy does not consist in the act of taking an object from another person or of occupying another person's land illegally. Rather, piracy consists of illegally copying—and/or profiting from the copies of—an artwork, sound, or visual experience. In short, piracy is an unauthorized replication of an 'idea'.

How does one police the reproduction of ideas? While the fall-back position for anti-piracy campaigners was originally to stress the importance of physical reproductions, the copies which are sold on the streets of many developing cities like Johannesburg are now usually the rump end of a long, complex, and largely 'intangible' process of illegal copying. The most powerful form of production and dissemination of illegal copies of music and film in today's market are peer-to-peer torrent sites where a global array of anonymous 'distributors' and 'users' simultaneously upload and download component parts of files online. So, regardless of the tangible trade in disks, it is unlikely that policing could significantly stamp out piracy without in some way limiting South Africans' access to the internet itself. Contemporary piracy cannot be meaningfully tackled without extensive cooperation from internet service providers and monitoring of broadband internet usage. To make matters worse, anti-piracy laws do not provide law-enforcement officials with an effective means of prosecuting offenders. In South Africa, the owners of copyright must launch a suit in order to gain a conviction, and experts or trained police officers must be prepared and willing to make the case in court.

Facing this difficult scenario and lacking the expert knowledge or resources to generate a meaningful response to copyright infringement, the Johannesburg police have simply responded in the manner they know best, by focusing their attention on the tangible manifestation of the problem on the city streets. This is a characteristically South African law-enforcement response to a difficult societal problem: including regulation of the sex industry, deterioration of the housing stock, pedestrian traffic congestion in the inner city, etc. Most South African observers are so familiar with this high manpower, raiding mentality that they tend to rationalize raids as unremarkable cases of 'how we do things here' or simply 'what the police do'. This stems from an ingrained habit of seeing criminality as a form of infestation or spatially fixed disorder, and simultaneously viewing high intensity operational policing as a limited but necessary means of combating such infestations and restoring order. What is often not noticed is that the principal power of the dragnet which the police deploy in these crime sweeps are their collective capabilities in enforcing laws regarding illegal forms of physical *movement*. Effectively, the knee-jerk response of the police is to deploy a set of laws to a situation which enable them to configure the ostensible suspects as 'out of place', thereby partially absolving themselves of the need to construct the more complex story of a commercial crime. In this process, the act of emptying out the market stands in for the less achievable goal of cleansing the internet. Evasive-yet-manageable people serve as proxies for uncontainable ideas.

Summary and Conclusion

This chapter has, in an exploratory fashion, sought to develop a more nuanced understanding of the relationship between the policing of mobility and crime. I have argued that by studying the way in which ordinary officials construct and deploy narratives of criminalized mobility we can better explain what happens when policy makers call upon their officials to simultaneously police immigration and criminal laws. In all of the cases I have discussed, narratives of criminal mobility serve as a way of simplifying complex enforcement problems. By profiling mobile people as perpetrators, presenting migrants as victims, and using human mobility to make intellectual property crimes tangible, officials create simple and replicable policing habits for dealing with deeply complex social realities. While prejudice and profiling constitute one important way in which officials simplify the difficult task of detecting potential perpetrators among diverse populations, I have argued that this is only part of the story. Mobility is commonly made the object of criminal suspicion in a variety of other ways and with a number of other indirect effects. In the human trafficking example, I showed that by encouraging teacher trainers to focus on stories of migrant victimhood, the IOM materials encouraged officials to shut off their attention to the perpetrators of trafficking. In the intellectual property example, I showed that by focusing on traders' illegal occupation of inner-city spaces, police raids allowed officials to avoid the more complex problem of dealing with the production of illegal copies of music and film.

The reasons why mobility narratives become such evocative and 'common-sense' simplifications for ordinary officials is not self-evident, but is itself an important object of explanation. As I have shown in this discussion, developing a narrative of criminal mobility is a subtle and complex discursive exercise, requiring the exercise of an official's imagination. The question then becomes why issues such as where an individual has come from, in what direction he or she is going, or how quickly and regularly he or she has moved take precedence over, or begin to displace, other lines of investigation such as an individual's line of work or social networks, or other forms of surveillance and detection which do not focus on human bodies but take physical property, personal testimony, data registers, etc as their primary source of evidence. As the discussion above suggests, South African officials' tendency to privilege mobility narratives over other ways of scripting a potential crime may be partly explained by their highly unique historical context: as inheritors of the apartheid tradition of policing separateness. However, I have also suggested that global policing agenda may provide a new context in which such highly localized practices might 'thrive'. The Convention on Transnational Organized Crime presents human mobility in particular, but cross-border mobility in general, as a potential vector of criminal activity, networks, and ambition. The impact of the Convention may hinge on the degree to which the various institutional formations and initiatives which have been developed under its broad rubric feed into and strengthen the tendency of law-enforcement officials to take questions about an individual's movements as the first step in any investigation of a potential crime.

References

Agustin, L.M. (2007) *Sex at the Margins: Migration, Labour Markets and the Rescue Industry*. London: Zed Books.

Batton, C. and Kadleck, C. (2004) 'Theoretical and Methodological Issues in Racial Profiling Research', *Police Quarterly* 7(1): 30.

Berman, J. (2003) '(Un)Popular Strangers and Crises (Un)Bounded: Discourses of Sex Trafficking, the European Political Community and the Panicked State of the Modern State', *European Journal of International Relations* 9(1): 9.

Brewer, J.D. (1994) *Black and Blue: Policing in South Africa*. Oxford: Clarendon.

Doezema, J. (2010) *Sex Slaves and Discourse Masters: The Construction of Trafficking*. London: Zed Books.

Engel, R.S., Calnon, J.M., and Bernard, T.J. (2002) 'Theory and Racial Profiling: Shortcomings and Future Directions in Research', *Justice Quarterly* 19(2): 239.

Gould, C. and Fick, N. (2008) *Selling Sex in Cape Town. Sex Work and Human Trafficking in a South African City*. Pretoria: Institute for Security Studies.

Hathaway, J. (2008) 'The Human Rights Quagmire of "Human Trafficking"', *Virginia Journal of International Law* 49(1): 25.

Herbert, S.K. (1997) 'Territoriality and the Police', *Professional Geographer* 49(1): 86.

Landau, L. and Vigneswaran, D. (2007) 'Shifting the Focus of Migration Back Home: Perspectives from Africa', *Development* 50(4): 82.

Starn, R. (1982) *Contrary Commonwealth: The Theme of Exile in Medieval and Renaissance Italy*. Berkeley: University of California Press.

Vigneswaran, D. (2013, forthcoming) *Territory, Migration and the Evolution of the International System*. Palgrave.

Vigneswaran, D. (2011) 'Incident Reporting: A Technique for Studying Police Corruption', *Policing and Society* 21(2): 190.

Vigneswaran, D. (2011) 'Taking out the Trash: A Garbage Can Model of Immigration Policing', in L. Landau (ed), *Exorcising the Demon Within: Xenophobia, Violence and Statecraft in Contemporary South Africa*. Johannesburg: WITS University Press.

Vigneswaran, D. (2008) 'Enduring Territoriality: South African Immigration Control', *Political Geography* 27: 783.

Vigneswaran, D. (2007) 'The Territorial Strategy of the Italian City-State', *International Relations* 21(4): 427.

Vigneswaran, D., Araia, T., Hoag, C., and Tshabalala, X. (2010) 'Criminality or Monopoly? Informal Immigration Enforcement in South Africa', *Journal of Southern African Studies* 36(2): 465.

Walters, W. (2010) 'Deportation, Expulsion, and the International Police of Aliens', in N. De Genova and N.M. Peutz (eds), *The Deportation Regime: Sovereignty, Space, and the Freedom of Movement*. Durham, NC: Duke University Press.

7

Human Trafficking and Border Control in the Global South

Maggy Lee[1]

Introduction

The promotion and development of international counter-trafficking norms and programmes over recent decades have transformed human trafficking from 'a poorly funded, NGO women's issue in the early 1980s' into 'the global agenda of high politics' of the United States Congress, the European Union, and the United Nations (Wong 2005: 69). To many policy makers and law enforcers, such expansion of trafficking control exemplifies a 'global prohibition regime' (Nadelmann 1990: 526) directed at activities which threaten 'the safety, welfare and moral sensibilities of international society'. Yet as Andreas and Nadelmann (2006) remind us, historically, through international prohibition efforts (for example, against slavery and drugs), metropolitan powers export their own definitions of crime for political and economic reasons as well as to promote their own morals from the metropolitan 'centre' to the 'periphery'. To paraphrase Aas (2011a), criminal justice 'exports' are not a natural, functional response to human trafficking as a growing crime problem; instead, they are infused with 'geo-political imbalances of power' between 'exporters' and 'importers' of particular discourses and practices of crime and crime control.

In the field of human trafficking, critics have pointed to a Eurocentric framing of the issue and its troubling consequences, notably through the intersection of trafficking and immigration control. There is now a growing body of criminological literature on the criminalization and securitization of trafficked victims, refugees, and asylum seekers (Green and Grewcock 2002; Pickering 2004; Huysmans 2006; Gerard and Pickering 2012). Considering human trafficking as an immigration crime problem casts those who are trafficked as unwanted 'Others', to be dealt with first and foremost as illegal immigrants who have to be 'rescued' and returned

[1] I am indebted to Katja Franko Aas and Mary Bosworth for their insightful suggestions and extremely helpful comments on earlier drafts of this chapter. I would also like to thank Sharon Pickering and Marie Segrave for their support and Ben Bowling and many others for their feedback at the Borders of Punishment Conference, University of Oxford, April 2012.

home, to where they belong or, better still, immobilized before they arrive at the borders in the global North. Within this milieu, border policing is widened into 'border spaces that are not primarily defined by territory'; it 'becomes global and predictably homes in on the most vulnerable and the most desperate for the unmitigated use of force and practices of exclusion' (Pickering 2004: 221).

This chapter seeks to add to the critical work on criminology of mobility by examining trafficking control and border policing currently taking place in the global South. To date, most of the criminological literature on trafficking control has tended to focus on Western models of border policing, the fortification of border surveillance in a global regime of mobility control, and the violent technologies of state control and collateral damage brought on by the 'war on trafficking'. Criminologists have paid relatively little attention to those international programmes, transnational migration and development aid agencies, and non-state actors whose business it is to implement and promote particular norms and standards about border control in the name of trafficking prevention and migration management, notably in what Walters (2011) has termed the 'humanitarian border' in the global South. It is here, in the unstable zones of the world system—or what Mark Duffield has termed the global 'borderlands'—where one can witness a significant 'internationalisation of public policy, privatisation and marketisation' (Duffield 2001: 309) via the thickening of public-private contractual and international aid networks between metropolitan and borderland areas, the growing involvement of non-state and private organizations, and the casting of the border as a particular terrain of expert knowledge and intervention. Metropolitan states may be reluctant to intervene directly in the internal affairs of third countries, but they are learning to govern the borderlands 'at a distance' through a reworking of international power and its projection through 'new non-territorial networks' and new technologies of control within the broad framework where security is redefined as development (Duffield 2001: 310–314).

To some extent, the lack of criminological attention to the global borderlands may reflect what critics have referred to as the longstanding Northern epistemic hegemony and geopolitical imbalances of academic knowledge production (Agozino 2003; Connell 2006; Cunneen 2011; Aas 2012). As Chen (2010: 237) suggests in the context of Asian cultural studies, 'Western-centrism' and its discourse of universality has constituted a 'solid structure of desire and knowledge', but this should not stop us from exploring ways to advance an alternative mapping of criminology that foregrounds the situated context of mobilities and control in Asia. As a tentative response to the rallying call to expand criminology's geopolitical imagination and 'to see from the peripheries' (Aas 2012: 11), this chapter considers the dominant human trafficking discourse, norms, logics, and forms of border control that have been extended from countries of destination in the North to countries of origin in the South. How does the dominant trafficking discourse become dispersed and institutionalized, especially through international agencies and non-state actors? How can we make sense of the novel alliances and power configurations that international agencies and non-governmental organizations bring into play in border policing in the Asian context? And how can the development of a 'peripheral vision' of trafficking and border control inform a truly global criminology of (im)mobility?

Human Trafficking as Illegal Immigration Crime

Human trafficking is not new. There are historical continuities in the commodification of people—from the sophisticated, state-sponsored slave trading systems and other forms of labour servitude that thrived in the seventeenth and eighteenth centuries, when Britain dominated the highly profitable trade of transporting Africans to the colonies and the plantations and mines of the Americas; the moral panic over the trade of white women and girls in Europe for prostitution from the nineteenth century; to the modern global traffic in men and women and body parts (Keire 2001; Scheper-Hughes 2001; Miers 2003; Bales 2005). As many commentators have noted, much of the impetus behind the contemporary rediscovery of the human trafficking problem and the global 'crime crusade' against trafficking lies in the (re)casting of human trafficking as an illegal immigration crime problem (Segrave, Milivojevic et al 2009; Lee 2011). Indeed, the political discourse of trafficking-as-immigration crime has featured prominently since the 1990s in numerous statements by 'professionals of the management of unease' (Bigo 2008: 23), such as criminal justice and policing agents, immigration and border control specialists, anti-terrorist and intelligence experts, and in risk assessments of transnational organized crime groups and ever spiralling estimates of trafficking figures (UNICRI 1999; Allred 2006; Europol 2008). The acknowledgement of internal trafficking[2] has done little to challenge the dominant understanding of trafficking as a problem of inter-state illegal immigration.

In the United Kingdom, for example, anti-trafficking measures are to be mainstreamed into the UK's immigration control system through an 'enhanced ability to act early, before the harm has reached the UK' and to prevent 'traffickers and migrants, who are particularly vulnerable to trafficking, from coming to the UK'. Within the European Union, human trafficking has been criminalized and actively reframed as one form of 'unauthorised immigration' at least from the late 1990s (European Council Joint Action 97/154/JHA). It is to be dealt with as part of the 'Unionwide Fight Against Crime' through 'border management', 'pre-frontier measures', Europol, and other appropriate penalties and enforcement actions aimed at 'dismantling criminal networks' (EU Council 2002).

The articulation of human trafficking as an immigration crime problem requiring transnational law enforcement is most clearly embodied in the United Nations Trafficking Protocol under the 2000 UN Convention Against Transnational Organised Crime, which now sits at the very heart of the contemporary trafficking legislation and international counter-trafficking discourse. This dominant discourse of trafficking now permeates a plethora of international and regional legal

---

[2] The UN Convention's definition of trafficking does not require the victim of trafficking to be a foreign national or that international borders be crossed in the commission of the offence. There have been a number of documented cases of internal trafficking or trafficking of EU nationals within the EU and cases of trafficking of US citizens as well as migrants with valid work permits in the US.

instruments, bilateral and multi-lateral treaties, and agreements aimed at the 'prevention, suppression and punishment of trafficking in persons' (UN Trafficking Protocol, preamble), intelligence gathering and data sharing (for example to share information about the identification of 'possible victims' in transit: UN Trafficking Protocol, Article 10), and training and technical assistance (for example 'to ensure the integrity and security of their travel documents': UN Trafficking Protocol, Article 12). The discourse draws upon particular assumptions about the need to 'deter' illegal immigrants—from imposing strict visa requirements for those coming from developing countries deemed a 'risk' for immigration abuse, to detaining and prosecuting trafficked persons as immigration offenders on a range of travel and identity documentation offences. It also draws upon gendered notions of victimhood based on a specific constellation of sexual exploitation and signs of raw suffering dominated by psychiatric and psychological knowledge (Doezema 2000; Aradau 2004). Yet these 'signs' of trafficking are rarely clear in transit or self-evident at the policing of borders. Given that the use of force, debt bondage, or exploitation may not be apparent until later stages of migratory movement (and even then, the meaning of 'exploitation' is highly contested as in labour exploitation), this allows for lumping together trafficked persons with various 'crimmigrant' others in the new global regime of border control (Stumpf 2006; Bosworth and Guild 2008; Welch 2010).

Policing-at-a-distance

The dominant discourse of trafficking has legitimized a shift of border functions and new technologies of policing unauthorized mobilities. Scholars have noted an externalization of migration control prerogatives to a patchwork of civil servants (immigration officials, consulate personnel) and private businesses (airline carriers, security agencies, transport companies), and an expansion of pre-emptive strategies aimed at identifying and immobilizing 'risky' populations and preventing the exit of trafficked persons at source. In the process, new dynamics and new logics of frontiers control—what Guiraudon (2002) and Bigo and Guild (2005) have termed 'remote control' or 'policing at a distance'—are set in motion as multiple state and non-state actors intervene 'upstream', by risk-profiling and targeting specific groups of vulnerable populations.

The dispersal and diffusion of border policing can be seen as an intrinsic feature of the way in which metropolitan states imagine and pursue trafficking control. Each state, separately or in collaboration with others, tries to disperse the locus of control upstream to block or deter the will to travel in the country of origin, and to displace the burden of controlling unwanted mobility and insecurity onto others. Much of the existing policing-at-a-distance literature has focused on Western models of 'pre-frontier' strategies, the creation of 'buffer zones' in Eastern and Central Europe, and the dispersal of control functions away from the usual border settings and their relocation to a de-territorialized terrain (notably in offshore processing as part of Australia's now partially disbanded 'Pacific Solution') (Anderson and Bigo 2002; Pickering and Gard 2004; Salter and Zureik 2005; Pickering and Weber 2006; Grewcock 2007; Mountz 2010). The debate has generally been about the creation of a legal vacuum, in which the constitutional or international hindrances to scrutiny are effectively eclipsed.

What seems to be missing in existing analyses of trafficking control is a critical examination of the emerging nature and practices of policing-at-a distance from the Southern perspective. Although the global division of policing labour has driven international institutions and donor countries to build up the surveillance resources in the South, there are inherent limitations and contradictions in these efforts to export metropolitan models of border control. On the one hand, countries of origin that resist the export drive are deemed 'deviant' in the fight against trafficking and 'backward' in the paths to modernity; on the other hand, those too eager to import the surveillance technologies are dismissed for making 'egregious requests' for technological hardware and border patrol equipment and criticized for treating donor assistance programmes as 'an equipment-bearing gift horse' (Gavrilis 2009: 2). Given the realities of lack of telecommunication facilities and information communications capacity and border surveillance infrastructure in Asia (including unreliable electricity supply, manual record-keeping and data sharing) (International Organisation of Migration 2009), much of the cutting-edge technoscience of border control which has proliferated in the global North can at best be described as 'surveillance fantasies' (Aas 2011b) in the South. So what does policing-at-a-distance look like if we shift our criminological gaze to the spaces of border control in the periphery?

The Geopolitics of Trafficking Control

First, we may want to consider precisely how trafficking control norms and practices are exported from the metropolitan centre and enacted in countries of origin in the borderlands. Huge efforts have been made by state and international institutions to promote the global reach of UN-sponsored understandings of trafficking and its control under the three themes of 'prevention, protection, and prosecution' (commonly known as the '3Ps' under the UN Trafficking Protocol). Strategies include the promotion of a vast array of international and regional frameworks, anti-trafficking legislation, action plans, minimum standards, best practices, and toolkits; the ranking of states in terms of calculable risks and their compliance in trafficking control; and donor assistance in extensive programmes of technical expertise, capacity building, and modernization of 'border management' (Chemonics International 2009; United Nations Office on Drugs and Crime 2009). In the process, trafficking control norms from countries of destination are exported to countries of origin, with a view to aligning the migration policies of the global South with the migration control norms and aspirations of the global North. Countries which fail to conform (for example, those that do not produce trafficking convictions) are seen as uncooperative and 'deviant' in the global fight against trafficking. Such an approach overlooks the inherent limitations of the UN Trafficking Protocol's enforcement-led model in responding to the social context of trafficking and the structural conditions conducive to the 'feminisation' and 'illegalisation' of cross-border migration patterns within the 'circuit of globalised economies' (Sassen 2002; Anderson 2007) in Asia.

This model of risk assessment and actuarial mapping of conduct by metropolitan powers is particularly apparent in the ranking of state compliance in the US Department of State Trafficking in Persons Report annual review process. Much has been written about the 'Americanization' of global trafficking control, notably through the US-defined minimum standards for the elimination of trafficking in its Trafficking in Persons (TIP) Report annual review process and the ranking of individual states' compliance with those standards in the annual TIP Report. Annually, around 150 countries are evaluated and ranked into four tiers (Tier 1, Tier 2 and Tier 2 Watch List, and Tier 3). As Segrave et al (2009: 20) have argued, while each nation is assessed ostensibly 'according to its efforts related to "prevention", "protection" and "prosecution", the assessment process has largely sought the development and implementation of domestic and cross-border criminal justice efforts'. The creation of anti-trafficking national legislation, action plans and task forces, the increase in arrests and prosecution figures, and anti-trafficking and border control agreements are taken as indicators of effort and cooperation in the global fight against human trafficking.[3] States that flout these norms are subject to unilateral US foreign assistance sanctions[4] and, perhaps more importantly, risk the reputational effects of being seen as 'a weak link in the security chain or … a "failed state" where disorder breeds, spilling over into the international community' (Andrijasevic and Walters 2010: 990).

Different elements of the TIP Report—from the 'lack of clarity in the tier ranking process', 'inconsistent application of the minimum standards', to the 'superficial country assessments'—have been the subject of extensive critique (Kempadoo 2005a; Global Alliance Against Traffic in Women 2007; Wyler and Siskin 2010). The rankings of states have been described as 'ideologically and politically motivated rather than rooted in hard facts about trafficking'; they serve 'as a major diplomatic tool' for advancing American foreign policy and various commercial interests (Kempadoo 2005b: 24). As Kempadoo (2007) suggests, the ranking constitutes part of American foreign policy to 'demonise' and 'isolate' states such as Cuba, Iran, Burma, North Korea, Syria, and Zimbabwe—all of which fall into US categories of 'rogue' states. In contrast, the US Government found justification for waiving all sanctions against Malaysia (alongside Kuwait and Saudi Arabia) in the lowest Tier 3. The geopolitical considerations are clearly evident in the TIP Report:

The granting of a full waiver of sanctions against Malaysia is in the national interest because it will permit continued security cooperation and the promotion of democratic principles

---

[3] Examples in Asia include the ASEAN 'Declaration Against Trafficking in Persons Particularly Women and Children' and the multilateral agreement between the Philippines, Malaysia, and Indonesia to share lists of airline passengers and refusals at visa-issuing offices and fingerprint databases.

[4] For example, Tier 3 countries are made subject to sanctions in the form of termination of non-humanitarian, non-trade-related assistance and loss of US support for loans from international financial institutions.

and will allow continued dialogue and engagement to combat human trafficking ... A full waiver has been granted in the national interest of allowing for the uninterrupted continuation of important military-to-military security cooperation programs and to allow for military sales in order to advance regional efforts to confront terrorist activities, eliminate the proliferation of weapons of mass destruction, and work with regional partners to ensure the security of critical maritime areas, including the Strait of Malacca and the Sulu and Sulawesi Seas. (US Department of State 2009)

Clearly, relations of international power influence the designation of which Southern countries in a global hierarchy of states are deemed 'at risk' of immigration abuse, disorderly, non-compliant, and, therefore, deserving of sanctions. The corollary is that any concerns about disruptive and violent border policing practices in the borderlands become sidestepped in the name of the global fight against trafficking. Arbitrary and repressive treatment of unauthorized migrants in countries of origin, including the use of mass arrests, detention, and deportation in Asia (notably in Malaysia, Thailand, and along the Thai-Burma border), has been well documented by organizations such as Human Rights Watch and the Global Detention Project.

By extending our criminological gaze from 'defensive policing' in metropolitan states to 'offensive intervention' in countries of origin, we can begin to understand how 'security narratives' and 'state-sponsored borderlands performance' (Pickering 2006: 55–56) have reinvigorated and reshaped border policing efforts in the global South, in order to prevent 'risky' populations from entering metropolitan countries *and* from exiting their countries of origin. As Megoran et al (2005: 733–734) wrote in relation to the militarization of border controls in the Central Asian state of Uzbekistan, border controls are essential elements of state crafting, and part of that 'performance of statecraft' is to demonstrate 'success' by arrests and apprehensions. Increased 'input' into border policing (including donor assistance) may demand more 'output', creating 'an imperative to play not only for the national audience, but an international one'—with 'knock-on effects' in terms of violence against petty cross-border traders and migrants alike (Megoran et al 2005: 734). All this highlights the urgent need to interrogate the 'increased material and political power' of border policing efforts that occur in spaces less visible to the Northern audience, the changing patterns of state violence, and the extent to which these have been legitimized and transformed in a 're-imagined internal, external and extended policing borderland' (Pickering 2006: 56).

The Technocratic Politics of Border Management

The multiple power relations and new tactics of policing-at-a-distance are also evident in the seemingly mundane space of public-private contractual networks of aid and in the extension of a depoliticized language of management based around technical norms, standardization, benchmarking, and performance auditing. As Andrijasevic and Walters (2010: 985–987) have argued, framing borders as 'a problem of management' entails a 'new imagination of the governmental space of borders' that involves a 'heterogeneous domain' of expertise and intervention associated with 'new public management' techniques and styles of reasoning within programmes and schemes of international authority.

Indeed, there has been an intensified export of the norms and practices of trafficking control and border management from metropolitan states—asserting 'expert' knowledge and professional routines in producing statistics and profiles of potential at-risk behaviour; promoting technological and audit capacity; expanding international intervention in 'social technologies' (Andrijasevic and Walters 2010) of facilitation and capacitation (for example, capacity building, study visits, 'train-the-trainers', and distribution of manuals and toolkits on border management for project managers, evaluators, and donors). In an inventory of anti-trafficking projects and initiatives within the UN Economic and Social Commission for Asia and Pacific (UNESCAP) region in 2001, there were at least six projects run by UNESCAP itself, eight by the International Organisation of Migration (this increased to at least 20 by 2004), four by UNESCO, four by the UNHCR, 32 by UNICEF, and many more (Piper 2005). Through providing funding, technical, and logistical support in a climate of geopolitical normativity, donor countries and international institutions such as the United Nations Office on Drugs and Crime, the World Bank, and The Asia Foundation export particular trafficking control norms, institute legislative models and 'best practices', and institutionalize information management systems in the generation and flow of data for (self)-monitoring of performance, within the broader project to modernize and securitize the diverse regions of Central, South, and South East Asia. Many of the anti-trafficking programmes and initiatives are donor country driven, channelling funds and disseminating norms and standards through transnational and donor agencies, not just in crime control but also in the development sector (such as the United Nations Development Programme, the Department for International Development (DFID) in the United Kingdom, the Australian Government Overseas Aid Program (AusAID), and the United States Agency for International Development (USAID)[5]), and through international NGOs that are trafficking-specific (such as End Child Prostitution, Child Pornography, and the Trafficking of Children for Sexual Purposes (ECPAT)) or have positioned themselves as migration experts (such as the International Organisation for Migration (IOM)).[6]

The scale and activity of donor and international agencies, and the elaborate interconnected public-private contractual networks in the development sector and

---

[5] Between 2001 and 2009, the US government invested an estimated US$686 million on international anti-trafficking programmes primarily through the State Department and USAID, including 30 anti-trafficking programmes in South and South East Asia and Central Asia (Chemonics International 2009).

[6] Representing itself as 'the migration agency', the IOM now operates as a major source of advice, assessment, intelligence, and technical assistance in connection with human trafficking, migration management, border policies, and practices. It is said to have an annual operating budget of close to US $1 billion and some 5,400 staff working in over 100 countries. It is reported to have implemented over 200 counter-trafficking projects in 84 countries and assisted over 14,000 victims of trafficking worldwide (<http://www.iom.int>). For a detailed analysis of the role of the IOM in the managerialization and international government of borders, see Andrijasevic and Walters (2010).

trafficking control in Asia, is best illustrated by three brief examples. First, the UN Inter-Agency Project in Human Trafficking (UNIAP) was set up in the Greater Mekong Sub-Region in 2000, funded by multiple donors, and included over 250 local and international partners and NGOs across Cambodia, China, Lao People's Democratic Republic, Myanmar, Thailand, and Vietnam (Cunnington and Hung 2009). Second, in Central Asia Republics, the European Union has exported its 'Integrated Border Management' (IBM) model to control cross-border crime such as drug trafficking, arms trafficking, and trafficking in human beings in a region where drug trafficking, undocumented migration, terrorism, and other security issues were seen to be rife (Gavrilis 2009). As a flagship EU programme and 'the most significant EU intervention in border management to date' (Czerniecka and Heathershaw 2010: 77) and a budget of over 33 million euros between 2003–2014, the EU-funded 'Border Management Programme for Central Asia' (<http://www.bomca.eu>) is implemented by the United Nations Development Programme. It involves multiple implementing partners and private contractors (for example the International Centre for Migration Policy Development, IOM, and EU experts) and numerous projects that aimed at providing capacity building and training for border security services and border troops, funding key technology and infrastructure assistance, creating mobile border control units, and promoting legal and institutional reform to support joint border management by Central Asian states.

Crown Agents provide the third example. As an 'international development specialist' in the private sector, Crown Agents promoted its security knowledge and expertise on 'integrated border management' (in Asia, Africa, and Eastern Europe and beyond) to 'facilitate the legal movements of goods and persons, whilst combating transnational crime, illegal migration and people trafficking' (<http://www.crownagents.com>). Crown Agents' website claims that its expert consultancy on the EU-ASEAN 'Migration and Border Management Programme' exemplifies 'the management of globally included and excluded populations', typically through the implementation of technical solutions, standards (performance indicators), awareness-raising seminars and training in countries of origin; exchange of information between Interpol and the Association of Southeast Asian Nations (ASEAN); promotion of European Standardised Operating Procedures for travel document and ID control at the border; developing 'smart card' formats for regular border commuters in pilot zones; and enhancing border control capacities by providing equipment such as national databases on travel documents, UV lamps, and electronic Cross Border Passes at selected border crossing points.

Clearly, governing through international assistance networks and private associations creates new forms of interaction and dependency between metropolitan and borderland areas and between states and non-state actors via contracts, technical norms, public auditing, and partnerships. It constitutes 'novel and flexible forms of strategic alliance' that cut across 'traditional institutional, professional and sector boundaries' (Duffield 2001: 318). These programmes and tactics of international expertise and intervention and networks of aid illustrate current trends of securitization of international assistance and the 'managerialisation of borders' (Andrijasevic and Walters 2010: 986). They also exemplify some of the more subtle mechanisms by which Southern state and non-state actors are encouraged to take up the work of border management themselves, enhancing their control capacities and, in the process, becoming key actors in the contemporary (re)making of borders.

Novel Assemblages of Border Policing

The emerging alliances between state and non-state organizations and international institutions in the South can be understood as 'novel assemblages' (Sassen 2008). As Sassen (2008: 67) suggests, these 'assemblages' are 'not exclusively national or global but are assemblages of elements of each'; they are 'partial' and often 'highly specialized formations', centring on single purposes or particularized normative orders. In this context, even 'resource-poor and *immobile* individuals or organizations' (Sassen 2008: 66) can tap into new digital technologies and public-private contractual networks (notably through cooperation with resource-rich international NGOs in the North) to become 'part of a global public space' and 'part of a type of horizontal globality centered on diverse localities'.

The role of NGOs in these novel assemblages of border policing is particularly pertinent to our discussion. As Walters (2011: 154) reminds us in his analysis of the border as 'a space of humanitarian government', border policing has become much more complex and polymorphous, as border regimes now combine elements of control with practices of pastoral care, aid, and assistance. Much has been written about the rapid growth of the aid industry throughout the late 1980s and 1990s, where NGOs have been viewed as 'doing good' in opposition to authoritarian or corrupt governments by some commentators, but as facilitators for privatizing foreign assistance by others (Keck and Sikkink 1998; Lewis and Wallace 2000; Walters 2011). In Indonesia, for example, the number of officially registered NGOs was said to have increased from 130 in 1981 to somewhere between 4,000 and 10,000 by 1994 (Clarke 1998). Their relations with the state are ambiguous and contingent, characterized by overlapping personnel, co-option, and control in some cases and opposition to the state in others (Lindquist 2004).

In the field of human trafficking in Asia, the ebb and flow of donor funding and dense patchworks of anti-trafficking alliances have transformed particular types of local NGOs into key actors in the border management and international development industry. In Indonesia, local NGOs redefined their expertise from HIV/AIDS prevention to counter-trafficking in order to fit into changing donor interests and priorities of international organizations such as USAID, the International Catholic Migration Commission (ICMC), Asia Foundation, United Nations Development Fund for Women (UNIFEM), and *Terres Des Hommes* Netherlands. Although the clients (or 'risk groups') and the nature of work on the ground may seem unchanged (ie outreach programme targeting sex workers and female migrants), the layers of contractual relationship and public management techniques of standardization and performance auditing reveal the institutionalization of the dominant trafficking discourse as well as the complex and precarious nature of these alliances.

One example is YMKK (Yayasan Mitra Kesehatan dan Kemanusiaan), an NGO that shifted the focus of its work from HIV prevention and reproductive health to trafficking in Indonesia. In practice, this new remit meant 'adding questions about whether the woman being interviewed during outreach work has been "trafficked" and if she wants to leave the place she is working, usually a place of prostitution' (Lindquist and Piper 2007: 149). The information collected by outreach workers through a standard questionnaire is turned over to data-entry staff in order to compile reports that are presented to donors as a basis for evaluating their work. As Lindquist and Piper (2007: 150–151) pointed out, anti-trafficking alliances between YMKK and other organizations are fraught with difficulties and dilemmas:

Clearly short-term and long-term goals are potentially in conflict, as the concern with finding victims stands in opposition to NGOs' aim to gain the trust of women and pimps in the brothel areas. Although the Program Officer at the Counter-trafficking unit at IOM clearly stated that they were not supporting 'rescues,' it is not clear that their partner NGOs use the same form of reasoning … NGOs who report trafficking victims are reimbursed by IOM once the guidelines have been accepted. In each case it is the head of the counter-trafficking unit at IOM in Jakarta who makes the final decision. It is therefore not possible to send individuals who have not directly been defined as victims by IOM. Even though there are limited funds available, IOM's 'victims of trafficking' project has led to some competition for victims among NGOs on Batam, with NGOs complaining to [the author] that other NGOs were 'taking' victims in their target areas.

Similarly, in Nepal, donor assistance in sex trafficking has significantly increased the number of NGOs in the field: an estimated 57 NGOs were said to have been involved in anti-trafficking, even though many were unable to provide any evidence of their anti-trafficking work or what they did with their funds (Kaufman and Crawford 2011). The resulting forms of unaccountable power and consequences of local NGO intervention can be deeply troubling, especially when they are cloaked in the name of protecting women and girls. In Burma, for example, women were forbidden to cross borders in the name of trafficking prevention:

Since 1997, unaccompanied young women between 16 and 25 in Eastern Shan State have been forbidden to travel to the Thai border. … This has limited the rights of young women and placed them further under the control of others. Young women forced to leave home to work in Thailand to support themselves and their families have simply ended up paying more to bribe officials to reach the border. Since 2004, young women in this area have also needed a recommendation letter or permit from the local Myanmar Women's Affairs Federation to travel to the border, supposedly to prevent possible cases of trafficking. In reality, this process has turned into a means for MWAF to extort money. In early 2006, the cost of a MWAF permit was 200,000 Kyat (about $200). (Women's League of Burma 2008: 23–24)

Local NGOs with diverse agendas have been able to claim expert knowledge and expertise in counter-trafficking work and to tap into extensive regional and global networks and professional alliances. In Taiwan, local anti-trafficking NGOs and conservative women's groups with middle-class social disciplinary agendas were able to tap into international NGOs and intergovernmental organizations' networks for 'exchange of skills, information, and advocacy purposes between organizations in the developed countries and those in the developing countries, which quickly and dramatically enhance the effectiveness of local efforts as well as their power of influence … [and] give strength and credibility to local groups' (Ho 2005: 96). In the process, international organizations were able to put pressure on the Taiwan government to reform its national laws and practices in broad areas of children's welfare, thus 'consolidating the "global governance" that the UN is aspiring for' (Ho 2005: 96). At the same time, NGOs that were once deeply localized actors have become transformed into actors aligned with the objectives of global govern-ance. Some may even enter into unexpected alliances with policing bodies, for example border militia, private security, and village-based vigilance groups that monitor women's freedom of movement, leading to deeply divisive and disem-powering consequences.

One example of the emerging novel assemblages in border policing is Maiti Nepal, a local NGO which claimed to have rescued and rehabilitated 'more than 12,000 women and girls' in Nepal through patrolling the border to intercept suspected trafficking victims (<http://www.maitinepal.org>). This organization and its founder have received widespread international attention from Prince Charles, Oprah Win-frey, and the media (CNN 'Hero of the Year' 2010 award), and its work has been featured in a documentary produced in cooperation with International Justice Mission. Here, in the open border between India and Nepal, Nepalese citizens have traditionally been able to travel back and forth without immigration control for family visits, buying and selling goods, conducting religious pilgrimages and so on as a mundane part of their everyday life. But while male migration has been a longstanding and accepted practice in Nepal, female migration is now heavily scrutinized, policed, and stigmatized in the name of trafficking prevention.

In Nepal, Maiti Nepal collaborates with the border police and employs traffick-ing survivors as 'border guards' in surveillance teams that work with border police and private security guards at official border crossing points to observe daily crossings and to intercept women and girls in 'suspicious circumstances' (Crawford 2010). In the name of paternalistic protection, any female crossing the border has to bear the burden of proving that she is not being trafficked. If a woman cannot provide a satisfactory explanation for her travel, she may be intercepted and detained. Indeed, women and girls have been forcibly intercepted and 'rescued' by Maiti Nepal 'border guards' and returned to their villages against their will or institutionalized in 'transit homes' or 'care homes' for an indefinite period:

[T]rafficking is determined from conflicting or hesitant answers being given by the 'suspects' (adult women as well as minors) to the NGO workers and police. For example, if a group of three girls are crossing together and they all give conflicting accounts of what they are doing, then they may be detained on suspicion of trafficking. This is a common sense strategy, but it has never been systematically evaluated to assess its accuracy. While recogniz-ing a well-intentioned desire to protect women's rights, the present ad hoc system could possibly limit a person's freedom or right to mobility. This is particularly the case with respect to adult women. NGO workers who were interviewed for this report noted that women are sometimes 'very angry' and ask, 'Why have we been stopped?' Some women in the transit homes need to be 'convinced' that they were about to be trafficked. (Evans and Bhattari 2000: 22)

Border interceptions of this kind are predicated on particular gender stereotypes that identify women and girls as inherently vulnerable and unable to interrogate and deflect the deception of traffickers. Border policing efforts—and information campaigns for trafficking prevention in general—target particular at-risk population groups (ie women) in countries of origin and employ messages that discourage migration, with the aim of convincing aspiring female migrants of the dangers of sexual exploitation and abuse abroad. The net results have been to decrease viable migration options for women, by enabling Southern state and non-state actors to increase measures to control and deter the movement of female migrants. Indeed, a gender-specific ban on migration (eg banning Nepali women to emigrate for work in the Gulf states) has been justified in the name of trafficking prevention. But rather than reduce the problem of exploitation, such movement restrictions have brought troubling consequences. They tend to reduce whatever oversight and protection women might have had as legal migrants and push them into the hands of more organized criminal groups, more dangerous routes (eg travelling to the Gulf states via India or Bangladesh), and more vulnerable situations (Sanghera and Kapur 2000). In this context, what may seem to be a secure border from the point of view of the border police and NGOs may in fact be a space of insecurity for the local population (especially girls and women) and a stimulus for further criminalization and securitization.

Conclusion

The contemporary discourses of trafficking control have been dominated by anxieties about unwanted migratory flows from the global South to the North and constructed on problematic assumptions about 'at risk' groups and 'success' in intervention. While many scholars have examined state-centred responses to trafficking within the law-and-order and immigration control frameworks, there has been relatively little scrutiny of the role that a wide range of non-state actors, NGOs, private organizations, and international agencies now play in the control of cross-border mobility of human subjects. As we have seen, the scale, depth, and forms of the connections between metropolitan and borderland areas and between state and non-state actors have gone through significant expansion and transformation. Border policing in Asia is important because it illustrates current global trends of the managerialization of borders, securitization of international assistance, and the meshing of border control and development aid in particularly stark terms. Clearly, the schemes, programme initiatives, and networks of aid under the remit of 'stopping the traffic' in the South have been largely driven by a reworking of international power and new technologies for governing at a distance, notably through a reformulation of borders as a problem of management, dissemination of norms and standards through transnational and donor agencies, and the spread of new public management techniques. Furthermore, the alliances between local NGOs and other non-state actors in counter-trafficking work make up what can be described as novel assemblages in border policing. Through creating profiles of suspicious persons and behaviour, enforcing gender norms of social discipline, and intercepting and immobilizing migrants in their countries of origin, these novel assemblages in border policing are at the heart of the new geographies of exclusion in a divided global order.

So, how can these critical insights into trafficking control and border policing in the South inform a global criminology of (im)mobility? A study of these emergent forms of border management within the extended policing borderland illuminates the configurations and contestations of power within the emerging system of global governance of migrations and mobilities. As Samers (2004: 20) argues, the 're-scaling of control to third countries is a way to shift the less palatable (and less easily legitimated) dimensions of border and visa control onto third countries where legitimacy may be less of an issue'. Third countries which lack strong and established sovereignty may be of particular theoretical interest to criminologists and social theorists 'by offering a springboard for reflection on the nature of the state globally ... under a general trend towards waning sovereignty' (Aas 2012: 15); they may, so to speak, be at the forefront of developments within a global polity of new hierarchies among states and between states and non-state actors that governmentality scholars have been describing (see, for example, Neumann and Sending 2010).

Seen in this light, the global borderlands constitute an important site for constructing theoretical accounts which diverge from the Western notions of statehood and sovereign modes of governing and examining cases where a state's ability to 'ultimately call the shots' on its territory is challenged by non-state and trans-state actors and by neo-liberal economic imperatives (Aas 2012: 16). One important dimension in future criminological work on the making of borders, therefore, lies in the study of the varied modes of governing, the meshing of border management and development aid in the global web of power relations, and the hierarchies of mobility and access to citizenship not only in countries of destination but also in countries of origin. Through exposing the contradictions and consequences of policing 'at a distance', we can begin to go beyond the state-oriented trafficking control discourse, to interrogate the norms and forms and power configurations of global political order, and to reveal the realities of border policing in settings outside criminology's traditional geographical boundaries.

References

Aas, K.F. (2012) '"The Earth is One but the World is Not": Criminological Theory and its Geopolitical Divisions', *Theoretical Criminology* 16(1): 5.

Aas, K.F. (2011a) 'Visions of Global Control: Cosmopolitan Aspirations in a World of Friction' in M. Bosworth and C. Hoyle, *What is Criminology?* Oxford: Oxford University Press.

Aas, K.F. (2011b) '"Crimmigrant" Bodies and Bona Fide Travelers: Surveillance, Citizenship and Global Governance', *Theoretical Criminology* 15(3): 331.

Agozino, B. (2003) *Counter-Colonial Criminology: A Critique of Imperialist Reason.* London: Pluto.

Allred, K.J. (2006) *Combating Human Trafficking*, NATO Review, Summer 2006 <http://www.nato.int/docu/review/2006/issue2/english/analysis.html>.

Anderson, B. (2007) 'Motherhood, Apple Pie and Slavery: Reflections on Trafficking Debates', Centre on Migration, Policy and Society, Working Paper No 48. Oxford: University of Oxford.

Anderson, M. and Bigo, D. (2002) 'What are EU Frontiers for and What Do They Mean?', in K. Groenendijk, E. Guild and P. Minderhoud, *In Search of Europe's Borders*. The Hague: Kluwer Law International.

Andreas, P. and Nadelmann, E. (2006) *Policing the Globe—Criminalization and Crime Control in International Relations*. New York: Oxford University Press.

Andrijasevic, R. and Walters, W. (2010) 'The International Organization for Migration and the International Government of Borders', *Environment and Planning Digest: Society and Space* 28(6): 977.

Aradau, C. (2004) 'The Perverse Politics of Four-letter Words: Risk and Pity in the Securitisation of Human Trafficking', *Millennium—Journal of International Studies* 33(2): 251.

Bales, K. (2005) *Understanding Global Slavery*. Berkeley: University of California Press.

Bigo, D. (2008) 'Globalized (in)Security: the Field and the Ban-opticon', in D. Bigo and A. Tsoukala, *Terror, Insecurity and Liberty. Illiberal practices of liberal regimes after 9/11*. New York: Routledge.

Bigo, D. and Guild, E. (2005) 'Policing in the Name of Freedom', in D. Bigo and E. Guild, *Controlling Frontiers. Free Movement into and within Europe*. Aldershot: Ashgate.

Bosworth, M. and Guild, M. (2008) 'Governing through Migration Control: Security and Citizenship in Britain', *British Journal of Criminology* 48: 703.

Chemonics International (2009) *USAID Anti-Trafficking in Persons Programs in Asia: A Synthesis* <http://pdf.usaid.gov/pdf_docs/PDACT220.pdf>.

Chen, K.H. (2010) 'Asia as Method—Overcoming the Present Conditions of Knowledge Production', in K.H. Chen, *Asia as Method. Toward Deimperialization*. Durham: Duke University Press.

Clarke, G. (1998) *The Politics of NGOs in South-East Asia*. London: Routledge.

Connell, R. (2006) 'Northern Theory: The Political Geography of General Social Theory', *Theoretical Sociology* 35: 237.

Crawford, M. (2010) *Sex Trafficking in South Asia*. London: Routledge.

Cunneen, C. (2011) 'Postcolonial Perspectives for Criminology', in M. Bosworth and C. Hoyle, *What is Criminology?* Oxford: Oxford University Press.

Cunnington, P. and Hung, S. (2009) United Nations Inter-Agency Project in Human Trafficking in the Greater Mekong Sub-Region, Phase III (2007–2010), Mid-Term Evaluation Report—Executive Summary, UNIAP (<http://www.no-trafficking.org>).

Czerniecka, K. and Heathershaw, J. (2010) 'Security Assistance and Border Management', in A. Warkotsch, *The European Union and Central Asia*. London: Routledge.

Doezema, J. (2000) 'Loose Women or Lost Women? The Re-emergence of the Myth of White Slavery in Contemporary Discourses of Trafficking in Women', *Gender Issues* 18 (1): 23.

Duffield, M. (2001) 'Governing the Borderlands: Decoding the Power of Aid', *Disasters* 25(4): 308.

European Union Council (2002) *Proposal for a comprehensive plan to combat illegal immigration and trafficking of human beings* <http://europa.eu/legislation_summaries/other/l33191b_en.htm>.

Europol (2008) *Trafficking in human beings in the European Union—A Europol perspective*. Serious Crime Overview Factsheet. The Hague: Europol <http://www.europol.europa.eu.>.

Evans, C. and Bhattari, P. (2000) *A Comparative Analysis of Anti-trafficking Intervention Approaches in Nepal*. Kathmandu: Asia Foundation and Population Council.

Gavrilis, G. (2009) 'Beyond the Border Management Programme for Central Asia (BOMCA)', EUCAM Policy Brief No 10, EU-Central Asia Monitoring, November.

Gerard, A. and Pickering, S. (2012) 'The Crime and Punishment of Somali Women's Extralegal Arrival in Malta', *British Journal of Criminology* 52(3): 514.

Global Alliance Against Traffic in Women (2007) *Collateral Damage: The Impact of Anti-Trafficking Measures on Human Rights around the World*. Bangkok: GAATW.

Green, P. and Grewcock, M. (2002) 'The War against Illegal Immigration: State Crime and the Construction of a European Identity', *Current Issues in Criminal Justice* 14(1): 87.

Grewcock, M. (2007) 'Shooting the Passenger: Australia's War on Illicit Migrants', in M. Lee, *Human Trafficking*. Cullompton: Willan.

Guiraudon, V. (2002) 'Before the EU Border: Remote Control of the "Huddled Masses"', in K. Groenendijk, E. Guild, and P. Minderhoud, *In Search of Europe's Borders*. The Hague: Kluwer Law International.

HM Government (2011) *Human Trafficking: The Government's Strategy*. London: Home Office <https://www.gov.uk/government/publications/human-trafficking-strategy>.

Ho, J. (2005) 'From Anti-trafficking to Social Discipline: Or, the Changing Role of "Women's" NGOs in Taiwan', in K. Kempadoo, *Trafficking and Prostitution Reconsidered. New Perspectives on Migration, Sex Work, and Human Rights*. Boulder, CO: Paradigm Publishers.

Huysmans, J. (2006) *The Politics of Protection: Sites of Insecurity and Political Agency*. London: Routledge.

International Organisation of Migration (2009) *ASEAN and Trafficking in Persons—Using Data as a Tool to Combat Trafficking in Persons*. Geneva: IOM.

Kaufman, M. and Crawford, M. (2011) 'Sex Trafficking in Nepal: A Review of Intervention and Prevention Programs', *Violence Against Women* 17(5): 651.

Keck, M.C. and Sikkink, K. (1998) *Activists Beyond Borders: Advocacy Networks in International Politics*. Ithaca, NY: Cornell University Press.

Keire, M. (2001) 'The Vice Trust: A Reinterpretation of the White Slavery Scare in the United States, 1907–1917', *Journal of Social History* 35(1): 5.

Kempadoo, K. (2007) 'The War on Human Trafficking in the Caribbean', *Race and Class* 49: 79.

Kempadoo, K. (2005a) 'Victims and Agents of Crime—the New Crusade against Trafficking', in J. Sudbury, *Global Lockdown*. New York: Routledge.

Kempadoo, K. (ed) (2005b) *Trafficking and Prostitution Reconsidered. New Perspectives on Migration, Sex Work, and Human Rights*. Boulder, CO: Paradigm Publishers.

Lee, M. (2011) *Trafficking and Global Crime Control*. London: Routledge.

Lewis, D. and Wallace, T. (2000) 'Introduction', in D. Lewis and T. Wallace, *New Roles and Relevance. Development NGOs and the Challenge of Change*. Bloomfield, Connecticut: Kumarian Press.

Lindquist, J. (2004) 'Putting Transnational Activism in its Place. HIV/AIDS in the Indonesian-Malaysia-Singapore Growth Triangle and Beyond', in N. Piper and A. Uhlin, *Transnational Activism in Asia. Problems of Power and Democracy*. London: Routledge.

Lindquist, J. and Piper, N. (2007) 'From HIV Prevention to Counter-trafficking: Discursive Shifts and Institutional Continuities in South-East Asia', in M. Lee, *Human Trafficking*. Cullompton: Willan.

Megoran, N., Raballand, G. et al (2005) 'Performance, Representation and the Economics of Border Control in Uzbekistan', *Geopolitics* 10: 712.

Miers, S. (2003) *Slavery in the Twentieth Century. The Evolution of a Global Problem*. Walnut Creek, CA: Alta Mira Press.

Mountz, A. (2010) *Seeking Asylum: Human Smuggling and Bureaucracy at the Border*. Minneapolis: University of Minnesota Press.

Nadelmann, E. (1990) 'Global Prohibition Regimes: The Evolution of Norms in International Society', *International Organization* 44: 479.

Neumann, I. and Sending, O.J. (2010) *Governing the Global Polity. Practice, Mentality, Rationality*. Ann Arbor, MI: University of Michigan Press.

Pickering, S. (2006) 'Border Narratives', in S. Pickering and L. Weber, *Borders, Mobility and Technologies of Control*. Dordrecht: Springer.

Pickering, S. (2004) 'Border Terror: Policing, Forced Migration and Terrorism', *Global Change, Peace and Security* 16(3): 211.

Pickering, S. and Gard, M. (2004) 'Everybody's Business: The Privatisation of Women's Imprisonment', in S. Pickering and C. Lambert, *Global Issues, Women and Justice*. Sydney: Federation Press/Institute of Criminology Monograph Series.

Pickering, S. and Weber, L. (eds) (2006) *Borders, Mobility and Technologies of Control*. Dordrecht: Springer.

Piper, N. (2005) 'A Problem by a Different Name? A Review of Research on Trafficking in South-East Asia and Oceania', *International Migration* 43(1/2): 203.

Salter, M. and Zureik, E. (eds) (2005) *Global Policing and Surveillance: Borders, Security, Identity*. Cullompton: Willan.

Samers, M. (2004) 'An Emerging Geopolitics of Illegal Immigration in the European Union', *European Journal of Migration and Law* 6(1): 27.

Sanghera, J. and Kapur, R. (2000) *An Assessment of Laws and Policies for the Prevention and Control of Trafficking in Nepal*. New Delhi: Asia Foundation, Nepal and Population Council.

Sassen, S. (2008) 'Neither Global nor National: Novel Assemblages of Territory, Authority and Rights', *Ethics and Global Politics* 1: 61.

Sassen, S. (2002) 'Women's Burden: Counter-geographies of Globalization and the Feminization of Survival', *Nordic Journal of International Law* 71: 255.

Scheper-Hughes, N. (2001) 'Commodity Fetishism in Organs Trafficking', *Body and Society* 7(2–3): 31.

Segrave, M., Milivojevic, S. et al (2009) *Sex Trafficking—International Context and Response*. Cullompton: Willan.

Stumpf, J. (2006) 'The Crimmigration Crisis: Immigrants, Crime and Sovereign Power', Bepress Legal Series. Working Paper 1635 <http://law.bepress.com/expresso/eps/1635>.

US Department of State (2009) Memorandum of Justification Consistent With the Trafficking Victims Protection Act of 2000, Regarding Determinations With Respect to 'Tier 3' Countries. Washington DC: US Department of State <http://www.state.gov/j/tip/rls/other/2009/129593.htm>.

United Nations Interregional Crime and Justice Research Institute (1999) 'New Frontiers of Crime: Trafficking in Human Beings and New Forms of Slavery'. Verona: 26–29 October.

United Nations Office on Drugs and Crime (2009) *Global Report on Trafficking in Persons*. Geneva: UNODC.

Walters, W. (2011) 'Foucault and Frontiers: Notes on the Birth of the Humanitarian Border', in U. Bröckling, S. Krasmann, and T. Lemke, *Governmentality: Current Issues and Future Challenges*. New York: Routledge.

Welch, M. (2010) 'Jailing in Post-9/11 America: The Convergence of Terror, Crime, and Immigration Control', in S. Stojkovic, *Managing Special Populations in Jails and Prisons*. Kingston, NJ: Civic Research Institute.

Women's League of Burma (2008) *In the Shadow of the Junta—CEDAW Shadow Report.* Chiang Mai, Women's League of Burma <http://womenofburma.org/Report/IntheShadow-Junta-CEDAW2008.pdf>.

Wong, D. (2005) 'The Rumor of Trafficking', in W.V. Schendel and I. Abraham, *Illicit Flows and Criminal Things—States, Borders, and the Other Side of Globalization.* Bloomington, IN: Indiana University Press.

Wyler, L.S. and Siskin, A. (2010) *Trafficking in Persons: U.S. Policy and Issues for Congress,* US Congressional Research Service, CRS Report for Congress <http://fpc.state.gov/documents/organization/147256.pdf>.

PART III

IMPRISONMENT

8

Can Immigration Detention Centres be Legitimate? Understanding Confinement in a Global World

Mary Bosworth[1]

Does it really do any justice really, being here? (Pause). I'd like to say that detention maybe eases society of a bit of cost, but then I think there's more people that shouldn't be in this country that are on the outside than there are detained ... I think that it just comes down to how much people that shouldn't be in this country cost the country. I think that's the purpose. I could see why foreign nationals should be locked up if they've done a crime, and sent back to their country. But as for the poor person who comes over to make his, you know, to try and make his life better or to get educated, I don't think it does a great deal for the country, detaining people really. (Alana, DCO, TH)[2]

Introduction

Almost 20 years ago Richard Sparks (1994) asked 'Can prisons be legitimate?' At that time prisons in England and Wales were facing a series of challenges. Rocked by a wave of riots, they had been blamed for failing to secure order or justice (Woolf 1990). The prison service had been reorganized as a semi-autonomous agency

[1] I gratefully acknowledge the assistance of Blerina Kellezi with whom I worked in gathering the interview material on which this chapter draws. I would also like to thank Katja Aas, Hindpal Singh Bhui, Richard and Michal Bosworth, Matt Gibney, Emma Kaufman, Ambrose Lee, Arjen Leerkes, and Ian Loader, for their feedback on an earlier draft. A paper from that draft was presented at the Borders of Punishment conference on 20 April 2012 at the Centre for Criminology at the University of Oxford and benefited from comments I received. The research was funded by a British Academy Research Development Award, the Nuffield Foundation, and by the Oxford University Press John Fell Fund. I am grateful to Alan Kittle, formerly Head of the Returns Directorate at the UK Border Agency (UKBA), for granting me research access and to all of the custodial and UKBA staff and detainees who participated in the project.
[2] All respondents have been anonymized appearing with a pseudonym, their nationality or, in the case of staff, their officer grade, and the centre where the interview was conducted. The centres are abbreviated: TH = IRC Tinsley House; CB = IRC Colnbrook; BH = IRC Brook House; YW = IRC Yarl's Wood; and CH = IRC Campsfield House.

within the Home Office and had acquired a new director-general from the business sector. The government had announced its intention to privatize a series of new penal establishments and the era of new public management had begun.

This chapter starts with a similar question, posed under equivalent conditions of institutional and political disarray: can immigration detention centres be legitimate? Whereas Sparks, and others who followed him (for example Sparks, Bottoms, and Hay 1996; Liebling 2004; Crewe 2009), argued that penal power in its application and its effect is constrained by the need to be legitimate, the power of the state in detention seems almost unfettered. There is no automatic judicial oversight of the decision to detain and no statutory limit on the period for which a person can be held. Despite the fact that over one-third of detainees stay for longer than a month and six per cent have been held for more than a year (Home Office 2012), there is no obvious purpose of detention that inheres in the institution, leaving it hard to justify developing any particular regime or treatment programmes for these people. The message seems clear: detainees are going to be deported; they are not coming back; and the UK state is not responsible for preparing them to return to their country of origin.

In practice, of course, matters are more complex. Power does not flow entirely without check. Immigration removal centres (IRCs) are not, as some would argue, sites of 'bare life' or modern iterations of the Camp (Agamben 2005; De Genova 2010; Fassin 2011). Senior management and individual custody officers often go out of their way to assist—bringing specific food and cultural items for religious holidays, inviting in local charities, and, in one establishment at least, setting up an arrangement with a local credit union to help detainees access their savings that were otherwise unobtainable.[3] The people within detention centres are neither abject nor unrecognizable. Many are long-term UK residents, some of whom attended school in Britain and have family members here as well. Despite the emphasis on removal and deportation, nearly one-third of the population is released each year into the community either on temporary admission by the UKBA or bailed by an immigration judge. Detention centres are marked by resistance and creativity (Bosworth 2012) as well as by the vulnerability of their residents. They are sites where exclusionary migration policies clash with the long history of immigration to the United Kingdom and its resultant diversity.

Part of the challenge in understanding IRCs—and at least one reason why criminological accounts of legitimacy may falter—relates to this inconsistency in the expression and nature of state power. As sites of border control, the state is at the same time more intrusive and, paradoxically, sometimes impotent. Many of the administrative goals of detention—documentation, deportation, or removal[4]— require the agreement of another sovereign power (see Aas, Chapter 1 in this

---

[3] IRC Yarl's Wood works with the Bedford Credit Union to help detainees transfer funds from savings accounts in banks that require them to present their savings book in person to a cashier.

[4] Although these last two have the same effect of forcible ejection from the UK and a time restriction on future return, legally they are different categories. Usually ex-prisoners are deported whereas visa overstayers or failed asylum seekers are removed.

volume).[5] At the more local level, detainees may not be able to avoid deportation indefinitely, but they can, in quite banal ways, resist it for some time. They may destroy their documents or provide a false name, address, or nationality—simple acts which make it taxing for the state to prove their identity and obtain travel documents, both of which are necessary for deportation.

In short, IRCs reveal how, under conditions of mass mobility, state power is both enhanced and, simultaneously, diminished. The question that then arises is whether the notion of 'legitimacy', with its intellectual roots in liberal communitarian philosophy, is still useful as a tool either of understanding or critique. Does this concept, which assumes a 'congruence between a given system of power and the beliefs, values, and expectations that provide it justification' (Beetham 1991: 11), work in an unbounded and mobile world? On what basis would the legitimacy be determined of an institution like an IRC that transcends the sovereign state in which it is located? Who would have a say, when the community in detention (not to mention those who are affected by their custody) are not fellows of a single political community (Fraser 2007)? How would they register their views and by what means would we recognize them as such?

Such questions are part of a broader debate about whether the liberal political project extends to foreigners (Honig 2001; Benhabib 2004, 2006; Bosniak 2006; Fraser 2007, 2008; see also Gibney, Chapter 12 in this volume). In this chapter I explore matters more narrowly, documenting how staff and detainees make sense of immigration detention. Drawing on 18 months of fieldwork across five British IRCs,[6] I find considerable confusion and ambivalence in their testimonies and a striking reliance on the prison to make sense of where they are and what they are doing. Their accounts unsurprisingly reveal an extensive legitimacy deficit facing detention. However, this deficit does not lead to the crises that criminological scholarship would lead us to expect, suggesting perhaps that we need a new critical vocabulary for understanding the power in and of such places.

Immigration Detention: An Overview

Purpose-built detention centres have existed in the United Kingdom since the Harmondsworth Immigration Detention Unit opened with 40 beds adjacent to London's Heathrow Airport in 1970. At that time, Harmondsworth housed Commonwealth citizens denied entry at the border who were given in-country right of appeal by the Immigrant Appeals Act 1969. Much has changed since then.

---

[5] Detainees and UKBA staff regularly reported India and China being particularly slow in this regard.

[6] Over this time, together with Dr Blerina Kellezi, I spent more than 1,600 hours in the field. Using mixed methods, I designed and we administered a survey to around 200 detainees, informally interviewing and chatting with many more. We also conducted 80 structured interviews with staff. Our mixed methods have produced a mass of data, from which various themes are emerging. This chapter concentrates on just a handful. The overall project is written up in detail elsewhere (Bosworth and Kellezi 2012, 2013a, 2013b; Bosworth 2012, 2014, forthcoming).

Most obviously, the immigration detention system is significantly larger; from the original 40 beds in a single establishment, there are now 10 centres (11 if we include the 'pre-departure accommodation' used for families) holding between 200 and 615 people each. Detainees may also be kept in prison post-sentence, or for up to five days in a police cell or a short-term holding facility (STHF).[7] In total, 3,000 men and women, as well as a handful of children, are confined in IRCs and STHFs, while as many as 800 ex-prisoners remain in prison after their sentence ends (Vine 2011: 19). There are no available statistics for those in police custody, nor is there consistency in the time detainees are held. Although the duration of their detention should be restricted by the likelihood of deportation, the varying period for which people are confined suggests that this legal requirement functions haphazardly. While the majority of detainees are removed, deported, or released within six months, a growing number are held for much longer (Phelps 2009; Home Office 2012).

IRCs confine a diverse mix of people. As a designated fast-track site,[8] Harmondsworth still contains some recent arrivals whose claims are being assessed, though today they identify as asylum seekers rather than as visitors or prospective workers. It also holds ex-prisoners, visa-overstayers, the undocumented, and those whose asylum claim has been rejected. In all IRCs, some detainees are long-term British residents with friends and family members in the local community. Others have just arrived. The primary factor such people have in common is their lack of British citizenship. Most of them—around 90 per cent—are adult men.

The immigration system itself, armed with its tribunals, judges, and caseworkers, has also grown in size, in response to numerous pieces of immigration and asylum legislation (Thomas 2011; Wilsher 2011). Matters that used to be considered purely administrative—overstaying or working without a visa—have been criminalized (Aliverti 2013), while any non-EEA national sentenced to more than 12 months in prison faces mandatory deportation. All foreigners with a criminal record of any sort can be considered for deportation (Bosworth 2011b; see Gibney, Chapter 12 in this volume).

Some key elements, however, have remained constant. As Harmondsworth was in 1970, most detention centres today are contracted out to the private sector. Indeed, the same company—then called Securicor, now known as G4S—still runs two of them: Tinsley House and Brook House, as well as Cedars, the institution for families. So, too, the lingering effects of empire remain visible in the disproportionate numbers of Commonwealth citizens held under Immigration Act powers. although the population in detention is drawn from all over the world, those

---

[7] Others may also be detained in hospital or, if under 18, post-sentence in a juvenile prison.

[8] For a small number of individuals, removal centres enable the state to ascertain people's identity or to rule on their asylum claim. Since March 2000 the UK has operated a fast-track asylum process. The first processing centre was Oakington, which has since closed. From 2003 a detained fast-track process began at Harmondsworth for men and, in 2005, at Yarl's Wood for women. Men on the fast track may also be held in Colnbrook and Campsfield House. Yarl's Wood and Harmondsworth both include an Asylum and Immigration Tribunal adjacent to the detention accommodation, where such cases are heard and determined, usually within a matter of weeks. (For more details, see Refugee Council 2007.)

from former British colonies make up the majority (Bosworth 2012; Kaufman and Bosworth 2013).[9]

Justifying Detention

In terms of government policy, IRCs are considered a necessary part of border control—both a right and an obligation of the British state. For critics of detention, however, matters are not so clear. IRCs, they point out, cause long-term psychological distress (Fazel et al 2011), are often used arbitrarily, and are expensive and inefficient. There is little evidence that removal centres deter migration, and plenty of proof that they cause considerable damage. Some argue that they should be abolished altogether, while others seek to cap the period for which an individual may be detained (Phelps 2009).

Detainees, though rarely seen or heard in either account, are also critical of removal centres. Over the past 10 years in the United Kingdom they have burned to the ground parts of Campsfield House, Yarl's Wood, and Harmondsworth (twice), while seriously damaging sections of Brook House. There have been a number of high-profile hunger strikes as well as a handful of suicides and at least one large-scale escape (from Campsfield).[10] Although the number of individuals seeking asylum in the United Kingdom has dropped from its peak in the 1990s, estimates of those living in the community without documents remain high (Global Detention Project 2011). The ongoing crisis throughout the Middle East, an area of the world with a legacy of British formal and informal empire, has generated new waves of mass migration, at least some of whom seek a new life in Britain.

Somewhat unexpectedly, given the vociferous debate that surrounds them, it is difficult to find a clear articulation of the official purpose of these policies There is no statutorily defined goal of detention, nor do the 2001 Detention Centre Rules provide much detail, stating instead that the purpose of detention is 'to provide for the secure but humane accommodation of detained persons' (para 3(1)). Unlike other agencies of government, the part of the UKBA with oversight of the detention centres has no official statement of purpose, 'mission', or 'values', opting instead, at least for a time, for a slogan: 'detain, protect, remove'.[11] Most matters are dealt with administratively, set out in the 2001 Rules, the 2003 Operating Standards, and a small number of Detention Service Orders (Bosworth 2007). Although such documents provide useful guidelines and benchmarks for administering detention

---

[9] In March 2011, for instance, the largest population in detention was from Pakistan followed by India, China, Nigeria, Afghanistan, and Bangladesh.

[10] According to one former centre manager, detainees frequently try to escape and sometimes succeed. Unlike prisoners, however, such events are rarely noted in the national press unless they involve a significant number.

[11] At the time of writing, the UKBA is undergoing another structural reorganization. IRCs now fall under the purview of the Returns Directorate, Crime and Enforcement Team.

centres, they give little sense of the nature or purpose of such places.[12] For that information, we need to look inside.

Life in Detention

Although most detainees speak some English, they find it difficult to read documentation relating to their case or understand the signs around the removal centres advertising courses or events. Many are confused about why they are detained and nobody knows how long they will be there. Even with the widespread availability of mobile phones, not everyone is able to maintain contact with their families and, though centres arrange family-day visits, few take this option. Detainees are often unable to obtain an effective immigration solicitor. Fewer and fewer are entitled to legal aid. Many are frustrated by the limited amount of paid work and education in detention, particularly if they have served a prison sentence elsewhere during which they have taken advantage of a wide range of courses and programmes. Health care remains a source of great anxiety (HMIP 2011; Bosworth and Kellezi 2012, 2013a).

Compounding matters, life in detention, at least in terms of the formal provision of activities, is limited. IRCs offer very little to do, keeping people in idleness, preparing them neither for return nor release. There is almost no paid work other than cleaning or serving food. In each centre I visited a core group of detainees were actively involved in art and craft classes and the gym, but they were the exception. Most detainees while away their time in their rooms watching television or sleeping. Steve explained:

I go late night asleep, yeah, watch the telly till three o'clock. Get up half past eleven, that's half the day gone. Then I have my food, then I just go in the library, read every single paper. Then go on internet for hour or so. And that's about it. And chat on the phone. (Pakistan BH)

Unsurprisingly, many detainees complained of being bored. Others, however, felt that additional options would make little difference to them. 'I cannot do anything each day', Stone commented, 'because am just thinking about my [immigration] case' (Sri Lanka CH). Such concerns, they recognized, made it hard to forge a united 'inmate community' familiar to prison sociologists (Sykes 1958; Sparks, Bottoms, and Hay 1996; Crewe 2009). 'Immigration issues fill our minds', Storm pointed out, 'so each man is alone' (Eritrea CH).

Matters are made worse by a lack of clarity over the reason for detention. Officially, foreigners are confined to expedite their documentation, removal, and/ or deportation. Whereas the UKBA presents this facilitation in utilitarian and bureaucratic terms, detainees frequently describe their detention as punitive and unexpected (see also Leerkes and Broeders 2010). Some were arrested when they reported as normal to the UKBA, adhering to the terms of their asylum case. Others were seized when the immigration authorities were looking for someone else. Those who came from prison had finished their sentence and were not always

---

[12] According to a number of UKBA and custodial staff I interviewed, they may also come into conflict with contractual arrangements, particularly if the contract in question is old.

aware that they were subject to deportation proceedings. Even those who acknowledged that detention had been a known risk, given their lack of immigration status,
challenged the length of their confinement, their conditions, or its efficacy: 'I will
just come back', Samir announced. 'Algeria is close to Europe' (Algeria CB).

In trying to make sense of where they were, women and men looked for suitable
comparisons. Some turned to the language of slavery: 'why it always got to be black
people locked up?', Lexi demanded angrily (Jamaica YW). In this view, detainees
were critical of the interdependence between the state and the private custodial
companies, and the irony that they had been unable to work legally in the community, but were expected to serve food or clean in the detention centre. More
commonly, in response to their material environment, staff and detainees compared
their experiences in detention to prison. Designed with the logic of prison architecture, or reused former penal institutions, they are run by staff who work for the same
companies that incarcerate offenders. How the institutions measured up, however,
was far from consistent.

For some, they were effectively the same. Housed together in institutions
redolent of penal power, with cells, uniformed staff, and razor wire fences, it is
no surprise to hear the constant refrain, 'I feel like I am in prison', across all IRCs.
Yet, for others, being in prison would have been preferable. Steve explained:

In the prison, everybody know their bird, they're doing their things, we don't talk about it.
Everybody got their work, you understand. Everybody put their head down. Somebody
[with] long bird, they know they're staying in the prison. You understand—you know
what your date coming and you're going home. Detention centre, like you think
'What's happening to me? When I gonna go home?' [There] is no fixed time limit or
anything … thing drags on and on and on. (Pakistan BH)

As Steve appreciates, prisons, however painfully, offer a predictable life. They are,
for him at least, recognizable in their form and content.

Yet, there were some good things about detention, he said: 'Like you out at half
past six till half past eight in the evening. And you have all the fax, internet. You can
phone, and your kids can send you picture on your email address, all that.' Another
man, who had served a prison sentence 'behind the door' in an overcrowded
London prison (ie who had been locked in his cell 23 hours a day, seven days a
week) agreed. Life in Brook House was much easier, Turis claimed: 'It is better
here, like they are not lock everyday, a complete hours lock. That's the difference
and another difference is that here is use the mobile and communication is a bit
better than prison' (Pakistan BH). Whatever their opinion of detention, each of
these men relied on a comparison with the prison to understand their confinement
(Kaufman and Bosworth 2013). The detention centre, they suggest, makes no
sense without the prison.

Such a view recurs in the staff interviews. Custody officers are, if anything, even
less clear about where they are working and what their jobs entail. Few of those
I interviewed had sought a career in detention. Most had simply stumbled into the
work due to redundancy or boredom with their previous employment. They came
from a range of occupations including retail, factory, and the armed forces. On a few
occasions they had not realized what they were applying for, mistakenly thinking they

were applying for a job in another part of the company. For some, working as a detention custody officer (DCO) was intended to be a launching pad for a better-paid and more secure position in the police or prison service. While others eschewed the prison altogether, both in terms of their own career plan and in relation to removal centres, it was, as with the detainees, always a defining comparator.

Officially, the duties of a DCO are 'to prevent escape, to prevent, deter or report on an unlawful act, to maintain good order and discipline, and to attend to a detainee's well-being' (UKBA 2011). Although this statement emphasizes security, placing 'well-being' last on the list of responsibilities, many officers asserted a different balance of priorities, with one member of the senior management team at Yarl's Wood, Scot, going so far as to claim that 'care is more important than security' (SMT YW). Others, lower down the staff hierarchy, agreed, making it clear that security was not the heart of their job, as they imagined it might be in prison. Landon claimed: 'Those officers who treat them like prisoners don't work. You need to treat them like human beings. What they need is someone to talk to. Talk to them like you would talk to your friends' (DCO TH).[13]

'Our main job', Stan asserted:

is to, you know, support them, giving them an ear hole when they wanna talk, proverbial shoulder to cry on, so it's just being there for them, reassuring them that, you know, this isn't a prison, you know, we're, we're there, as I said, not just to lock doors but to help them. (DCO YW)

In addition to offering such emotional support, Stan explained, officers spend a lot of time engaged in practical assistance, sending faxes, and trying to communicate across languages and cultural divides to an anxious and vulnerable population. In the library, for instance, he describes, there are folders listing:

legal representation, different companies that deal with their type of cases like the immigration and stuff like that, so you know, then they pick out half a dozen or more of them, we fax the correspondence to these people and then we're there to do the communication for them, like they give us a fax, we send it off, when the fax comes through, it goes in their appropriate pigeon hole and when they come into the office and ask if they got any faxes then we, you know, if we got them, then we give them to them, same as any other letters and correspondence they get, we hand them out. ... so yes, support and ... if we can't answer their questions then we find out someone who can. (DCO YW)

On the one hand this representation of the work of a DCO was clearly self-justifying. Who could criticize a custody officer for trying to help? On the other hand, Stan's lengthy account illuminated an important paradox within the centres that generated considerable ambivalence among custodial staff: many detainees seek legal remedy to get out of detention. The individuals who are charged with assisting them in pursuing these remedies are also those who must keep them securely in

---

[13] Though foreign nationals are meant to be 'risk assessed' by the Home Office before being placed in detention, the IRC estate has no official security classification system. Three male establishments, Harmondsworth, Colnbrook, and Brook House, are built to 'category B' prison security standards, and so tend to house more ex-prisoners than some of the alternative centres.

detention—the DCOs. Under these circumstances, it becomes more understandable why some staff members disagreed with the official emphasis on security, seeking to craft a more nuanced understanding of their labour.

Just as detainees equated themselves to prisoners, many staff compared themselves to prison officers. Generally in this comparison they came up short, complaining that their pay and prestige were lower and their job more burdensome. Most commonly, and in some tension with their alleged commitment to care, staff frequently complained about the unavailability of formal sanctions. Though, at the time of the research, most IRCs operated with an 'incentives and privileges' scheme, whereby detainees lost access to certain items if they broke detention centre rules, there are no 'adjudications' in IRCs, and no sentences that can be imposed to maintain order. While detainees can be removed from association, they are usually only held in segregation for up to 24 hours. Even then, their removal has to be authorized by the UKBA contract manager; the power of the custody officer rests solely in the demand for punishment, they cannot enforce it. Detainees considered ungovernable are removed to prisons (Kaufman and Bosworth 2013).

On occasion, staff attempted to articulate what their job entailed in terms that were not punitive. According to Roby, who had worked in Yarl's Wood for a decade:

I've always maintained you should never use prison and detention in the same sentence because they're very far removed from each other. You have to treat these people who have committed no crime according to the law with the, the, the dignity that they deserve; it's as simple as that. We, we shouldn't be compared to prison.

As he tried to explain why, however, his reasoning faltered: 'We've got locked doors, we're a secure environment and we've got a big fence around us.' Perhaps, 'that big fence could come down', he wondered, before concluding somewhat inexplicably, 'on the other hand that big fence out there is to stop those people on the outside coming in' (DCO YW).

As with the earlier testimonies from the detainees, staff found it hard to identify a vocabulary for understanding their work and its rationale in terms that were not penal. When asked about this relationship, one senior uniformed member of staff suggested that the distinction between the two institutions (and thus the appeal of the positive comparisons), lay in the prison's common-sense and widely held[14] moral and legal justification: 'I can't say for certain but perhaps in prison there is this underpinning thing, "You've broken the law"', Lela observed, 'whereas here, you know, that's softened' (DCM YW). Whereas criminal law offers a common-sense justification of incarceration, for this woman at least, immigration law lacked such impulse.

Ambivalence about the justification of detention went further. Even in the UKBA, in remarkable contrast to its official rhetoric and policies, staff at high levels in the administration expressed doubt about the legal framework that underpins and justifies such places: 'It's not like they're real offenders', one senior civil servant told me; 'It's just, you know, they might have worked without a

---

[14] Though not undisputed (Mathiesen 2006; Sim 2009).

passport or something'. That such confusion emanates from all levels of the institution, from detainees to DCOs and immigration officers, provides compelling evidence of the legitimacy deficit with which removal centres operate. At the same time, it is not clear that IRCs are in any immediate danger of being closed down or reformed. They are not, in other words, in crisis.

While some suggest that reforms simply await a bigger, more dramatic 'catastrophe', as an ex-IRC manager cynically put it, such an expectation is premised on an assumption that legitimacy matters. The current situation is simply not bad enough; the crisis has not been reached. Yet, what would it take to reach this tipping point? Or is the notion of 'crisis', with its inward gaze on life in detention, a false trail? Whereas prison scholars argue that there is a close relationship between the interior life of the prison and its external legitimacy (Sparks, Bottoms, and Hay 1996; Liebling 2004), this relationship simply is not as clear in detention centres. Not only do many aspects of a person's experience of detention rely on decisions made elsewhere (by the UKBA or other nation states), but, in a system where the vast majority of people without immigration status are not detained, the very justification of removal centres itself is unclear. Either those in detention are a special case for whom only a custodial environment will suffice—and there is no compelling evidence for that claim—or there is a profound gap between the operation of these institutions and their purpose. That gap troubles the assumption inherent in much criminological literature that we can understand what custodial institutions are *for* by examining what they are *like* (Crewe 2009). It also draws into question whether legitimacy is at all essential to the system of immigration detention.

Legitimating Detention

In criminological accounts of prisons,[15] legitimacy is a necessary quality of the state and a concept used to interrogate, critique, and understand power. Methodologically, writers interested in legitimacy draw together analytic and normative questions about the exercise of power while emphasizing the importance of the views and experiences of the subordinate. According to Sparks and Bottoms (2007: 104), legitimacy 'can be studied as a property of social systems but it is also in an important sense their *goal*'. A concern with legitimacy thus directs 'attention to how things work and fail to work. But it should also make us more sharply aware of the gap between things as they are and as they might be' (Sparks and Bottoms 2007: 204).

Conceptualizing penal power as a negotiated settlement between prisoners and staff (as representatives of the state) transformed prison studies, injecting a healthy critique into what was at risk of becoming an exclusively descriptive domain. Yet, notwithstanding its important contributions, this work has always had its limitations. The emphasis on order, as well as the genealogy of the concept of legitimacy that flowed from the studies by Sparks and Bottoms, inadvertently

---

[15] And elsewhere in a related body of literature on policing (eg Sunshine and Tyler 2007).

contributed to a gender-blind approach to penal power that not only rarely featured women but failed to consider how power relations structure and are shaped by matters like race, gender, and citizenship (Bosworth and Kaufman 2012). Similarly, and not unrelated to its lack of engagement with matters of identity, much of the literature assumed a notion of agency where prisoners are able to withhold consent. As Eamonn Carrabine (2005) suggests, to conceive of power as under negotiation may overstate prisoners' agency and overlook other, more banal reasons why people 'obey the law' or follow rules. In Carrabine's view, prisoners may be compliant out of what he terms 'dull compulsion', caught up in the routines and requirements of prison life, unable or unwilling to deviate from these norms, yet not in agreement with them.

There are two main challenges to legitimacy apparent in the detention centre, both of which spring from the question of identity. First, as one ex-IRC centre manager observed, detention centres are places of 'hyper diversity', where there are slim grounds for the shared group membership assumed by those traditions of liberal political theory on which most criminological understanding of legitimacy is premised (Bosworth and Kellezi 2013b). They house foreign women and men, whose cultural beliefs and expectations will, by definition, diverge from those in power, under conditions of great uncertainty. As such, they force us to consider whether our working assumptions about the negotiation of power have assumed some level of (cultural/ethnic or racial) homogeneity. Secondly, the coercive nature of state power is different in detention centres. Not only is it imbricated in and subverted by its dependence on other state actors and NGOs, but it is more absolute. These intersections between power and identity raise questions about detainees' capacity for the agency assumed by much legitimacy literature.

Detainees are governed by a range of persons not all of whom agree on the purpose of their job. Whereas the day-to-day responsibilities of removal centres are contracted out to private companies or the prison service, decisions about immigration matters are made off-site by UKBA 'case owners'.[16] On-site UKBA staff monitor the contract and pass information between the detainees and their case owners. They play no role in decision making. In these places the state has both retreated, governing at a distance through the private companies, and split in two, between internal and off-site immigration agents. Complicating matters further, a range of transnational state and non-state actors play a role in determining the outcome for detainees. 'Power' in detention thus springs from a number of sources, many of which are located not only beyond the removal centre but in another country altogether. Some states, like China and India, are very slow to document their nationals, leading to long-term detention while the wheels of bureaucracy creak forward. Others, like Somalia or the Democratic Republic of Congo, are in no position to identify their citizens. NGOs like the International Organisation of

---

[16] Each UKBA case-owner has responsibility for a number of different case files each of which corresponds to an individual in detention. Current research is being conducted into the decision-making processes of these UKBA employees (Bosworth and Bradford, forthcoming).

Migration (IOM) administer transnational financial incentive schemes to persuade detainees to leave voluntarily and return to their place of birth.[17]

The global reach of the institution and the uncertainty over the completion or outcome of detention raises new questions about how to understand and judge its legitimacy if only by asking: legitimate for whom? As Nancy Fraser testily asserted (2008: 94) in her critique of the literature on legitimacy and governance in political theory, 'Engrossed in disputing the "how" of legitimacy, the contestants apparently felt no necessity to dispute the "who"'. Globalization, she argues, changes the frame and the scale of power and justice as well as how we understand them (see also Aas, Chapter 1 in this volume). In a system designed to determine who may move freely, and to immobilize and eject those who may not, matters of identity are central. To comprehend border control, in other words, we must start with the relationship between identity and the state. In terms of immigration detention, this relationship narrows further to one between identity and carceral power.[18]

The 'hyper diversity' of detention centres raises fundamental questions about the possibilities for 'congruence' in beliefs, values, and expectations inherent in traditional accounts of legitimacy. Basic issues stand in the way of communication and negotiation from varying levels of proficiency in English, high rates of depression among the detainees, and the inconsistent and unpredictable duration of detention. The high levels of depression in the detained population and their exclusion from many of the rights (for example of due process) and protections (for example legal oversight) accorded to citizens raise significant questions about their capacity to act on their own behalf in meaningful fashion. They have very little agency (Bosworth 2011b, 2012; Bosworth and Kellezi 2012).

In Margalit's terms (that are, however ironically, echoed by HM Prison Service), this is not a 'decent' system (Margalit 1999). Holding someone indefinitely in idleness fails to recognize them as fully human beings. Whereas the dignity and self-worth of detainees should be protected by international human rights instruments, detainees find it difficult to appeal to such safeguards (Bosworth 2011b). Their lack of citizenship is compounded by intersections between race and gender that effectively diminish their right to have rights, at least in an everyday sense. For example, some of the men in detention seeking relief under Article 8 of the European Convention on Human Rights, the right to privacy and family life, have to overcome not only practical matters in regards to providing birth certificates and evidence of their intimate relationships, but also racialized assumptions about black men's lack of commitment to their female partners and children. The impact of these views, one man in Campsfield House makes clear, is painful. Sylas, a singer-songwriter from Jamaica, who had overstayed a visitor's visa, came to the attention of the UKBA only after living undocumented in the United Kingdom

---

[17] For more on the role of NGOs in border control, see Walters 2010; and Johansen and Lee, Chapters 14 and 7 respectively in this volume.

[18] The growth of foreign national prisoners across many jurisdictions suggests that citizenship is also a constitutive part of penal power in prisons (Bosworth 2011a; Bosworth and Kaufman 2012; see Melossi and Kaufman, Chapters 15 and 9 respectively in this volume).

for eight years. He was in a long-term relationship with a British woman with whom he had fathered two children. As with many Jamaican immigrants, Sylas's links to Britain did not stop there: 'In this country now, I've a family, he said. I've got granddad, I've aunts, I've uncle, cousins, all that.' Facing imminent and likely permanent separation from these loved ones, Sylas pointed out that his goals were commonplace: 'I want that freedom of speech, our rights, just like any normal family, yeah.' He recognized that his status as a detainee, however, rendered such an outcome unlikely: 'we can't get that' (Jamaica CH).

Like Sylas, women seeking protection are held to gendered expectations about their behaviour in the United Kingdom, even when such beliefs conveniently overlook their prior experiences of gendered violence: 'I was told I didn't have properties here, because I have no children, because I am not married', Nya reported sadly. 'But there are some things I cannot do because of what happened to me' (Uganda YW).

In these legal and institutional encounters, the power of the state is magnified and the individuals' capacity for agency diminished, making it hard to believe that their relationship is, in any meaningful sense, negotiated. Notwithstanding the doubts of individuals within the centres or even in the UKBA, the state, when faced with detained non-citizens, has so much more coercive power at its disposal than it does against its citizenry. Under these circumstances all too often the concerns of legitimacy theorists seem irrelevant.

What does it mean, however, to consider a carceral institution as existing outside the boundaries of 'legitimacy'? Why bother with the term at all? If the injustice is so great, why not simply argue for abolition? Certainly that is one route out of this dilemma. Yet it is not one that has had much success and, indeed, abolition may itself require an engagement with legitimacy in order to make its claim. Why, other than that an institution is unfair, unjust, or illegitimate, would one argue for its closure?

The conceptual difficulty of removal centres is profound, leading to intractable moral and normative questions. We possess no proper vocabulary for understanding, challenging, or reforming them because they have no justification in their own terms. Unlike their constant penal comparator, removal centres are not an end in themselves. They are instead a midway point, or 'no-man's-land' (Barker, Chapter 13 in this volume) between the polity and the globe, a holding zone for those awaiting removal or deportation (on which see Gibney 2008, and Chapter 12 in this volume).

However punitive they may feel, IRCs are not designed to punish. Under conditions of globalization, they do little to deter. While some might argue that, as a group, those without immigration status 'deserve' to be detained, the arbitrary nature of the detention process makes this claim hard to sustain for individuals. In any case, the usual constraints on desert—that a coercive state response is 'proportional' to the action being sanctioned—are eroded in a system that has no upper limit to the duration of detention and in which the nature and extent of the original 'harm' (immigration status) is unclear.

Under these circumstances, the constant comparison with the prison can be better understood as an attempt at legitimation. Unable to grasp the purpose of where they work or are held, staff and detainees turn to the institution with which they are more familiar; the material similarities between prisons and IRCs are such that they do not have to have worked or been held in a prison to make this connection. Such institutional blurring is highly productive. Not only does it inhibit institutional imagination but it casts IRCs as 'hybrid spaces' of sovereign and disciplinary power (Pratt 2005), in which the population is marked out and governed by their precariousness (Butler 2009; see also Weber and Pickering 2011); always, already detainable. Under these conditions, the usual restraints of liberal political power are too often suspended and concerns over legitimacy irrelevant.

Conclusion

For Sparks (1994: 16), the 'conceptual power' of legitimacy 'lies in the connections which it illuminates between the interior life of penal systems, and the social relations that characterize them, and the centrally important "external" issue of the conditions under which it is judged appropriate to impose prison sentences in the first place'. In this view, legitimacy is critical for directing our attention inside prisons by reminding us their external purpose and justification can be undermined by inadequate or unjust actions within them. The legitimacy of prison, Sparks and Bottoms rousingly proclaim, is called into question at every instance 'of brutality in prison, every unwarranted bureaucratic delay, every inedible meal, every arbitrary decision to segregate and transfer without giving clear and well-founded reasons, every petty miscarriage of justice, every futile and inactive period of time' (Sparks and Bottoms 1995: 607).

Immigration detention centres routinely fail to measure up according to this formula. Yet, the poor food, the language barriers, and concerns about health care matter very little relative to the unequal global distribution of security and opportunity, or the family ties people have established in Britain. These are the factors that are far more important causes of people's reluctance to leave and they, for the most part, fit with difficulty into a conceptual framework that assumes that legitimacy inheres in an institution.

In the age of mass mobility it is not possible to stop people from coming to Britain. However, states remain committed to ever deeper border control. Even as much of their role is symbolic, IRCs, for the people within them, intrude deeply, representing an absolute form of coercive state power. Holding individuals indefinitely until they agree or are forced to go, such institutions operate outside the usual expectations of legitimacy. As such, they require a new vocabulary. Matters of identity are clearly important. So, too, are issues of dignity and decency (Margalit 1999; Henry 2011).

Criminologists also need to think about time and space, following our colleagues in geography and anthropology (Hall 2012; Moran 2013). Unlike prisons, where staff and detainees tend to focus on life within the walls, in detention centres the issues being contested are, for the most part, located elsewhere. Removal centres are a temporal and geographical threshold standing between the past and the future (Stumpf 2011). They are places that simultaneously join Britain to, and separate it from, the rest of the world. As a result, questions over their justification and effect are not limited to the positives or negatives of specific sites of bricks and mortar.

Above all, IRCs reveal a dramatic erosion of rights for non-citizens under conditions of globalization (Cole 2007; Zedner 2010; Bosworth 2011b). Though protected by international human rights, detainees endure a lack of access to basic rights that makes it difficult for non-citizens to make normative and ethical claims on us. Their vulnerability in that regard explains why detention centres flourish even though they are unable to fulfil many of their basic tasks. The normative question that remains then is how to make the case for non-citizens (Cole 2007). As Landon, a particularly critical DCO, put it:

They put so much money in here, it is a waste. It is not a solution. There are so many people who will come from the North Africa now. How are they going to sort the problem? By building more places like this? This is not a solution. They spend so much money and it does not help any of them in anyway. People need more than detention. (DCO TH)

References

Agamben, G. (2005) *State of Exception*. Chicago: University of Chicago Press.

Aliverti, A. (2013) *Crimes of Mobility: Criminal Law and the Regulation of Immigration*. Abingdon: Routledge.

Aliverti, A. (2012) 'Making People Criminal: The Role of the Criminal Law in Immigration Enforcement', *Theoretical Criminology* 16(4) 417.

Beetham, D. (1991) *The Legitimation of Power*. London: Macmillan.

Benhabib, S. (2006) *Another Cosmopolitanism*. Oxford: Oxford University Press.

Benhabib, S. (2004) *The Rights of Others: Aliens, Residents and Citizens*. Cambridge: Cambridge University Press.

Bosniak, L. (2006) *The Citizen and the Alien: Dilemmas of Contemporary Membership*. Princeton, NJ: Princeton University Press.

Bosworth, M (2014, forthcoming). *Inside Immigration Detention: Foreigners in a Carceral Age*. Oxford: Oxford University Press.

Bosworth, M. (2012) 'Subjectivity and Identity in Detention: Punishment and Society in a Global Age', *Theoretical Criminology* 16(3): 123.

Bosworth, M. (2011a) 'Human Rights and Immigration Detention', in M.B. Dembour and T. Kelly (eds), *Are Human Rights for Migrants? Critical Reflections on the Status of Irregular Migrants in Europe and the United States*. Abingdon: Routledge.

Bosworth, M. (2011b) 'Deporting Foreign National Prisoners in England and Wales', *Citizenship Studies* 15(5): 583.

Bosworth, M. (2007) 'Immigration Detention in Britain', in M.Lee (ed.), *Human Trafficking*. Collumpton: Willan Publishing: 159.

Bosworth, M. and Bradford, B. (forthcoming) *UKBA Case-Worker Decision-making: Findings from a Pilot Study*. Oxford: Centre for Criminology.

Bosworth, M. and Kaufman, E. (2011) 'Foreigners in a Carceral Age: Immigration and Imprisonment in the U.S', *Stanford Law and Policy Review* 22(1): 101.

Bosworth, M. and Kellezi, B. (2013a) 'Developing a Measure of the Quality of Life in Immigration Detention', *Prison Service Journal* 205: 10.

Bosworth, M. and Kellezi, B. (2013b) 'Citizenship and Belonging in a Women's Immigration Detention Centre', in C. Phillips and C. Webster (eds), *New Directions in Race, Ethnicity and Crime*. Abingdon: Routledge.

Bosworth, M. and Kellezi, B. (2012) *Quality of Life in Detention: Results from the MQLD Questionnaire Data Collected in IRC Yarl's Wood, IRC Tinsley House and IRC Brook House, August 2010—June 2011*. Oxford: Centre for Criminology.

Butler, J. (2009) *Frames of War: When is Life Grievable?* New York: Verso.

Carrabine, E. (2005) 'Prison Riots, Social Order and the Problem of Legitimacy', *British Journal of Criminology* 45(6): 896.

Cole, D. (2007) 'Against Citizenship as a Predicate for Basic Rights', *Fordham Law Review* 75: 2541.

Crewe, B. (2009) *The Prisoner Society: Power, Adaptation, and Social Life in an English Prison*. Oxford: Oxford University Press.

Fassin, D. (2011) 'Policing Borders, Producing Boundaries: The Governmentality of Immigration in Dark Times', *Annual Review of Anthropology* 40: 213.

Fazel, M., Reed, R., Panter-Brick, C., and Stein, A. (2011) 'Mental Health of Displaced and Refugee Resettled in High-income Countries: Risk and Protective Factors', *The Lancet* 379(9812): 266.

Fraser, N. (2008) *Scales of Justice: Reimagining Political Space in a Globalizing World*. New York: Columbia University Press.

Fraser, N. (2007) 'Transnationalizing the Public Sphere: On the Legitimacy and Efficacy of Public Opinion in a Post-Westphalian World', *Theory, Culture and Society* 24(4): 7.

De Genova, N. (2010) 'The Deportation Regime: Sovereignty, Space and the Freedom of Movement', in N. De Genova and N. Peultz (eds), *The Deportation Regime: Sovereignty, Space, and the Freedom of Movement*. Durham, NC: Duke University Press.

Gibney, M. (2008) 'Asylum and the Expansion of Deportation in the United Kingdom', *Government and Opposition* 43(2): 146.

Global Detention Project (GDP) (2011) *Global Detention Project Online* <http://www.global-detentionproject.org/countries/europe/united-kingdom/introduction.html#c1968>.

Hall, A. (2012) *Border Watch: Cultures of Immigration, Detention and Control*. London: Pluto Press.

Henry, L.M. (2011) 'The Jurisprudence of Dignity', *University of Pennsylvania Law Review* 160(1): 169.

HMIP (2011) *Report on a Full Announced Inspection of Brook House Immigration Removal Centre*, 15–19 March. London: HMIP.

Home Office (2012) *Immigration Statistics April–June 2012* <http://www.homeoffice.gov.uk/publications/science-research-statistics/research-statistics/immigration-asylum-research/immigration-q2-2012/>.

Honig, B. (2001) *Democracy and the Foreigner*. Princeton, NJ: Princeton University Press.

Kaufman, E. and Bosworth, M. (2013) 'The Prison and National Identity: Citizenship, Punishment and the Sovereign State', in D. Scott (ed), *Why Prison*. Cambridge: Cambridge University Press.

Leerkes, A. and Broeders, D. (2010) 'A Case of Mixed Motives? Formal and Informal Functions of Administrative Immigration Detention', *British Journal of Criminology* 50: 830.

Liebling, A. (assisted by H. Arnold) (2004) *Prisons and Their Moral Performance*. Oxford: Oxford University Press.

Margalit, A. (1999) *The Decent Society*. Cambridge, Mass: Harvard University Press.

Mathiesen, T. (2006) *Prison on Trial* (3rd edn) Winchester: Waterside Press.

Moran, D. (2013) *Carceral Geography: Prisons, Power and Space*. Aldershot: Ashgate.

Phelps, J. (2009) *Detained Lives*. London: London Detainee Support Group.

Pratt, A. (2005) *Securing Borders: Detention and Deportation in Canada*. Vancouver: UBC Press.

Refugee Council (2007) *The New Asylum Model: Refugee Council Briefing* <http://www. refugeecouncil.org.uk/Resources/Refugee%20Council/downloads/briefings/Newasylummodel.pdf>.

Sim, J. (2009) *Punishment and Prisons: Power and the Carceral State*. London: Sage.

Sparks, R. (1994) 'Can Prisons be Legitimate? Penal Politics, Privatization and the Timeliness of an Old Idea', *British Journal of Criminology* 34(5): 14.

Sparks, R. and Bottoms, T. (2007) 'Legitimacy and Imprisonment Revisited: Some Notes on the Problem of Order Ten Years after', in J. Byrne, F. Taxman, and D. Hummer (eds), *The Culture of Prison Violence*. London: Prentice Hall.

Sparks, R., Bottoms, A.E., and Hay, W. (1996) *Prisons and the Problem of Order*. Oxford: Oxford University Press.

Sparks, R. and Bottoms, A.E. (1995) 'Legitimacy and Order in Prisons', *British Journal of Sociology* 46(1): 45.

Sunshine, J. and Tyler, T.R. (2003) 'The Role of Procedural Justice and Legitimacy in Shaping Public Support for Policing', *Law and Society Review* 37: 555.

Stumpf, J. (2011) 'Doing Time: Crimmigration Law and the Perils of Haste', *UCLA Law Review* 58: 1705.

Sykes, G. (1958) *Society of Captives*. Princeton, NJ: Princeton University Press.

Thomas, R. (2011) *Administrative Justice and Asylum Appeals: A Study of Tribunal Adjudication*. Oxford: Hart Publishing.

UK Border Agency (2011) *Detention Custody Officer Certification, June 2011*. London: Detention Services <http://www.ukba.homeoffice.gov.uk/sitecontent/documents/policyandlaw/detention-services-orders/detainee-custody-officer-cert?view=Binary>.

Vine, J. (2011) *A Thematic inspection of how the UK Border Agency manages foreign national prisoners*. London: Independent Chief Inspector of the UK Border Agency.

Walters, W. (2010) 'Foucault and Frontiers: Notes on the Birth of the Humanitarian Border', in U. Bröckling, S. Krasmann, and T. Lemke (eds), *Governmentality: Current Issues and Future Challenges*. London: Routledge.

Weber, L. and Pickering. S. (2011) *Globalization and Borders: Death at the Global Frontier*. London: Palgrave Macmillan.

Wilsher, D. (2011) *Immigration Detention: Law, History, Politics*. Cambridge: Cambridge University Press.

Woolf, Lord Justice (1991) *Prison Disturbances: April 1990: Report of an Inquiry*. London: HMSO.

Zedner, L. (2010) 'Security, the State and the Citizen: The Changing Architecture of Crime Control', *New Criminal Law Review* 13(2): 379.

9

Hubs and Spokes: The Transformation of the British Prison

Emma Kaufman

The foreign national prisoner crisis began in 2006. On 25 April of that year, British Home Secretary Charles Clarke announced that over the preceding seven years more than 1,000 'non-citizens' had been released from prison without being considered for deportation (BBC 2006a). Clarke's revelation prompted a media frenzy: 'Home Office Blunders Left Foreign Rapists in the UK' (*Daily Mail* 2006a); 'We May Never Find Foreign Murderers and Rapists' (Johnston 2006); 'Foreign Criminals "on the Loose"' (*Daily Mail* 2006b). Even the relatively staid BBC ran a series of stories describing how 'foreign criminals', notably 'murderers and rapists', had been 'allowed to walk free' (BBC 2006d). Ten days later, Clarke was dismissed.

The Home Secretary's dramatic departure provided a superficial conclusion to the prisoner 'crisis'. Behind the scenes, however, the scandal continued long after the presses stopped. In the weeks and months following Clarke's dismissal, the government initiated a wide-scale restructuring of both its migration control apparatus and its prison system. These efforts culminated in a broad new policy on foreign national prisoners, which establishes special prisons for 'non-citizens' and deputizes prison staff to act as quasi-immigration agents (Ministry of Justice (MoJ) and UK Border Agency (UKBA) 2009). Dubbed 'hubs and spokes', the new policy also 'embeds' immigration officials in penal institutions and obliges prisons to hold prisoners beyond the length of their criminal sentences (MoJ and UKBA 2009).

This chapter asks how such an expansive penal policy came to pass and what it can tell scholars about the meaning of imprisonment. How and why did hubs and spokes develop from a heated political scandal? What does this story reveal about the relationship between immigration and incarceration? How do policies like hubs and spokes affect the purpose of the prison? These questions guide the chapter and, in the process, situate a relatively short-lived political scandal within a wider set of concerns about the regulation of mobility in a global world. Drawing on a year of fieldwork in and around five men's prisons, I examine both the origins of the prisoner 'crisis' and its aftermath in penal policy and practice. Ultimately, I argue that the prison is a key—and too often overlooked—site for migration control.

The Crisis

The hubs and spokes policy originated in a few lines of a government report. Though most prison officials recall 'the foreign prisoner crisis of April 2006', the scandal actually commenced relatively quietly in July of 2005, when the National Audit Office (NAO) published a report on failed asylum seekers (NAO 2005). In that report, the NAO noted that immigration authorities could not provide figures on the number of foreigners who had been released from prisons because 'removal could not be arranged' (NAO 2005: 13). The report suggested, in other words, that some prisoners who 'should' have been deported were instead released. This claim caught the attention of MP Richard Bacon, who was at the time running for re-election in the constituency neighbouring Charles Clarke's Norwich South (Public Accounts Committee 2006).

Eager to position himself against the Home Secretary, Bacon decided to make the deportation of 'foreign criminals' a focal point of his campaign (BBC 2006a). Over the next five months, he publicly questioned the Home Office and repeatedly pressed for the release of statistics on foreign national prisoners (BBC 2006a). These efforts precipitated Clarke's announcement, which pre-empted a parliamentary hearing on the issue. Nine days after that announcement—and just one day after Labour's poor showing in the local elections—Charles Clarke was replaced as Home Secretary by John Reid. In tendering his resignation, Clarke presented the prisoner scandal as a problem of failed bureaucracy. 'The issue is not people going free', he explained, but rather 'getting the various aspects of our operation functioning properly' (BBC 2006b).

The media saw it differently. In contrast to Clarke, many reports framed the release of 'foreigners' as a dangerous national crisis (Johnston 2006; *Daily Mail* 2006a; BBC 2006d). Most accounts of the scandal, including the one penned by the Home Office, adopted the choice term 'foreign criminal' to describe the released prisoners (Home Office 2007). As Hindpal Bhui notes, this language 'conjure[s] up over-dramatic and frightening "underworld" images' to distinguish a largely unexceptional group within the prison population (2007: 379). The Home Office's own statistics suggest that rates of recidivism, violent, and sexual offences among foreign nationals are either comparable or lower than those of British nationals (Bhui: 379; MoJ 2012). Of the 1,023 foreign nationals released under Clarke's watch, only 36 had committed offences classified as 'most serious' (Vine 2012: 7).[1] Moreover, if they are released, foreign nationals are subject to the same supervision arrangements as British citizens. Nevertheless, the coverage of Clarke's dismissal proclaimed—or as Stuart Hall would remind us, created—a widespread crisis of governance (Hall et al 1978).

These accounts overshadowed Clarke's reading of the 'problem' and laid the groundwork for an aggressive response from a New Labour administration keen to

---

[1] 'Most serious' offences include murder, manslaughter, rape, and child sex offences (Vine 2012: 7).

assert its seriousness about both crime and migration control (Loader 2006; Zedner 2010). In the wake of the frenzy over 'foreign criminals', the British government made a series of public overtures: it petitioned the European Court of Human Rights to reconsider the ban on deporting people to countries where they could face torture of death (BBC 2006c); it invested more money in the 'problem' of failed asylum seekers (BBC 2006a); and Parliament passed legislation expanding the use of deportation for foreign national prisoners (UK Borders Act 2007; see also Bosworth and Guild 2008; Gibney 2008). Less publicly, the government also initiated a transformation of its bureaucratic machinery.

Shortly after Clarke's dismissal, the Prison Service and the UKBA entered into a long (and by all accounts tense) series of negotiations about how to handle the 'problem' of foreign prisoners. Those meetings resulted in the hubs and spokes agreement, which creates a panoptic model for the management of incarcerated 'foreigners' (MoJ and UKBA 2009). Under this new policy, foreign nationals, who make up 13 per cent of the total prison population, are concentrated in prisons known as hubs, each of which is 'embedded' with full-time immigration staff (MoJ and UKBA 2009; MoJ 2012).[2] The agreement also created two 'dedicated foreign national-only prisons' meant to hold non-citizens facing deportation.[3] In effect, the policy redistributed the prison population according to nationality. This redistribution involved hundreds of prisoner transfers, many of which took place overnight the day after hubs and spokes took effect.[4]

In addition to reorganizing the penal estate, the hubs and spokes policy also established guidelines for the relationship between immigration and prison staff. Among those guidelines is a mandate: where immigration officials are not 'embedded' within a prison, prison staff are obliged to identify all foreign nationals to the UKBA (MoJ and UKBA 2009; Kaufman 2012a). Building from those referrals, the UKBA then determines which prisoners will face deportation.[5] In this sense, the hubs and spokes policy inaugurated an inter-agency effort to identify the 'foreigners' in British prisons. The new policy also required that prisons 'maximize'

[2] In 2009 the hub prisons were: HMP Risley; HMP Hewell; HMP Morton Hall; HMP The Mount; HMP The Verne; HMP Wandsworth; and HMP Wormwood Scrubs (MoJ and UKBA 2009). Morton Hall was 'reroled' as a men's Immigration 'Removal' Centre in May 2011.

[3] In 2009 the 'foreign-only' prisons were HMP Canterbury and HMP Bullwood Hall (MoJ and UKBA 2009). HMP Huntercombe has since been added to that list.

[4] These transfers were challenged under the 1976 Race Relations Act but were ultimately upheld (*EHRC v Secretary of State for Justice* [2010] EWHC 147 (Admin)).

[5] In making this determination UKBA caseworkers follow the 2007 UK Border Act. Under that Act, all non-citizen prisoners are automatically considered for deportation, while non-European nationals sentenced to at least one year and European Economic Area nationals sentenced to at least two years face mandatory deportation. While these guidelines determine who will face deportation, they do not dictate which prisoners will ultimately be deported. Often, prisoners identified for 'removal' are released into the UK because they qualify for temporary leave to remain, because the UKBA cannot procure travel documents from their country of origin, or because they win an appeal on human rights grounds (Vine 2012).

the immigration detention estate by holding some ex-prisoners as immigration detainees (MoJ and UKBA 2009: 9).[6]

This last requirement is the most contentious among prison staff and, at least in terms of legal trends, is one of the most notable aspects of the new policy. According to the hubs and spokes agreement, the Prison Service is expected to hold 'time-served' immigration detainees—that is, prisoners facing deportation whose criminal sentences have expired—until they are released, transferred to one of the UKBA's 'removal' centres, or 'removed' from the UK (MoJ and UKBA 2009: 9). These ex-prisoners are held in prisons under administrative (rather than criminal) powers.[7] This form of detention is indefinite in theory, though not in practice, and has led to ex-prisoners being detained 'pending deportation' for years.[8] As of early 2012, there were 760 ex-prisoners held in British prisons, which is 500 more than the government's 'performance target' for imprisoned detainees (MoJ and UKBA 2009; Vine 2012: 19).

The indefinite imprisonment of a hundreds of ex-prisoners raises concerns about the use of administrative law and the related erosion of due process rights. This practice also compels a critical examination of the government's reaction to the prisoner 'crisis'. In a matter of months after the scandal emerged, Home Secretary Reid reshuffled the Home Office, orchestrated communication between state agencies, and funnelled both money and energy into the 'problem' of foreign prisoners.[9] This response affirmed Charles Clarke's proclamation that the challenge of the scandal was 'to [get] ... our operation functioning properly' (BBC 2006b). On a deeper level, it also evinced an actuarial understanding of crime control that prioritizes the classification and expulsion of a risk posed to the state. This time, the risk was 'the foreign criminal' and the goal was to identify and 'remove' him or her from the United Kingdom. As is often the case, this actuarial approach converged with sensationalist media reports, legitimating and propelling the expansion of state control (O'Malley 1999; Bosworth and Guild 2008; Zedner 2008, 2010).

Specifically, the hubs and spokes policy deployed the power of *the prison* toward the state's efforts to control its borders. While the enabling exchange between actuarial logic and popular punitivism is not new, the prison's particular role in this

---

[6] Prisons have long been used to detain people both pre- and post-sentence (Bosworth 2008a, 2008b; Bosworth and Kaufman 2011). The hubs and spokes agreement does not inaugurate this practice, but rather continues and condones it in explicit terms.

[7] The authority to hold deportees stems from the 1971 Immigration Act (UK).

[8] In theory, the UKBA has the power to detain non-citizens indefinitely in immigration removal centres (IRCs) or prisons 'for the purpose of removing them from the UK' (Vine 2012: 19). While this power is not limited to a specific timescale, detention is only lawful where there is a 'reasonable prospect' of removal within a 'reasonable timescale' (*R v Governor Durham Prison ex p Hardial Singh* [1984] 1 WLR 704 at 706D). Several prisoners have challenged their post-sentence detention in prison, arguing that it constitutes a form of false imprisonment. See, eg *Lumba (WL) v Secretary of State for the Home Department* [2011] UKSC 12; *AP (Trinidad & Tobago) v Secretary of State for the Home Department* [2011] EWCA Civ 551; *RU (Bangladesh) v Secretary of State for the Home Department* [2011] EWCA Civ 651.

[9] In the two years after the foreign national prisoner scandal, the UKBA's budget increased by £40 million, while its Criminal Casework Directorate, the division responsible for handling criminal cases, expanded to 35 times its original size (MoJ 2007: 2).

story warrants further scrutiny. Taken as a whole, the hubs and spokes policy amounts to a new vision of the prison's place in migration control. Under this policy, the prison becomes a site for border control measures and imprisonment becomes a constitutive piece of the government's wider deportation strategy. In this context, the practice of imprisonment works to delineate and reinforce the boundaries of the British nation state (Kaufman 2012a, 2012b; Kaufman and Bosworth 2013).

That is not to say, however, that the new policy altogether transforms the prison's purpose. There are still more than 75,000 British citizens incarcerated in England and Wales and the traditional justifications for imprisonment—deterrence, incapacitation, rehabilitation—continue to shape penal discourse (see, for example, HMPS 2012; MoJ 2012). The hubs and spokes policy does not negate these goals; it supplements and revises them by prioritizing migration control. In this sense, the policy implicates the prison in what Matthew Gibney calls 'the deportation turn', an historical moment in which the 'problem' of migration is increasingly understood through the solution of detention (2008; see also Bosworth and Kaufman 2011). The question that remains is how this conceptual 'turn' plays out in practice.

Immigration Postmen

Like many penal policies, hubs and spokes takes on a life of its own in the actual prison setting. Inside the prisons I visited, the new-found emphasis on border control was evident on a number of different levels. Perhaps most obviously, the policy recasts Prison Service staff as quasi-immigration officers. From day to day, prison line staff may be called upon to collect prisoners' travel documents, to search their cells for passports, and to promote the government's deportation schemes. Foreign national coordinators, the staff members assigned to manage 'foreign' prisoners, regularly contact embassies, mediate between prisoners and immigration officials, and serve foreign nationals with legal notices on behalf of the UKBA (HMPS 2008). In these ways and others, prison staff members sit in 'structured subordination' to the project of migration control (Hall 1978).

This endeavour is shaped not only by the UKBA's mission, but also by its method. In one Prison Service Order published in response to the prisoner scandal, for instance, the UKBA provides detailed instructions on how prison staff should serve immigration documents to foreign national prisoners (HMPS 2008). 'If you are asked to date a notice, please do so', the order reads:

At worst a failure to date the notice can lead to serious problems at the appeal; at best, it gives the appellant's legal representatives an easy way of casting doubt on Home Office competence. (HMPS 2008: 31)

This directive frames the Prison Service, a division of the Ministry of Justice, as ambassador and defender of the Home Office's legitimacy. As that section of the Order bluntly concludes, 'You are, essentially, the postman' (HMPS 2008).

In enlisting Prison Service staff as UKBA 'postmen', the new foreign national prisoner policies extend the practical reach of migration control deep into the penal estate. These policies also situate the prison as a symbolic site for migration control. Under hubs and spokes, 'foreigners' are identified, concentrated, and incarcerated in prisons until the UKBA approves their release (MoJ and UKBA 2009). Since the scandal, moreover, the UKBA has spent an increasing proportion of its time and budget on the management of the 'criminal' population (MoJ and UKBA 2009; Vine 2012). Within this frame, release from prison becomes a certification of legal residency and finding 'foreign criminals' becomes a guiding—and self-fulfilling—goal for the UKBA. The hubs and spokes policy thus figures the prison as an immigration net, an integral site at and through which migration is policed.

The counterpoint to this rhetorical process is that prisons are actual physical sites for incarcerating foreign prisoners. British prisons currently hold between 11,000 and 13,000 foreign nationals, many of whom face deportation (MoJ 2012).[10] In housing these prisoners, particularly those who have completed their criminal sentences, prisons extend the immigration detention estate. Prisons also provide a controlled space for interaction between foreign nationals and immigration authorities. In accordance with new penal policies, prisons now host regular meetings between UKBA officials and prisoners who have been identified as 'foreigners' (HMPS 2006, 2008). Such meetings, which inside the prison are called 'immigration surgeries', give border agents an opportunity to fingerprint and photograph prisoners and to use what one official called 'assertive interviewing practices' and 'police techniques' to determine prisoners' nationalities. At least in some cases, border agents also employ the threat of imprisonment to achieve their aims. In one surgery I attended, a UKBA representative told a 'non-compliant' prisoner—that is, a man who would not agree to his own deportation—that unless he acquiesced to deportation proceedings, immigration could 'hold him in prison as long as we want'. In situations like these, the prospect of imprisonment becomes a practical tool for immigration staff.

Yet, while hubs and spokes figures the prison as a means of border control, the policy is also less popular and more piecemeal than it can seem from outside prison walls. Behind bars, it is clear that the new approach to 'foreigners' has its detractors and that the overlap between immigration and imprisonment is incomplete. While the policy establishes specific hubs and spoke prisons, many prisons diverge from this script. Some spoke prisons employ full-time immigration staff, others incarcerate a significant number of foreign nationals, and the role that immigration personnel play within the prison differs in each institution. In a few prisons, the staff assigned to manage foreign nationals had never heard of hubs and spokes.

---

[10] The number of foreign national prisoners varies depending on the size of the remand and 'time-served' populations and the number actually 'removed' from the UK is even more difficult to track. Official statistics place the foreign national population at 11,077 (MoJ 2012a). That statistic includes neither the 760 ex-prisoners currently held in prison nor the more than 1,500 prisoners listed as 'nationality not recorded', many of whom are likely foreign nationals (Bhui 2007; Vine 2012).

The meaning of the new policy thus took on a local character when realized within the penal institution. So, too, did the interactions between prison and immigration staff. This bureaucratic relationship was one of the targets of the hubs and spokes agreement, which makes plain that the foreign prisoner scandal was caused, at least in part, by poor communication between state agencies (HMPS 2006, 2008). In most of the prisons I visited, UKBA and prison staff communicated according to the dictates of that agreement and were both cooperative and cordial with each other when doing so. In individual interviews, however, the conflicts between these groups emerged. Both prison and UKBA staff worried that their missions were too different for the new system to work. In several cases, prison staff members complained that they had little knowledge and less control over prisoners' immigration cases, a situation that they found especially frustrating when handling 'difficult' time-served prisoners.[11] Prison staff also worried about how the UKBA's priorities affected the nebulous balance of power within the prison.

One foreign national coordinator recounted the problems created when border agents introduce immigration casework into the prison system and then leave prison staff to maintain order. 'If you're coming with bad news, I'm giving it to [the prisoners]', she said. 'You're not coming into my prison and giving my prisoners bad news.' Articulating a blend of protectiveness, defensiveness, and ownership over the prison and its prisoners, this staff member suggested that hubs and spokes disrupts the daily organization and hierarchies of prison life. More senior Prison Service officials reiterated this argument on a grander scale, noting that the new policy transposes the demands of migration control onto a penal estate already arranged by security classification and pinched by overcrowding. As one Prison Service policy maker put it, hubs and spokes necessitates prisoner transfers and particular prison assignments when 'we are already bursting at the seams'.

These criticisms illuminate the tensions underlying the new penal policy. They also clarify the Prison Service's own perception of its purpose. Prison officials' complaints about hubs and spokes reflect an interest in maintaining their authority, both within the prison and within the broader government bureaucracy. Inside the prison, this goal takes the form of localized debates about the limits of immigration staff power. Such debates typically centre on the balance between immigration 'removal' targets and 'the need to maintain order', a concept that holds great sway in prison staff members' articulations of the drawbacks of hubs and spokes. Throughout my interviews, prison officials asserted the primacy of the need for order, and with it, the import of existing classification systems. These claims suggest that the Prison Service understands itself through the lens of order and, at least in some cases, sees that paradigm as incompatible with the notion of 'removal'.

Prison staff also expressed concerns about the treatment of prisoners under hubs and spokes. One staff member, for instance, predicted that the policy would

---

[11] Ex-prisoners held under immigration powers tend to be more vocally angry, resistant, and frustrated than prisoners who know their date of release. For a psychological account of the pressures of indefinite detention as they relate to tendencies toward self-harm, see Borrill and Taylor (2009).

ultimately fail because the two organizations had distinct approaches to prisoners. As that official put it, 'the difference between the Prison Service and the UKBA is that we see them as people and they see them as numbers'. This is a biased perspective, of course, but it nonetheless illustrates the philosophical conflicts at play in the implementation of penal policy. According to one official familiar with the relationship between the UKBA and the Prison Service, these conflicts were part of the reason that the hubs and spokes agreement took three years to negotiate. That official said that the policy was created 'for UKBA convenience' and that during the negotiations the National Offender Management Service (NOMS), the umbrella organization that includes prisons and probation, voiced fears about its capacity to uphold a 'decency agency' while indefinitely detaining deportees.[12] The UKBA, on the other hand, was singularly focused on the effort to 'detain and deport'.

The two agencies tapped to manage the foreign prisoner 'crisis' thus had distinct and sometimes conflicting goals in creating hubs and spokes. This distinction was acknowledged in the government report commissioned in response to the scandal (MoJ and UKBA 2009). That report found that 'NOMS and UKBA are ultimately working toward different objectives in managing F[oreign] N[ational] P[risoners]'. NOMS, according to its mission statement, exists both 'to protect the public' and 'to reduce re-offending rates' (MoJ 2010b). While the Prison Service is not explicit about how it intends to reach these goals, its official emphasis on 'reducing re-offending' by helping prisoners lead 'good and useful lives during and after release' suggests a conceptual investment in the connection between offenders and the British polity.[13] The UKBA, in contrast, is by definition interested in 'controlling the border' by increasing the annual number of deportations.

The clash between the two agencies' aims plays out on the ground in the subtle but constant tension between immigration and prison staff. That tension is then more than bureaucratic boundary drawing; it is a window into the problems that arise when governments attempt to merge immigration with imprisonment. On paper, policies like hubs and spokes appear to blend border control with punishment practices, and in doing so, to police both migration and crime. But behind closed doors and prison walls, these policies prompt debates about transfers and prisoner treatment—debates that are, at their base, about the purpose of the prison and the legitimacy of the UKBA's presence behind bars. Accordingly, one official advised me to 'hesitate when talking about any "integration" of the UKBA and the

---

[12] The 'Decency Agenda' was introduced by Prison Service Director General Martin Narey in 1999. While there is no consensus on what this agenda entails, Alison Liebling argues that it is an explicit move away from notions of 'justice' and 'liberality' and toward concepts like 'fairness, minimum standards, security, order, the challenging of offender behaviour, and a reduction in the availability and use of drugs' (2004: 478). Prison officials and staff regularly cite this agenda, despite its conceptual ambiguity, when they are asked to explain the purpose of the prison.

[13] To be clear, my suggestion is not that the Prison Service is actually or sufficiently concerned with the prison's broader place in society, or even with offender resettlement. The point here is a limited one: given its stated objective, the Prison Service is conceptually connected to prisoners' continued presence on British soil in a way that the UKBA is not.

Prison Service'. Instead, criminologists ought to rethink the relationship between immigration and imprisonment.

The Criminalization of Immigration

Typically, scholars have critiqued the overlap between migration control and imprisonment as evidence of the criminalization of immigration, or as Juliet Stumpf calls it, 'crimmigration' (Stumpf 2007; see also Cole 2003; Preston and Perez 2006; Bosworth and Guild 2008; Sheikh 2008; Stumpf, Chapter 3 in this volume). This formulation has a number of merits, chief among them its focus on the concerning spread of imprisonment practices beyond the realm of the criminal law. However, notions like crimmigration can also suppress some of the key distinctions between border control and punishment. Examining those distinctions raises questions about the purpose of the prison.

This critique of crimmigration springs from an appreciation of its contributions. As a conceptual framework, crimmigration has propelled academic enquiry into the nature of contemporary punishment practices. Stumpf's portmanteau captures how the language and machinery of criminal justice gets transposed onto discussions of migration, effectively criminalizing foreign nationals for their mere presence in a foreign nation (Stumpf 2007). Her description of recent legal trends has motivated scholarship on the transformation and expansion of administrative law (Stumpf 2007; Zedner 2010), the decline of national sovereignty (Garland 1996; Brown 2010), and the obfuscation of due process rights (Cole 2003).[14] Scholars have explored how the criminalization of immigration recasts racism in new forms, enabling incarceration and further marginalizing migrant communities (Simon 1998; Weber 2006; De Giorgi 2011; Pallida 2011; Bosworth 2011a). The concept of crimmigration has also provided solid ground to critique the securitization of immigration, and with it, the oft-drawn link between criminality, migration, and terrorism (Cole 2003; Huysmans 2006; Zedner 2010).

While it helps to illuminate these issues, however, the crimmigration framework can also elide notable aspects of policies like hubs and spokes. The concept of crimmigration tends to encourage an overemphasis on the process of criminalization, which is only one of several emergent patterns in migration legislation and policy. The crimmigration paradigm highlights the expansion of the criminal law into the realm of migration, the use of criminality to describe migrants, and the development of policing practices along the national border. These processes are important to understanding the treatment of migrants in the twenty-first century, but they are also accompanied by a series of non-criminal trends, such as the

[14] Cole's *Enemy Aliens* (2003) and Garland's early writing on sovereignty (1996) precede Stumpf's article on 'crimmigration' (2007), but tackle many of the same questions about the collusion of administrative and criminal legal paradigms. My claim is not that the term 'crimmigration' inaugurated a new line of thought, but rather that it captured a set of concerns about migration control that had been percolating in Anglo-American criminology and legal scholarship since the mid-1990s.

expansion of administrative detention and the curtailment of due process for non-citizens (Cole 2003; Bosworth and Guild 2008). Indeed, in many ways contemporary migration control practices depend less on a connection between immigration and crime than on the particularly non-criminal nature of foreignness (Cole 2003; Bosworth and Guild 2008). By foregrounding the process of crimin-alization, the crimmigration framework can suppress this crucially non-criminal element of the relationship between crime and border control.

The crimmigration paradigm can also obscure the specific role the prison plays in migration control. Over the past decade, a number of scholars have noted the growing overlap between the imprisonment and border policing (Leerkes and Broeders 2010; Zedner 2010; Bosworth and Kaufman 2011; Bosworth 2011a). Much of this work focuses on the emergence of the immigration detention centre, a technology that fuses migration control with incarceration practices (for example Simon 1998; Leerkes and Broeders 2010). Writing in this vein, Jacqueline Stevens has documented the incarceration of migrants under prison-like circumstances throughout the United States and particularly along the US-Mexican border (Stevens 2009, 2010). Leanne Weber (2006) has explored a similar phenomenon in Australia, where immigration detention centres have sprung up at a rapid clip since the mid-1990s. This scholarship suggests that the boundary between immi-gration and criminal incarceration has been blurred by migration control policies that emphasize detention.

With the creation of policies like hubs and spokes, it is clear that this account of imprisonment holds true in England and Wales (see also Bosworth 2011a). There are multiple ways in which British prisons and immigration 'removal' centres support and mirror one another: these institutions are constructed to the same architectural blueprint; they hold many of the same prisoners; they share 'perform-ance targets' and policy makers; and with immigration officials 'embedded' within the prison, they share staff as well (MoJ and UKBA 2009; Vine 2012).[15] On both conceptual and practical levels, prisons and detention centres are involved in the same project: they are two arms of the government's effort to 'shore up' national borders and reinforce a waning sense of national sovereignty (Weber and Bowling 2004; Bosworth and Guild 2008; Brown 2010; Bosworth and Kaufman 2011). From this perspective, the institutions of criminal justice and migration control appear to be part of a particular and shared late modern moment.

In a different and important sense, however, prisons are *not* a part of the immigration estate, nor are they completely consistent with the project of migra-tion control. This inconsistency is worth noting, for it highlights the tensions that emerge when prisons get used to police mobility. While the hubs and spokes model seems to integrate border control with imprisonment, this policy also depends upon and preserves the prison's distinct character as an institution—namely, one defined by the totality of its control over its inhabitants and bounded, at least in theory, by the criminal law. That is to say, there are key differences between prisons and

---

[15] See Bosworth and Kaufman on the parity between the immigration and penal systems in the United States (2011).

detention centres and these differences matter to the operation of both institutions. One UKBA policy maker I interviewed appreciated this fact. That official explained that the prison is a unique site for border control: 'You can look at their property, their phone calls, their visitors', she said of foreigners held in prisons. 'In a prison regime', information about a prisoner's nationality 'is easier to get. Removal centres are a different regime'.

Technically, ex-prisoners held under immigration powers have the same legal status as detainees and are treated as remand prisoners inside the penal institution (HMPS 2008). In this context, the prison is not a separate legal sphere from the detention centre and obtaining information about prisoners' nationalities should not be much 'easier to get' in prison. Yet this policy maker presented the penal institution as an especially controlled, and hence desirable, environment for the UKBA project. This articulation of border control is revealing, not so much because it exposes a dubious practice, but because it captures the prison's conceptual role in the effort to 'manage' migration. Whether or not prisoners are actually treated differently in prisons and detention centres, it is clear that the prison occupies an important position in the Border Agency's understanding of itself. Prisons are institutions that look a certain way, where practices such as keeping people behind bars and searching their cells become normal. These practices, and the very idea of the penal institution, hold a particular place within the UKBA imagination. The prison is the paradigm against which the Border Agency compares its own activities and makes sense of its mission.

The distinction between prisons and 'removal' centres is then both salient and substantive (see also Bosworth 2011b, 2012). While there is no question that the prison is a practical site for migration control and that prisons increasingly function as de facto detention centres, the prison also serves as a conceptual foil to the detention centre and as an aspirational model of incarceration for the UKBA. In other words, the discursive relationship between immigration and imprisonment is analogic rather than exact. The prison and the detention centre are related by analogy—and for that matter, through an imperfect analogy that elides the differences between administrative and criminal incarceration. The detention centre is a replica of the prison devoid of the criminal law. The prison is a symbolic representation of the criminal sanction. In practice, these two regimes often look and function similarly. In principle, they exist in contrast to one another. Ultimately, there is a conceptual gap between the prison and the detention centre, and that gap works to legitimate the existence of both incarceration regimes (Bosworth 2011b; Kaufman and Bosworth 2013).

Again, this phenomenon is clearest in the actual prison. In the institutions I visited, prison staff chafed against their role as aides to the UKBA. Staff members drew contrasts between prisons and detention centres, particularly when discussing the detention of ex-prisoners. Several foreign national coordinators told me that they did everything they could to limit the number of detainees held in prisons, a practice that made them 'uncomfortable'. These efforts, which constitute a form of resistance to the hubs and spokes policy, included lobbying officials at 'removal' centres to take detainees from the prison, offering to 'trade' ex-prisoners across the two estates, and advocating for more frequent UKBA visits. One prison staff member who had tried these methods told me that she was frustrated by ex-prisoners' continued presence within the prison and that this problem was 'just an immigration capacity issue'.

This claim captures how the concept of the prison forges a link between migration and crime control. On the one hand, the assertion that indefinite detention is 'an immigration issue' appears to clarify the boundaries and purpose of the penal institution. This staff member seemed to think, and wanted to make clear, that the prison should be a place only for those people who are serving criminal sentences. That sentiment echoes the objections Prison Service policy makers voiced during the hubs and spokes negotiations: the prison is not a detention centre and should not, in so far as it is possible, be used as such. This articulation of hubs and spokes defines the prison in contrast to other incarceration regimes. For these prison staff and policy makers, the UKBA's presence in the prison made it more urgent that the penal institution be a reflection of the criminal law.

On the other hand, these staff members' claims enable the blurring of criminal and administrative law—the very trend they aim to resist. The prison worker who said that detaining ex-prisoners is 'just an immigration capacity issue' is technically correct, for under hubs and spokes it is the UKBA and not the Prison Service that decides when a foreign national prisoner gets released (MoJ and UKBA 2009).[16] This policy allows the UKBA to detain more people and, to the extent that the most 'difficult' prisoners remain in prisons, to avoid the problems created by its own policies. However, if it divorces the Border Agency from the consequences of its own work, the UKBA's control over detainee casework also lets prison staff defer responsibility for the foreign national prisoners whose lives they 'manage' from day to day. Insisting that the problems of foreign nationals are 'just immigration issues' places ex-prisoners who threaten suicide and foreign nationals who resist 'removal' outside the scope of the prison. Yet these people remain within the prison and their concerns become a part of prison life. The sense of the prison as a unique and bounded institution—one where certain people are held and only certain problems are handled—allows those who manage prisons to ignore what is actually happening within the penal institution and how that institution has changed.

Given the overlap between prisons and detention centres, maintaining a sharp conceptual distinction between these two institutions creates a cyclical problem. Policy makers and staff members rely on the theoretical differences between imprisonment and detention; they assume that these regimes have different goals. This assumption allows the people who craft and implement penal policy to sidestep unanswered questions about the purpose of incarceration and the meaning of punishment. On a practical level, the distinction between prisons and detention centres also facilitates the existence of a separate immigration detention estate to

---

[16] This broad power to determine a detainee's date of release is checked by the judiciary, which can order an ex-prisoner's release. However, the High Court has, for the most part, upheld detention 'pending deportation' under the 1971 Immigration Act. See fn 8.

detain 'non-criminal' migrants. In the end, there is a reinforcing exchange between Prison Service practices and UKBA policies.

Bureaucratic exchanges like these reveal the inherent paradoxes of imprisonment in an age of mass mobility. The effort to police and punish 'foreign criminals' depends as much on the prison's theoretically bounded scope as it does on the blurring of legal realms. Indeed, the hubs and spokes policy operates *through* the tensions and distinctions between migration control and punishment, detention centres, and prisons. This policy aims to ingrate migration control with incarceration and to expand the detention regime—in this sense, it is a case of 'crimmigration'. Yet, at the same time, the trend toward 'crimmigration' is also met with resistance by prison staff and complicated by the unique and often particularly egregious treatment of 'non-citizens' whose very lack of citizenship enables the obfuscation of due process. These developments in the practice of imprisonment deserve further attention, for they suggest that while immigration has been criminalized in recent years, the apparatus of criminal justice has itself been transformed by the push to find, punish, and banish 'foreign criminals'.

Conclusion

In the past two decades, criminologists have become increasingly engaged with debates about sovereignty and migration control (Garland 1996; Simon 1998; Aas 2007; Loader and Sparks 2007; Bosworth et al 2008). Academics, particularly those who are interested in globalization, have applied criminological theories to topics ranging from immigration detention and asylum to risk assessments and airport security (Bloch and Schuster 2002; Murdolo 2002; Malloch and Stanley 2005; Gibney 2008; Bowling 2011). This work has gone a long way towards incorporating concerns about mobility and its regulation into the criminological canon. However, scholars have not always brought the insights of a 'global' criminology to bear on studies of the penal institution. With notable exceptions (Bhui 2007; Bosworth 2011a), the prison tends to remain a place where criminologists study legitimacy, rehabilitation, and recidivism without asking critical questions about citizenship and border control.

This trend can and should be reversed, for immigration and imprisonment are intertwined. Originally, the penal institution was crafted for the domestic polity and focused on the reform of criminals who come from and return to a national space (Foucault 1977). Today, the purpose and boundaries of the prison are far less clear. Like its counterparts in the United States (Bosworth and Kaufman; Simon 1998), Australia (Weber 2006), and Western Europe (Van Kooten 2008), the contemporary British prison is used not just to punish, but also to police migration, to expand immigration detention, and to determine whom among us does not belong. While on paper the prison remains an institution of the criminal law, the hubs and spokes policy imports—indeed literally builds—border control into the structure of the penal estate. This policy recasts prison staff as agents of border control and, at least for some prisoners, makes deportation rather than release the conclusion of life behind bars. Hubs and spokes turns the prison into one border of the British nation state.

As is often the case, this approach to punishment disproportionately affects people of colour. Foreign national prisoners constitute more than half of the black and minority ethnic population in British prisons and studies show that the effort to identify incarcerated 'foreigners' is shaped by racialized assumptions about the meanings of foreignness (Bhui 2004; Kaufman 2012a). Whether understood as migration control or a new form of punishment, the treatment of this prisoner population thus raises longstanding questions about the relationship between race, ethnicity, and state power. To get at those questions and to raise new ones, scholars concerned with the stratifying effects of border control should turn our attention to the prison, and for that matter, towards the other sites of criminological enquiry traditionally viewed as national in purpose and scope. Today's prisons are not simply domestic criminal justice institutions. They are places where global power dynamics unfold and where the boundaries of the nation state are resisted and rewritten every day.

References

Aas, K. (2007) 'Analysing a World in Motion: Global Flows Meet "Criminology of the Other"', *Theoretical Criminology* 11(2): 283.

BBC (2006a) 'How the Deportation Story Emerged', *BBC News Online* <http://news.bbc.co.uk/1/hi/uk_politics/4945922.stm>.

BBC (2006b) 'In Quotes: Clarke and Deportation', *BBC News Online* <http://news.bbc.co.uk/1/hi/uk_politics/4945736.stm>.

BBC (2006c) 'UK Seeks Human Rights Law Review', *BBC News Online* <http://news.bbc.co.uk/1/hi/uk_politics/5000238.stm>.

BBC (2006d) 'Foreign Criminals "Not Deported"', *BBC News Online* <http://news.bbc.co.uk/1/hi/uk_politics/4942886.stm>.

Bhui, H.S. (2007) 'Alien Experience: Foreign National Prisoners after the Deportation Crisis', *Probation Journal* 54(4): 368.

Bhui, H.S. (2004) *Going the Distance: Developing Effective Policy and Practice with Foreign National Prisoners*. London: Prison Reform Trust.

Bloch, A. and Schuster, L. (2002) 'Asylum and Welfare: Contemporary Debates', *Critical Social Policy* 22(3): 393.

Borrill, J. and Taylor, D. (2009) 'Suicides by Foreign National Prisoners in England and Wales 2007: Mental and Cultural Issues', *Forensic Psychiatry and Psychology*. 20(6): 886.

Bosworth, M. (2012) 'Subjectivity and Identity in Detention: Punishment and Society in a Global Age', *Theoretical Criminology* 16(3): 123.

Bosworth, M. (2011a) 'Deporting Foreign National Prisoners in England and Wales', *Citizenship Studies* 15(5): 583.

Bosworth, M. (2011b) 'Human Rights and Immigration Detention', in Marie-Bénédicte Dembour and Toby Kelly (eds), *Are Human Rights for Migrants? Critical Reflections on the Status of Irregular Migrants in Europe and the United States*. Abingdon: Routledge.

Bosworth, M. (2008a) 'Immigration Detention and Foreign Nationals in Prison', *Prison Service Journal* 180: 18.

Bosworth, M. (2008b) 'Border Control and the Limits of the Sovereign State', *Social and Legal Studies* 17: 199.

Bosworth, M. and Guild, M. (2008) 'Governing Through Migration Control: Security and Citizenship in Britain', *British Journal of Criminology* 48: 703.

Bosworth, M. and Kaufman, E. (2011) 'Foreigners in a Carceral Age: Immigration and Imprisonment in the United States', *Stanford Law and Policy Review* 22(1): 429.

Bosworth, M., Bowling, B., and Lee, M. (2008) 'Globalization, Ethnicity and Racism: An Introduction', *Theoretical Criminology* 12(3): 263.

Bowling, B. (2011) 'Transnational Criminology and the Globalization of Harm Production', in M. Bosworth and C. Hoyle (eds), *What is Criminology?* Oxford: Oxford University Press.

Brown, W. (2010) *Walled States, Waning Sovereignty.* Cambridge, MA: Zone Books.

Cole, D. (2003) *Enemy Aliens: Double Standards and Constitutional Freedoms in the War on Terrorism.* New York: The New Press.

Daily Mail (2006a) 'Home Office blunders left foreign rapists in UK', *Mail Online* <http://www.dailymail.co.uk/news/article-384183/Home-Office-blunders-left-foreign-rapists-UK.html>.

Daily Mail (2006b) 'It's not only the foreign criminals who've vanished, but also any pretence that Britain controls its borders or, indeed, its very destiny', *Mail Online* <http://www.dailymail.co.uk/debate/columnists/article-384284/Its-foreign-criminals-whove-vanished-pretence-Britain-controls-borders-destiny.html>.

De Giorgi, A. (2011) 'The U.S. Penal Experiment', in S. Palidda (ed), *Racial Criminalization of Migrants in the 21st Century.* Surrey: Ashgate.

Foucault, M. (1977) *Discipline and Punish: The Birth of the Prison* (A. Sheridan (trans)). New York: Vintage.

Garcia, J.A.B. and Bessa, C.F. (2011) 'The Construction of Migrants as a Risk Category in the Spanish Penal System', in S. Palidda (ed), *Racial Criminalization of Migrants in the 21st Century.* Surrey: Ashgate.

Garland, D. (1996) 'The Limits of the Sovereign State: Strategies of Crime Control in Contemporary Society', *The British Journal of Criminology* 36(4): 445.

Gibney, M. (2008) 'Asylum and the Expansion of Deportation in the United Kingdom', *Government and Opposition* 43(2): 146.

Hall, S. (1978) 'Racism and Moral Panics in Post-War Britain', in *Five Views of Multi-Racial Britain.* London: Commission for Racial Equality.

Hall, S., Critcher, C., Jefferson, T., Clarke, J., and Roberts, B. (1978) *Policing the Crisis: Mugging, The State and Law and Order.* London: Palgrave MacMillan.

HM Prison Service (2012) 'About HM Prison Service', *MoJ Online* <http://www.justice.gov.uk/about/hmps>.

HM Prison Service (2008) *Prison Service Order 4630: Immigration and Foreign Nationals in Prison.* London: MoJ.

HM Prison Service (2006) *Prison Service Order 4630: Immigration and Foreign Nationals in Prison.* London: MoJ.

Home Office (2007) *A Review of the Failure of the Immigration & Nationality Directorate to Consider Some Foreign National Prisoners for Deportation.* London: Home Office.

Huysmans, J. (2006) *The Politics of Insecurity: Fear, Migration, and Asylum in the EU.* Abingdon: Routledge.

Johnston, P. (2006) 'We May Never Find Foreign Murderers, Says Home Office', *Telegraph Online* <http://www.telegraph.co.uk/news/uknews/1516747/We-may-never-find-foreign-murderers-says-Home-Office.html>.

Kaufman, E. (2012a) 'Finding Foreigners: Race and the Politics of Memory in British Prisons', *Population, Space and Place* 18(3): forthcoming.

Kaufman, E. (2012b) 'Foreign Bodies: The Prison's Place in a Global World', Unpublished Doctoral Dissertation, University of Oxford.

Kaufman, E. and Bosworth, M. (2013) 'Prison and National Identity: Citizenship, Punishment and the Sovereign State', in D. Scott (ed), *Why Prison*. Cambridge: Cambridge University Press.

Liebling, A. (2004) *Prisons and Their Moral Performance: A Study of Values, Quality, and Prison Life*. Oxford: Oxford University Press.

Leerkes, A. and Broeders, D. (2010) 'A Case of Mixed Motives? Formal and Information Functions of Administrative Immigration Detention', *British Journal of Criminology* 50: 830.

Loader, I. (2006) 'Fall of the "Platonic Guardians": Liberalism, Criminology and Political Reponses to Crime in England and Wales', *British Journal of Criminology* 46: 561.

Loader, I. and Sparks, R. (2007) 'Contemporary Landscapes of Crime, Order, and Control: Governance, Risk, and Globalization', in M. Maguire, R. Morgan, and R. Reiner (eds), *The Oxford Handbook of Criminology* (4th edn). Oxford: Oxford University Press.

Malloch, E. and Stanley, M. (2005) 'The Detention of Asylum Seekers in the UK: Representing Risk, Managing the Dangerous', *Punishment and Society* 7(1): 53.

Ministry of Justice (2012a) *Offender Management Caseload Statistics 2011*. London: MoJ.

Ministry of Justice (2010b) 'NOMS: About Us', *Ministry of Justice Online* <http://www.noms.homeoffice/gov.uk/about-us/>.

Ministry of Justice (2007) *Letter from Maria Eagle, MP, to Mr. John Shine, Chair of the Independent Monitoring Board*, 20 September.

Ministry of Justice and UK Border Agency (2009) *Service Level Agreement to Support the Effective and Speedy Removal of Foreign National Prisoners*, 1 May.

Murdolo, A. (2002) 'Keeping "Our" Women Safe: Containing Australian Fear and Danger though Immigration Detention', *Hecate* 28(1): 123.

National Audit Office (2005) *Returning Failed Asylum Applicants*. London: National Audit Office.

O'Malley, P. (1999) 'Volatile and Contradictory Punishment', *Theoretical Criminology* 3: 175.

Palidda, S. (2011) 'Introduction', in S. Palidda (ed), *Racial Criminalization of Migrants in the 21st Century*. Surrey: Ashgate.

Preston, P. and Perez, M. (2006) 'The Criminalization of Aliens: Regulating Foreigners', *Critical Criminology* 14: 43.

Public Accounts Committee (2006) *Hearing of Commons Committee of Public Accounts, Thirty-fourth Report of Session 2005–6*, HC 620. London: PAC.

Sheikh, I. (2008) 'Racializing, Criminalizing, and Silencing 9/11 Deportees', in D. Brotherton and P. Kretsedemas (eds), *Keeping Out the Other: A Critical Introduction to Immigration Enforcement Today*. New York: Columbia University Press.

Simon, J. (1998) 'Refugees in a Carceral Age: The Rebirth of Immigration Prisons in the United States', *Public Culture* 10(3): 577.

Stevens, J. (2010) 'America's Secret ICE Castles', *The Nation* <http://www.thenation.com/article/americas-secret-ice-castles>.

Stevens, J. (2009) *States Without Nations: Citizenship for Mortals*. New York: Columbia University Press.

Stumpf, J. (2007) 'The Crimmigration Crisis: Immigrations, Crime and Sovereign Power', Paper No 2007-2, Lewis and Clark Law School Legal Research Paper Series.

Van Kooten, H. (2008) *Conference Report: Foreigners in European Prisons—From 'Good Practices' to 'Good Policy'*. Nieuwersluis, Netherlands: MoJ.

Vine, J. (2012) 'Thematic Inspection of How the UK Border Agency Manages Foreign National Prisoners: February–May 2011', *Independent Chief Inspector of the UK Border Agency*. London: HMSO.

Weber, L. (2006) 'The Shifting Frontiers of Migration Control', in S. Pickering and L. Weber (eds), *Borders, Mobility, and Technologies of Control*. Dordrecht: Springer.

Weber, L. and Bowling, B. (2004) 'Policing Migration: A Framework for the Regulation of Global Mobility', *Policing and Society* 14(3): 195.

Zedner, L. (2010) 'Security, the State, and the Citizen: The Changing Architecture of Crime Control', *New Criminal Law Review* 13(2): 379.

Zedner, L. (2008) 'Terrorism, the Ticking Bomb, and Criminal Justice Values', *Criminal Justice Matters* 73: 18.

10

Seeing Like a Welfare State: Immigration Control, Statecraft, and a Prison with Double Vision

*Thomas Ugelvik**

[T]he state has always seemed to be the enemy of 'people who move around'
... Nomads and pastoralists (such a Berbers and Bedouins), hunter-gatherers,
Gypsies, vagrants, homeless people, itinerants, runaway slaves, and serfs have
always been a thorn in the side of states.

James C. Scott, in *Seeing Like a State*

Scandinavia[1] is probably the corner of the world where citizens have the highest degree of heartfelt confidence and trust in the central government and its various agencies (Christensen and Lægreid 2005; Brochman and Hagelund 2010). Although not entirely uncritical, Scandinavians in general believe that their state is able and willing to solve problems and influence society in beneficial ways and that their civil servants are looking out for their best interests. Scandinavian government agencies, for their part, expect citizens to participate in state governance willingly and efficiently (Neumann 2003). We Scandinavians are expected to manage and control ourselves. We report all kinds of information voluntarily to the relevant government agencies and embrace ever more advanced and sophisticated examples of schemes belonging to that family of power technologies Foucault (2007) called 'governmentality'—a population management strategy where members are governed indirectly through their own free will.

* The research leading to this article has been generously funded by the European Research Council. The author would like to express his thanks to Mary Bosworth, Kjersti Lohne, Coretta Phillips, John Pratt, Victor Shammas and Synnøve Ugelvik for valuable comments at different stages of the writing process.
   [1] Scandinavia is a geographical area consisting of Denmark, Norway, and Sweden. These countries have a common cultural heritage and can understand each other's languages. The Nordic countries, on the other hand, also include Iceland and Finland. Although part of the same linguistic family, most Scandinavians cannot understand Icelandic. Finnish, being part of a totally separate family of languages, is, as the proverb goes, like Greek to Scandinavians, although Greek is actually a closer linguistic relative. In common English usage, however, the difference between Scandinavia and the Nordic countries is often blurred.

A generous and universally available welfare system aimed at enhancing individual autonomy, maximizing labour force participation, promoting gender equality, and creating a generally egalitarian social structure is often referred to as the Nordic model (Esping-Andersen and Korpi 1987; Pratt 2008a, 2008b). The welfare state, understood, following Rugkåsa (2011), as a constellation of (1) political ideals about a well-functioning society, (2) institutional mechanisms, and (3) principles for the allocation of resources, can be said to constitute a sort of general social frame in these countries. In Denmark, it has been called a secular religion (Brochman and Hagelund 2010); in the current Norwegian context, it is almost a total social phenomenon in the Maussian (1995) sense. The welfare state is everywhere, and everywhere it is trusted and regarded as mostly benevolent. In general, the welfare state is a source of Norwegian pride and identity and, as a national symbol and rhetorical trope, all-important for the legitimacy of many state initiatives. 'The state' may be criticized, but 'the welfare state' is beyond reproach.

Even prisons are regarded as part of the welfare state system in Norway. With ambitious goals set before them, like rehabilitation and the creation of a society with less crime, the correctional services' employees work hard to re-connect prisoners with the law-abiding parts of the Norwegian society outside the prison's walls. What happens to such a system and its ambitious goals when increasing numbers of foreigners arrive to take their share of its resources? According to official statistics, the proportion of foreign nationals in the prison population has been increasing rapidly in recent years, from one in five in 2006, to one in three in 2011.[2] The welfare-oriented rehabilitation machine that the Norwegian prison system is supposed to be is facing the challenge of having to cope with increasing numbers of non-citizens.

In this context, a new table was added to the most recent Correctional Services' year statistics report (2011). Its caption reads 'Prisoner transfers (to homeland)', and it states that 52 prisoners were transferred in 2011 from Norway to prisons in their countries of origin to serve the rest of their sentence there. Fifty-two individuals may look like a small drop in the ocean, even in Norway, a country with a relatively modest prison population of 3,600. But it all adds up; according to the new table, the transfer of these individuals meant that the Correctional Services managed to save the taxpayers the cost of 34,498 days of prison time, or roughly 100 prison years.

Why did the new table become part of the system's public information about itself in the 2011 report? What suddenly made this information an important part of the state's knowledge production and self-narrative? This chapter will discuss and analyse the development behind this statistical novelty. I will argue that the more fundamental question to ask is this: What happens to an ambitious and generous welfare state system when unknown and increasingly often unwanted outsiders arrive? How can a historically relatively homogeneous welfare state understand and

---

[2] Correctional Services' year statistics 2006–2011, figures collected on 1 March each year <http://www.kriminalomsorgen.no/index.php?cat=78464>.

handle a new situation with an unprecedented queue of potential new welfare state subjects that threatens to take up its resources?

I will explore how the changing situation in Norwegian prisons may be seen as part of a more general development where a universally generous welfare state responds to globalization. For those welfare state subjects with citizenship, the entire welfare safety net is available when needed. For non-citizens, on the other hand, this safety net is increasingly likely to be replaced by a system explicitly working towards returning them to their place of origin, voluntarily (through incentive schemes) or involuntarily (using force). With the promotion of return as the fundamental goal in these cases, an important practical and philosophical shift has happened. A welfare-oriented system with inclusion as its fundamental logic has been accompanied by an alternative substitute system where exclusion is the desired end. I will argue that the Norwegian welfare state (and its prisons) seems to be wearing bifocals, making a kind of double vision with two different points of focus simultaneously possible.

Seeing Like a Welfare State

Scandinavian countries are often taken to epitomize the well-functioning welfare state. They are among the most financially and socially egalitarian in the world, with a narrow field of class differences (Moene and Barth 2004). According to Esping-Andersen and Korpi (1987), the Nordic model is *comprehensive, institutionalized,* and *universal.* The welfare schemes are (in principle at least) available to all irrespective of social or geographical position. The safety net is strong and wide; comparably low levels of unemployment are backed up by generous unemployment benefit schemes, liberal social welfare schemes, a universal right to secondary level education, a free public health care system, free and easy access to higher education, and so on. The level of what Rugkåsa (2011) has called 'welfare ambitiousness'— the scope of responsibilities the state assumes for the welfare of its citizens and the extensiveness of the welfare system—has been and (to varying degrees) still is second to none. Compared to almost everywhere else, the Scandinavian countries have high expectations when it comes to their goals of modifying and engineering social conditions so as to create a just and healthy society for all citizens, regardless of background—a factor that undoubtedly helps them consistently to do well on the UN Human Development Index.[3] In recent years some critics have registered a tendency towards increased income differences, but this is because the wealthiest have increased their relative wealth, not because the segment of the least well-off has grown or been marginalized further (Prieur 2003).

The neo-liberal decimation of the welfare state and the connected growth of the penal state reported in other countries (Bourdieu 1999; Wacquant 2001, 2008, 2009) has not happened in this northernmost part of Europe, at least not to the

---

[3] In the 2011 report, Norway is ranked 1, Sweden 10, and Denmark 16 out of the 187 countries listed. See <http://hdr.undp.org/en/media/HDR_2011_EN_Table1.pdf>.

same extent and in the same ways as elsewhere. Wacquant employs Bourdieu's analytical distinction between a left hand and a right hand of the state, where the left hand typically takes care of 'social functions' like public education, health, housing, welfare, and labour law, and the right hand is charged with enforcing budget cuts, fiscal incentives, economic deregulation, as well as managing the courts, the police, and the prisons (Wacquant 2009). In his analysis, under neo-liberalism the left hand withers into a feeble and impotent version, a shadow of its former self. With a lack of symmetry typical of societies in a state of advanced neo-liberalism, the right hand is stronger than ever, becoming a pumped up and muscular version on steroids. Compared with many other jurisdictions, where such a focus on penal rather than social measures and workfare rather than welfare has been the trend, Norway may very well be seen as an exception. Wacquant himself employs the Scandinavian countries as exceptions to the rule (2009: 303). Other scholars, such as Lacey (2008) and Pratt (2008a, 2008b; Pratt and Eriksson 2011a, 2011b) also see the Scandinavian countries as exceptions to the international rule of convergence towards a more or less global punitive neo-liberal model.

The higher the degree of welfare state ambitiousness, the more state agencies will want to initiate schemes to normalize and civilize the subjectivities of citizens. The immigrant women in Rugkåsa's (2011) study, potential citizens going through a programme for foreign denizens to help them integrate into Norwegian society, were learning not only the ins and outs of Norwegian professional life but also taught that they should change their underwear daily and that deodorant is needed in a Norwegian workplace. In ambitious welfare states, generous care and intrusive social control often are two sides of the same coin. This is what Sejersted (2005) has called the paternalistic paradox. Such intrusions into personal life and integrity obviously need to be explained and made legitimate somehow. The Norwegian answer has been a welfare state ideal and ideology of goodness, good intentions, and the perfect society of equals (Witoszek 2011). As part of a project of 'doing good', the state has entered the private sphere in several ways: managing child rearing, the relationship between spouses, and citizens' general way of life (Brochman and Hagelund 2010). This tendency is what prompted Huntford (1971) to give his famous analysis of Swedish society in the 1960s the title *The New Totalitarians*. More welfare-ambitious states interfere in citizens' (and non-citizens') lives more readily and more profoundly than states with lower ambitions.

There are (at least) two sides to everything. On the one hand, the familiar notion that care must be at a level low enough to make sure that only those who really need it and thus are morally worthy of help apply, has, in the Nordic model, been replaced with an idea of welfare state aid as a universal right. On the other hand, all welfare systems—even universally generous ones—need mechanisms to identify people in true need of assistance, and sort them out from the people who seek benefits illegitimately. A high level of welfare ambitiousness as a universal right is not universal in an absolute sense. Even the most generous forms of welfare aid, like the Norwegian maternity leave, is of course dependent on the recipient actually having a child at a certain age (Brochman and Hagelund 2010). In fact, every kind of social care system will need a form of optic of differentiation to be able to distinguish people eligible for a certain form of good/care/intervention from those who are not. As part of the construction of the wide and strong safety net, the state needs to produce knowledge, to gather information, to be able to focus its resources where they are actually needed (Foucault 2007). For a welfare state, part of 'seeing like a state' (Scott 1998) is employing a specific optic which makes it possible to focus on the truly needy in a way that makes them separable from people merely wanting to play the system. The more ambitious a state is, the more complex information it needs to gather for this purpose, and the more elaborate forms of social control it may want to employ.

The inclusive rhetoric of the Nordic model became hegemonic in the two decades following the Second World War (Brochman and Hagelund 2010). The array of welfare state responsibilities widened drastically with the increase in resources required with such a development. The welfare state became professionalized and institutionalized. The question of individual moral fibre has become manifestly less important in laws and official policy documents. The Norwegian welfare state now runs on need, not merit or social position, and, importantly, all forms of need are legitimate. Even though the state must still identify cheats and freeloaders, the focus has moved to a rhetoric of individual rights and individuals' resources or lack thereof, not moral worth. A person cannot refuse to seek employment and then expect to receive unemployment benefits. But in contrast to earlier regimes and those in operation elsewhere,[4] the Norwegian welfare system looks for a solution *for everyone*, even people who refuse to better themselves. Or, in the words of Esping-Andersen and Korpi: 'The welfare state is meant to integrate and include the entire population rather than target its resources toward particular problem groups' (1987: 32).

Immigration to Norway at a Glance

An important question, then, is how one should understand the phrase 'the entire population'. Norway has historically been a relatively homogenous country with a tradition of emigration rather than immigration. In troubled times, Norwegians have flocked to other shores in search of a better life. In 1920, Chicago, Illinois housed the third largest Norwegian population in the world, after the capital city of Kristiania (renamed Oslo in 1925) and Bergen on the country's western coast.[5] This all changed in the 1960s, when Norway, thanks to a deliberate *gastarbeiter* policy, saw the beginning of a new era of immigration from countries like India, Pakistan, and Vietnam (Brochman and Hagelund, 2010). Since the early 1970s, Norway has, together with its Scandinavian sibling societies (albeit to different degrees), become natural laboratories for students of rapid population change. The situation has lasted to this day, a general stop on labour migration since 1975

---

[4] For example the logics underpinning the British or French systems, according to Prieur (2003).
[5] According to the Norwegian Centre for Emigrants <http://www.utvandrersenteret.no/index.cfm?id=157425>.

notwithstanding. These days, 13 per cent of the population (around 655,000 out of about five million) are counted as immigrants by the national official statistics agency Statistics Norway (SSB), meaning that they either have migrated from another country themselves, or have two parents who have done so.[6] The population of Oslo is the most extreme case with 23 per cent of Oslo residents listed as immigrants or children of immigrants following SSB's definition. Oslo has always been a city with an east–west divide, symbolically marked by the Akerselva River crossing the city north to south. Today, the river divides the population along ethnic as well as class lines. The population on the eastern side is more ethnically diverse, has a shorter average life-expectancy, and reports lower income. People living there are also more often unemployed, on welfare, have more serious health problems, and so on (Barstad and Skardhamar 2006).

In the early days of what is sometimes referred to as 'new immigration', the newcomers, in principle, had most of the same rights to welfare benefits as the general population (Brochman and Hagelund 2010). At the same time, it soon became clear that the earlier assumption—that migrants would stay for a time, work hard, wait for conditions in their homeland to improve, and then return voluntarily—was inaccurate. The early immigrants did not leave. Furthermore, they brought their families. The official end to the labour migration schemes in 1975 was followed by an unparalleled influx of people to the country.

In Norway, the period near the end of the 1960s has been called the 'the social democratic society's happy moment' (Sejersted 2005). Equal opportunities in life seemed to have become more than a lofty ideal. The egalitarian welfare state's safety net was finally wide enough to catch all who fell, and strong enough to carry them. It was a time of unparalleled optimism. It could not last. By the late 1980s, criticism had mounted and the political climate shifted. The 1987 parliamentary election saw the Progress Party (*Fremskrittspartiet*, FrP), until then a marginal right-wing political party based on the struggle for a general tax reduction, soar to 12 per cent of the votes largely because of its new-found vocal immigration scepticism—not bad in an election system where seven or eight different political parties typically make it into parliament. The Progress Party explicitly campaigned for the removal of welfare benefits from non-citizens, a standpoint that was universally shunned by the other parties at the time, but which was to gain a strong political momentum subsequently. In fact, the 1987 Progress Party campaign material in many ways reads like a fairly accurate description of what has become political doxa 25 years on. According to Brochman and Hagelund (2010), 1975 should instead be understood as the beginning of a selective and exclusive immigration policy that is still in effect. The aim was (and is) to limit unskilled labour migration from developing countries, and facilitate the recruitment of the skilled labour force needed by, for example, the burgeoning oil industry. Refugee and family migration has also contributed to net migration in the period since 1975.

[6] See <http://www.ssb.no/innvandring/>.

Norway must be understood within a wider European context. The country decided to remain outside the European Union on two occasions. In both referenda (in 1972 and 1994) opposition to joining the European Union won by a narrow margin (Brekke 2011). Although not a full member, Norway cooperates closely with the European Union, both on informal and formal levels. Arguably (and frustrating both for supporters of the Union and those who oppose it), one might say that Norway enjoys a hybrid position between full membership and so-called third country status. As a member of the European Free Trade Association (EFTA), Norway is part of the European Economic Area (EEA). It is a signatory to both Dublin Conventions and has agreed to implement the EU Returns Directive.[7] Norway is also, importantly, part of the Schengen area, making the Norwegian land border with Russia an EU/Schengen outer border. The association agreement making Norway part of the Schengen cooperation makes Norway equally responsible for the effective deployment of the various compensatory measures deemed necessary to reduce the negative effects of the free movement of persons within the Union. Nevertheless, after the 2004 and 2007 EU expansions eastward, the country has, like most other Western European countries (Boswell and Geddes 2011), seen increased EU migration, even though the 1975 general labour migration stop has never been formally lifted.

Immigration is an issue perpetually on or near the top of the political agenda. The proportion of the population which thinks that immigrants contribute positively to society is decreasing, while the proportion which feels that it should be more difficult to get citizenship is increasing (Blom 2009). Progress Party politicians publicly claim that the sitting Labour Party-dominated coalition government will 'tear the country apart' with their lenient policies.[8] Internet debate forums are filled with reactions on reactions on reactions, many reiterating a frustrated sense of living in a country once pure, but now slipping into impurity—a world view that was at least part of the causal complex leading to the horrors of the terrorist attack in Oslo and at Utøya on 22 July 2011. A recurring question in such debates is whether immigrants are 'more criminal' than the 'true Norwegian population'. Whatever the answer is to that question,[9] the dangerous 'criminal immigrant' certainly is an important figure in political and media discourses (Cere et al 2013).

Today, foreigners, asylum seekers, and third country nationals have become and are increasingly becoming important foci of state and supra-state control and administration (Aas 2007a, 2007b; cf Weber and Bowling 2008). The result is well known and not particular to Norway or indeed to Scandinavia. The state has to

---

[7] Directive 2008/115/EC of the European Parliament and of the Council of 16 December 2008 on common standards and procedures in Member States for returning illegally staying third-country nationals.

[8] See <http://www.aftenposten.no/meninger/kronikker/article3783373.ece>.

[9] Studies indicate that non-Western immigrants are disproportionally represented in the crime statistics. If allowance is made for demographical differences in the two populations, however, most of the difference disappears (cf Gundersen et al 2000; Skardhamar 2006). How the remaining disproportionality should be interpreted is controversial. One possibility is that it is the result of the specific control culture and its resulting 'police gaze' (Finstad 2000; Sollund 2006).

cultivate a form of double vision: more sophisticated systems of control and exclusion for some, alongside more open borders and a higher degree of mobility for others (Bosworth 2008). Increased labour migration from EU countries means stricter border control for third country nationals. A massive transnational apparatus has been and is developing for this purpose. The systems for evaluation, classification, and either integration or exclusion of the queue of outsiders at our doorsteps are becoming more and more advanced. At the same time, an estimated 18,000 irregular migrants (Zhang 2008) are denied anything more than the most basic welfare provisions (Johansen, Chapter 14 in this volume). Even providing emergency medical aid for this group has been controversial, but recent court decisions seem to confirm that giving such aid at least is not a crime.

To sum up so far: the neo-liberal 'rolling in of the social state' described by Wacquant (2009) and others has not (yet) happened in Norway. The welfare state is still going strong; it is, perhaps, stronger and more multi-faceted than ever. This is not to say that neo-liberal influences do not exist. There is a new focus on incentives schemes and the collection and implementation of new forms of power/knowledge. But these developments also have long histories and have existed since before the welfare state came into being in the modern sense. At the same time, Norway is part of Europe, and the world. The generous welfare state has been and is constantly being challenged by the arrival of non-members in larger and larger numbers. How can generosity and ambition be reconciled with the need to spread resources over a wider and wider field?

A State with Double Vision?

When the governmentality strategies typical of advanced welfare regimes break down, and members of the population show that they are unable efficiently to self-govern, the Scandinavian societies have an alternative to fall back on. Even a welfare state primarily focusing on indirect forms of power needs its prisons. Subjects who have shown that they are unable to self-govern efficiently must be guided and controlled more directly, for the good of the totality. They must be identified, isolated, and attended to so as to minimize their risk potential.

Norwegian prisons are not just a last resort when other forms of welfare state power have failed, however. The prison is in itself understood as an integral part of the ambitious Norwegian welfare state (Ugelvik 2011), an institution on the same level as schools and hospitals. Following the distinction between the left hand and the right hand of the state, one could argue that the Norwegian prison is an ambidextrous institution: it is supposed to be able to use its left hand as well as its right. Behind the barbed wire and concrete walls, welfare agencies are expected to communicate and cooperate efficiently with each other, ensuring that the health care, unemployment services, and education opportunities inside a prison are at least on a par with those on the other side of the walls.

The current Norwegian welfare regime thus stretches its safety net particularly wide; prisoners are supposed to be the beneficiary of the welfare state policies and prisons are run according to a logic of universal right to welfare. Even prisoners, in other jurisdictions subject to exclusion and simple warehousing, are still regarded as part of the social community. The morally deficient remain included; the black sheep are still part of the flock.

Prisoners are of course, in most cases, incarcerated and thus physically removed from society. But their sequestration is only temporary, designed to make it possible to include them again as quickly and effectively as possible. Such a view is encapsulated in the current Correctional Services strategy document (Fagstrategien 2004: 4) that sets out the following vision statement:

The convict should when the sentence is served be better prepared[10] for a life without crime. Everything we do will be measured against this standard. The sentence will be a turning point. Our goal is more specifically that:
A convict, when the sentence is served:
- Is drug-free or has control over his drug use
- Has a suitable place to live
- Can read, write and do basic math
- Will have a chance on the labour market
- Can relate to her/his family, friends and society in general
- Knows how to seek assistance if problems arise after release
- Can live an independent life.

These are indeed ambitious welfare state goals, given that the average Norwegian prison sentence is only around 100 days, but that is beside the point here. On the level of discourse, the vision statement says a lot about what a prison is supposed to be and the position Norwegian prisons have as part of a general welfare state system of care/control.

The ambidextrous prison is a tool to change flawed welfare state subjects unable to self-govern properly, whose success or failure is measured out on the level of the population as a whole (Ugelvik 2011). Being a prisoner in this context means being positioned as a subject of the welfare state, temporarily forcefully excluded from the community of free subjects on the other side of the walls, but still fundamentally included or at least *includable* in this community. The responsible prisoner must take advantage of and utilize the opportunities accorded him by the state and its prison; he must participate wholeheartedly in his own rehabilitation, recreating himself as a regular, law-abiding citizen (Bosworth 2007). The prison, on the other hand, must strive to make this transformation as effective and as easy as possible.

Internationally, this logic is far from the rule. Sparks (1996; cf Simon 1993; De Giorgi 2010) describes a rhetorical figure or trope which is frequently encountered in a certain penal culture context where deterrence is centre stage among justifications for punishment: to act as an efficient deterrent, prisons are supposed to convey a feeling of severity; they are symbols of a moral order returned, of a balance restored. Sparks argues that this logic of less eligibility has been both practically necessary and morally compelling, as seen from the point of view of a citizen

---

[10] Literally *bedre skodd*, meaning better shod.

outside the prison walls. The prison is supposed to *work*, and in a context where most of the weight is put on deterrence, a prison will not work if it is so comfortable that people prefer it to the world outside.

In a context like the Norwegian one, on the other hand, a life imitating life outside is considered an important rehabilitative and inclusionary tool. This so-called principle of normality is reflected in the material conditions accorded to prisoners,[11] and in the fact that prisoners retain all civil rights while imprisoned, apart from the obvious fact that they are held behind prison walls. Prisoners may, for example, vote in elections and they have the same right to secondary education as other citizens. In terms of legal status, prisoners are not fundamentally different from other people.[12] In the ambidextrous welfare state prison, the historically important notion of less eligibility has been replaced by a variety of techniques of penal inclusion. In contrast to the situation in many other jurisdictions, these inclusionary techniques and goals have been and are still by far the most important in current prison discourses. The arguments calling out for more austere and punitive conditions and a general return to 'real punishment' are not totally absent in public discourse on such matters, but they are pushed way into and beyond the margins, at least when laws and policy documents are concerned.

The relatively sober penal discourse may come under pressure in the future, however. A third of the prisoners and over half of those on remand in Norway are currently foreign nationals. When those imprisoned are not part of the 'us' to begin with, when they are citizens of other states (and, to make matters even worse, countries outside the EU), not at any time legitimate members of the community of liberal self-governing individuals, will prisons still be welfare-oriented rehabilitation and reintegration institutions?

The Correctional Services has created a special separate wing in Oslo Prison for foreign prisoners who face deportation at the end of their sentence. Another similar wing is being planned for Ullersmo Prison. According to the state budget for 2012,[13] the purpose of this new wing is to ease and facilitate the quick transfer of foreign criminals to prisons in their native countries or, if this is impossible, to make deportation after the full sentence is served in Norway as efficient as possible. The wing will explicitly be shaped by the fact that it will hold non-citizens for whom rehabilitation is not a main goal. 'Foreign prisoners', the document makes clear, 'who are being expelled will not be reintegrated back into Norwegian society,

---

[11] Norwegian prisons are famous for being humane institutions with decent living conditions or, depending on whom you ask, notorious for being soft and hotel-like (Pratt 2008b, 2008a; Ugelvik 2012).

[12] It is not a given that prisoners should retain full rights as citizens while incarcerated. In classic contract theory, for instance, a person who fails to live up to his or her side of the social contract cannot expect to reap the benefits. Rousseau famously states that '[S]ince every wrongdoer attacks the society's law, he becomes by his deed a rebel and a traitor to the nation; by violating its law, he ceases to be a member of it; indeed, he makes war against it. ... Trial and judgment are the proof and declaration that he has broken the social treaty, and is in consequence no longer a member of the state' (Rousseau 1968 [1762]: 79).

[13] See <http://www.regjeringen.no/nb/dep/jd/dok/regpubl/prop/2011-2012/prop-1-s-20112012/2.html?id=657408>.

and they can therefore not partake in many of the rehabilitation measures fitted to the Norwegian context.'[14] The Parliamentary Standing Committee on Justice commended this new development in their comments to the budget. The following paragraph perfectly illustrates a welfare state prison with double vision:

The majority [of the committee members] are satisfied with the fact that the Cabinet is continuing the work of increasing the overall prison capacity. … The majority would like to point out that Norway is the Nordic country with the lowest recidivism rate and emphasize that a correctional system which provides a meaningful content to the sentence, like education, vocational training and other activities, will contribute to an improved reintegration into society and reduce the risk of reoffending. … The majority is satisfied with the fact that the Cabinet is suggesting a special wing at Ullersmo prison for foreign prisoners who are going to be expelled, and who thus will not be rehabilitated and brought back to Norwegian society.[15]

As already detailed, the voluntary or involuntary return of foreign prisoners to prisons in their countries of origin has recently been made a priority. In a related development, the Ministry of Justice has proposed to finance the building of prisons in other jurisdictions (for example Poland[16]) to ease the early transfer of foreign prisoners to their home countries. The transfer of foreign nationals will also be made more efficient by permanent agreements made between the Norwegian Ministry of Justice and the governments of Romania, Lithuania, and Latvia.[17] Furthermore, a project is underway that aims to improve the cooperation between the police, the correctional services, and the Directorate of Immigration, making the expulsion of foreign prisoners on release more effective.[18] Ideally, the agents of the deportation system should have everything ready and meet with the prisoners even before release to plan everything.[19]

It has also been common in Oslo Prison, conveniently situated close to the largest international airport in Norway, to deny parole release if the police are not available to take responsibility for the parole-eligible prisoner-deportee.[20] A citizen will be paroled; a foreigner, on the other hand, must wait until the police have time to collect him[21] and put him directly on a plane. Because they are regarded as absconding risks, prisoners awaiting deportation will not be considered for transfer

---

[14] This and the following quote are translated from the Norwegian by the author.
[15] See <http://www.stortinget.no/no/Saker-og-publikasjoner/Publikasjoner/Innstillinger/Stortinget/2011-2012/inns-201112-006/?lvl=0>.
[16] See <http://www.dagbladet.no/2010/11/27/nyheter/utenriks/soning/kriminalomsorg/fengsel/14472702/?commentId=5125370#comment_5125370>. This is not a development unique to Norway; in fact, it seems to be becoming the international norm. Australia has helped fund prisons in Indonesia, and the UK has recently funded a prison wing in Nigeria. Various EU Member States have also built immigration detention centres 'out of area'.
[17] See <http://www.regjeringen.no/nb/dep/jd/aktuelt/taler_og_artikler/ministeren/justisminister_knut_storberget/2011/flere-skal-sone-i-hjemlandet.html?id=641552>.
[18] Høringsforslag—Endringer i utlendingsloven om adgangen til frihetsberøvelse mv (7 July 2010).
[19] Utlendingsforskriften § 14-3 første ledd.
[20] This practice has been controversial; cf the State Ombudsman's statement on the matter: 64: Prøveløslatelse av utenlandske innsatte med forbehold om effektuering av utvisningsvedtak.
[21] Oslo Prison is an all-male prison.

to more open regimes. Thus, they do not enjoy the so-called 'ladder of progression' intended to aid in the rehabilitation of the imprisoned citizens.

The planned prison wing at Ullersmo is not yet operational. It is hard to know what it will look like in practice. Will it still be a prison wing—meaning, in the Norwegian context, a form of institution part of a larger welfare system where people are put *as* punishment, but also *for* rehabilitation and positive personal change—or will it be something else? The Conservative Party Høyre, currently at the top of the opinion polls and favourites to form a new government after the election later this year (2013), possibly in coalition with FrP, recently made prison conditions for foreign prisoners part of its vision for a new and improved Norway. Vice Chairman Bent Høye explained to the daily *Aftenposten* that: 'We do not need to use resources on the rehabilitation of convicts who will not be released back into Norwegian society. ... Nor do we need to provide education or other forms of help for these people, or prepare them for a future life in Norway.'[22]

If the ambitious welfare state goals of rehabilitation and reintegration in an ambidextrous prison give way to the more clean-cut security goals of incapacitation and deportation combined with the creation of an effective deterrent, one might, following Agamben (2005), say that imprisoned foreigners are not quite put in a prison, not quite in what he calls a camp. In that case, even though non-citizen prisoners are still subjected to the normal judicial system, it will choose to ignore its own fundamental welfare-oriented goals. As such, the foreign prisoners-only wings could be seen as places where a specific form of a state of exception may be a permanent feature (see also Kaufman, Chapter 9 in this volume). The important question is perhaps what the imprisoned non-citizens in these wings will look like from the perspective of the state. Will the optic employed permit them to be observable as future resourceful and productive state subjects, potential members of a community of taxpayers? Or will the prison optic only be able to see them as security problems to be returned as quickly and efficiently as possible? According to Scott (1998), certain forms of knowledge and control require a narrowing of vision. What will come into focus on the foreign prisoners-only wings? And what will be left out of view?

Conclusion: Welfare State Crafting

Why have states, for as long as they have existed, been preoccupied with the administration of and control over groups and individuals who move (Scott 1998)? Some have asserted that the state may be losing its importance as its traditional power base erodes in a context of globalization (Bauman 1998). Ulrich Beck has even argued that the state in a certain sense no longer exists, that it is a category lacking a referent in the real world:

---

[22] *Aftenposten*, 18 September 2012, p 3.

All the distinctions that make up our standard picture of the modern state—the borders that divide domestic from international, the police from the military, crime from war and war from peace—have been overthrown. It was precisely those distinctions that defined the nation state. Without them, it is a zombie idea. It still looks alive, but it is dead. (Beck 2002)

Whether it is really (un)dead or merely dying, or just thriving in new ways (Neumann and Sending 2010), we are living in a time when the state is actively looking for new ways of reproducing itself and its power and legitimacy. The politics of territory and (im)mobility, encompassing related practices like border control, immigration control and administration and immigration removal and deportation, are an important field from this perspective (Turner 2007; Salazar and Smart 2011; Aas, Chapter 1 in this volume). These are practices that, although they have by no means lost their instrumental function, have important symbolic implication, not least in mainland Europe, where the intended borderlessness of the Schengen area might make it look like the state indeed has finally abdicated. The presence of large numbers of unwanted immigrants clearly indicates that nation states are no longer able to completely regulate the number of immigrants entering a country (Engbersen 2009). Border control and immigration administration practices should in such a context be understood as the enactment of sovereignty, and thus as important tools in state crafting (Schinkel 2009).

The shrinking of the welfare state and its transformation into a lean and nimble workfare state is often described as a consequence of neo-liberalism. This development seems not to be happening in Norway. It is true that the generous and universal kind of welfare state typical of the Scandinavian countries are both invasive and expansive (and expensive), but not in the way observed in the United States, where the right hand is growing at the expense of the left. Today, however, the Norwegian state has to deal with problems arising from governing a society that is more heterogeneous than before, and where foreigners are showing up in unprecedented numbers.

According to Pratt and Eriksson (Pratt 2008a, 2008b; Pratt and Eriksson 2011a, 2011b), one of the foundations of what they have labelled 'Scandinavian exceptionalism' is the strong standing of the principle of normalization and an accompanying penal philosophy where prisoners are seen as fellow citizens. Those in prison may have committed a crime, but this has not fundamentally altered their status vis-à-vis the state. Pratt and Eriksson ask, however, whether Scandinavia may be standing at a crossroads as a culture of equality shared by a relatively homogeneous Scandinavian population is ending. The question that remains to be answered is whether and how this situation will impact on the traditional exceptional welfare state with its exceptional welfare-oriented prisons.

The agents of the Norwegian welfare state seem to be exploring their options in the new situation. In this chapter I have shown just one example: the tendency to create two separate but parallel systems, one for citizens, another for non-citizens. What happens with an ambitious welfare state when its ambitious goals are suspended for certain groups? In general, Norway seems to be resisting a development where the rhetorical, symbolic, and practical justification for punishment focuses more on punitive measures than welfare-oriented goals like rehabilitation. A more punitive approach is, however, easy enough to find in discourses about immigration control, the effective return of asylum seekers, and the possible warehousing of foreign prisoners who, as stated in the Parliamentary Standing Committee on Justice Comments to the State Budget, 'will not be rehabilitated and brought back to Norwegian society'. 'The bright line' between worthy and unworthy poor (Wacquant 2009: 295) is not new; in fact, it has a long history. Today, it is intertwined with two other lines: one separating Norwegian citizens from EU citizens, and the other separating EU citizens from the citizens of the rest of the world.

All Norwegians are worthy of welfare benefits and forms of public social aid. These schemes are universal. Some EU citizens may be worthy; others are not (for example depending on their employment status and the length of their stay). Third country nationals are also divided into worthy and unworthy. Recognized refugees are worthy; their arrival compels the state to fire up its increasingly sophisticated apparatus of integration and nationalization. Failed asylum seekers and non-citizens convicted of serious crimes, however, are illegitimate welfare subjects, and are therefore transferred to the parallel alternative system. The result, however, of different police strategies and different prisons with different goals for the two populations will undoubtedly be the consolidation of a society where the difference between citizens and non-citizens is particularly salient. A high level of welfare state ambitiousness seems to be necessarily exclusive. For those excluded, less eligibility—often reformulated in the neo-liberal age as incentive structures—is necessary to keep non-citizens from coming. Great ambitions and universal coverage simply do not fit together well in the real world. The answer to this dilemma may not be a general erosion of the welfare state, however, but a dusting off of an old hierarchy based on a division between the worthy and the unworthy needy.

References

Aas, K.F. (2007a) 'Analysing a World in Motion: Global Flows Meet "Criminology of the Other"', *Theoretical Criminology* 11(2): 283.

Aas, K.F. (2007b) *Globalization and Crime*. London: Sage.

Agamben, G. (2005) *State of Exception*. Chicago, London: The University of Chicago Press.

Barstad, A. and Skardhamar, T. (2006) *Utviklingen av levekårene i Oslo indre øst*. Oslo: SSB.

Bauman, Z. (1998) *Globalization: The Human Consequences*. New York: Columbia University Press.

Beck, U. (2002) 'The Terrorist Threat: World Risk Society Revisited', *Theory, Culture and Society* 19(4): 39.

Blom, S. (2009) *Holdninger til innvandrere og innvandring 2009*. Oslo: Statistisk sentralbyrå.

Boswell, C. and Geddes, A. (2011) *Migration and Mobility in the European Union*. Basingstoke: Palgrave Macmillan.Bosworth, M. (2008) 'Border Control and the Limits of the Sovereign State', *Social and Legal Studies* 17(2): 199.

Bosworth, M. (2007) 'Creating the Responsible Prisoner', *Punishment and Society* 9(1): 67.

Bourdieu, P. (1999) *The Weight of the World: Social Suffering in Contemporary Society.* Cambridge: Polity Press.

Brekke, J.-P. (2011) *Migrasjon og integrasjon: Norges tilknytning til EU.* Oslo: Europautredningen.Brochman, G. and Hagelund, A. (2010) *Velferdens grenser: Innvandringspolitikk og velferdsstat i Skandinavia 1945–2010.* Oslo: Universitetsforlaget.

Cere, R., Jewkes, Y. and Ugelvik, T. (2013) 'Media and Crime: A Comparative Analysis of Crime News in the UK, Norway and Italy', in S. Body-Gendrot, R. Lévy, M. Hough, S. Snacken, and K. Kerezsi (eds), *The Routledge Handbook of European Criminology.* Abingdon: Routledge.

Christensen, T. and Lægreid, P. (2005) 'Trust in Government: The Relative Importance of Service Satisfaction, Political Factors and Demography', *Public Performance and Management Review* 28(4): 487.

De Giorgi, A. (2010) 'Immigration Control, Post-Fordism, and Less Eligibility', *Punishment and Society* 12(2): 147.

Engbersen, G. (2009) 'Irregular Migration, Criminality and the State', in W. Schinkel (ed), *Globalization and the State.* Basingstoke: Palgrave.

Esping-Andersen, G. and Korpi, W. (1987) 'From Poor Relief to Institutional Welfare States: The Development of Scandinavian Social Policy', in R. Erikson (ed), *The Scandinavian Model: Welfare States and Welfare Research.* Armonk: Sharpe.

Fagstrategien: Strategi for faglig virksomhet i Kriminalomsorgen 2004–2007. Oslo: Kriminalomsorgens Sentrale Forvaltning.

Finstad, L. (2000) *Politiblikket.* Oslo: Pax.

Foucault, M. (2007) *Security, Territory, Population: Lectures at the Collège De France 1977–1978.* Basingstoke and New York: Palgrave Macmillan.

Gundersen, F. et al (2000) *Innvandrere og nordmenn som ofre og gjerningsmenn.* Oslo: Statistisk sentralbyrå.

Huntford, R. (1971) *The New Totalitarians.* London: Allen Lane.

Lacey, N. (2008) *The Prisoners' Dilemma: Political Economy and Punishment in Contemporary Democracies.* Cambridge: Cambridge University Press.

Mauss, M. (1995) *Gaven: Utvekslingens form og årsak i arkaiske samfunn.* Oslo: Cappelen akademisk.

Moene, K. and Barth, E. (2004) 'Den skandinaviske likhetsmodellen', *Plan* 3: 30.

Neumann, I.B. (2003) 'Innledning: Regjeringsbegrepet og regjeringens historiske fremvekst', in I.B. Neumann and O.J. Sending (eds), *Regjering i Norge.* Oslo: Pax.

Neumann, I.B. and Sending, O.J. (2010) *Governing the Global Polity: Practice, Mentality, Rationality.* Ann Arbor: University of Michigan Press.

Pratt, J. (2008a) 'Scandinavian Exceptionalism in an Era of Penal Excess: Part I: The Nature and Roots of Scandinavian Esceptionalism', *The British Journal of Criminology* 48(2): 119.

Pratt, J. (2008b) 'Scandinavian Exceptionalism in an Era of Penal Excess: Part II: Does Scandinavian Exceptionalism Have a Future?', *The British Journal of Criminology* 48(3): 275.

Pratt, J. and Eriksson, A. (2011a) 'In Defence of Scandinavian Exceptionalism', in T. Ugelvik and J. Dullum (eds), *Penal Exceptionalism?: Nordic Prison Policy and Practice.* Abingdon: Routledge.

Pratt, J. and Eriksson, A. (2011b) ' "Mr. Larsson is Walking out Again": The Origins and Development of Scandinavian Prison Systems', *Australian and New Zealand Journal of Criminology* 44(1): 7.

Prieur, A. (2003) 'Senmoderne Elendighet: En Kommentar Om Relevansen Av Bourdieus Bok *La Misère Du Monde* I Norden I Dag', *Sosiologisk tidsskrift*: 300.

Rousseau, J.-J. (1968 [1762]) *The Social Contract*. London: Penguin.

Rugkåsa, M. (2011) 'Velferdsambisiøsitet, sivilisering og normalisering: Statlig velferdspolitikks betydning for forming av borgeres subjektivitet', *Norsk antropologisk tidsskrift* (3–4): 245.

Salazar, N.B. and Smart, A. (2011) 'Introduction: Anthropological Taks on (Im)Mobility', *Identities: Global Studies in Culture and Power* 18(6): i.

Schinkel, W. (2009) 'Dignitas Non Moritur?: The State of the State in an Age of Social Hypochondria', in W. Schinkel (ed), *Globalization and the State: Sociological Perspectives on the State of the State*. Basingstoke: Palgrave Macmillan.

Scott, J.C. (1998) *Seeing Like a State: How Certain Schemes to Improve the Human Condition Have Failed*. New Haven: Yale University Press.

Sejersted, F. (2005) *Sosialdemokratiets tidsalder: Norge og Sverige i det 20. århundre*. Oslo: Pax.

Simon, J. (1993) *Poor Discipline: Parole and the Social Control of the Underclass, 1890–1990*. Chicago: University of Chicago Press.

Skardhamar, T. (2006) *Kriminalitet gjennom ungdomstiden blant nordmenn og ikke-vestlige innvandrere: En analyse av fødselskullet 1977*. Oslo: Statistisk sentralbyrå.

Sollund, R. (2006) 'Racialisation in Police Stop and Search Practice: The Norwegian Case', *Critical Criminology* 14: 265.

Sparks, R. (1996) 'Penal "Austerity": The Doctrine of Less Eligibility Reborn?', in R. Matthews and P. Francis (eds), *Prisons 2000: An International Perspective of the Current State and Future of Imprisonment*. Basingstoke: Macmillan.

Turner, B.S. (2007) 'The Enclave Society: Towards a Sociology of Immobility', *European Journal of Social Theory* 10(2): 287.

Ugelvik, T. (2012) 'The Bellman and the Prison Officer: Customer Care in Imperfect Panopticons', in O. Moufakkir and Y. Reisinger (eds), *The Host Gaze in Global Tourism*. Wallingford: CABI.

Ugelvik, T. (2011) 'Hva er et fengsel?: En analyse av manualen til en sosial teknologi', *Retfærd* 34(1): 85.

Wacquant, L.J.D. (2009) *Punishing the Poor: The Neoliberal Government of Social Insecurity*. Durham NC: Duke University Press.

Wacquant, L.J.D. (2008) *Urban Outcasts: A Comparative Sociology of Advanced Marginality*. Cambridge: Polity Press.

Wacquant, L.J.D. (2001) 'The Penalisation of Poverty and the Rise of Neo-Liberalism', *European Journal on Criminal Policy and Research* 9(4): 401.

Weber, L. and Bowling, B. (2008) 'Valiant Beggars and Global Vagabonds: Select, Eject, Immobilize', *Theoretical Criminology* 12(3): 355.

Witoszek, N. (2011) *The Origins of the 'Regime of Goodness': Remapping the Cultural History of Norway*. Oslo: Universitetsforlaget.

Zhang, L.-C. (2008) *Developing Methods for Determining the Number of Unauthorised Foreigners in Norway*. Oslo: Statistisk sentralbyrå.

PART IV

DEPORTATION

11

The Social Bulimia of Forced Repatriation: A Case Study of Dominican Deportees

David C. Brotherton and Luis Barrios

Frank Madera sits in a wheelchair facing the judge in an immigration appeals courtroom housed in a deportee detention center in upstate New York. Frank is 57 years old, blind due to lack of medical attention for cataracts while in prison, has suffered 5 strokes in the last couple of years, sits paralyzed down his right side, was diagnosed as bipolar a decade ago, suffers from Type 1 chronic diabetes, and is functionally illiterate. Frank has just served three years in a New York State prison after trying to burgle a house in the Bronx on the orders of local drug dealers. Frank came to the United States more than 50 years ago and lives with his 80-year-old mother. Frank has an estranged wife and a 21-year-old daughter. Frank's lawyer, a pro-bono corporate attorney, tells the judge that if Frank is deported it will be a 'death sentence.' For six hours the judge listens intently to the appeal and to the government's case. Finally he reads his decision. He concludes that there is no merit to Frank's case and that while he might not receive adequate medical attention this does not amount to torture by the Dominican government. Therefore, he has no recourse but to forcibly repatriate Frank to what will be a speedy end to his life. (Field note, 8 February 2012)

I (DB) wrote these words after providing testimony as an expert witness, describing the likely state of public health services awaiting Frank in the Dominican Republic. His story encapsulates the extraordinary punitive and vindictive sanctions that are regularly meted out to deportable aliens throughout the United States. Such sanctions, which Daniel Kanstroom (2007) calls 'post-entry social control', emerged in the wake of the 1986 Immigration Reform and Control Act, before increasing greatly after the Illegal Immigration Reform and Immigrant Responsibility Act (IIRIRA) and the Antiterrorism Effective Death Penalty Act, both of 1996.

It is important to understand what these pieces of legislation have meant for Dominicans in the United States, a community that has long been the subject of 'targeted enforcement', racial profiling, saturated policing, and intergenerational poverty (Northern Manhattan Coalition for Immigrant Rights 2007). It is also important to consider their implications for criminological and sociological perspectives on the immigration-crime connection. In this chapter we examine both these issues through the concept of social bulimia (Young 1999, 2007, 2011). Drawing on 98 life history interviews with Dominican deportees (86 men and 12 women[1]) conducted in the Dominican Republic and the United States during the years 2002–2010, as well as *in situ* field observations of deportees and archival research related to Dominican deportation and the settlement of that community (see Brotherton and Barrios 2011), we focus on three stages of the bulimic cycle as they apply to the immigration/deportation process: (i) the seduction of the American Dream, Integration, and Othering; (ii) blurred boundaries, drifting, and pathways to crime; and (iii) the vindictiveness of prison and deportation.

Social Exclusion, Bulimia, and Agency

According to Jock Young (1999), threats against immigrants are a particular form of Othering in late modern capitalism, a process of circumscribing or thwarting social citizenship that he describes as bulimic rather than as just exclusionary. Advanced capitalist societies culturally include yet socially exclude large sections of the population, particularly those from the lower classes and so-called 'minorities'. This highly contradictory process is exhibited through a number of intersecting dynamics:

(i) the pushes and pulls of the global political economy with its restructuring of work and cross-national labour markets, irrational rewards system, increase in relative deprivation, and sharpening of class divisions;

(ii) the evolution of the social control industry with its expansion of gulags, laws, surveillance systems, constraints on civil and democratic liberties, and their vindictive applications;

(iii) the role of Othering as a form of social exclusion and stigmatization; and

(iv) the porous and fluid nature of all physical, social, and cultural borders.

Together, these processes make it difficult for individuals to formulate a coherent sense of self, leading to a ubiquitous condition of 'ontological insecurity'. Based on a set of beliefs about the pathological nature of criminals, and other socially constructed human pollutants, and buoyed by an economic commitment to a free market mythos, a brave new world of governance through crime and fear has emerged (Simon 2007). In this world the state must take pre-emptive action and exact extreme punishments to ensure that risks to the good, the pure, and the healthy never materialize (Douglas 1966). The deportee is a perfect example of the bulimic subject/object, the dehumanized outcome of three conjoining moral crusades: the war on drugs, the war on terrorism, and the war on the immigrant (Kanstroom 2007).

---

[1] Sixty of the deportees had been documented residents while 38 were undocumented, including 18 who had returned illegally.

However, is it all such one-way social control traffic? Both theoretically and empirically it is important to locate agency in these chaotic and contradictory processes and not to relinquish the presence of social and political will to obsessions with the indices of social order or received wisdoms about social reproduction (Bauman 2004). Acknowledging the possibility of agency, however attenuated, helps to underscore and articulate the tensions in the dialectic rather than simply emphasize the delineation of opposites, or what Young calls 'the binary' (Young 2007: 18). In other words, we need to (re)consider the many overt and covert acts of individual and collective defiance performed by immigrants, mindful that such actions and vocabularies of motive (Mills 1940) contrast with the tropes of adaptation and acculturation found in much of the assimilationist literature (Ngai 2004) as well as with a criminological literature that sees a world of good and bad immigrants outside the lived contradictions of culture and the state.[2]

In the following we address these issues in describing and analysing key aspects of the bulimic process as it is lived, felt, and experienced by deportees. Through their complex and often opaque histories those men and women reveal a layered and often contradictory life course as neo-colonial subjects. Thrice removed—from their original homeland, from US civil society, and from the US sovereign state—and multiply punished for their original transgression, they are incarcerated again for the same crime in immigration detention camps before enduring stigmatization, discrimination, and social exclusion on being repatriated to the Dominican Republic (Brotherton and Barrios 2009).

Leaving, the Seduction of the American Dream, and Othering

DB: Tell me about where you were born ...

Danny: I was born here in Santo Domingo on October 22nd 1962 and on August 8th 1963 my father took me to New York ... I grew up there all my life. I came back here in 1966 for a couple of months and in 1981 and 1991 for a few weeks. Then I came back here deported in 1999. I was born here but I really don't remember anything from here. (7 February 2006)

As Danny's account attests, immigrants frequently feel displaced, both socially and culturally, even though they may eventually become 'acculturated' or even 'assimilated'. This *dialectically social and historical process* of concurrent cultural inclusion and socio-economic exclusion is an essential feature of life for many transnational working-class families in the contemporary global marketplace. These contradictions of separation and reintegration, cultural loss and economic gain are constant sites in the formation of a renewed identity and become experiential markers as subjects form and reconstitute their sense of self in the new society.

---

[2] Hence both old and new Chicago Schools see immigrants remarkably free of punitive state interventions with little attention paid to complex lived, hybridized, and often criminalized immigrant (sub)cultures, or the opportunity structures of closely knit formal and informal economies in certain immigrant communities.

Some of our respondents, like Danny, were too young to remember much about the decision-making process of the past other than that they were compelled to join their parents or their grandparents '*alla en Nueva York*'. Their mobility was linked to the familial struggle for economic survival and the quest for a political future after the overthrow of the constitutional government of Juan Bosch in 1963 and the subsequent civil war and invasion of 42,000 US marines and paratroopers in 1965. For others, leaving was a means to negate the past, the psycho-social colonial legacy of fatalism (Fanon 1965), and a common fate befalling regime opponents: disappearance.

Framing these repressive experiences are the long-term dependency relations between the United States and the Dominican Republic, exemplified in the Monroe Doctrine.[3] These profoundly asymmetrical historical relations inscribe and circumscribe processes of development while providing the political economic and ideological context in which the notion of the 'American Dream' has had such seductive influence on dependent populations.[4] Thus, among our respondents the theme of the Dream was prominent, particularly for those who had emigrated to the United Status in their teens or later. Others who emigrated earlier spoke mostly of their parents or of other family members who were attracted to the promise of a better life somewhere 'over there'.

Messages of American prosperity and superiority are omnipresent in the swirl of First and Third World themes and images that constitute the urban Dominican's daily semiotic fare. Blaring from the television screens in *colmados* (neighbourhood grocery stores) and in many homes there is a constant diet of media productions foregrounding middle-class lifestyles in Los Angeles, New York City, and Chicago. Similarly, Hollywood films are the staple diet of most Dominican cinemas although the cost of entry is generally too prohibitive for working-class residents of the capital. More prosaically, the American Dream is communicated through social networks of family members and friends who are more inclined to talk of their 'positive' American transition than of the difficulties of settlement and any notions of 'failure'.

While the idea of American prosperity is alluring, no one can predict how it might be realized. For some, the dream can be achieved legitimately as they study, enter the labour market after graduating from high school, 'keep their noses clean', and generally follow the examples of their hard-working parents. But for many of those we interviewed, especially long-term legal residents continuing to struggle in the lowest tiers of the segmented labour force, the only way to attain their Dream was through the informal economy.

---

[3] In 1823, the US proclaimed Latin America to be free of European colonization. Over time, this has rationalized the right of the US to intervene whenever and wherever it wants in the Americas.

[4] Cullen (2003) argues that the concept of the American Dream has at least four connotations: (i) it filled the imaginations of early religious dissenters seeking a space to practise their own particular worship; (ii) it is in the notion of upward mobility and part of America's dominant culture and ideology (Adams 1931); (iii) it is contained in the notion of home ownership as in the Homestead Act of 1862 but more recently in the suburbanization of America; and (iv) it conveys the notion of personal fulfilment.

The process of moving towards the Dream has been described in the immigration literature but relatively little is heard from those who have seen the process go into reverse, such as Celio:

DB: Why did you emigrate? Was it for the American Dream?

Celio: The idea came from my brother-in-law. He was in Puerto Rico and at that time had an amnesty. He was always telling us, 'You've got to go, you've got to go'. Until he damaged my mind and I went. But I don't regret it, in spite of losing everything. I learned a lot and I've got something that every man wants to have, a son. He's not with me, but I have him. God and I are witnesses that he is there. I helped my family a lot when I was over there. It may have been drug money, but I helped them. I was my family's economic support when I was in the United States ... in Puerto Rico.[5] I say these days that I don't regret it, because I did bad things but also I did good things—the lottery for many undocumented immigrants. (2 December 2002)

Celio's reference to his mind 'being damaged' captures his disquiet and ambivalence. It also speaks to the unsettling impact of American power and the vulnerability of a people whose efforts at independence have been consistently denied by Washington. Perhaps both meanings are present, as the immigrant/emigrant constantly pieces together the narratives of a transnational journey in search of something approaching a unified self (Brotherton and Barrios 2009). Despite losing 'everything' and remaining separated from his child, Celio outwardly retains some of the hope behind his original journey.

In contrast, Manolo waxes nostalgic about his childhood, a time when he was living the American Dream as part of a working-class immigrant family in the early 1960s:

DB: Did you miss the DR?

Manolo: I didn't miss the DR for nothing, I was basically too excited to be over there rather than over here. It was plenty over there, but specially the train. My mother used to take us down to Macy's. She ... and my father used to get paid and would say, 'Let's get the kids', you know. Specially when winter time was coming ... the coats, the boots, the long johns to protect us. We used to go down in the train. My mother used to hold on to me tight and my father used to hold on to the little girls, and we'd go inside those big department stores ... all that stuff specially at Christmas. My God, Lord have Mercy ... bags for the kids, trying on new clothes with my mother who used to take up her hair special. And then with all this she'd get us ready for school, to go out in the snow. And then the weekends, the ice skating ... Man, it was very exciting, man, wow! (2 April 2003)

Economic security and educational possibilities are both important elements of the Dream for deportees as evidenced by Alex, who wistfully remembers his experience of public schooling and its promise of social ascent. For Alex, it was easy to take the Dream for granted, as if this revelation late in his life might have saved him from himself and the pitfalls of his immediate neighbourhood during the 1970s:

---

[5] Puerto Rico is a 'colonized' unincorporated territory of the United States and is geographically close to the Dominican Republic.

Alex: God bless them [the United States] ... they offer you a lot of things. They offer you school, they give you money while you're going to school, you know, they give you free college and things. I don't know how they call it but you have a lot of opportunities over there. But when you're young you don't realize those things, especially when you don't have no family next to you that can give you the proper guidance. (5 March 2003)

Nonetheless, the Dream did not produce the same bounty for everyone. Some of the respondents recounted how betrayed they felt and the dislocation and disruption caused by their ultimately futile attempts to succeed:

Julio: What happened is that I went crazy with the idea of seeking the American Dream. And therefore I left the country. If I had stayed and not been carried off by the American Dream I would have gone on to study. I would have gone to college and I would be a professional by now. Instead, I was in Puerto Rico from '89 to '96, between Puerto Rico and New York, that's practically 7 years. In those years I could have graduated here, but seeking the American dream I lost it all, except my life which is most important! (3 March 2003)

Settlement and integration are, for many, complicated and concurrent in the process of emigrating and immigrating (Sayad 2004). Both matters can be usefully examined through the *dialectics of the bulimic process* in order to appreciate how immigrant hope and positive momentum contend with social and racial ordering (ie Othering), processes of downward mobility, and the unpredictability of segmented assimilation.[6]

For those whom we interviewed, the experience of settling ranged greatly. It was contingent on a number of factors including the intact status of the family (50 per cent of New York Dominicans were living in single, female-headed households in the mid-1990s), the age of the immigrant/emigrant, the crime and immigration politics and laws of the host society, the race-ethnic climate of the receiving society and the state of its political economy, and the comparative condition of the ethnic community. Those who left as children often recalled the good things, describing an arc of life that at one time pointed positively toward security and prosperity. They remembered rejoining their families, relishing basic necessities as food, electricity, and hot water, and the novelty of consumer items such as refrigerators and televisions (with real channels). For older 'documented' deportees their memories were more conflicted as they recounted their feelings of social and cultural loss in their longing for the Caribbean tropical heat, their preference for the slow rhythms of island life, and their nostalgia for the more communal warmth of *la gente*. Undocumented deportees often focused on the relief of arriving safely and on the hopes for a successful if unpredictable process of settling and, importantly, the lifelong family obligations they were committed to in their homeland.

This comparison in the memories of Manolo and Juan (below) was typical of many:

---

6 Portes and Zhou (1993) developed the notion of 'segmented assimilation', combining several models of integration with a strong emphasis on the intersection of social and economic capital. They argued that significant cohorts of second generation immigrants might find themselves excluded on a more permanent basis and therefore become downwardly mobile.

DB: When you think about those early years, how do you remember them?

Manolo: I wished I just could go back again with the mentality I have now. Those years were the best years in my life, compared to now … Back then it was very good. We had programs, we did things together, we used to have tournaments … it was incredible: Yankee Stadium, Shea Stadium, Madison Square Garden, the New York Knicks. I've seen everything: football, the Giants, everybody. (2 April 2003)

DB: When you arrived in the States, how was that?

Juan: When I arrived that was very bad, I was trying to stay for a year to bring my wife and family. But I saw that New York wasn't good for them.

DB: What did you see?

Juan: I saw a lot of guys in the streets selling drugs and they used to do it freely. I thought that was a bad environment for my kids. (1 March 2003)

While some deportees told of a rich, fruitful new beginning, others struggled from the very beginning, battling impoverishment, the seduction of neighbourhood subcultures and inadequate schools, family, or the church. For everyone, their class, ethnic, and gendered backgrounds, and the ways their human, social, and cultural capitals intersected with the opportunity structures of the receiving society, were situated in an especially punishing epoch of neo-liberalism (Wacquant 2008; Hochschild 2012). The lingering effect of this period of rampant outsourcing, privatization, securitization, and growing class divides can still be felt, as recent comparative research conducted in New York has demonstrated, with second generation Dominicans the least likely to see upward social mobility (Kasinitz, Waters, Mollenkopf, and Holdaway 2008).

The threat of downward or levelled out mobility was highlighted in many of the deportees' work and educational histories. Sixty-five men and women whom we interviewed had spent a major part of their early socialization in the United States but only three of them had attended college.[7] We found almost no strong bonds with teachers even though nearly all had attended large public high schools.[8] Further, during their period of adolescence at least 10 had been members of street gangs, joining local deviant youth subcultures for reasons such as: 'fitting in', 'peer pressure', 'defending my culture', 'excitement', and 'you had to do it in my neighborhood'.

Such downwardly mobile pressures were particularly evident in accounts of their years of paid labour, with nearly all of the respondents finding work in marginal blue collar occupations or low status positions in the service industry. Only one deportee had held a white collar job, in this case as a bank teller. It was not difficult to see the cultural mismatch between these Dominican working-class products of the barrio and the middle-class work environments of the office where most of the recent jobs growth occurred in New York (Bourgois 1991; Castells and Mollenkopf 1999).

---

[7] In 1996 54.7% of Dominicans had no educational diploma while 25% had less than high school (US Department of Commerce 1997).

[8] One woman went to a private school.

Nonetheless, perhaps none of these downward pressures would matter inter-generationally if the respondents did not also face a barrage of race- and class-inflected laws (Reinarman and Levine 1997). Segmented assimilationists are largely silent about the mutually reinforcing and intricate relationship between the criminal justice and the deportation systems often referred to as 'crimmigration' (Stumpf 2006). Yet such matters are crucial if we are to understand the ways in which policing, sentencing, and adjudication have been imagined and applied to the Dominican and other immigrant communities of colour over time (Noguera 1999). The results are amply reflected in the following, bearing in mind that most of those we interviewed were adjudicated in the 1990s:

- Between 1985 and 2007 the foreign-born inmate population in New York State increased by 148 per cent, of which Dominicans made up approximately one-third, the majority imprisoned on drug charges with sentences growing longer and parole more difficult to attain.

- Nationally the imprisonment rate of Latinos tripled from 1980 to 1993 (from 163 to 529 per 100,000) reflected in the overall New York State Prison population increasing from 22,000 in 1980 to 71,500 in 1996: 91 per cent of state inmates are either Black or Latino.

- In 1986 the Anti-Drug Abuse Act passed by Congress set the now familiar 100–1 mandatory sentencing guidelines for the sale of crack versus powdered cocaine (ie someone guilty of possession with intent to sell more than five grams of crack received five years' imprisonment versus the same sentence for more than 500 grams of powdered cocaine)—by the end of the 1990s more than 50 per cent of all inmates were incarcerated for non-violent, often drug-related crimes and this rose to more than 80 per cent of all federal inmates.

- Federal drug laws compounded the draconian precedents in New York State of the 1973 Rockefeller anti-drug legislation which first mandated prison for drug possession.

- Rikers Island, the biggest prison in the world, located in the middle of New York City's East River, regularly registered 20,000 inmates during the early 1990s—it was known as one of the most violent prisons in the nation with Blacks and Latinos constituting 92 per cent of the population.

- The racially and ethnically selective anti-drugs crusade has continued and recent marijuana arrests in New York City increased by 1,000 per cent, with more than 500,000 during 1996–2010 apprehended for the lowest level of marijuana possession (Levine and Siegel 2010).

- Finally, the punitive and racially discriminatory practice of detention and arrest can be seen in the NYPD's practice of 'stop and frisk' which began in the early 1990s as the then police chief William Bratton rejected the community policing approach in favour of a new 'efficient and effective' scientific management. In 2011 more than 680,000 mostly young Blacks and Latinos (87 per cent) were the targets of this policy.

All of these policies of selective policing and coercive social control have had a profoundly negative and disruptive impact on the Dominican community. Nonetheless, our respondents exhibited a surprising lack of fatalism. While some spoke of missed opportunities, musing, 'If only I knew then what I know now', few regretted their US experience even when it was cut tragically short. For most it remained their shot at 'making it', their time spent hanging out with characters on the block, their schooldays, their participation in the 'crazy' years of New York, and their lived memories of family, parents, siblings, grandparents, and children.

Blurred Boundaries, Drifting, and Pathways to Crime

Blurred boundaries between mainstream and deviant behaviour, between socio-geographic and cultural domains, and between the formal and informal economies are critical ingredients of the socially bulimic condition. The participants in our study were constantly negotiating within and across such boundaries as they made their way transnationally through risk-filled environments in a risk-based, highly policed society. Many of the deportees were raised in New York's most socially and economically underserved neighbourhoods. These are the urban spaces where the immigrant proletariats and precariats (Standing 2011) attempted to settle, reminiscent of what the Chicago School would call 'interstitial areas'.

The community of Washington Heights, where a substantial number of the interviewees had previously resided, experienced some of the highest rates of poverty and crime throughout the 1970s, 1980s, and 1990s.[9] It is also one of the geographic centres of the New York drugs trade, occupying a prime location abutting the George Washington Bridge, a major transit hub that linked the area to the white middle classes of New Jersey who made up a significant proportion of the illicit drug market's customer base. The Dominican Republic itself was and is a major conduit for Colombian drug cartels and was considered by the US Drug Enforcement Agency to be one of the leading sites of money laundering for the drugs trade in the world (Brotherton and Martin 2009).

This is not to say that such structural, spatial, and cultural conditions predetermined involvement in crime but rather that the opportunities to do crime, the social networks that lead to it, the subcultures that seduce people into crime, as well as the legal and social definitions that make crime and/or transgression normative made such a pathway difficult to avoid. Rarely did anyone refer to the guiding hand of a parent (socially and emotionally some parents were there but none of them possessed the cultural capital to enable their upward ascent). No one mentioned an intervention in prison steering them to a different path if and when they returned to civil society. School was often disappointing and nobody spoke of mentors in the community from their family or elsewhere.

---

[9] By the mid-1990s almost 46% of Dominicans were living in households below the poverty line and were the only ethnic group to experience a rise in poverty (by 10%) during the early 1990s (Hernández and Rivera-Batiz 1997).

Among our respondents, instead, we heard different versions of an inexorable drift into the life worlds of low-level crime. Not the well-organized worlds of the mafia or even mid-level drug dealers (with a few exceptions), but rather the loose, peripheral edges of the local informal economy that included drug dealing, small-time burglaries, other relatively minor felonies, and 'off the books' work. Men often committed crime in a bid for economic niches, social spheres of belonging, and the chance to create and add meaning and edge to their early adult barrio lives. Some were simply caught in the wrong place at the wrong time with inadequate legal representation due to their immigrant status. Women, in contrast, were mostly led into crime by their male partners or criminalized by their undocumented working status. The social and cultural context for most was from the mid-1970s to the mid-1990s—a subculturally effervescent period that spawned hip-hop amid the bank-ruptcy of New York (see Chang 2005) followed by an era encompassing the 'crack attack' (Reinarman and Levine 1997). In such contexts it is important to bear in mind that in certain city locales the deviants outnumbered the straights.

But what can we say about the process and progression of these pathways? We found that they were not sudden and are not easily compartmentalized into neat life course stages. Rather they transpired as a layered if somewhat predictable process of multiple marginalization (Vigil 1988), occurring in neighbourhoods that were the site of increased policing and surveillance, 'geographies of exclusion' (Sibley 1995), and sustained disinvestment by local and central governments. Boundaries were porous, with multiple links to local and global surroundings not least of which were those workers recruited to support the lifestyles of the adjacent middle classes:

Quisqueya: A friend of mine got me this job. They know I'm undocumented and that I have been deported ... They are a lovely family with a daughter and a son. It's been two years that I've worked with them and when I started the girl was three years old and the boy one year old. I speak a little English but they always told me to only speak Spanish to the children. I don't know how the hell they learned Spanish in such a short time and I keep trying with this f***ing English that I sometimes know and sometimes don't know what the hell I am saying!

For legal permanent residents (LPRs) the process of social maginalization often started in their teens. It was usually a gradual progression, moving from experimenting with soft drugs such as marijuana to small-time, peripheral roles in the drugs trade, until they eventually become more independent market players buying and selling a range of 'product' including marijuana, powdered cocaine, crack cocaine, and heroin, sometimes accompanied by sustained using. For others, the drugs trade was complemented by robberies and burglaries, but these were a small minority and such practices were not self-initiated but were strongly influenced by their peers and older acquaintances. In most cases, the deportees drifted into crime and often drifted out again (Matza, 1964). Some, however, took a more focused entrepreneurial path, building delinquent and criminal careers, lured and encouraged by lucrative drug profits and the felt need to sustain a conspicuous lifestyle, a barrio version of the American Dream (Bourgois 1991; Nightingale 1993). A similar number (eight) participated in the illicit economy for what they claimed were altruistic reasons, doing it for their parents, usually their mothers, helping to get them out of poverty and make the financial contributions their fathers were incapable or unwilling to do.

Among those who were living in the United States during the height of the 'crack epidemic' there was a great deal of positioning, what might be called a situated ambivalence, between the street and the mainstream. Chino, for a time, at least, appears to handle the two worlds:

DB: Did you go back to Washington Heights?

Chino: Yeah.

DB: Same neighborhood?

Chino: Same neighborhood. And then, you know what was waiting for me over there? The boom of the crack, everybody was going nuts, what the fucking thing is this! Everybody going up and down the building, roaching here, roaching there. I said, 'What's this man?' And then I said, 'Everybody's making money!' Bam, bam, bam, like that. And then I went to take a course, like I told you, as a bank teller. I wanna get a job, bam, bam, and then I went to the streets. I use both of them the streets and the bank.

But the rule enforcers were not so hermetically sealed off from the deviants. Again the blurred boundaries between the in and out group, the decent and the corrupt were highlighted as subjects testified to the hypocrisies and ironies they have witnessed. To those involved in the drugs economy everybody is potentially seduced by the cash nexus. Since so much of this political economy depends on bribery and corruption the following forms of informal social control should not surprise us.

DB: And how many guys did you have working for you?

Luis 3: About 30.

DB: Did you manage to put any money away, save anything?

Luis 3: They took a lot of money from me, the cops. When they first arrested me, they took $250,000 and jewelry and they kept the drugs, they kept everything. They did a stick up and said go away. About 6 months later they came back again and took another $270,000, cars, jewelry, everything but never put me in jail. It was like they were robbing me! (10 June 2003)

The Vindictiveness of Prison and Deportation

Regardless of their crime, both legal and undocumented subjects found them-selves incarcerated in the United States and thrust into what for some was an assembly-line process of arrest and confinement followed by deportation. Others saw a slower pathway to permanent exile (except for the 18 who came back illegally). Whatever the speed of the process, their transnational social exclusion felt vindictive, irrational, disconnected from rehabilitation or even effective social control. Humiliation, shock, trauma, violence, depression, extreme isolation, and intimidation are all the felt effects of incarceration (including prisons and jails) and sentencing. Young (2007) calls this the sociology of vindictiveness and links the penchant for state punishments to the rising resentment of the middle classes in an era of deep economic precariousness and late modern liquidity (Bauman 2004). The following are just a few examples of multiple testimonies by deportees based on their experience of the interlocking US crimmigration systems.

Elixida was an undocumented worker in Manhattan employed in a clothing store whose Russian owners laundered money and imported drugs from 'Colombian' drug cartels. She was picked up as an 'accessory' and sent to Rikers Island while pregnant, later giving birth to her first son there. After being held for two years all charges against her were dropped but she was ordered deported anyway despite the fact that her Dominican husband had tried to kill her twice:

Elixida: They took me to X Hospital. There I had my son, foot-cuffed, tied all the time. Only when I was pushing the baby did they let me free, but then at once they handcuffed me and I had two policemen with me, one in front and one behind, looking at me, with the pain and everything, always.

GE: As if you were going to run away?

Elixida: They sent me back with the baby to prison. I filled out an application because I didn't want them to take away my son. There I lasted one year. After the child was one year old, they sent him home. That's what hurt me the most in my life. (8 June 2006)

Guido entered the criminal justice system for the first time in his mid-twenties. He had been working in a warehousing job but got involved in small-time cocaine distribution selling to his workmates. Guido had lived in the New York area since he was two and was an LPR after his father was assassinated in the Dominican Republic by revolutionaries. His father had given information about clandestine activities to CIA operatives who had threatened to kill and torture his entire family (this was during the armed struggle of the mid-1960s).

Guido: When I went for sentencing, my lawyer told me, 'if you go in front of this other judge you're f*****d'. This guy gave me 50 years, and I think it was 2 years for the firearms charge. I was scared. I'd never been in trouble in my life and it led to this. He gave me 52 years! Before I was thinking I would be out in 2 years. (22 May 2003)

Mauricio was a 'short timer', an LPR who had lived in Washington Heights for almost all his life. He had worked as a janitor but was serving three years for drug possession and sales and sent to an upstate prison where he experienced the following:

DB: And how was the prison where you were?

Mauricio: You know Ku Klux Klan people? Something like that.

DB: KKK were working there?

Mauricio: Yeah, with the fucking tattoos here (he shows his forearm), with the blacks on the trees. Plus when you work in there the whole day they give you $1 dollar a day!

DB: One dollar a day?

Mauricio: One dollar a day! And if you don't work you get locked up.

DB: And did they beat the inmates there too?

Mauricio: Yeah! A lot of people, … they don't give a f*** what happens to you … This motherf***er … uses the club, smacking, putting you in the SHU. When the family go there he say you're not even there. If I get put in the hole, I can't even send you my number. (2 June 2003)

Pedro was an LPR doing a significant 'bid', 15 years for his role as a 'collector' for Colombian drug cartels in Brooklyn. Pedro had also worked for a number of years in construction and had mastered several specialized trades. He had been in five upstate prisons (Pedro was eventually assassinated by the Dominican police after investigating the sexual abuse of minors by a police captain):

> Pedro: The mindset with those guys was different. They're like out of a movie. I see some of the guards with tattoos of black babies hanging off trees! I said, 'What the hell?' And they are all big, like 6'3"and they'll break you up. They broke my ribs. Ask a medical doctor how difficult it is to break the ribs … Mine actually separated. (10 June 2003)

Having served their sentences these people faced the deportation system. Quickly, they had to confront odds stacked against them in trying to win relief and a modicum of justice for themselves and their families. They had already spent years incarcerated, felt the discriminating pinch of segmented labour opportunities, and discovered that school was often little more than a tracking device for the skilled and the unskilled. Fermin describes the humiliation of getting picked up by the then Immigration and Naturalization Service (INS):

> Fermin: My kids went to see me when immigration caught me. They took me back to Hudson County Jail and the guy from immigration and the guy from the jail picked me up and sent me to another immigration jail far away, near Trenton. They said my kids were running after the van. Priscilla was running after the van, 'Mommy, mommy', but I didn't wanna see it. It was awful … (the interviewee is weeping). (7 May 2006)

We also consistently heard complaints about the quality of legal representation. Ten of the original 65 people we interviewed claimed to have been defrauded by their lawyers. Of the total respondents, only three spoke positively of their representation:

> Luis 2: … the lawyer that I had, I sued … he told me, 'Get me $2,500 … I'm getting you out'. Then he lied to me … and didn't help me at all. Instead he continued working for the court and took my money. The court answered saying that the lawyer had been suspended for a year due to malpractice. I couldn't continue with the suit because of my English and lack of experience … I stopped the whole thing because I didn't have, how do you it say it, the means! (2 April 2003)

Consequently, many felt 'tricked' into signing their deportation papers since they did not fully understand both the immediate and long-term consequences of their action. Their main complaints were that they: (i) were rarely given time to think about their choices; (ii) had few people with the appropriate knowledge with whom they could consult; (iii) were unable to consult with family members; and (iv) lacked education and knowledge of the English language.

None of the deportees spoke positively about the immigration detention facilities; rather they recalled overcrowded conditions, lack of recreational opportunities, abuse by prison guards, a general atmosphere of despair among the detainees, and the gradual if not immediate understanding that their experience of the justice system would not improve. Juan sums it up:

DB: Was jail any different to the prison?

Juan: That was worse! They used to have riots over there all the time and they do things just to bother inmates.

DB: What sort of things?

Juan: Lots of different things. The food was very bad, they got a lot of rules, they were abusive to most of the people that go there from prison or from the feds. They're accustomed to work with guys from the street. They think that people from prison have to be treated in the same way. But most of the people that go to immigration prison just want to leave and get out. We're just tired of being in custody. (10 March 2003)

There were, however, 10 individuals who decided to fight their case, taking the system at its word and making use of the appeals process. Four did so with the aid of a lawyer and six tried without professional representation. To take on such a responsibility requires a great deal of self-confidence and courage. It also requires a level of formal education that was usually lacking. In addition three participants fought to have their sentences reduced in prison arguing that they had been inadequately represented. These were all successful towards the end of their sentence, which might have been helped by judges responding to the increased pressures to reduce prison costs and overcrowding:

Juan: My lawyer said that it was a better idea not to talk during the trial, and then she changed her mind ... I was very confused and I never got a good explanation ... she said that if I weren't Spanish it would be better. She said that a lot of white guys on the jury are prejudiced against drugs and Spanish people. I say, ok, we try to make a better case in the appeal. She said that that was a good case, but we lost it. We took it to the Supreme Judicial Court of the State ...

DB: How long did all that take?

Juan: ... about 2 years.

DB: When you finally lost everything what were your thoughts?

Juan: I never gave up. I still thought there would be a moment that I was going to make it. I used to tell myself, until the last day I spend in here I'm gonna take this case back to court, because I knew I didn't do it! I was trying that for 5 years and then finally after 10 years I got the right to go to a new trial. (1 March 2003)

Conclusion

There is a much to learn from the deportation process in coming to terms with the irrationality and inhumanity of society's rules. For deportees, it ran counter to their understanding of being 'American' and of everything that identity constitutes, including legal legitimacy, justice, due process, democracy, and opportunity. Their families came from a country that, in their experience, had none of these qualities and was an important reason for their original departure. To have the United States so wilfully fragment their family, an institution that remains the foundation of most Dominican socio-cultural life, while curtailing any possibility of rehabilitation and reintegration created an existential crisis from which they and their families may never social-psychologically recover.

The trajectory of these immigrants took a turn for the worse not simply because of what they did or did not do, but because the laws in the United States changed, turning the racialized communities from whence they came, their spaces, networks, survival mechanisms, and status into criminalizable units of control. In this we see the bulimic paradox, creating what Stumpf (2006: 352) calls 'an ever-expanding population of the excluded and the alienated'.

For the disciplines of criminology and sociology there are other important implications. First, most of these first and 1.5 generational immigrants saw themselves as 'fitting in' to the dominant culture, struggling to attain the American Dream through the extant opportunity structures. They did not enter the country as criminals (aside from the administrative status of a few) but as mainstream aspirants eventually making their way into the criminal justice system. In the past their individual mistakes might eventually have been corrected by a community's strengthening institutions. These days, however, the sovereign state's punitive immigration policies now overdetermine local processes of immigrant assimilation. Second, advocates of crime control policies such as 'broken windows' and 'zero tolerance' fail to consider the fragmentary effects on vulnerable immigrant populations and the increasing collateral damage to related families. Third, while some immigration sociologists correctly point to those local antisocial pressures that can reduce immigrant upward mobility, the depiction of these so-called oppositional forces is far too mechanistic and dualistic. This is particularly the case in a world of blurred boundaries, rampant Othering, and essentializing, When we pay closer attention to the life worlds of various immigrant groups and the different ways that racial, class, and gender codes of social control are applied to their 'kind' (both now and historically) we can better appreciate how such pressures help produce not just diminished mobility but a lifetime of exile, alienation, and a desperate struggle for survival.

References

Adams, J.T. (2001 [1931]) *The Epic of America*. Simon Publications: New York.

Bauman, Z. (2004) *Wasted Lives: Modernity and its Outcasts*. Hoboken, NJ: Polity Press.

Bourgois, P. (1991) *In Search of Respect: Selling Crack in El Barrio*. New York: Cambridge University Press.

Brotherton, D.C. and Barrios, L. (2011) *Banished to the Homeland: Dominican Deportees and Their Stories of Exile*. New York: Columbia University Press.

Brotherton, D.C. and Barrios, L. (2009) 'Displacement and Stigma: The Social-Psychological Crisis of the Dominican Deportee', *Crime, Media, Culture: An International Journal* 5(1): 29.

Brotherton, D.C. and Martín, Y. (2009) 'War on Drugs and the Case of Dominican Deportees', *Journal of Crime and Justice* 32(2): 21.

Castells, M. and Mollenkopf, J.H. (1991) *Dual City: Restructuring New York*. New York: Russell Sage Foundation.

Chang, J. (2005) *Can't Stop Won't Stop: A History of the Hip Hop Generation*. New York: St. Martin's Press.

Cullen, J. (2003) *The American Dream: A Short History of an Idea that Shaped the Nation*. New York: Oxford University Press.

Douglas, M. (1966) *Purity and Danger—An Analysis of Concepts of Pollution and Taboo*. London: Routledge Classics.

Fanon, F. (1965) *Wretched of the Earth*. New York: Grove Press.

Hernández, R. and Rivera-Batiz, F. (1997) *Dominican New Yorkers: A Socioeconomic Profile*. New York: Dominican Research Monographs—The CUNY Dominican Studies Institute.

Hoschschild, A. (2012) *The Outsourced Self: Intimate Life in Modern Times*. New York: Metropolitan Books.

International Human Rights Law Clinic (2010) *In the Child's Best Interest? The Consequences of Losing a Lawful Parent to Deportation*. Berkeley, CA.

Kanstroom, D. (2007) *Deportation Nation: Outsiders in American History*. Cambridge, MA: Harvard University Press.

Kasinitz, P., Waters, M., Mollenkopf, J. and Holdaway, J. (2008) *Inheriting the City: The Children of Immigrants Come of Age*. New York: Russell Sage Publication.

Levine, H. and Siegel, L. (2010) *$75 a year: the cost of New York City's Marijuana Arrests*. New York: Drug Policy Alliance.

Matza, D. (1964) *Delinquency and Drift*. New York: John Wiley and Sons.

Mills, C.W. (1940) 'Situated Actions and Vocabularies of Motive', *American Sociological Review* 5(6) 904.

Ngai, M.M. (2004) *Impossible Subjects: Illegal Aliens and the Making of Modern America*. Princeton, NJ: Princeton University.

Nightingale, C. (1993) *On the Edge*. New York: Basic Books.

Noguera, P. (1999) 'Exporting the Undesirable: An Analysis of the Factors Influencing the Deportation of Immigrants from the United States and an Examination of their Impact on Caribbean and Central American Societies', *Wadabagei: A Journal of the Caribbean and its Diaspora*, Winter/Spring (2)1: 1.

Northern Manhattan Coalition Report (2007) *Dominicano, Deportado, y Humano: The Realities of Dominican Deportations and Related Policy Recommendations*. New York: Northern Manhattan Coalition.

Portes, A. and Zhou, M. (1993) 'The New Second Generation: Segmented Assimilation and its Variants', *Annals of the American Academy of Political and Social Science* 22(2): 217.

Reinarman, C. and Levine, H. (1997) *Crack in America: Demon Drugs and Social Justice*. Berkeley, CA: University of California Press.

Sayad, A. (2004) *The Suffering of the Immigrant*. Massachusetts: Polity.

Sibley, D. (1995) *Geographies of Exclusion: Society and Difference in the West*. New York: Routledge.

Simon, J. (2007) *Governing Through Crime: How the War on Crime Transformed American Democracy and Created a Culture of Fear*. New York: Oxford University Press.

Standing, G. (2011) *The Precariat: The New Dangerous Class*. New York: Bloomsbury.

Stumpf, J P. (2006) 'The Crimmigration Crisis: Immigrants, Crime, and Sovereign Power', *American University Law Review* 56: 368.

US Department of Commerce (1997) *March 1997 Current Population Survey*. Washington, DC Bureau of the Census, October.

Vigil, J.D. (1988) *Barrio Gangs: Street Life and Identity in Southern California*. Austin: University of Texas Press.

Wacquant, L. (2008) *Urban Outcasts: A Comparative Sociology of Advanced Marginality*. Cambridge: Polity Press.

Young, J. (2011) *The Criminological Imagination*. London: Polity.

Young, J. (2007) *Vertigo in Late Modernity*. London: Sage Publications.

Young, J. (1999) *The Exclusive Society: Social Exclusion, Crime and Difference in Late Modernity*. London: Sage Publications.

12

Deportation, Crime, and the Changing Character of Membership in the United Kingdom

Matthew J. Gibney

Introduction

Of those subject to the expulsion power of contemporary liberal states, non-citizens convicted of criminal and terrorist offences seem to gain the least public sympathy. While local and national newspapers often feature stories about anti-deportation campaigns, typically centred around churches or schools, attempting to stop the expulsion of unsuccessful asylum seekers or visa overstayers, the deportation of criminals seems to proceed relatively unhindered, breaking into the news only when individuals escape deportation because of 'incompetent' public officials or 'liberal judges' using putatively absurd human rights laws (see Kaufman, Chapter 9 in this volume). Indeed, in the United Kingdom the tabloid press, reflecting the restrictive tastes of their audiences, routinely use such failures to call for deportation policies of unprecedented strictness (see, for example, *Sun* 2011).

It is tempting to attribute this enthusiasm for deporting criminals to a legitimate desire of sections of the public to protect themselves from those who would violate their personal and collective security: deported thieves, rapists, and murderers cannot rob, rape, or kill again in this country. Yet amongst the deported are many who have committed relatively minor crimes which cannot be said to threaten public security under circumstances that suggest that they are unlikely to break the law again. Deportation often seems like an unduly harsh response, not least because it typically follows a prison sentence (cf Kanstroom 2007).

However, something deeper is at work in public enthusiasm for deportation. Hostility to criminal migrants seems rooted in a widespread view that non-citizens convicted of crimes are particularly undeserving of sympathy because they have betrayed the hospitality of the society that let them enter and live in the state. The deportation of criminals may also draw its popularity from its role as a lightning rod for public hostility towards immigration in general, though relatively little research has been conducted on public attitudes to deportation. Irrespective of its drivers, support for the deportation of convicted non-citizens appears a salient feature of modern immigration politics. The UK Prime Minister Tony Blair felt sure enough of the support of the British public to make the extraordinary statement that 'it is now time that *anybody* who is convicted of an imprisonable offence and who is a foreign national is deported' in Parliament in 2006 (*Daily Mail* 2007; emphasis added).

Whether or not one accepts as legitimate the state's right to deport criminals, there is no denying the hardships deportation exacts from the foreign nationals concerned. Scholars have recently shed a great deal of light on the human costs of living life under the shadow of deportation (Sigona 2012), the role of detention and imprisonment by state authorities in facilitating deportation (Bosworth 2012), the limited procedural rights of deportees (Kanstroom 2007), the use of (sometimes fatal) coercion in the enforcement of deportation orders (Cohen 1994), and the appalling conditions that may await those deported in the countries to which they are sent (Brotherton and Barrios, Chapter 11 in this volume). But in this chapter I will look at deportation from a different angle: my focus will be on the implications of the deportation of criminals not for the non-citizen but for the citizen (see also Zedner, Chapter 2 in this volume).

The dominant and most intuitively plausible account of the relationship between deportation and citizenship sees deportation as facilitating the construction of the established boundaries of membership in contemporary states (Walters 2002; De Genova and Putz 2010; Anderson, Gibney, and Paoletti 2011). Deportation reinforces the normative unity of membership and the practical significance of citizenship. In terms of the former—citizenship's normative significance—deportation acts to reaffirm the values of the citizen community by effectively punishing, through expulsion, those residents who trangress its fundamental norms. Contemporary states do not portrary themselves simply as random collections of people thrown together by birth on the same territory, but as communities of *value*, people who share some common principles and beliefs (cf Honig 2003). Deportation reinforces these values—albeit negatively—by serving as a public statement of what kinds of behaviour are unacceptable and therefore at odds with this normative, idealized conception of the community. Hence, deportation tracks those whose practices and values are seen as antithetical to the community of value. While communists, Nazis, and prostitutes were commonly deported in 1930s America, Islamist extremists preaching jihad and sex offenders are a major target today. Arguably, this kind of affirmation of the citizen community is particularly important at times of large-scale immigration (Kanstroom 2007). Deportation serves both to reassert the value of social unity and reassure the public that immigration will be managed in a way beneficial to members.

Just as significantly, deportation serves as a practical reminder of the worth of citizenship (Anderson, Gibney, and Paoletti 2011). It does so because citizens are free from the state's deportation power. Unlike the non-citizen, whose presence in the state is conditional, the residence of the citizen is (in principle) unconditional. This unconditional right of residence is particularly salient in a context where migration is a contentious issue, where states trumpet their deportation power, and where the difference in rights and entitlements possessed by long-term legal residents and formal citizens are quite small in practice.

The deportation of criminal non-citizens, then, is a way in which citizenship may be affirmed and reaffirmed as a normatively meaningful and practially valuable status. Yet, in this chapter, I wish to point to some other, less intentional effects of the use of deportation. I will show that recent efforts to deport criminals also serve to underline citizenship's fragility and its contested nature. Drawing upon the example of the United Kingdom, I show how, at key moments, governments have effectively redrawn the boundaries of membership to bring some groups of people previously accepted as members into the reach of deportation power, generating controversy and contention.

My mechanism for highlighting the changing historical contours of deportation is examination of the parliamentary discussions surrounding four pieces of UK legislation that relate to the British state's deportation power. The first is the Commonwealth Immigrants Act 1962, which made it possible for the first time to deport Commonwealth citizens. The second and third are the Nationality, Immigration and Asylum Act 2002 and the Immigration, Asylum and Nationality Act 2006, which together extended the state's power to strip citizenship from birthright UK citizens (with a second nationality), thus making them vulnerable to deportation. Finally, I consider the UK Borders Act 2007 which made deportation orders mandatory for non-citizens (from outside the European Union) who were imprisoned for a year or more or were imprisoned for committing certain categories of serious offences. This Act in effect curtailed the discretion of the courts and the Home Secretary to recognize the membership claims of individuals who, due to their length of residence in the state and other hallmarks of integration, are recognized as having a strong moral claim to be considered nationals.

The discussion in this chapter will proceed as follows. In the next section, I briefly discuss the history and significance of the norm that states should not deport their own citizens. I then move to discuss a set of relatively recent legislative encroachments into the insulation from deportation that members of the United Kingdom have traditionally enjoyed. I begin with legislation relating to Commonwealth citizens and move on then to discuss birthright dual nationals and conclude with long-term permanent residents or 'virtual nationals' (Berry 2009). It is important to note two things at the outset. First, the pieces of legislation I discuss here represent relatively recent (post-1960) examples of the changing reach of deportation power in the United Kingdom. They could have been supplemented with other, less contemporary examples, such as debates over the deportation of Irish nationals in the 1940s or debates over the denaturalization of Germans by descent in 1918 legislation. However, the examples I give provide a cross section of how pressures to deport affect a range of different categories of membership, for example Commonweath citizens, dual nationals, and virtual nationals. Moreover, the fact that my examples are relatively recent increases the likelihood that they have something relevant to say about contemporary UK citizenship.

Second, as is already obvious, I move in this chapter (potentially imprudently) between using the terms 'citizen' and 'member', and thus between legal, moral, and historical conceptions of belonging. My imprecision is largely intentional. One of my aims in this chapter is to show that just who is entitled to protection from deportation is a matter of debate and dispute because membership is not merely a legal category and is not simply confined to formal citizenship. It needs also to be understood as a normative and historical category if we are to understand its social meaning and political importance.

Banishment and the Norm against Expelling Citizens

Before I examine some specific examples of how the boundaries of who is deportable in the United Kingdom have changed over time, I want briefly to consider the norm that animates this chapter: the restriction on states deporting their own members. This norm, underlined in international law by the duties of states to readmit their own nationals (citizens) and to prevent the creation of statelessness, is of great significance for contemporary states for two major reasons. First, it represents, to all intents and purposes, an *absolute* prohibition on certain activities by states. Even the most disreputable and dangerous of a state's citizens enjoy its protections. Convicted mass murders, serial rapists, and even terrorists may be imprisoned for life and even, in some countries, put to death by the state, but if they are citizens of the state concerned they may not be expelled or banished from the country (Gibney 2013).

Second, the norm is notable because, as I have suggested, it is a distinctive entitlement of modern citizenship. In recent years, political scientists and sociologists have observed a diminution in the privileges and entitlements of citizens vis-à-vis (particularly permanent) resident non-citizens in Western states, depriving citizenship of much of its significance (Soysal 1994; Hansen 2002; Joppke 2011). Resident non-citizens typically enjoy rights to vote in local elections, access to welfare on a par with nationals, greater security of residence, and most other social, economic, and civil rights. In the midst of this eclipse of the distance between citizens and non-citizens, the right not to be deported has, along with the right to vote in national elections, emerged as a distinctive entitlement of citizens. Moreover, the significance of this right has grown with the turn to deportation across Western states in recent years (Gibney 2008).

Despite its role as a key aspect of contemporary citizenship, the protection of members from expulsion power is a relatively new phenomenon. The revoking of citizenship, almost inevitably accompanied by physical expulsion through banishment, was a common practice in the ancient world. Indeed, the word 'deportation' comes from the Roman practice, *deportatio*, of expelling citizens to the outer edges of the Empire (Starn 1982: 21). Before the 1800s, banishment existed in many guises and across all parts of Europe (Spierenburg 1997; Coy 2009). In eighteenth-century France, for example, banishment was a common way of dealing with criminals when courts believed there were mitigating factors or doubts about their guilt (Kingston 2005). Banishment could be permanent or temporary, applied to a single jurisdiction or to the kingdom as a whole. While there were moves to eliminate the practice in the aftermath of the 1789 Revolution, the French regime's desire to expel political enemies proved irresistible and the practice continued (Kingston 2005).

In England, those who wished to escape prosecution by fleeing to a sanctuary could avail themselves of opportunities for self-banishment (abjuration) until the time of James I. Involuntary banishment was also provided for under a number of Acts of Parliament, including the Vagabonds Act 1597, which allowed justices to banish 'dangerous Rouges ... out of the Realm' and prescribed the death penalty for their unlawful return. The Roman Catholic Relief Act 1829 also allowed for the banishment of Jesuits from England, requiring that anyone joining this society 'shall be sentenced and ordered to be banished from the United Kingdom for the term of his natural life'. The numbers expelled under such laws, however, paled into insignificance against convicts subjected to the punishment of transportation in the eighteenth and nineteenth centuries. Transportation first to America and subsequently to Australia involved the forced exile in chains of hundreds and thousands of Britons. Unlike other forms of banishment from England, transportation involved being sent to a particular place rather than simply expulsion from the realm (Hughes 1986). Indeed, in one famous Scottish case of the early 1800s, two individuals (Mr Muir and Mr Palmer) sentenced under a 1703 Act which forbade leasing-making (the uttering of lies about the sovereign) appealed to the fact that the Act cited 'banishment' as the appropriate punishment and thus were required simply to leave the realm rather than be 'transported' to Australia (*Hansard* 1794–1795: 267–280). They lost the case and were duly transported. If any distinction was to be drawn between transportation and banishment, it was not one that authorities accepted.

In many ways, transportation was banishment's last hurrah, as by the early 1800s a number of developments were putting an end to the practice. Banishment was increasingly seen by liberal theorists, like Bentham, as an arbitrary punishment that should be replaced by modern prisons meting out punishment and suffering more equitably (Jackson 1989). Prisons were seen as offering greater potential for deterring criminal activity and reforming men's souls, important considerations in a new age of mass enfranchisement and modern citizenship (Gibney 2013). At the same time, the rise of nationalism was hardening the state into a more defined membership unit in which insiders needed clearly to be distinguished from outsiders: not only did states become more reluctant to accept undesirable foreigners dumped on their territory but the claim that each state was the state of a distinct and unique people made it difficult for states to engage in the kind of absolution of responsibility central to banishment (Gibney 2013). This responsibility not to deport was reinforced by the fact that developing rules of international society in the nineteenth century included duties by states to accept the return of their own nationals as a necessary correlative of the power to expel foreigners (Noll 2005).

By the 1900s, the norm that states could not deport their own citizens was widely accepted both at international level (as necessary to protect the right of states to control the entry and residence of foreigners) and in popular understandings of citizenship. In the post-Second World War world, freedom from the state's expulsion power was conceptualized as a human right held by citizens, as evident in the 1948 Universal Declaration of Human Rights' enumeration of the right of individuals to leave and return to their country of nationality.

That said, protections against expulsion have long existed in an uneasy relationship with the right of states to define their own rules for membership (nationality or citizenship) acquisition (Gibney 2013). From the beginning of the 1900s, but particularly during the febrile environment of the First World War, many countries in the Empire and North America passed new laws enabling the stripping of citizenship (denaturalization) from naturalized or native-born citizens deemed disloyal, criminal, or a threat to the national security or order (Gibney 2012). It was evident that if states could not deport those who held their own citizenship, they could, under certain circumstances, transform them into non-citizens, and through this make them vulnerable to deportation power. Thus, by manipulating the basis for the acquisition and continued holding of citizenship, states could decide who was deportable.

Commonwealth Citizens

It is just this kind of manipulation of membership status for the purposes of rendering citizens vulnerable to expulsion that I will consider in the rest of this chapter. While one might be tempted to see the vulnerability of members to deportation—or, more controversially, 'banishment'—as a thing of the past, a closer look at recent practices by the United Kingdom shows that this is far from being the case. My first example considers the circumstances under which Commonwealth citizens in the United Kingdom became subject to deportation power, an event that occurred in the early 1960s.

Before the Commonwealth Immigrants Act 1962, citizens of Commonwealth countries could freely enter and reside in the United Kingdom and were, along with Britons born there, immune from deportation power. Their rights were consistent with a conceptualization of membership that emphasized subjection to the British Monarch rather than national citizenship as the basis for belonging. Under this conception, membership was based not on citizenship in the British nation but rather 'allegiance between individual subjects and the King'. 'These ties of allegiance', moreover, 'knit together the British Empire not the British nation' (Brubaker 1989: 11). Put simply, immunity from deportation for members of the Commonwealth, and rights to reside in the United Kingdom, reflected a conception of common imperial subjection rather than civic membership. Commonwealth citizens' insulation from deportation power stood in stark contrast to the situation of (non-Commonwealth) non-citizens—aliens—resident in the United Kingdom. Since the beginnings of the First World War, they had been subject to frequently renewed Alien Orders which meant that their right to reside in the United Kingdom could be revoked whenever a Home Secretary deemed their presence—whether or not recommended by a court in sentencing—not conducive to the public good (McDonald and Toal 2010).

Parliamentary consideration of the extension of deportation power to Commonwealth citizens from 1958 was sparked by widespread public concern over rising immigration to the United Kingdom from the so-called New Commonwealth countries of India, Pakistan, and the West Indies. Under the British Nationality Act 1948, almost one billion members of the Commonwealth had the right to settle in the United Kingdom. Before 1945, however, few such people had availed themselves of the right. Things changed dramatically after 1948, when the number of non-white entrants started to grow from several hundred a year to 11,000 by 1954 to well over 100,000 annually by 1961 (Hansen 2000). This test of the Commonwealth idea of membership sparked social and political anxieties about competition for jobs, public housing, and the possibility of integration reflecting, amongst other things, racist attitudes amongst large sections of the British public and elite. Yet, in the face of such public concern, as Hansen notes, the Conservative government was extremely reluctant to legislate restrictions because of its desire not to impede the entrance of people from the Old Commonwealth countries—Australia, Canada, South Africa, etc—and to avoid the appearance of entrance restrictions based on race (Hansen 2000).

The mounting pressure on the government for restrictive legislation during the late 1950s was reflected in parliamentary debates. One manifestation was a push by parliamentarians in favour of immigration restriction ('restrictionists') for new legislation that would, for the first time, enable the deportation of Commonwealth immigrants convicted of crimes in the United Kingdom. This push was led initially by two conservative MPs with a track record of racist hostility towards the New Commonwealth migrants: Cyril Osbourne and Norman Pannell. In defence of new deportation powers, Osbourne argued that New Commonwealth immigrants were disproportionately involved in 'organized prostitution and the traffic in dangerous drugs' (HC Debates, col 199, 29 October 1957). Pannell, on the other hand, produced statistics attempting to show that 'practically the whole of drug trafficking in the country' was attributable to 'Colonial and Commonwealth immigrants' (HC Debates, col 1967, 17 February 1961).

The focus on deportation by restrictionists was a strategic move on their part to attack Commonwealth immigration at its most vulnerable point. Somewhat disingenuously, restrictionists presented criminal deportation provisions as beneficial not just to the indigenous British public, but also to the Commonwealth immigrants themselves because 'evil men' put a smear on 'all the people with coloured skins' (HC Debates, October 1958). The initial parliamentary response of the government was to reject this call on the grounds that Commonwealth immigrants were members: 'the Mother country does not deport British people of this sort' (HC Debates, cols 545–547, November 1957). However, the emphasis on deporting criminals successfully exposed the limited commitment of inclusionists to seeing the Commonwealth entrants as members. For, in response to the call for deportation powers, many who supported wide-ranging entrance rights conceded that any right to reside should be conditional on good behaviour. Once the conditionality of residence had been conceded, the claim that Commonwealth citizens were equal in entitlements and rights to UK-born citizens started to erode.

Other restrictionists used the concession as the basis from which to argue for different, more expansive grounds to deport. Martin Lindsay claimed that 'the unfit' should also be expelled and 'those who prefer to live on National Assistance here rather than in poverty in their own country' (HC Debates, col 1561, 5 December 1958). By the late 1950s the government too was conceding that the case for deporting criminals was 'reasonable'.

By 1962 the government had drafted and introduced to Parliament a Commonwealth Immigrants Bill that, in addition to controlling Commonwealth migration by requiring that immigrants possess work vouchers before arriving, proposed that the Home Secretary be given the power to deport Commonwealth immigrants if they were convicted of an offence punishable by imprisonment and a court recommended their deportation. This proposal might have made Commonwealth citizens closer to aliens in their vulnerability to deportation power, but they still possessed a distinct and elevated status. The position of the government was summed up by McColl, who noted in debate on the Bill that 'we want to reduce to the absolute minimum the power of deportation of Commonwealth citizens. It is profoundly distasteful' (HC Debates, col 534, 7 February 1962). The real question in the debate that followed was where Commonwealth citizens should be located on the spectrum from national citizens to aliens in terms of the state's power to deport.

Those hostile to new controls on Commonwealth citizens—'inclusionists'—took issue with a proposal in the government's Bill that the age that an individual should become vulnerable to deportation power be 17, proposing instead that the age be 25. Michael Foot argued that it was unjust to expel people of such youth as 'they are criminals who are manufactured here and sent there' (HC Debates, col 523, 7 February 1962). While an amendment to raise the age limit was not successful, another issue was a matter of concern to the inclusionists: at what point in their residence should Commonwealth citizens be treated as full members and thus freed from deportation power?

The inclusionists argued that the period be 24 months. One MP suggested that 'if a person has established himself here as a resident for a couple of years, even though he may commit an offence ... he should, as a member of the Commonwealth, have the same protection against deportation as a native born British subject or anyone else who has made this country his home' (HC Debates, col 547, 7 February 1962). However, restrictionists pushed back, and sought to make deportation power for Commonwealth citizens virtually equivalent to that applied to aliens generally. In the midst of this heated discussion, the government's position of five years took on the appearance of a compromise and subsequently won the day (HC Debates, col 557, 7 February 1962).

When the 1962 Act received Royal Assent, Commonwealth citizens became, for the first time, deportable. However, as is evident from the previous discussion, they were not thrust unambiguously into the status of aliens. Unlike non-citizens in the United Kingdom who were not from Commonwealth countries, Commonwealth citizens could only be deported if recommended by a court after being convicted of an imprisonable offence; moreover, they were subject to deportation power only during the first five years of their residence. Unlike aliens, they were not subject to the discretionary judgment of the Home Secretary that their presence was not conducive to the public good. The status of Commonwealth citizens thus looked like something of a compromise, one that treated them neither as fully citizens nor as non-citizens. However, this position as quasi-members of the British state was a precarious one and it was not to last. In 1969 the Home Secretary acquired the power to 'initiate deportation proceedings against Commonwealth citizens'. And with the Immigration Act 1971, the position of aliens and Commonwealth citizens in the United Kingdom was made 'broadly the same' (McDonald and Toal 2010: 1272).

Dual Nationals Born into UK Citizenship[1]

My second example of the creep of deportation power across the boundaries of membership emerges from the Labour government's legislative attempts in 2002 and 2006 respectively to extend denaturalization (deprivation of citizenship) provisions to native-born citizens (with a second nationality) and to lower the standard necessary to use this power.

Denaturalization, the state-initiated withdrawal of citizenship, typically due to acts perceived to violate the fundamental norms of good citizenship, such as treachery or disloyalty, is not equivalent to deportation. An individual can be deprived of citizenship and yet may be allowed to go on living in the state. However, the loss of citizenship always makes an individual vulnerable in principle to deportation power (by turning a national into an alien) and, in practice, denaturalization is often used hand in hand with attempts either to expel particular individuals or to prevent them from re-entering their country of former citizenship.

UK governments have long had denaturalization powers at their disposal. British nationality Acts in 1914 and 1918 respectively allowed for denaturalization on a range of grounds including trading with an enemy state, residing outside the United Kingdom for more than seven years, and remaining a subject of a state at war with His Majesty. Yet these powers applied only to naturalized UK citizens, not to citizens by birthright. Moreover, denaturalization power was rarely used after the 1920s and had fallen into desuetude by the 1960s. Indeed, in the four decades before Tony Blair's Labour government came to office, denaturalization power had been used only once (in 1971) (Gibney 2013).

In 2002, the Blair government introduced a Bill to Parliament proposing to reform UK denaturalization powers. The main changes to be proposed under the

---

[1]   My discussion in this section draws in part from Gibney (2012).

new Nationality, Immigration and Asylum Bill were three. First, the standard required for deprivation of citizenship was to be changed from an enumerated list of acts, such as treachery, trading with the enemy, and commission of a serious criminal act within five years of having been naturalized, into the single standard that the Secretary of State considered that an individual's holding citizenship was 'seriously prejudicial to the vital interests' of the United Kingdom. This new standard was taken from Article 7 of the 1997 European Convention on National-ity. A second change was that deprivation power was, for the first time, now to apply to *all* types of British citizens—native born as well as registered and natural-ized. This dramatic change was, however, mitigated by a third: the Secretary of State now could not deprive if it would make an individual stateless (save for those cases in which an individual's citizenship was gained through fraud or misrepresentation).

This new Bill was drawn up and presented to Parliament in an environment informed to a great extent by the 9/11 terrorist attacks in the United States in 2001. This event led the British government to become increasingly concerned with Muslim extremists in the United Kingdom and, in particular, extremist preachers, like Abu Hamza, who were seen as inciting violent anti-Westernism. But the new proposals were also consistent with the government's stated concern with social cohesion and efforts to make citizenship more than simply a bureaucratic status. Indeed, when the Act was passed and a deprivation order was served on Abu Hamza, David Blunkett, the Home Secretary, stated that Parliament had supported new denaturalization powers to 'make holding our citizenship worth something' (*BBC News* 2003).

The new denaturalization provisions were controversial in Parliament, particu-larly in the House of Lords. The government defended its innovations by arguing that deprivation of citizenship was an important and necessary state power, though one that would be used sparingly. In presenting the Bill to the Lords, Lord Filkin argued that the deprivation power was necessary to express 'public abhorrence at treasonable conduct and to demonstrate that the disloyalty shown is incompatible with being regarded as a member of the British family' (HL Debates, col 279, 9 October 2002). Lord Filkin went on to state that the new deprivation provisions would 'deter and prevent future conduct' and provide 'an additional sanction' against 'treason and subversion', even when an individual was not convicted of a crime. Connecting deprivation powers to the government's new citizenship measures, he asserted, 'we believe that it is consistent with our approach to citizenship ... namely, that it is an extremely important privilege' (HL Debates, col 279, 9 October 2002).

The new denaturalization *standard* was justified by the new terrorist threats associated with Al Qaeda's attacks in the United States. In Committee, the Home Office Minister, Angela Eagle, told members that 'the Bill modernises the ... [deprivation] procedure in terms of national security threats and non-state threats, such as those from organisations that are organised globally but are not states' (HC Committee, col 56, 30 April 2002). But the change in who was *subject* to deprivation power to dual nationals was justified quite differently. This was presented entirely as an anti-discrimination measure. The new law, the government argued, would put all citizens 'on an equal basis' (HL Debates, col 279, 9 October 2002). Because citizenship is so important to the government, 'it ... should be respected without discrimination as to the route it was received'. The old deprivation laws, by singling out the naturalized, risked reducing their citizenship to 'a second class status' (HL Debates, col 279, 9 October 2002).

It was immediately apparent to critics in Parliament that this way of dealing with the invidious distinction between the naturalized and the native born only created a new citizenship hierarchy. The Bill, argued Lord Goodhardt, 'simply creates a new form of discrimination towards British citizens by birth who hold no other citizenship and British citizens by birth who happen to hold the nationality of a second country' (HL Debates, col 275, 9 October 2002). The government's response to this criticism was revealing. Departing from historical practice, it did not attempt to justify marking out dual nationals as possessors of a contingent citizenship on the basis of principle. Rather, the government lamented its inability to make *all* British citizens contingent citizens due to the practical problem of not violating the norms on statelessness. The government's proposals also faced criticism on other grounds. Unconsciously echoing worries expressed in debates over almost all previous deprivation legislation, Lord Goodhardt claimed that deprivation should be beyond the power of the Home Secretary: 'Any removal of citizenship—if it is justified at all—should be a matter for decision by the courts' (HL Debates, col 275, 9 October 2002). Earl Russell took issue with the government's description of citizenship as a 'privilege'. 'For those born here', he argued, 'citizenship was a right' (HL Debates, col 281, 9 October 2002). The appropriate way to challenge threats to the state's vital interests, he believed, was through the courts. Extending his argument to the naturalized, Russell stated: 'If we are to have equality, let us not have ... equality of misery. Let us have an equality of rank giving proper value to the concept of citizenship' (HL Debates, col 508, 8 July 2002).

In the end, the parliamentary debates made virtually no mark on the final legislation. The government was true to its word, however, in not using the power rashly. Only one deprivation order was made under the provisions of the Act. The individual concerned was none other than the aforementioned Abu Hamza, a British and Egyptian national who had naturalized into UK citizenship.

Less than four years after the passing of the Act, the government again put forward legislation to amend its denaturalization powers. The last legislative change to the UK's deprivation provisions was made in 2006, again by Blair's government. An amendment to the Immigration, Asylum and Nationality Bill introduced in Committee on 25 October 2005 reduced the standard required for deprivation. The new standard required only that the Home Secretary show that someone's holding citizenship was 'not conducive to the public good'.

This change was indeed a direct response to terrorism, specifically the bombings on 7 July 2005, in which four British Muslims detonated bombs that killed 56 people in the heart of London. In a major press conference less than a month after the attacks Tony Blair announced that the 'rules of the game are changing' with regard to expulsion. Blair warned that 'people who want to be British citizens must share our values and way of life'. 'If you come to our country from abroad,' he stated, 'don't meddle in extremism … [or] you are going to be back out again' (*Guardian* 2005). Blair's warning to immigrants crossed over into a warning for citizens when, in the same speech, he announced, as part of a package of new rules, that the government would seek further powers to 'strip citizenship' to make the current procedures 'simple and more effective' (PM Press Conference 2005).

The amendment of deprivation law emerged after some intensive pre-legislative negotiations over new anti-terrorism measures during the summer. In Parliament, the government defended the new 'not conducive to the public good' standard as 'necessary to fight the domestic terrorist threat' (HL Debates, col 1190, 14 March 2006). In Committee discussions it became clear that the government aimed to make deprivation compatible with a list of 'unacceptable behaviours' that the Home Secretary, Charles Clarke, had announced on 25 August 2005 (*BBC News* 2005). These behaviours, put forward as grounds for the exclusion and deportation of immigrants, included fomenting, justifying, or glorifying terrorist violence and fostering hatred that 'might lead to inter-community violence'. Collapsing the distinction between citizens and non-citizens, the Minister for Security, Counter-Terrorism, Crime and Policing, Tony McNulty, stated in Parliament that it is 'now essential that we have similar powers to withhold and to remove British nationality … where an individual is found to have engaged in [unacceptable behaviours]' (HC Committee, cols 244–245, 27 October 2005).

The horror of the 7 July 2005 attacks appeared to mute criticism of the government's changes in Committee. Nonetheless, a number of parliamentarians criticized the new proposal largely on the grounds that it made depriving an individual of citizenship as easy as deporting a non-citizen. The new clause, said Lord Dholakia, 'amounts to an equation of deprivation of citizenship with the deportation of aliens. It is a huge leap to move from identifying a basis for excluding or deporting a foreign national from the UK to using that same test as the basis for depriving a person of citizenship he or she may have held since birth' (HL Debates, col 268, 19 January 2005).

The Immigration, Nationality and Asylum Act received royal assent on 30 March 2006. The latest piece of deprivation legislation departed radically from the seminal piece of deprivation legislation of the twentieth century, the British Nationality and Status of Aliens Act 1918. In that Act, the 'conducive to the public good' standard was an additional requirement on top of others necessary for depriving legislation. After the 2006 Act, the requirement became the only thing that stood between dual national UK citizens and non-citizenship. Since the passing of the Act, no fewer than 14 British nationals have been deprived of their citizenship and thus either excluded from the United Kingdom or rendered vulnerable to deportation power.

Long-term Permanent Residents

My final example of the creep of deportation power into the domain of members does not involve individuals who are formally citizens of the British state but rather those who have variously been described as long-term permanent residents, denizens (Hammar 1990), 'virtual nationals' (Berry 2009), and even 'aliens by the barest of threads' (Foster 2009). The UK Borders Act 2007 introduced (amongst a raft of other changes) what the Labour government described as 'automatic deportation' or 'mandatory deportation' for non-citizens convicted of a range of imprisonable offences. Specifically, the Act required that the Secretary of State order the deportation of any foreign national 'who is sentenced to 12 months or more in prison, or imprisoned for any length for any one of the serious offences covered under the 2002 Act'. This new duty to deport, which was constrained by the country's human rights commitments and duties to EU nationals, was intended, according to the government, to make it clear to foreign nationals and the UK public that 'a breach of Britain's hospitality leads to deportation' (HC Debates, col 213, 9 May 2007). The powers in this Act are relevant to our consideration of the changing sphere of deportation power because they are insensitive to a special category of members in the liberal state: non-citizens who have been resident in the United Kingdom for much of their lives and hence possess deep roots in British society.

The Bill owes its provenance largely to the foreign national prisoners release scandal of April 2007 when it came to light that just over 1,000 non-citizens held in British prisons (some of whom had committed violent crimes) had been released at the end of their sentences without being considered for deportation (see Kaufman, Chapter 9 in this volume). The scandal led eventually to the forced resignation of the Home Secretary Charles Clarke and greatly damaged the Labour government's attempts to paint itself as tough on crime and strict on immigration.

In an attempt to reassure the public in his government's ability to assert immigration controls against criminals, the Prime Minister, Tony Blair, announced that 'it is now time that anybody who is convicted of an imprisonable offence and who is a foreign national is deported' (*Daily Mail* 2007). The 2007 Bill, which instantiated a somewhat toned-down version of this ethos, came on the heels of a frantic attempt by the government to find and return to jail foreign nationals who had been released from prison without being considered for deportation. This hunt for former prisoners involved, according to the then Chief Inspector of Prisons, Anne Owers, 'a trawl' that 'was so undiscriminating that it included some British citizens' (*Telegraph* 2007).

In the House of Commons, a government minister, Liam Byrne, presented the new Bill as part of an 'ambitious plan for reform' by the government. Its provisions on 'mandatory deportation', he argued, illustrated the fact that 'public protection is (the Home Secretary's) No. 1 priority' (HC Debates, col 598, 5 February 2007). In the debate in Parliament, the Bill's novelty was questioned, with one Conservative claiming that 'the Bill doesn't give the Home Secretary' any deportation powers 'he doesn't already have' (HC Debates, col 605, 13 June 2007), especially given that there already existed 'a rebuttable presumption in favour of deportation'. Consequently, the Conservative opposition discussion in the Commons (and in Committee) focused almost entirely on ways the Bill could be made even tougher (HC Debates, 13 June 2007).

Damien Green, the Opposition immigration spokesperson, rejected claims that the Bill would lead to automatic deportation given the exceptions allowed, and argued that the Bill's mandatory provisons (such as they were) should be extended to those who commit crimes against 'immigration officials' (HC Debates, col 199, 9 May 2007). Green argued that 'it is not credible that a Bill that purports to protect our borders excludes from ... automatic deportation ... those who commit serious crimes against immigration officials and those who seek to enter our country illegally' (HC Debates, col 199, 9 May 2007). Green also argued that individuals given a suspended sentence that was then activated in all or in part should be included in the provisions of the Bill. Such relatively minor extensions of the scope of the Bill were not enough to satisfy the Conservative MP David Davies who railed against the human rights exception in the Bill. 'There should be', he proclaimed, 'no country in the world considered so dangerous that we should not deport people to it if they are persistent criminals or have committed serious crimes such as rape' (HC Debates, col 207, 9 May).

Nonetheless, some concerns were expressed that the deportation provisions were too harsh. Under the Bill, the individual's age (18 years) at the time of *conviction* for an offence rather than his or her age when the offence was *committed* determined eligibilty for deportation. This led to concerns about the possibility of deporting juvenile offenders. In the House of Lords, Lord Judd questioned whether such provisions were consistent with Britain's obligations under the Convention on the Rights of the Child. Lord Hylton stated outright: 'there should be no automatic deportation of children when they reach 18; each case should be considered on its merits' (HL Debates, 13 July 2007). In the House, a proposal to amend the Bill to the 'fairer' position of determining eligibility for deportation to the age of an individual when the offence was committed was supported by both Damien Green and the Labour parliamentarian Keith Vaz (HC Debates, col 201, 9 May 2007). It was left to David Davis— and the government minister—to give a contrary view. The key question, Davis suggested, was whether the government was to look after 'the wishes and conveniences of a 16 or 17 year old serious offender' or 'protect members of the public who, in major cities, are facing an onslaught of criminality' (HC Debates, col 441, 27 March 2007).

The question was whether there was a category of non-citizen entitled to insulation from the state's deportation provisions because his or her length of residence and attachment to British society. When concerns about the harshness of the Bill were expressed, they tended to be concerned with the seriousness of the crime which might trigger the deportation of such people. For example, the Liberal Democrat, John Hemming, was worried that minor offences such as 'not paying Council Tax' would lead to mandatory deportation 'for someone who had been living in this country for 30 years' (HC Debates, col 203, 9 May 2007). The minister agreed, stating that he wanted 'to avoid a situation where someone who has spent all his life here and who is convicted and sentenced for something quite minor—such as the proverbial charge of Council Tax non-payment—is deported to a country that they have not been to in their living memory' (HC Debates, col

207, 9 May 2007). Nonetheless, how such injustices were to be avoided was left largely unexplained.

If insulating long-term residents from deportation was raised only gingerly in the House of Commons, the debate in the Lords was a feistier affair, with direct criticism of automatic deportation. The Liberal Democrat peer Lord Avebury announced that his party believed that taking 'away entirely the court's discretion over recommendations for deportation is wrong in principle' (HL Debates, 13 June 2007) and similar to mandatory sentencing for crimes. But the most detailed critique of the Bill was offered by Lady Stern who alone attempted to articulate the perspective of those individuals who would be at risk of deportation. Roundly critical of the Home Office's panicked response to the foreign prisoner scandal, she accused the government of failing to treat non-citizens convicted of crimes as 'individual human beings ... with rights, needs and maybe even a contribution to make, rather than a political problem'. She argued that the Bill would continue this pattern, noting that it was 'rigid, harsh and would lead to many injustices' (HL Debates, 13 June 2007). Citing the case of Sakchai Makao, a 23-year-old, resident in the United Kingdom since he was 10, but ordered deported by the UK authorities after his conviction for arson, she stated: 'He was not just a "foreign criminal". He was also a sportsman, a member of a family, a worker, a taxpayer, a member of a community and a constituent whose MP was very active on his behalf.' 'What would happen to him under the Bill, and any other similar young people', she asked; 'Is he the sort of person we do not want in the UK under any circumstances?' (HL Debates, 13 June 2007).

The final Act passed by Parliament reflected elements of the preceding discussion, but the measures to soften the legislation failed. The government included individuals given suspended sentences in the scope of its automatic deportation provisions, but attempts to change the government's proposal that the age of conviction for an offence was the relevant one in determining deportation power failed.

How should one understand the significance of the debate over the mandatory deportation provisions? One way is by seeing the government as attempting to impose in legislation a conceptualization of non-citizens that makes them, in Daniel Kanstroom's words, 'eternal guests' (2007) in the polity: people whose continued residence in the state is contingent on their good behaviour regardless of the length of their stay in the United Kingdom or their degree of social integration. This is certainly the view implicit in Blair's idea that any foreign national who commits an offence should be deported. Yet this view of the eternal guest was contrasted, particularly in the Lords debate, with a more nuanced and fine-grained view of non-citizens which left scope for the recognition of some non-citizens as de facto members of the state (virtual nationals) who had a moral claim not to be deported difficult to distinguish from that of legal British citizens.

Yet this contrast may be too strong. While the government wanted to portray itself as unyielding in its toughness on non-citizens convicted of what it considered serious crimes, it was doing so in a context where the state's commitment not to transgress the human rights standards of the European Convention on Human

Rights (ECHR)—in particular the duties not to inflict 'cruel, inhuman or degrading treatment' and the respect for family life—offered some protection to non-citizens from the more draconian implications of the Act. These legal obligations thus served to mitigate the harshness of the legislation while not directly implicating the government in acts of leniency towards individuals who committed crimes. This distancing was important at a time when the 'right to a family life' and protections against cruel and degrading treatement in the ECHR were seen by some sections of the British media and the public as mechanisms abused by dangerous foreigners. The interesting (but ultimately unanswerable) question is whether the government would have even proposed its mandatory deportation provisions if a human rights framework for protecting certain non-citizens from state deportation power had not existed.

Interpreting the Changing Boundaries of Deportation

What can we conclude from this examination of the parliamentary debates surrounding these four pieces of legislation? The preceding discussion highlights the fact that UK governments have in recent history expanded the boundaries of the deportable to include groups previously immune from deportation power. Legislation has not simply changed the kinds of crimes and behaviours for which a non-citizen can be deported; it has literally changed who is subject to deportation power. Before 1962, Commonwealth citizens could not be deported; after the Commonwealth Immigrants Act, they could. Before 2002, birthright citizens could not have their citizenship revoked and thus be made deportable; after the Immigration, Nationality and Asylum Act, they could. Before 2007, long-term non-citizen residents could rely on the courts or the Home Secretary to consider the case for considering them (effective) members and thus free from deportation power; after the UK Borders Act, their deportation was mandatory in certain circumstances.

Citizenship (and membership, more broadly) in the United Kingdom is evidently a fragile status and, as a consequence, any protection it offers against deportation is also precarious. Concerns about crime and security have been able to undermine prevailing conceptions of unconditional or secure membership. In the debates over Commonwealth immigrants, restrictionists used anxieties over crime (which were themselves racially loaded) successfully to test the extent to which their parliamentary colleagues really saw those from Commonwealth countries as equal members and thus as entitled to unconditional residence. Widespread public concern and governmental anxiety about terrorism in the United Kingdom played a key role in legitimating the extension of deportation powers to birthright citizens by enabling denaturalization. Finally, the desire to assure the public that protection from criminals was the government's 'No. 1' priority legitimized the passage of mandatory deportation legislation in 2007.

Yet while the discussion here shows how some citizens (and members) have come to hold a less secure status, the ability of government officials to redraw the boundaries of membership are still subject to important constraints. Changes in the realm of expulsion have been influenced and, in some cases, mitigated by the political controversy provoked by attempts to redraw citizenship. The debates discussed above illustrate the existence of competing accounts of who is actually a member of Britain (legally, historically, and morally) and who thus should be insulated from the state's deportation powers. For example, supporters of Commonwealth citizens invoked Britain's role as a 'Mother Country' in a way that constructed such entrants, albeit paternalistically, as part of the UK family. Supporters of the claims of birthright dual national citizens argued that even those who were categorized as terrorists could not be treated as if their citizenship was a mere privilege—that they were no longer members of the 'British family'; they deserved to be tried in the courts and subject to criminal sanctions, like other British citizens. Finally, opponents of mandatory citizenship attempted to contest the government's proposal by presenting a richer picture of those who may be subject to the new powers. In this picture, the non-citizen participated in, contributed to, and relied upon British society as much as any formal citizen and thus seemed entitled to equal protection (or, at least, better protection) from deportation. Rather than creating a more unified vision of who belongs in the United Kingdom, the government's attempt to expand the reach of deportation power brings to the surface significant divisions among the political elite and presumably amongst the public at large (Anderson, Gibney, and Paoletti 2011).

Furthermore, the 'members' I have looked at here—Commonwealth citizens, birthright citizens with dual nationality, and virtual nationals—all have an important feature in common: they have a country to which they can be deported. All of them have nationality in another state, even if that nationality may be nominal rather than symbolic of a genuine and effective link to the country concerned. Most UK citizens, by contrast, enjoy no such second nationality or membership, and thus do seem to be completely immune from deportation power. The selective nature of the expansion of deportation suggests that the UK governments (perhaps increasingly) see the 'do not deport citizens' norm not as a principled commitment to the idea that people have a (human) right to reside in the place where they have deep roots, historical attachments, or have made their lives in spite of the way they behave. Instead, their commitment stems from the practical difficulties involved in getting other states to take their own former members and from the recognition of the dangers of undermining international law duties (such as those against the creation of statelessnessness) that impose burdens on other states (though cf Aas, Chapter 1 in this volume).

Conclusion

The intimate connection between crime and national security, membership and expulsion outlined in this chapter inevitably raises the question of how far the modern United Kingdom has really moved from the nineteenth-century practice of banishment. Certainly, Britain no longer uses expulsion as a direct punishment for crime: it is, at best, a collateral consequence of conviction for—or suspicion of having committed—some offences for people holding certain statuses. That said, the fact that one can be denaturalized and deported without ever being convicted of a crime makes the current state of affairs (particularly post-9/11) in some respects even more dubious than using banishment as a direct punishment. If recent developments of citizenship in the United Kingdom do not signal the return of banishment in its traditional form, they do illustrate, starkly and clearly, the ways that social and political anxieties about crime and terrorism redefine the idea of citizenship and the community of those enjoying its protections.

References

Anderson, B., Gibney, M.J., and Paoletti, E. (2011) 'Citizenship, Deportation and the Boundaries of Belonging', *Citizenship Studies* 15(5): 547.

BBC News (2005) 'Clarke Unveils Deportation Rules', 24 August <http://www.news.bbc.co.uk/1/hi/uk_politics/4179044.stm>.

BBC News (2003) 'Cleric Stripped of Citizenship', 5 April <http://www.news.bbc.co.uk/1/hi/uk/2919291.stm>.

Berry, E. (2009) 'The Deportation of "Virtual National" Offenders: The Impact of the ECHR and EU Law', *Journal of Immigration Asylum and Nationality Law* 23(1): 11.

Bosworth, M. (2012) 'Deportation and Immigration Detention: Globalising the Sociology of Punishment', *Theoretical Criminology* 16(2): 123.

Brubaker, R. (1989) *Immigration and the Politics of Citizenship in Europe and North America*. Lanham MD: University Press of America.

Cohen, R. (1994) *Frontiers of Identity: The British and the Others*. London: Longman.

Coy, J.P. (2008) *Strangers and Misfits*. Leiden, The Netherlands: Brill.

Daily Mail (2007) 'You can't deport 3,000 criminals, EU tells Britain', 28 May <http://www.dailymail.co.uk/news/article-458040/You-deport-3-000-criminals-EU-tells-Britain.html>.

De Genova, N. and Peutz, N. (eds) (2010) *The Deportation Regime: Sovereignty, Space, and the Freedom of Movement*. Durham NC: Duke University Press Books.

Foster, M. (2009) 'Alien by the Barest of Threads—The Legality of the Deportation of Long-Term Residents from Australia', *An Melb UL Rev* 33: 483.

Gibney, M.J. (2013) 'Should Citizenship Be Conditional? The Ethics of Denationalization', *Journal of Politics* (forthcoming).

Gibney, M.J. (2012) '"A Very Transcendental Power": Denaturalisation and the Liberalisation of Citizenship in the United Kingdom', *Political Studies* <http://www.onlinelibrary.wiley.com/doi/10.1111/j.1467-9248.2012.00980.x/full>.

Gibney, M.J. (2008) 'Asylum and the Expansion of Deportation in the United Kingdom', *Government and Opposition* 43(2): 146.

Guardian (2005) 'Blair Vows to Root Out Extremism', 6 August <http://www.guardian.co.uk/politics/2005/aug/06/terrorism.july7>.

Hammar, T. (1990) *Democracy and the Nation State*. Aldershot: Avebury.

Hansen, R. (2002) 'Globalization, Embedded Realism, and Path Dependence: The Other Immigrants to Europe', *Comparative Political Studies* 35(3): 259.

Hansen, R. (2000) *Citizenship and Immigration in Post-war Britain: The Institutional Origins of a Multicultural Nation*. Oxford: Oxford University Press.

Honig, B. (2003) *Democracy and the Foreigner*. Princeton: Princeton University Press.

Hughes, R. (1986) *The Fatal Shore*. New York: Vintage.

Jackson, R.V. (1989) 'Bentham's Penal Theory in Action: The Case Against New South Wales', *Utilitas* 1(02): 226.

Joppke, C. (2010) *Citizenship and Immigration*. Cambridge: Polity Press.

Kanstroom, D. (2007) *Deportation Nation*. Cambridge, MA: Harvard University Press.

Kingston, R. (2005) 'The Unmaking of Citizens: Banishment and the Modern Citizenship Regime in France', *Citizenship Studies* 9(1): 23.

McDonald, I. and Toal, R. (2010) *McDonald's Immigration Law and Practice*. London: LexisNexis/Butterworths.

Noll, G. (2005) 'Readmission Agreements', in M. Gibney and R. Hansen (eds), *Immigration and Asylum: Volume 1*. Santa Barbara: ABC-Clio.

PM (Prime Minister's) Press Conference (2005) 5 August <http://www.number10.gov.uk>.

Sigona, N. (2012) '"I Have Too Much Baggage": The Impacts of Legal Status on the Social Worlds of Irregular Migrants', *Social Anthropology* 20(1): 50.

Soysal, Y.N. (1995) *Limits of Citizenship: Migrants and Postnational Membership in Europe*. Chicago: University of Chicago Press.

Spierenburg, P. (1997) 'The Body and the State: Early Modern Europe', in *The Oxford History of the Prison*. New York: Oxford University Press.

Starn, R. (1982) *Contrary Commonwealth: The Theme of Exile in Medieval and Renaissance Italy*. Berkley and Los Angeles: University of California Press.

Sun (2011) 'The 5000 Crooks We Can't Deport', 27 October.

Walters, W. (2002) 'Deportation, Expulsion, and the International Police of Aliens', *Citizenship Studies* 6(3): 265.

13

Democracy and Deportation: Why Membership Matters Most

Vanessa Barker[1]

Democracy and Deportation

Global mobility is made possible by the strict control of territory and social membership. The flow of people across borders is much more regulated and stratified than commonly assumed and has many more negative impacts on migrants than universal human rights principles should allow. Researchers in the emergent field of the criminology of mobility, including many of the contributors to this book, have been at the forefront of identifying these trends, systematically documenting the retraction of rights and the stratification of mobility as they unfold. They have shown how criminal justice tools such as classification and segregation have been used to separate those with free movement from those perceived to be 'other,' particularly poorer ethnic minorities, who are increasingly subject to control, containment, expulsion, and, in some cases, crude violations of their human rights to safety and security. The field has highlighted the global reach of these targeted and regressive movements, exposing empirical patterns that undercut the post-war trend towards equality and the expansion of rights. This work has fractured our understanding of what constitutes an 'open' or 'closed' border demonstrating how borders may be open for some but closed for others, semi-permeable for some and inescapable for others. The field has brought to the surface deep currents that are reshaping our world in ways we might not recognize, understand, or sanction.

What the criminology of mobility has been especially good at is revealing the interconnections between the criminalization process, including its historical roots and contemporary practices, and the field of immigration (Simon 1998; Wacquant 1999; Melossi 2003; Calavita 2005; Aas 2007, 2011a; Bosworth 2008; Zedner

[1] I am indebted to Katja Aas and Mary Bosworth for their editorial might and critical interventions. Special thanks to David Nelken and the participants at the Borders of Punishment Workshop for helpful feedback. Research for this project was partially funded by the National Science Foundation Law and Social Science Program, US and Stockholm University Linneas Center for Integration Studies (SULCIS).

2010; Pickering and Weber, Chapter 5 in this volume; Kaufman, Chapter 9 in this volume). It has productively shown how certain aspects of immigration control have adopted and taken on the practices and language of security, order, and crime control, not eliminating but certainly suppressing a human rights paradigm of mobility. The criminology of mobility has also shown the limits of its own conceptual framework, suggesting that the 'criminalization of migration' only takes us so far in understanding the global dynamics of these trends (Aas, Chapter 1 in this volume), and perhaps, more importantly, illustrating how criminalization in certain instances would actually improve the status and legal protection of migrants, who in many cases fall outside the real protections of due process that are embedded in criminal law but are absent in administrative law (see Dauvergne 2008; Stumpf, Chapter 3 in this volume; Zedner, Chapter 2 in this volume).

This chapter aims to bring together some of the current thinking about the reasons behind these regressive developments. By building on the literature on mobility and membership (Benhabib 2004; Bosniak 2006; Stumpf 2006; Bosworth and Guild 2008; Anderson, Gibney, and Paoletti 2011), it suggests that democracy itself may ultimately be responsible for the convulsions and control of mobility we see today. It is vital to understand from the outset that democracies are inherently exclusionary entities even though we usually think of them as preferred modes of government based on universal principles of equality. But as Seyla Benhabib (2004) explains, democracies are inherently exclusionary because the presumed *universal* principles apply *only* to members. Universal principles in theory apply to everyone because we are human; placing limits around them is inconsistent and problematic. She goes on to explain how democracies are exclusionary because they are bounded communities: they are limited and marked by territory and membership. On the inside, members can access equality, rights, and benefits and fulfil their obligations, but on the outside, non-members are on their own, left to grasp at the ideals of equality, justice, freedom, and human dignity. How democratic states handle this fundamental paradox has major consequences for the degree to which they rely on restrictive approaches to mobility and incorporation. Democracies have historically relied on the criminal law, penal sanctioning, and immigration policy to mark membership and justify social inclusion and exclusion (Calavita 2005)—these public policy tools are effective social sorters, classifying, marking, designating, claiming, and refusing membership. As Juliet Stumpf (2006) explains in her seminal piece on the 'crimmigration crisis', both immigration and criminal law function as 'gatekeepers of membership' in which criminal sanctions often result in segregation within the society while immigration sanctions can result in the separation from the society in a dramatic severing of ties through expulsion. And as Mary Bosworth has argued, the grafting of criminality onto immigrants has not only marked but demeaned non-members as 'threatening and dangerous', further justifying their exclusion (Bosworth 2008: 208).

Global mobility has exposed the contradictions of democracy (Benhabib 2004). Since the 1990s in Europe, for example, the massive influx of new members has strained traditional channels of incorporation and exposed the legacies of differential treatment for non-members. It has exposed the fissures in the very foundation of these societies. Some democracies handle these cracks better than others, while some cannot or are unwilling to cope with the new social reality (especially in the face of growing economic crisis and restructuring). I argue that it is the structural contradictions of democracy that create the conditions conducive to deportation. European democracies unable or unwilling to apply full rights and protections to non-members, particularly to racial and ethnic minorities within and without the European Union, increasingly turn to more coercive measures to resolve this tension. By literally casting out non-members, European governments simultaneously reassert the primacy of national belonging and national sovereignty and weaken international and transnational claims and protections. As David Garland (1996) has shown in the field of crime control, increased penalization is an effective way for states to reassert political authority under threat. Bosworth and Guild (2008) have shown that border control may be functioning in similar ways.

I suggest that the reassertion of national belonging and membership may be even more central to mobility control, working in line with Bridget Anderson, Matthew Gibney, and Emanuela Paoletti (2011). They explain how deportation, despite its repressive character, is actually constitutive of the formal and normative boundaries of citizenship and membership in nation states. In order to be recognized as a rights-bearer, it is vital to belong to a particular place, to claim membership in a political community. This axiom is as relevant today as it was when Hannah Arendt (2009 [1951]) captured this dilemma in the aftermath of the Second World War, over half a century ago. What is more, there is no universal right to residency, anywhere. Even in the European Union, only people working in another EU Member State and their family members have a right to reside in that country: residency is conditional and not fundamental (European Commission 2012). This absence of migrants' rights to settlement further compounds the precariousness of mobility for certain social groups as they face even steeper barriers to membership through which rights are accessed and recognized. As Thomas Ugelvik explains (Chapter 10 in this volume) the return of the nineteenth-century principle of 'less eligibility', especially in the affluent welfare states of Northern Europe, has made it even more difficult for poorer migrants to cross these barriers, as they now face a double burden of demonstrating economic viability and moral worthiness to access membership (also see Di Giorgi 2010). For those other than global elites, the transnational principles of cosmopolitanism (see Soysal 1994; Hudson 2008; Aas 2011b) and the protection of international human rights norms have been threatened by the proliferation of detention centres, border camps, transit zones, forced deportation, and lives lost at sea.

Democracy may be central to our understanding of mobility control but it has been sidelined by criminology's traditional reliance on global capitalism, particularly neo-liberalism, and postcolonial racism as key explanatory factors (see Barker 2012). These concerns are not misplaced but they may be interfering with our ability to develop a deeper structural analysis through which economic and racial dynamics are filtered and made meaningful. Although deportation can function to maintain a flexible, disciplined, and exploitable labour force in some places under certain conditions (De Genova 2010; Di Giorgi 2010; Hansen 2010), the practice itself would not be possible without the elaborate system of nation states and territorial sovereignty (Cornelisse 2010). There must be somewhere for outcasts to go on a map of the world already known, divided, and fixed. The historical development of democracies depended on the fusing of sovereignty, population, and territory in order to establish legitimacy as a new form of governance (Halfmann 2000). Likewise, while deportation can maintain racial hierarchies by regulating and refusing entry to poorer people of colour from the Global South, blocking or limiting access to membership, work, or welfare in the Global North (Fekete 2005; Weber and Bowling 2008; Fekete and Webber 2010), racism itself is more nationalized than global or uniform. The constricted mobility of the Roma all across Europe has very little to do with the racial dynamics between the Global North and South. The Romani people are EU citizens and still subject to social marginalization, including deportation from other EU Member States. Contrariwise, Silicon Valley is happily awash with migrants and money from South East Asia. Who counts as 'other' is heavily dependent on national experience, socio-economic status, cultural specificity, and the particular conditions of membership and incorporation that are shaped by varying democratic institutions and practices. A civic conception of national belonging based on political subjectivity (exemplified but not fully realized in France or the United States) nevertheless processes and interprets racial and ethnic identities differently than an ethnocultural view of national belonging based on shared experience, culture, and blood (Brubaker 1992), or in democracies where national belonging is based on a mosaic of multiculturalism, as in Canada (Banting 2000; Koopmans et al 2005).

Furthermore, we should note that debates over immigration are at their core debates about *national* belonging and *national* identity (Anderson et al 2011, emphasis added). The rise of neo-nationalism across Europe and the surge of welfare-nationalism in Northern Europe are direct responses to conflicts over the very conceptions of national belonging and national identity: they are conflicts about membership, who is worthy to fulfil the obligations of citizenship, and who is worthy to gain access to the social investment state. In Northern Europe, the stakes are high and the barriers steep. There is no doubt that global economic conditions and long-term racial dynamics are critical to understanding the stratification and control of mobility. However, all of these forces clash and must grapple with the resilience of the nation state and the lure of democracies as prime destinations and prime structural forces in determining the rights and mobility of migrants even as these relationships are being remade by globalization.

This chapter examines three major structural features of democracies that restrict and stratify mobility, features that in some cases undermine human rights (for review, see Dembour and Kelly 2011). By drawing upon key analytical dimensions that have been identified by scholars in such divergent fields as international relations, migration law, political theory, social theory, and criminology, the chapter then aims to bring out their application and relevance for the criminology of mobility. Specifically, it analyses:

(1) the nation state form of sovereignty, with emphasis on democracy and territorial sovereignty;
(2) the paradox of democracy as a bounded community based on universal principles, with emphasis on differential treatment;
(3) the persistence of racialized hierarchies and ethno-cultural membership (discussed in the Roma case).

The nation state form, the paradox of democracy, and racialized hierarchies are problematic for all democracies, but how each democracy deals with these inconsistencies tends to vary by the particular institutional and cultural context. Criminalization is often called upon to resolve these tensions, but rather than alleviating inconsistencies the reliance on state coercion tends to reaffirm the steep barriers to belonging. 'This is a flawed solution to the problem of order', note Leanne Weber and Benjamin Bowling (2008: 360). I refer to general patterns but use concrete examples to illustrate how these structural features are manifest in empirical cases.

In the last section, I then turn to a specific case of deportation of Roma in Sweden to highlight what is at stake when democracies rely on coercive forms of power to restrict mobility. As a relatively egalitarian welfare state with a tradition of a human rights approach to mobility, Sweden, with its inclusionary mechanisms firmly in place, is an unlikely place to see such regressive approaches to mobility and, as such, it represents a *critical case* to understand the scale and depth of the phenomenon; it allows for strategic and analytical leverage into the problem (see Flyvjerg 2011: 307). The case highlights some of the neo-nationalistic pressures rather than neo-liberalism or distant global forces that have resulted in the forced deprivation and eventual removal of those who are perceived not to belong or who are deemed unworthy (Khosravi 2009; Johansen, Chapter 14 in this volume; Ugelvik, Chapter 10 in this volume).

One case may seem innocuous or anomalous, but when we consider the sheer weight of examples presented in this book and their collective impact, we can see how mobility control is burning a hole in our societies, weakening democratic values, violating human rights, and undermining international law. In its most extreme outcome, this pattern of regressive mobility control, particularly in the forms of camps, detention centres, extra-territorial border control, refusal of entry in international waters, and deportation, creates a legal limbo, or *no-man's-land*. This state of being is beyond the law's protection but subject to its repressive force, what Leanne Weber and Sharon Pickering (2011) have identified as a *frontier zone*, a wilful gap between national sovereignty and international law, and what Giorgio Agamben (1998) has named *bare life*, when human beings are banned from human society and all that remains is their total subjection to sovereign power. This is a clear and present danger to our societies.

Main Structural Features of Democracy that Restrict Mobility

Nation state and territory

First, why is the nation state a problem for mobility? As noted, it is difficult to understand how deportation is even possible without fully grasping the historical development of democracies in which political communities were both nationalized and tied to a territory. In a new configuration of sovereignty, modern states claimed authority over a population based on space or territorial markers rather than exclusively by blood ties, tribe, or religious affiliation (Halfmann 2000: 39). This process, the fusing of states, population, and territory, as Galina Cornelisse (2010: 107) explains, created a new but quickly essentialized world order based on borders, with clear distinctions between the 'inside and outside', between insiders and outsiders, and between 'us' and 'them', where mobility itself becomes problematic as people traverse borders and immigrants forge settlement, disrupting the natural order of things and places. The map of the world based on sovereign nations responsible for distinct population on that territory reinforces the idea that people belong to place. Deportation is based on the idea of restoring the natural order of place and people. This tension was compounded by the nationalization of political communities. Democracies offered nationals a set of natural and universal rights, forging an alliance to this new form of governance and establishing the concept of political community as one based on citizenship and membership—moves that undercut a more inclusionary concept of shared community based on humanity rather than citizenship (see Cornelisse 2010). As Jost Halfmann explains: 'the price which states and people had to pay for their territorial coexistence was, therefore, the nationalization of the state-people relationship' (2000: 42). Nationalized citizenship reinforces the boundaries of belonging and limits access to rights. Describing these types of exclusionary mechanisms embedded in modern states, Charles Tilly writes:

Internally, states undertook to impose national languages, national education systems, national military service, and much more. Externally, they began to control movement across frontiers, to use tariffs and customs as instruments of economic policy, and to treat foreigners as distinctive kinds of people deserving limited rights and close surveillance. (Tilly, in Halfmann 2000: 42)

Democratic state development created strong institutional configurations and path dependencies that continue to shape access to rights and limit mobility today. People must be tied to a territory as a citizen or resident, or officially recognized as a protected refugee to fully realize their rights. Even as states allow for dual, or multiple, citizenship, a relatively recent phenomenon and not a fundamental right, human rights are accessed through residency in a particular place. To be sure this scenario loosens but has not untied this historical bind. Instead, international human rights that are based on the principle of common humanity are realized and constricted vis-à-vis nation states, filtered through nation-specific institutions and practices. Human rights are *embedded* in domestic legal systems and the nation state is charged with upholding those rights for persons within its jurisdiction on its territory (Benhabib 2004; Bosniak 2006; Somers 2008; Cornelisse 2010; Noll 2010).

It is critical to note that transnational entities such as the European Court of Human Rights do uphold international principles of human rights and have been at the forefront of protecting individuals against human rights violations at the national level. However, access to the Court is predicated on exhausting all domestic legal channels first. Individuals cannot bring a complaint directly to the Court but must begin at the national level and reach a decision from the highest domestic court (European Court of Human Rights 2012). In the case of the Roma, the Council of Europe found that 'many did not know how to approach ombudsmen and other national human rights institutions' (Council of Europe 2009).

It is nation-specific institutions that shape legal protection of human rights, incorporation, labour market participation, political participation, and social inclusion, including two of the most important factors in gaining membership and rights: naturalization and residency. In other words, 'people enjoy protection of their human rights by the state exactly because they are citizens of that state' (Cornelisse 2004: 106). Human rights tend to be recognized through contractual rights through social membership by birth (*jus soli*), by blood, (*jus sanguinis*), by naturalization, or by belonging. This institutional configuration is especially problematic for people who fall outside membership and territory. With no universal right to residency or permanent settlement anywhere, for some these structural barriers are impermeable.

The situation for stateless people is especially precarious. The Council of Europe estimates that there are at least 32,000 stateless Romani people in South Eastern Europe: 10,000 in Bosnia Herzegovina; 17,000 in Serbia; over 4,000 in Slovenia; and 1,500 in Montenegro (Council of Europe 2009). Thousands of Romani from the former Yugoslavia and former Czechoslovakia have not been recognized as citizens of the new state formations despite long-term residency in the territory (Council of Europe 2009). Without birth certificates or proper administrative papers, many Roma cannot claim to belong anywhere. With the introduction of restrictive citizenship laws in the Czech Republic, Slovenia, Croatia, and the FYR Macedonia, thousands were left in legal limbo and without a nationality. These people:

face a double jeopardy—being stateless makes life even harder for those who are already stigmatized and facing a plethora of serious, discrimination-related problems. For those who happen to be migrants as well, their situation is even worse. (Council of Europe: Commissioner for Human Rights 2009; also see European Union Agency for Fundamental Rights 2009; Council of Europe 2010)

In Italy, statelessness has compounded the Roma's social exclusion and has been used as a way to suspend the law and justify their displacement (Sigona 2005). In his extensive fieldwork in Naples, Tuscany, and Emilia Romagna, Nando Sigona (2005) explains how local political discourse and public policy insisted that the

Roma were 'nomads', travellers, 'zingari' and could therefore be housed in temporary camps rather than permanent settlements. Their statelessness became a legitimate reason to reject them rather than a compelling political or moral reason to incorporate them, naturalize them, or provide them residency. What is more, Sigona explains, the social construction of nomadism contributed to common Gypsy myths about their presumed cultural and social distance—they are not like us, they do not really 'belong' to us, they are not Italians. Their presumed nomadism sparked anxiety, discomfort, and political debate precisely because it disrupted the naturalized patching of people and place.

Nomads who traverse borders invert what seems like clear markers of inside and outside. In the Italian case, this set of myths collided with local fears about 'order and security' quickly transforming what had been 'humanitarian camps' (however problematic) into places of policing, 'of control, surrounded by material—and immaterial—fences' (Sigona 2005: 752). The state response quickly crossed over from sympathy to hostility vis-à-vis security concerns and crime control. Here the conflation of nomads with criminality reaches back to the period of modernization and industrialization where harsh poor laws were designed to exact control and restrict mobility of labouring classes, particularly 'vagabonds' and 'beggars' who resisted the proletarianization of labour (Melossi 2003). The criminalization of 'suspect mobility' has a long history as Weber and Bowling (2008) connect these earlier practices to contemporary patterns of mobility control designed to 'select, eject, and immobilize' modern-day 'global vagabonds', sorting and selecting desirables from unwelcome 'others' (Weber and Bowling: 359). In the Italian case, there were clearly racial and ethnic factors at work contributing to the construction of the Roma as 'other' and undeserving (discussed below), but here I want to highlight how their 'suspect mobility', to use Weber and Bowling's term, their presumed nomadism and statelessness created their precarious legal and social status and eased their eventual removal from the country.

The nation state form of sovereignty, particularly as it is tied to territory, can leave those without citizenship, particularly poorer people who are mobile, in a precarious situation, subject to social exclusion and even state coercion. This institutional arrangement becomes problematic, especially in the case of migrants, when nation state sovereignty—that is, the state's power and prerogative to regulate its population and territory—conflicts with or takes precedence over the rights of individuals, particularly individuals who are denied access or rights to the territory itself. The universal human rights of undocumented, *sans papiers*, *papperslösa*, or 'paperless' migrants or failed asylum seekers, for example, are suppose to be recognized and enforced by the very same nation state that seeks their speedy removal from the territory. International law and supranational entities, including the European Court of Human Rights, have been surprisingly weak in the protection of the rights of migrants, particularly the most vulnerable, undocumented migrants (see Dauvergne 2008; Noll 2010; Dembour and Kelly 2011).

This vulnerable legal situation has been further compounded by shifts in the criminalization process. By making paperless migrants' presence a criminal rather than administrative violation—or by making administrative sanctions 'mimic criminal ones', many European governments have not only changed the character of the interaction but justified a more punitive response to it. In Sweden, for example, residents without proper documentation, *papperslösa*, can be imprisoned for up to a year (Aliens Act, Chapter 20, section 2) and may be 'expelled from Sweden if he or she is staying in this country but lacks a passport or the permits required to stay' (Aliens Act Chapter 8, section 7). More research is needed to firmly establish how often this new power is used, but for now we can note its rhetorical and political significance in reshaping the state's relation to migrants. If a failed asylum seeker refuses to leave the territory or to cooperate with the Migration Board, the police take over repatriation and, as the Migration Board reminds us, 'the police have a right to use force in order to make you leave the country' (Migrationsverket 2010: 2). As the Council of Europe Commissioner on Human Rights (2008) stated:

I have observed with increasing concern a trend to criminalize the irregular entry and presence of migrants as part of a policy of migration management. Such a method of controlling international movement corrodes established international law principles. It also causes many human tragedies without achieving its purpose of genuine control.

By linking criminality with immigration violations, state authorities can then justify a policing or security response rather than a human rights approach (Guild 2009). Jef Huysmans (2006) calls this process the 'securitization of migration', whereby migration is recast as a security issue, one to be control and contained.

Finally, the nation state is the ultimate rights-granting agency. It gives out one of the most precious of all rights: the right to residency—that is the right to papers (which in some cases is the functional equivalent of the right to safety, security, and life). Globalization has put people into motion but it is the nation state that ultimately decides their fate. Even global elites, who are tightly bound to global market forces, remain subject to and dependent on the nation state to ease their mobility, to grant their legal residency, and to guarantee their distinctive and elite status.

Paradox of democracy: differential treatment for non-members

Democracy itself poses barriers to mobility. As fundamentally bounded communities, democracies reaffirm the naturalness of population and territory, shoring up the idea that people and place belong together in a coherent fixed map of the world. Democracies rely on borders to distinguish between insiders and outsiders, members from non-members, to make clear distinctions between those who have access to rights and benefits and those who do not. In reality, these lines can be blurred: those on the inside can be marginalized and those without citizenship can be treated as partial members or as denizens (see Hammar 1990; Somers 2008). Bordering seeks to clarify and reaffirm distinctions. Moreover, the historical fusion between population and territory, particularly as it was nationalized and democratized, has established and legitimated the differential treatment of non-members, outsiders, and foreigners. While all democracies determine membership and access to the territory, this prerogative does not necessitate the differential treatment of non-members once they have accessed the territory.

In her legal analysis of immigration law and citizenship in the United States, Linda Bosniak (2006) asserts that personhood as distinct from membership or citizenship should guarantee rights. Democracies, after all, are meant to promote and protect principles of equal treatment regardless of race, religion, gender, sexual orientation, or place of origin. Yet, by maintaining the legal categories of citizen, resident, and alien, democracies maintain differential treatment and differential rights for citizens and non-citizens. This distinction creates a legal hierarchy of rights and protections that counter-pose democracy's equality principle (Bosniak 2006). Although the historical trend has been toward equalizing the rights of non-citizens, there are important areas where this legal distinction remains and has a major negative impact on non-citizens' equality and life chances, namely voting rights and deportation (Koopmans et al 2005). Voting rights are not superfluous to civil or social rights but are indeed the most basic rights to self-determination and freedom; these are denied to non-citizens. In addition, all democracies retain the right to deport non-citizens (with the exception of refugees facing torture or death upon return—the *non-refoulement* principle). All democracies engage in deportation to a lesser or greater scale.

The deportation of criminal aliens dramatically captures the paradox of democracy. The reason a criminal alien is deported is because of his or her alienage, because of his or her status as a non-citizen. Citizens who commit the same crime and serve the same time in the criminal justice system are not then subject to deportation; this sanction is reserved for non-nationals. Deportation, or expulsion, is one of the most extreme forms of state power—the state effectively cuts off all ties, connection, and any obligation to the person: deportation is a kind of civic death (on the historical development, see Gibney, Chapter 12 in this volume). Deportation, as Anderson et al (2011) explain, is a public act, a form of degradation ceremony, where the state forcefully removes a person's residency status denying the possibility of membership, forgiveness, or mercy. In the European Union, if a person is deported from one Member State, he or she is effectively expelled from all 27 countries within the EU. Some commentators see this as a double punishment (exclusively used against non-citizens)—the first served through a criminal justice sanction and the second through administrative sanction. In some countries, compulsory deportation for certain crimes is becoming the norm—'we are getting stricter on those who don't play by the rules' (UK Prime Minister in Anderson et al 2011: 550), while in others it is subject to intense debate because it is inherently discriminatory.

For example, paralleling the 'open and secure' policy of the European Union where Europe is open for some migrants but secured against others, immigration policy in Sweden has become more open in certain areas—such as labour migration (Ministry of Justice 2011)—but more restrictive in asylum policy and deportation. It has become much more selective in who it allows in and who it excludes. And, like many other EU Member States, Sweden has come to rely more on criminalization and deportation to produce and manage a more 'sustainable' and 'efficient' immigration policy (Ministry of Justice 2011). The Alliance-governing coalition made up of centre-right parties, including the Moderates and Liberal Parties, has taken credit for speeding up the deportation process (Ministry of Justice 2011; Migrationsverket 2012). Criminal aliens now make up the largest category of deportees from Sweden (Westfelt 2008).

A recent Parliamentary Commission report on migration and asylum policy provides insight into the debate about compulsory deportation for criminal aliens. Although these particular motions eventually failed, the debate makes visible the reasoning and motivation behind the practice. It is also instructive because the discourse was manifested in a controversial application of the Swedish Aliens Act, which led to the swift arrest and same day deportation of over 26 Roma from Sweden (discussed below). During the debate, the far-right party pushed for the compulsory deportation of criminal aliens: 'Expulsions should be the rule rather than the exception' (Socialförsäkringsutskottets 2010/2011: SfU6).

Jimme Åkesson, the young leader who spearheaded the Sweden Democrats' historic electoral success in 2000 by running on an explicitly anti-immigrant and neo-nationalist platform, insisted upon the differential treatment of non-nationals. In his motion (Sf385 claim 17:01) he stated that those without Swedish citizenship who were guilty of serious offences or repeated offences of a less serious nature 'should have their permits revoked and be deported' (2010/11: SfU6). His fellow party members in Parliament echoed his demands. Kent Ekeroth and Thoralf Alfsson stated:

The issue of deportation will be a mandatory part of the court to consider in criminal cases where the accused holds the nationality of a country other than Swedish or are stateless. We do not think it is legitimate for an alien to have the privilege to stay in Sweden if he or she cannot respect Swedish laws and regulations. (2010/11: SfU6)

They continued: 'the courts should not consider foreigners' living conditions or how long the foreigners have been in Sweden' as is current practice. And finally: 'A criminal alien's connection to Sweden must be considered to weigh less heavily than the need to provide victims with redress' (2010/11: SfU6).

This last construction is the familiar and effective zero-sum trope that pits criminals, in this case, criminal aliens—who are doubly unworthy both as criminals and as non-nationals—against worthy, honourable victims, and by extension Swedish society. The discourse on crime victims as a means to legitimate more punitive sanctions so effective in the US context has also had some traction in Sweden and elsewhere (Garland 2001; Simon 2007; Ljungwald 2011). In the Swedish context of criminal aliens, this construction differentiates between who belongs and who does not, demonstrating once again how criminalization legitimates the exclusion of foreigners.

Despite the government's support and increased use of deportation, Parliament nevertheless rejected all the motions for compulsory deportation of criminal aliens proposed by the Sweden Democrats. The government did not reject differential treatment of non-nationals; they merely wanted to maintain control and discretion over the system to allow certain aliens to remain while others could be deported.

We should also note that the Alliance preferred to frame the policies and practices of mobility control in terms of managerial efficiency and sustainability rather than reduce it to crude neo-nationalistic impulses toward expulsion—even though both approaches often lead to similar results.

Deportation, particularly of criminal aliens, reflects and reaffirms the fine distinctions between citizens and non-citizens, embodying the differential treatment of non-nationals and undercutting the equality principle so central to democracies. Here the criminalization process takes on an added weight as a powerful sorting mechanism, helping democracies overcome, if not legitimate, these internal inconsistencies.

Deporting Roma: A Critical Case in Sweden

No-man's-land

In the winter of 2010, the Swedish Border Police served refusal of entry orders to 26 Roma and initiated their immediate deportation (Justice Ombudsman 2011/12: JO1). En route to Romania by bus, the Roma were left on the Öresund Bridge, a 16-kilometre bridge that connects Sweden to Denmark, hovering 57 metres above the strait. The Öresund Bridge is a powerful marker of globalization, a technological feat that eases the flow of people and goods across places, connecting the continent to Northern Europe across the Baltic. Since 25 million people cross the bridge every year with little or no impediment and with no passport checks, the bridge represents the possible erasure of the border. Except that it does not. On the night of the deportations, the bridge became the border again, backed by the full force of the law, marking the Roma as 'foreign beggars', unwanted, unworthy, tinged by criminality, and, as such, subject to expulsion. They were literally cast out as violators of the Swedish Aliens Act, which prohibits the presence of non-nationals who cannot support themselves by 'honest means', an interpretation of the law that would later be found 'obsolete' and unlawful (Justice Ombudsman 2011/12: JO1, 728).

On that night, they were mobile poor people, global vagabonds, subject to scrutiny, selection, and ejection (Weber and Bowling 2008). The bridge became a twenty-first-century 'no man's land', a site where migrants were subject to the repressive side of criminal and immigration law but denied international law's protection of human rights to safety, security, and human dignity. It was enforcement without protection. In that moment, the Öresund Bridge became a 'frontier zone', a place where the rule of law is sometimes suspended but sometimes used strategically to create illegality (Weber and Pickering 2011). No-man's-land is not a legal black hole but instead is created by the presence and absence of law. As Catherine Dauvergne (2008) has shown, only the law can create an 'illegal' person. In this case, the Swedish Aliens Act engendered the illegal status by fusing criminality to mobility to justify the deportation. In so doing, it created what Agamben (1998) has identified as 'bare life', when human beings are banished from society but completely subject to sovereign power.

The deportation of Roma from a place like Sweden makes no sense. Sweden is well known for its human rights tradition and egalitarian values which propel public policy towards inclusion and make it an unlikely place for regressive mobility practices. And yet, the deportation makes perfect sense when we consider how Sweden is swimming in the paradox of democracy. The Roma expose this rift in society by making visceral the centrality of membership in contemporary democracies. Deportation was possible because they were not members and, with their removal, they were forcefully prevented from becoming members. Although this case certainly represents old forms of hostility and antipathy toward the Romani people, who have been subjected to some of the most aggressive forms of social marginality across Europe, including forced sterilization, homelessness, hate crimes, and mass extermination during the Holocaust, this particular case also signals new forms of exclusion. It is part of an emerging pattern of exclusion based on the criminalization of mobility, particularly for poorer ethnic minorities, whereby mobility is perceived to disrupt the naturalness of territory and people, and deportation is perceived to restore order, putting displaced people back in their rightful place.

The deportation of the Roma indicates the high price of non-membership. Consider that the indigenous Swedish Roma, who have been on the territory over 100 years while still subject to internal social marginality (despite their official designation as a recognized and protected ethnic minority), are in fact not subject to deportation—the repressive use of state power that severs all ties of obligation and demeans migrants' status. Similarly, Sweden has deported permanent residents who have committed a crime because, as Lisa Westfelt explains, the 'question of "belonging"' was not fully resolved until or unless they became Swedish citizens, 'affiliated with a new sovereign' (Westfelt 2008: 288). In the Roma case, the perceived offenders were outsiders, they were 'foreign beggars' with no right to remain, their presence on the streets of Stockholm an affront to Lutheran asceticism and violation of the principles of the welfare state where everyone works to build the society. Like worker ants, *arbetsmyra*, everyone works to build the nest, everyone benefits and everyone is equal. By begging, they had failed to show their contribution, their moral worthiness, and failed to uphold their moral obligations and duties that have been pivotal to the development of welfare states, as Ugelvik (Chapter 10 in this volume) has illustrated in the Norweigan case. It was their foreignness and presumed cultural distance that magnified the insult.

The dynamics of the welfare state intensify the centrality of membership. Historically, the boundaries of democracies became more fixed as membership became more meaningful, a move that countered an earlier nineteenth-century trend toward fluid and open borders and the relatively lower value of membership. With the expansion of the welfare state and social rights, the meaning of membership, along with its thicker sense of belonging and citizenship, raised the barriers to entry, forging stronger boundaries between insiders and outsiders. Ironically then, as democracies became more equal and welfare states expanded social rights even for non-citizens, they became more selective and more exclusionary in another sense, narrowing, restricting, and blocking entry. The welfare state may be universal and generous toward insiders but not necessarily for outsiders.

In the Swedish case, this situation is further compounded by the fractured nature of the welfare state itself, *Folkhemmet*—the People's Home. The People's Home is based on a split foundation of *demos* and *ethnos*: *demos*, the people, who are free and equal, is inherently inclusionary, whereas *ethnos*, a people by blood, is exclusionary (Trägårdh 1997). These dual and competing conceptualizations of membership and national belonging have major ramifications for the incorporation and exclusion of non-ethnic Swedes. In the inclusionary mode, Sweden resembles a republic of free and equal citizens regardless of origin or ethnicity. In the exclusionary mode, ethno-cultural blood ties and heritage impede incorporation and repulse outsiders. In its most extreme form, the ethnocultural mode essentializes democracy as an ascribed status of Swedishness—democracy is in the blood of the people, according to Prime Minister Hanson, founder of People's Home (Andersson 2009; Schall 2012). This construction becomes even more problematic when it seeps into the penal realm, defining crime committed by foreign nationals not as social or moral deprivation but as confirmation of difference, un-Swedishness, providing further reason to exclude or reject non-members (Barker 2013). This discourse underpins much of the platform of the far right party, including its demands for compulsory deportation for aliens: 'We do not think it is legitimate for an alien to have the privilege to stay in Sweden if he or she cannot respect Swedish laws and regulations' (Socialförsäkringsutskottets 2010/11: SfU6). It informed the speedy removal of the foreign Roma.

Conclusion: Membership Matters Most

To a certain extent, this particular case of Roma deportation fits into a general pattern of racialized mobility control across Europe. The summary deportation of Roma from France in the summer of 2010, the mass detention of North Africans fleeing the violence of the Arab Spring in Lampedusa, Italy in 2011 (see Campesi 2011), and, in 2010, Australia's refusal to rescue Afghani and Iraqi women and children whose boat broke apart at sea (Weber and Pickering 2011), are recent examples of the undeniably ethnic and racial dynamics at work. As Liz Fekete (2001, 2005) argues, the European 'deportation machine' effectively separates and excludes many third country nationals because of xeno-racism, fusing racial difference, socio-economic status, and foreignness, a toxic combination that denies non-members full rights and protections (see also Krasmann 2007).

Yet, I do not think we can fully understand the phenomena if we stop there and leave it as racism in Sweden or elsewhere. Our explanation is better served by examining how membership and modes of incorporation compound or minimize and constitute the very categories of ethnic and racial difference. That is to say, racial and ethnic difference is constituted by democracies themselves and understood in relation to national history rather than global dynamics. In Sweden, both *demos* and *ethnos* are operating, which explains a certain amount of ambivalence about ethnic relations in Sweden; it also helps to clarify why Swedish Roma, as qualified members, are not now subject to regressive mobility measures, while foreign Roma are.

Likewise, restricted and stratified mobility is not just a battle over scarce resources or a function of labour market dynamics. The deportation of the Roma as criminal aliens, failed asylum seekers, and children, for example, has very little do with the needs of flexible and expendable labour, although these factors play a role in some cases. What is at stake here is a struggle over national identity, membership, and belonging. Who belongs to the democracy club? Who is worthy to access the welfare state? Who will enjoy equal protection under the law? To understand these dynamics, the criminology of mobility needs to take into account the bounded nature of democracy itself to see how its restrictive character thwarts the realization of its ideals and principles. How will this paradox be resolved? Overcoming or reaffirming the paradox of democracy will provide the foundation for the future—will we move toward an equality of mobility and realize our ideals or continue to press for membership and dwell in our own hypocrisy?

References

Aas, K.F. (2007) 'Analyzing a World in Motion: Global Flows Meet Criminology of the "Other"', *Theoretical Criminology* 11: 283.

Aas, K.F. (2011a) ' "Crimmigrant" Bodies and Bona Fide Travelers: Surveillance, Citizenship and Global Governance,' *Theoretical Criminology* 15(3): 331.

Aas, K.F. (2011b) 'A Borderless World? Cosmopolitanism, Boundaries and Frontiers', in Bailliet and K.F. Aas (eds), *Cosmopolitan Justice and its Discontents*. London: Routledge.

Agamben, G. (1998) *Homo Sacer: Sovereign Power and Bare Life* (trans D. Heller-Roazen). Stanford, CA: Stanford University Press.

Anderson, B., Gibney, M., and Paoletti, E. (2011) 'Citizenship, Deportation, and the Boundaries of Belonging', *Citizenship Studies* 15: 547.

Andersson, J. (2009) 'Nordic Nostalgia and Nordic Light: The Swedish Model as Utopia 1930–2007', *Scandinavian Journal of History* 34: 229.

Arendt, H. (2009 [1951]) *The Origins of Totalitarianism*. New York: Harcourt Brace.

Banting, K.G. (2000) 'Looking in Three Directions: Migration and the European Welfare State in Comparative Perspective', in Michael Bommes and Andrew Geddes (eds), *Immigration and Welfare: Challenging the Borders of the Welfare State*. London: Routledge.

Barker, V. (2012) 'Global Mobility and Penal Order: Criminalizing Migration, a View from Europe', *Sociology Compass* 6: 113.

Barker, V. (2013) 'Nordic Exceptionalism Revisited: Explaining the Paradox of the Janus-faced Penal Regime', *Theoretical Criminology*: 17(1): 5.

Benhabib, S. (2004) *The Rights of Others: Aliens, Residents and Citizens*. Cambridge: Cambridge University Press.

Bosniak, L. (2006) *The Citizen and Alien: Dilemmas of Contemporary Membership*. Princeton: Princeton University Press.

Bosworth, M. (2008) 'Border Control and the Limits of the Sovereign State', *Social Legal Studies* 17: 199.

Bosworth, M. and Guild, M. (2008) 'Governing Through Migration Control: Security and Citizenship in Britain', *British Journal of Criminology* 48: 703.

Brubaker, R. (1992) *Citizenship and Nationhood in France and Germany*. Cambridge, MA: Harvard University Press.

Calavita, K. (2005) *Immigration at the Margins: Law, Race, and Exclusion in Southern Europe*. New York: Cambridge University Press.

Campesi, G. (2011) 'Arab Revolts and the Crisis on the European Border Regime: Manufacturing the Emergency in the Lampedusa Crisis', Plenary, European Group on the Study of Deviancy and Social Control 39th Meeting, Chambéry, France.

Cornelisse, G. (2004) 'Human Rights for Immigration Detainees in Starsbourg: Limited Sovereignty or a Limited Discourse', *European Journal of Migration and Law* 6: 93.

Cornelisse, G. (2010) 'Immigration Detention and the Territoriality of Universal Rights', in N. de Genova and N. Peutz (eds), *The Deportation Regime: Sovereignty, Space and the Freedom of Movement*. Durham, NC: Duke University Press.

Council of Europe: Commissioner for Human Rights (2008) 'It is wrong to criminalize migration'. Viewpoints <http://www.coe.int/t/commissioner/Viewpoints/080929_en. asp>.

Council of Europe: Commissioner for Human Rights (2009) 'Many Roma in Europe are Stateless and Live Outside Social Protections', 6 July <http://www.unhcr.org/refworld/ doci/4a7023c72.html>.

Council of Europe (2010) 'The Situation of Roma in Europe and Relevant Activities of the Council of Europe', Doc 12236 <http://www.assembly.coe.int>.

Dauvergne, C. (2008) *Making People Illegal: What Globalization Means for Migration and Law*. Cambridge: Cambridge University Press.

De Genova, N. (2010) 'The Deportation Regime: Sovereignty, Space and the Freedom of Movement', in N. de Genova and N. Peutz (eds), *The Deportation Regime: Sovereignty, Space and the Freedom of Movement*. Durham, NC: Duke University Press.

Dembour, M.-B. and Kelly, T. (2011) 'Introduction', in M.- B. Dembourand and T. Kelly (eds), *Are Migrants Rights for Migrants? Critical Reflections on the Status of Irregular Migrants in Europe and the United States*. London: Routledge.

Di Giorgi, A. (2010) 'Immigration Control, Post-Fordism, and Less Eligibility: A Materialist Critique of the Criminalization of Immigration across Europe', *Punishment and Society* 12: 147.

European Court of Human Rights (2012) 'Case Processing', <http://www.echr.coe.int/ ECHR/EN/Header/The+Court/How+the+Court+works/Case+processing/>.

European Union Agency for Fundamental Rights (2009) 'The Situation of Roma EU citizens moving to and settling in other EU Member States' <https://www.fra.europa. eu/fraWebsite/minorities/proj_romafreedommovement_en.htm>.

Fekete, L. (2001) 'The Emergence of Xeno-Racism', *Race and Class* 43: 23.

Fekete, L. (2005) 'The Deportation Machine: Europe, Asylum and Human Rights', *Race and Class* 47: 64.

Fekete, L. and Webber, F. (2010) 'Foreign Nationals, Enemy Penology and the Criminal Justice System', *Race and Class* 51: 1.

Flyvjerg, B. (2011) 'Case Study', in N. Denzin and Y. Lincoln (eds), *The Sage Handbook of Qualitative Research*. Los Angeles: Sage.

Garland, D. (1996) 'The Limits of the Sovereign State: Strategies of Crime Control in Contemporary Society', *British Journal of Criminology* 36: 445.

Garland, D. (2001) *The Culture of Control: Crime and Social Order in Contemporary Society*. Chicago: University of Chicago Press.

Guild, E. (2009) *Security and Migration in the 21st Century*. Cambridge: Polity Press.

Halfmann, J. (2000) 'Welfare State and Territory', in M. Bommes and A. Geddes (eds), *Immigration and Welfare: Challenging the Borders of the Welfare State.* London: Routledge.

Hammar, T. (1990) *Democracy and the Nation State: Aliens, Denizens, and Citizens in a World of International Migration.* Brookfield, VT: Gower.

Hansen, P. (2010) 'More Barbwire or More Immigration, or Both? EU Migration Policy in the Nexus of Border Security Management and Neoliberal Economic Growth', *Whitehead Journal of Diplomacy and International Relations* Winter/Spring: 89.

Huysmans, J. (2006) *The Politics of Insecurity: Fear, Migration and Asylum in the EU.* London and New York: Routledge.

Hudson, B. (2008) 'Difference, Diversity and Criminology: The Cosmopolitan Vision', *Theoretical Criminology* 12: 275.

Justice Ombudsman (2011) 'Redogörelse 2011/12: JO1'. Vällingby: Sweden.

Khosravi, S. (2009) 'Sweden: Detention and Deportation of Asylum Seekers', *Race and Class* 50: 38.

Koopmans, R., Statham, P., Giugni, M., and Passy, F. (2005) *Contested Citizenship: Immigration and Cultural Diversity in Europe.* Minneapolis, MN: University of Minnesota Press.

Krasmann, S. (2007) 'The Enemy on the Border: Critique of a Programme in Favour of a Preventive State', *Punishment and Society* 9: 301.

Ljungwald, C. (2011) 'The Emergence of the Crime Victim in the Swedish Social Services Act', PhD thesis, Stockholm University, Sweden.

Melossi, D. (2003) ' "In a Peaceful Life:" Migration and the Crime of Modernity in Europe/ Italy', *Punishment and Society* 5: 371.

Migrationsverket (2010) 'Refusal of Entry with Immediate Enforcement', Swedish Migration Board <http://www.migrationsverket.se>.

Ministry of Justice (2011) 'Migration Policy: Fact Sheet Ju11.02e–April 2011'. Stockholm, Sweden.

Noll, G. (2010) 'Why Human Rights Fail to Protect Undocumented Migrants', *European Journal of Migration and Law* 12: 241.

Schall, C.E. (2012) 'Democracy in the Blood? Ethnic and Civic Idioms of Swedish Nationhood and the Consolidation of Social Democratic Power, 1928–1932', *Journal of Historical Sociology* 25: 440.

Sigona, N. (2005) 'Locating "The Gypsy Problem." The Roma in Italy: Stereotyping, Labelling and "Nomad Camps"', *Journal of Ethnic and Migration Studies* 31: 741.

Simon, J. (1998) 'Refugees in a Carceral Age: The Rebirth of Immigration Prison in the United States', *Public Culture* 10: 577.

Simon, J. (2007) *Governing Through Crime: How the War on Crime Transformed American Democracy and Created a Culture of Fear.* New York: Oxford University Press.

Socialförsäkringsutskottets (2010/20 11: SfU6) 'Migration och Asylpolitik: Utvisning på grund av brott'. Swedish Parliament, Stockholm, Sweden.

Somers, M. (2008) *Genealogies of Citizenship: Markets, Statelessness, and the Right to Have Rights.* Cambridge: Cambridge University Press.

Soysal, J. (1994) *Limits of Citizenship: Migrants and Postnational Membership in Europe.* Chicago: Chicago University Press.

Stumpf, J. (2006) 'The Crimmigration Crisis: Immigrants, Crime and Sovereign Power', *Bepress Legal Series.* Working Paper 1635 <http://www.law.bepress.com/expresso/eps/1635>.

Trägårdh, L. (1997) 'Statist Individualism', in B. Stråth and Ø. Sørensen (eds), *The Cultural Construction of Norden.* Oslo: Scandinavian University Press.

Wacquant, L. (1999) '"Suitable Enemies": Foreigners and Immigrants in the Prisons of Europe', *Punishment and Society* 1: 215.

Weber, L. and Bowling, B. (2008) 'Valiant Beggars and Global Vagabonds: Select, Eject, Immobilize', *Theoretical Criminology* 12: 355.

Weber, L. and Pickering, S. (2011) *Globalization and Borders: Death at the Global Frontier.* Basingstoke: Palgrave Macmillan.

Westfelt, L. (2008) 'Migration som straff? Utvisning på grund av brott 1973–2003 med fokus på flykningskydd', PhD thesis, Stockholm University, Sweden.

Zedner, L. (2010) 'Security, the State, and the Citizen: The Changing Architecture of Crime Control', *New Criminal Law Review* 13: 379.

PART V

SOCIAL EXCLUSION

14

Governing the Funnel of Expulsion: Agamben, the Dynamics of Force, and Minimalist Biopolitics

Nicolay B. Johansen[1]

Introduction

Migration politics are emotionally charged. So too is much academic analysis of them. Presenting migration policies as 'politics of destitution' (Welch and Schuster 2005; Phuong 2006; Vitus 2010; Pinter 2012), scholars tend to discuss foreign nationals in terms of their (lack of) citizenship (De Genova 2002), stateless-ness (Blitz and Otero-Iglesias 2011), and absence of rights (Dembour and Kelly 2011). Migration control, in other words, is defined by deficit and deprivation.

Giorgio Agamben's (1998: 2005) work has been particularly influential in creating and maintaining this 'deficit paradigm' in migration research. His famous term 'homo sacer' (1998) describes a liminal figure 'reduced to bare life'. Power neglects and has no concern with homo sacer. Control is equated with abandonment.

While these arguments have many merits, I believe that the deficit paradigm does not do justice to the political ambiguities and subtle ways in which states manage unwanted foreign nationals. Rather than a politics of destitution, such issues are better captured by Khosravi's notion of 'hostile hospitality' (2009: 53). 'The detention apparatus in Sweden', Khosravi asserts:

does not operate in the form of simple acts of violence but as a complex and ambiguous set of regulations. Built on a 'hostile hospitality', it is partly caring, partly punitive; partly endangering (deportation), partly saving (protecting deportees from police brutality); partly forced, partly empowering; partly a site of hospitality, partly a site of hostility.

Following Khosravi's approach, this chapter describes and analyses the conditions of 'hostile hospitality' as they appear in strategies pursued by Norwegian authorities

[1] This text is, to some extent, a collective product. I would like to acknowledge contributions from the members of the research group Crime Control in the Borderlands of Europe and Ben Bowling. I am especially grateful for extensive assistance from Katja Franko Aas and Mary Bosworth.

to expel refused asylum seekers. Legally and politically, refused asylum seekers are not wanted—'they have no right' to stay, we are told—but refuse to leave voluntarily and resist deportation. While substantial numbers are deported every year,[2] the government is reluctant and sometimes unable to remove them without jeopardizing its humanitarian self-image and human rights commitments (Valenta 2012). The ambition is nevertheless to remove them, to make them leave by other means. In this respect, the handling of refused asylum seekers reveals broader and complex sets of strategies of social exclusion and expulsion directed at the 'unruly' inhabitants of the globalized world, forming a distinct field of politics, which I call 'the funnel of expulsion'.

While sharing the political objectives of deportation, the inner logic of expulsion is different and more finely tuned.[3] It is difficult to grasp its character within the framework of traditional divides of sovereignty since it is an area of politics that transcends the inside and the outside of the state (Aas, Chapter 1 in this volume). The governing of expulsion is indirect. As such, the strategies to expel refused asylum seekers have similarities with rationalities, like biopolitics, which concern the demos: citizens and the 'regular' population. However, the overall objective is to force the unenforceable, locking these people in a situation that is so unbearable that they 'choose' to leave. They must be the ones to make the choice to leave, yet they do so because their life situation is designed to be as deprived as (politically) possible. The refused asylum seekers are thus politically abandoned—left to themselves—to such an extent that a substantial number live in misery and destitution.

In what follows, the chapter sketches the complex and often contradictory interplay of exclusions and rights which define the funnel, focusing in particular on two main institutional domains: work and welfare. In addition, attention will be paid to the openings for aid. In the final section, the chapter examines how the 'funnel of expulsion' works in relation to Foucauldian concepts of governmentality and biopolitics. First, however, a brief comment on the (problematic) uses of Agamben within border studies.

The Borders of Agamben

Giorgio Agamben's (1998) analysis takes, as a starting point, the marginal figure of 'homo sacer'. Homo sacer was originally a concept in Roman law, designating a liminal status simultaneously inside and outside the polity. In Agamben's terms, homo sacer is someone who may be 'killed but not sacrificed'. In its oldest guise, homo sacer is a form of punishment, and Agamben analyses this social figure as a way of splitting the social and biological nature of the individual. Homo sacer is 'reduced' to 'bare life', deprived of social attributes: not defended by the state, not

[2] Since 2000, the number of people deported from Norway has varied between 2,300 and 7,000 (Mohn 2013).
[3] My use of the term 'expulsion' is in line with Walters (2010a) but differs from Gibney (Chapter 12 in this volume).

included in social circulations (the market), and of no religious value. Agamben argues that this social figure is immanent in liberal politics and, as such, inseparable from sovereignty.

Agamben presents homo sacer as a prism to disclose the inherent dilemmas and contradictions in liberalism. Homo sacer exists both inside and outside society, and thereby mirrors how sovereignty relates to the limits of law and territory. By the 'inclusive exclusion' of homo sacer, the state creates an 'exception'. This exception is both a threshold between the inside and outside and a defining entity for the law and the state (Agamben 1998: esp 18).[4]

How does homo sacer translate to modern societies? A succession of metaphors muddles the answers. It is clear that homo sacer constitutes a liminal figure. Homo sacer is both included and excluded. But what does that mean? The liberal tradition is famous for grappling with the problem of jurisdiction: what goes on 'beyond the pale' (the end of (national) territory) is of no interest to the sovereign (Brown 2010). This dilemma once provoked Carl Schmitt to highlight the issue of 'enemies' and 'foreigners' as an intrinsic part of liberal jurisprudence. However, it is worth noting that Schmitt's solution was not to let the outside, the exception, linger in a twilight zone of indistinction, but to subsume the outside under the inside, the exception under the rule (Schmitt 1996).[5] Agamben discusses these tensions in Schmitt's conceptualizations extensively (1998, 2005). The point here is to address the messy and perhaps misleading connotations of homo sacer. Is homo sacer an enemy, or something else?

The concept of homo sacer has gained considerable popularity. It is commonly used as a (more or less) shorthand reference to a politics of 'abandonment' and other forms of indifference equivalent to the land beyond the pale (Diken and Bagge Laustsen 2005; Andrijasevic 2010; Bhartia 2010; Cornelisse 2010; De Genova 2010; Kjærre 2010; Stenum 2010). In this view, migrants are treated as enemies and abandoned. American anthropologist Nicholas De Genova (2010), who has played an important role in popularizing Agamben in migration studies, uses the case of Elvira Arellano as a starting point for his discussion of 'deportation regimes'. Arellano had migrated illegally from Mexico to the United States. After being apprehended a second time for staying illegally on US soil, she took refuge in a church in Chicago. There, in her self-inflicted curfew, she provided a face for the many illegal workers and became, for a period, one of the most talked about persons in the United States. De Genova does not hesitate to classify Arellano's situation within the walls of the church as 'bare life' (De Genova 2010). Dutch sociologist Willem Schinkel (2010) cites another case. A prisoner at the Guantanamo Base was force fed after a hunger strike. Schinkel uses this example to illustrate a form of intermediary status, between insiders and outsiders. According to Schinkel, the

---

[4] For a more elaborate discussion of Agamben's position regarding refugees, see Rajaram and Grundy-Warr (2004).

[5] This strategy, it needs to be mentioned, contributed to the legitimacy of the Third Reich (Müller 2003).

prisoner is 'reduced' to nakedness, to 'bare life'.[6] In the same vein Prem Kumar Rajaram and Carl Grundy-Warr (2004) label detained irregular migrants in Australia, Malaysia, and Thailand as homo sacer.

Though these examples reveal troubling levels of disregard for fellow human beings, one must ask whether it is accurate to apply the term homo sacer to them all. No matter how grotesque their treatment, in each case there is actually someone looking after them. Arellano was cared for by the Church, and the prisoner at Guantanamo, cited by Schinkel, was saved from dying.

Who were homini sacri in the Roman penal code? Were they slaves? In the United States and parts of Europe irregular migrants seem, to some extent, to be at least tolerated in the labour market (Calavita 2005; Anderson and Ruhs 2010).[7] This is not the case in Norway, but even so there is no mention of exploitation of labour in Agamben's texts. What exactly does it mean to be sacrificed today? Can anyone at all be sacrificed? Sacrifice is obviously a metaphor, but for what?

Another possibility is that homo sacer is a person in exile. Thomsen also portrays exile as an earlier form of ostracism from Greece (Thomsen 1972), but exile is conspicuously absent in Agamben's analysis. Neither is it obvious to relate homo sacer to mediaeval forms of expulsion. Agamben mentions the figure of the *friedlose*, known in German law in the Middle Ages, but this is mentioned as a separate institution (Agamben 2005). Homo sacer may serve as a metaphor, but for what?

Although the politics of expulsion produces sickness and misery, understanding the treatment of irregular migrants requires more than a simple usage of metaphors and notions of abandonment. As systems of control 'de-compose' and borders shift, it is necessary to distance our understanding from Agamben's terminology and its reliance on insiders and outsiders. This chapter suggests that irregular migrants, in this case refused asylum seekers, are not simply outsiders or 'enemies'. Yet, to conceptualize them as insiders would be equally misleading. Rather, the politics regarding asylum in Norway are shaped in the *image of* the relationship between the state and the citizen, without the bonds and attachments that characterize biopolitics. The key to understanding this political field is to recognize that we are dealing with the emergence of a political field that transgresses the vision from the world order based on nation states, with insides and outsides.

Forcing the Unenforceable

While we should not forget the possibility of deportation that looms in the back of refused asylum seekers' consciousness (Valenta 2012), this chapter is concerned with the less dramatic mechanisms deployed by the state to enforce the unenforceable. These strategies are important both because there are a number of effective

---

[6] Schinkel must be partly excused for making this conceptual leap, as Agamben himself discusses Guantanamo as a present-day expression of the state of exception (Agamben 2005).

[7] Especially in the US, where it seems that irregular migrants are welcomed as a means to press down wages and widely tolerated as labour.

ways of eluding deportation and because the state often seems to prefer to use less forceful means. As will be revealed, the funnel of expulsion is defined by denial of access to the most basic societal institutions: work, welfare, and health care.

Work

Everyone wishing to participate in the Norwegian labour market must have a work permit. Those with citizenship and residence permits receive one automatically. Asylum seekers are eligible for provisional work permits for as long as their applications are being processed and as long as they provide a reliable identity. Someone who has lived in hiding may activate a work permit when appealing the rejection of his or her asylum application; however, the permit is lost once his or her legal remedies for asylum are exhausted (Vevstad and Brochmann 2010).

In Norway, exclusion from work is effective enough to define the life situation of most refused asylum seekers who come to the attention of researchers (Kjellberg and Rugeldal 2011; Øien and Sønsterudbråten 2011; Valenta 2012; Fangen and Kjærre 2013).[8] Still, some refused asylum seekers have jobs. Restaurants, auto repair shops, and cleaning companies are among the most likely businesses to employ irregular migrants, although we know little about their actions in this regard since this is not a properly researched area. Reports indicate that the payment irregular migrants receive is sometimes less than 10 per cent of ordinary wage rates (Øien and Sønsterudbråten 2011). On the other hand, there are also reports of employers who pay according to local tariffs (Kjellberg and Rugeldal 2011). Whatever the pay, workers do not receive benefits and rights, placing them in a vulnerable position.

According to the police, refused asylum seekers can be found in several sectors of the shadow economy and criminal activities, particularly in the drug trade and/or the sex trade (Sandberg and Pedersen 2011; Skilbrei 2013).[9] Their exclusion from legal income is not complete, as it is possible to find work both inside the ordinary labour market and in the black economy. However, these opportunities are limited, and dependent upon networks (Kjellberg and Rugeldal 2011). In this respect, the situation in Norway might differ from experiences in the rest of Europe and the United States (Anderson and Ruhs 2010), where irregular migrants and refused asylum seekers are, to a larger extent, tolerated in the labour market (Calavita 2005).

However, illegal earnings involve risks. If apprehended by the police for a crime, those working without a permit are likely to be deported. Thus, refused asylum seekers avoid areas known for illegal business (Valenta 2012). Illegal work is also

---

[8] However, it is possible that the research is designed in ways that are better at finding the people most deprived of work and other means. Note that this research is concerned with 'irregular migrants', which is a more general category than refused asylum seekers.

[9] At the same time, some commentators highlight the resistance among irregular migrants to commit crimes, to 'be criminals' (Kjellberg and Rugeldal 2011; Øien 2011).

risky, as authorities increasingly investigate the composition of the workforce. The Norwegian Labour Inspection Authority, which primarily targets health in workplaces, cooperates with other authorities including the police to monitor private businesses in their search for irregular migrants (Årsrapport 2011). In this cooperation, organizations providing welfare and aid play an important role channelling refused asylum seekers into the 'funnel of expulsion'.

Welfare and Aid

Citizens of welfare states, particularly in Scandinavia, can rely upon a variety of institutions offering economic security (see Ugelvik and Barker, Chapters 10 and 13 respectively in this volume). Refused asylum seekers are not eligible for financial support of this kind (Vevstad and Brochmann 2010). In some emergencies, they may qualify for ad hoc aid, but this has been politically unclear (Søvig 2013) and, reportedly, this form of support is rarely used.[10] Residents in asylum centres receive a small amount of money each week (60 euros). Though primarily filled with individuals whose cases are yet to be decided, such places also hold some who have already been rejected. Families with small children and the seriously ill are also eligible for food, shelter, and pocket money (Utlendingsdirektoratet 2008). Effectively, such groups are deprived of permanent housing facilities (Øien and Sønsterudbråten 2011; Valenta 2012; Fangen and Kjærre 2013).

In countries with weaker welfare states, families constitute the main social and financial security net. For refused asylum seekers, people from the same region or country and acquaintances may count as a network with similar potential. Some refused asylum seekers use contacts in this way, sleeping on the sofas of acquaintances in a more stable situation (Kjellberg and Rugeldal 2011). However, they are often reluctant to talk about how they actually cope (Valenta 2012). They are anxious not to overburden their relationships by asking for too much (Øien and Sønsterudbråten 2011), reportedly preferring to sleep outside than stay too long. They also withdraw from relationships so as not to bother others in their surroundings with their concerns (Kjærre 2010; Valenta 2012).

Some ethnic Norwegians assist refused asylum seekers. Idealists have set up networks of 'helpers' (Dahl 2008; Kjellberg and Rugeldal 2011) and there are several examples of local communities throughout the country embracing 'their' refused asylum seekers. According to newspaper reports, communities are frequently willing to disobey politicians and authorities when their local neighbours are threatened with deportation.

As in other European countries, supporting refused asylum seekers has been partly criminalized (Søvig 2013). Citizens who profit from their work with refused asylum seekers or aid such people in obstructing the enforcement of a legal decision, ie by hiding them, may be subject to criminal penalties. Although there

---

[10] Conversation with the leader of the health centre for irregular migrants in Oslo.

was a heated political debate in parliament, where strong voices were heard forwarding the message that all help was detrimental in making migration politics efficient, most forms of individual aid to irregular migrants were decriminalized in 2012. Obstructing police is still punishable (Søvig 2013).

In contrast to the loosening of controls over personal aid to refused asylum seekers, the provision of health care to this group is closely regulated and heavily restricted. For the most part, health care is for citizens. Only children of refused asylum seekers and adults in need of emergency medical attention can obtain it.[11] Even then, they are treated differently, generally directed to health centres run by NGOs and local municipalities, rather than allocated to a doctor.

Together, exclusion from the labour market, health care, and welfare institutions operate as effective mechanisms of control. There are nevertheless loopholes that undermine their capacity to determine people's behaviour. Control is not, in other words, absolute. The labour market absorbs an unknown quantity of labour from unregistered residents, and some hospitals do (informally) accept patients without payment. Politically, a limited amount of health care and non-profit aid for foreigners seems to be accepted by the population. Informal organizations and individual idealists combine to produce substantial (but typically unknown amounts of) aid. We might even say that to be 'irregular' activates some sort of rights (Fangen and Kjærre 2013). This aid does not dramatically relieve their life situation or reach all who need it. Nevertheless, it is enough to justify a more detailed scrutiny.

The Dynamics of the Funnel: Framing Choices

The main purpose of the control of work, health, and welfare is to set up a situation in which the state's preferred outcome is more attractive than the alternative. When faced with life without means to acquire food and other necessities, a rational person would find another place to stay. In other words, in the welfare state, the building blocks of control are incentives. The individual retains the final decision; however, the group is governed through obstacles designed to shape their choices. This is the mechanism we find in the funnel of expulsion.

Incentives are the preferred instruments in putting politics to practice in neo-liberal regimes. In post-welfarist societies, it is common to create situations that function in the same ways as markets (Dean 2010). As such, the politics regarding refused asylum seekers have the same characteristics as other forms of government and the indirect uses of force described above are in many ways a 'success'. The health centre for irregular migrants in Oslo reports widespread misery, both somatically and mentally (Johansen 2013).

This strategy also involves the elimination of loopholes. There should be no escape from the desired choice, so the incentives create a particular structure. On all

---

[11] Emergencies include abortion, childbirth, and cases of contagious diseases (Årsmelding 2011; Søvig 2013).

sides of the funnel there is a wall that is more or less impenetrable. At the bottom end there is a hole, which leads outside the territory. To complete the image of the funnel, the hole leading out is smeared with a lubricant. In the case of refused asylum seekers, the lubricant consists of government prizes and organizations that provide aid for those willing to leave.[12] In addition, migrants are offered financial rewards if they leave voluntarily (on average 3,300 euros per person).

Eliminating loopholes requires attention to detail. The labour market is large and complex, and private enterprises do not always conform to government rule. Refused asylum seekers can offer something valuable—inexpensive labour. It would be tempting, if one had a realistic hope of getting away with it, to hire a person without paying for the costs of social security and taxes. Such holes are plugged in several ways. For example, health and tax authorities regularly inspect bars, restaurants, and workplaces, with a particular eye to finding irregular migrants. In the winter of 2010, the tax authorities plugged another hole by comparing tax registers with the main population register. This step meant that more than 100 refused asylum seekers did not have their taxation forms renewed and could no longer hold the jobs they had or apply for new ones (Johansen 2013).

So far, we have seen a funnel of expulsion negatively constructed by institutions in nation states. In this view, the handling of refused asylum seekers may be understood as a part of internal, national policies. However, the field of politics identified as the funnel of expulsion transgresses the dichotomy of national and international policies. This becomes clear when we compare the characteristics of the funnel with Foucault's concepts of governmentality and biopolitics. First, to illuminate the anatomy of the funnel of expulsion, we may look at a certain, albeit short-lived, political solution to the problem of unruly visitors: the 'waiting camps'.

Waiting Camps: The Dynamics of Governing the Non-population

In 2006, rejected asylum seekers in Norway were offered a new form of 'assistance'. The so-called 'waiting camps' provided food and shelter. These were neither ordinary asylum centres nor detention centres, but shelters for people who had been denied permission to stay in the country and had no other place to live. Waiting camps were originally proposed to alleviate the harsh conditions under which irregular migrants found themselves when the right to housing in an asylum centre was withdrawn (Brekke and Søholt 2005; Brekke 2010). The government proclaimed that 'nobody should freeze or starve in Norway' (Department of Regional Administration 2005). The design of the camps illuminated the humanitarian ambitions within these policies. But they also turned out to be a microcosmic funnel of expulsion.

The camps were located in former asylum centres, without any major physical modification of the buildings. High fences surrounded the camps, and all traffic in

---

[12] The International Organisation for Migration (IOM) is the dominant player in assisting migrants to leave.

and out was registered electronically. The camps offered a room, three meals a day, and some equipment for table tennis. They were sparsely equipped and located far away from city centres. The camps prevented the residents from freezing and starving. However, there was nothing for the residents to do. Individuals could not even cook their own food. Considering that it would have been cheaper to let the residents make their own food, it seems obvious that the void of meaning was an intended part of the design of the waiting camps.

Inhabitants who stayed away for three days or more lost their rooms. The distance to nearby cities was too long to walk and too expensive to travel by bus regularly in light of the amount of allowance residents received (12 euros per week). Residents were practically closed in. Even though they could leave at any time, some stayed for years.[13] These people were fenced off from the rest of society through design, not force. The only force in function was that of their bodily needs: hunger and shelter.

There are important differences between waiting camps as a microcosm and control of refused asylum seekers more generally. In the big picture, misery took the form of insecurity and uncertainty in not knowing where the next meal and shelter would come from. In the smaller picture, misery took the form of 'empty time' (Bourdieu and Ferguson 1999).[14] The mood inside the camps was tense for long periods, and the administration attempted to keep the press away. The low living standards and the lack of meaningful occupation frustrated the residents. A mix of violence and retreat prevailed. In the end, some of the residents set both camps on fire (Kjellberg and Rugeldal 2011).[15]

Waiting camps were created to enforce expulsion. Although the White Paper that proposed them mentions human rights (Department of Regional Administration 2005), it is evident that they were consciously designed to persuade refused asylum seekers to return 'voluntarily'. The organization and localization worked in tandem with architecture to exacerbate meaninglessness and emptiness of existence. In the void of meaning, agencies promoting return, such as the IOM, had an opening to offer their services. According to one study, the employees in the camps were encouraged to use everyday encounters to talk about the 'possible way out' and to highlight the link between hopelessness and return (Folkeson 2009). Designed misery manipulated the residents directly.

When the waiting camps were closed in the summer of 2010, the political reaction was to blame the rioters. The arsonists were quickly identified and deported. 'How could they be so ungrateful and dissatisfied with the generous offer to stay in the waiting camps?' Those who had exhausted their legal remedies clearly did not 'really' need protection. If they did not choose to leave, such figures had to accept the responsibility for their experiences in the waiting camps. Any

---

[13] According to some, long-term residents were primarily those who were unwell or had other problems (Kjellberg and Rugeldal 2011).
[14] This situation differs from descriptions of detention centres in the UK (Burnett and Chebe 2010; Bosworth 2011, 2012).
[15] One may only speculate whether the fires were concerted (Brekke 2010; Kjærre 2010), but the phenomena of burning down similar institutions have also been known in the UK (Bosworth 2011).

suffering they may have endured rested unequivocally with the refused asylum seekers themselves.

Minimalist Biopolitics

There are obvious traits connecting the politics described above and the concept of governmentality established by Foucault (1997, 2007, 2010), and developed later by a number of scholars (Rose et al 2006). Governmentality is commonly summarized as 'indirect control' or 'conduct of conduct'. The funnel of expulsion fits well with this conceptualization. Instead of deportation, refused asylum seekers are placed in a situation where they are expected to make that move themselves. Their actions are governed through establishing a life situation where the only rational choice seems to be to leave.

Although governing through choice is an important aspect of Foucault's analysis, the emphasis put on material incentives here does not conform to the leading trends of the governmentality tradition (Rose et al 2006). One important aspect of the neo-liberal governmental rationality is to produce cognitive connections to specific goals. Dean terms such strategies 'programmes' (Dean 2010). Programmes take the form of binding theoretical knowledge and practical considerations. Thus, governmentality is a concept that first and foremost concerns control in a normative and epistemological sense. Governmentality, in this programmatic way, presupposes a disciplined population of docile individuals.

Thus, the analogy with governmentality seems to sit alongside the main currents in the tradition following Foucault. Still, the structure of incentives is important because it displays the dynamics of the field we investigate. We find a mechanism at work, tying the subjects of control to a certain situation. They are forced to make a certain choice. Since the dynamics in the funnel of expulsion resemble neo-liberal government, what kind of relationship is there then between the state and the political subject? Does the funnel of expulsion conform to the characteristics of biopolitics?

The emergence of biopolitics represented a shift in political strategies from regarding the population as a source of disorder to one of riches (Foucault 1997). In the biopolitical perspective, the population's growth is the goal of politics. Biopolitics enhances the health of the group. Avoiding sickness and strengthening the populace makes it more productive. By looking at the population as a living organism (Dean 2010) biopolitics sets a new form of rationality in motion. Concern for its well-being replaces the former perspective of regulating the territory. Thus, knowledge about the population becomes important. Biopolitics rose as a political strategy in the nineteenth century, in tandem with the new human and social sciences. Biopolitical awareness presupposes knowledge about humans and their relationships. Biopolitical rationalities become more important in tandem with the development of liberalism and the growth of sciences of man. The welfare state is the end product of biopolitical rationality (Ojakangas 2005).

The funnel of expulsion, on the other hand, does not promote health. On the contrary, the political goal of politics in this area is poor health and sickness, even death (Weber and Pickering 2011). The denial of access to social arenas produces patterns of illnesses (Johansen 2013). Thus, it would be unfair to characterize the politics of expulsion as biopolitics (Schinkel 2010; Aas 2011).

Nevertheless, there are elements of biopolitics in the funnel. The Norwegian Parliament accepted the establishment of a health centre providing acute assistance to irregular migrants. The waiting camps were also established in a rationale of care, explicitly referring to human rights. Albeit minimal, those refused asylum enjoy some rights. By looking at the control of these people as a combined and coordinated effort by different institutions and politics, a pattern emerges that is not really biopolitical but resembles some of the characteristics understood as biopolitics.

In this context, it might be more yielding to employ the term 'minimalist biopolitics', coined by Redfield (2005) and refined by Walters (2010b). Minimalist biopolitics refers to the activities 'devoted to monitoring and assisting populations in maintaining their physical existence' (Redfield, quoted in Walters 2010b: 144). Thus, these writers identify a sort of biopolitics which is not developed in the spirit of producing a healthy population but has the goal of reducing poor health. These are different political paradigms, but they do share a concern for health. Walters reveals an element of minimalist biopolitics in the way borders are developed. Beside securitization, he argues, a rhetoric of humanism increasingly inscribes borders, transforming them into 'humanitarian borders'. For example, the IOM presents its services as 'humanitarian assistance'. This rhetoric is more than glossy self-presentation; it expresses an 'uneasy alliance' of politics of alienation and care (Walters 2010b).

Minimalist biopolitics is most visible in military conflict zones, where medical organizations aim to 'save lives' (Fassin and Pandolfi 2010). However, military interventions are not isolated from the humanitarianism offered. Looking at it more broadly, it is evident that idealists and NGOs also define the nature of borders. NGOs are involved in the administration of minimalist biopolitical policies while simultaneously protesting the lack of responsibility shown by political authorities. In this way, NGOs are absorbed into the administration of liminal groups, and constitute an important element in the governing of borders (see also Lee, Chapter 7 in this volume). In an area often identified with securitization, force, and military means, Walters promotes the idea that there is another regime of politics developing in the area of border controls, which is also intrinsic to the growth of neo-liberalism. Citing the work of critical anthropologist Didier Fassin, Walters defines the humanitarian approach as 'the administration of human collectives in the name of a higher moral principle which sees the preservation of life and the alleviating of suffering as the highest value of action' (Fassin, quoted in Walters 2010b: 143). Humanitarianism in this context is not restricted to certain political ideologies, but is a political rationality, growing out of the activities of assemblages of organizations. Here, we are not really speaking of forcing nourishment into unwilling prisoners. Humanitarian government concerns itself with assistance, aid, and documentation of needs.

Key features of the funnel fit well with the characteristics outlined by Walters. State authorities provided financially for the waiting camps. Private enterprises and NGOs ran them. Some health services are provided to irregular migrants by the state, other health care is provided by NGOs. Aid is accepted as long as it does not obstruct policing. In addition, children of irregular migrants are allowed to attend kindergartens and schools. Although adults do not have rights to enter the market as workers, students, or clients, their offspring may attend educational institutions. Finally, idealists are running some of the asylum centres.

NGOs may complain about the lack of responsibility shown by political authorities (Baghir-Zada 2010; Hjelde 2010; Årsmelding 2011; Årsmelding 2012). Their ambition, they claim, is to become 'superfluous'. In their efforts, they nevertheless shape this area of politics, having become a substantial sector in their own right.

Walters' corrections of the dystopian images of borders seem well grounded. There are defining elements of humanism in contemporary border politics which transgress the political space of the nation state. The same humanism also characterizes the funnel of expulsion.

Conclusion

In terms of conclusion, I would like to point out the importance of the political dynamics within the field. In the age of globalism, migration flows challenge traditional conceptualizations of politics. A combination of forms of exclusion defines the politics regarding refused asylum seekers. They must endure terrible conditions and risk harsh treatment from authorities. There is no shortage of tales of inhuman and unjust experiences and examples of hostility. For some, the counter image of hospitality is hard to recognize, especially in Khosravi's own story (2009). Yet there are also in-built openings for aid and relief. They are neither left to themselves nor included in the demos: they are led into a position in which a certain dynamics operates.

This dynamic was outlined through the description of the funnel of expulsion, whose characteristics are also mirrored in the institution of the waiting camp. Although the waiting camps have been closed down, they still serve as an illustration of the political dynamics in the field more generally. In the waiting camps the most basic needs of irregular migrants were taken care of. The subjects were fenced in and put into a situation from which they were indirectly forced to leave. Despite the potential use of force that lies behind the treatment of refused asylum seekers, there is a political recognition that there is a certain lower limit to the level of destitution that can be tolerated. This is why the 'deficit paradigm' often misses the point and why the concept of minimalist politics seems to be more adequate. While recognizing the same principles of government that Foucault and the governmentality tradition found in neo-liberal regimes, Walters points out that important aspects of border politics display divergent elements of 'minimalist' rather than full-scale biopolitics. They are coined in the 'image' of it, but also subvert its objectives. The aim is the reduction of suffering rather than production of health.

However, the analysis of what I termed 'the funnel of expulsion' revealed also an additional dynamics of control that forces the subject to make a seemingly 'free' choice to leave. This dynamics reveals the blurring boundaries between several spheres of social control described in this volume. Historically, we have distinguished between internal and external sovereignty. In the face of globalization this distinction has become contested and 'destabilized' (see Aas and Bosworth, Chapters 1 and 8 respectively). Aas describes a transformation of penality. Migration control is expanding and has become interwoven with crime control. Control of the interior is mixed with control of the exterior. In this process, the traditional landscape of domestic and international politics is 'de-composed' (Aas, Chapter 1 in this volume). Globalization defines all areas of politics and, accordingly, decomposes the politics of expulsion. In contrast to the cases cited by Aas and Bosworth, expulsion is not restricted to the area of penal law, but is defined by demarcations in public law more generally, and even civil law. State organizations constitute the framework for the designed structure of incentives forced upon refused asylum seekers that is then supplemented by private and idealist parties.

The funnel of expulsion is a field of politics that has risen in the shadow of the conceptual horizons offered by nation states. Expulsion is not deportation, but rather force and humanism melted into a unique area of politics that must be understood as such. It is designed as a combination of inclusion and exclusion, which, despite all his metaphors of duality, is invisible through the lenses offered by Agamben.

References

Aas, K.F. (2011) '"Crimmigrant" Bodies and Bona Fide Travelers: Surveillance, Citizenship and Global Governance', *Theoretical Criminology* 4: 16.

Agamben, G. (2005) *State of Exception*. Chicago: University of Chicago Press.

Agamben, G. (1998) *Homo Sacer: Sovereign Power and Bare Life*. Stanford, California: Stanford University Press.

Anderson, B. and Ruhs, M. (2010) 'Migrant Workers: Who Needs Them? A Framework for the Analysis of Shortages, Immigration and Public Policy', in B. Anderson and M. Ruhs (eds), *Who Needs Migrant Workers? Labour Shortages, Immigration and Public Policy*. Oxford: Oxford University Press.

Andrijasevic, R. (2010) *From Exception to Excess*. Durham, NC: Duke University Press.

Baghir-Zada, R. (2010) 'Health and Illegality: The Case of Sweden', in T.L. Thomsen, J.B. Jørgensen, S. Meret, K. Hviid, and H. Stenum (eds), *Irregular Migration in a Scandinavian Perspective*. Maastricht: Shaker.

Bhartia, A. (2010) 'Fictions of Law', in N. De Genova and N.M. Peutz (eds), *The Deportation Regime: Sovereignty, Space, and the Freedom of Movement*. Durham NC: Duke University Press.

Blitz, K.B. and Otero-Iglesias, M. (2011) 'Stateless By Other Name: Refused Asylum-Seekers in the United Kingdom', *Journal of Ethnic and Migration Studies* 37(49): 657.

Bourdieu, P. and Ferguson, P.P. (1999) *The Weight of the World: Social Suffering in Contemporary Society*. Cambridge: Polity Press.

Bosworth, M. (2012) 'Subjectivity and Identity in Detention: Punishment and Society in a Global Age', *Theoretical Criminology* 16(2): 123.

Bosworth, M. (2011) 'Human Rights and Immigration Detention in the United Kingdom', in M.-B. Dembour and T. Kelly (eds), *Are Human Rights for Migrants?: Critical Reflections on the Status of Irregular Migrants in Europe and the United States*. Abingdon: Routledge.

Brekke, J.-P. (2010) *Frivillig retur fra Norge: en historisk gjennomgang*. Oslo: Institutt for samfunnsforskning.

Brekke, J.-P. and S. Søholt (2005) *I velferdsstatens grenseland: en evaluering av ordningen med bortfall av botilbud i mottak for personer med endelig avslag på asylsøknaden*. Oslo: Institutt for samfunnsforskning.

Brown, W. (2010) *Walled States, Waning Sovereignty*. New York: Zone Books.

Burnett, J. and Chebe, F. (2010) 'Captive Labour: Asylum Seekers, Migrants and Employment in UK Immigration Removal Centres', *Race and Class* 51(4): 95.

Calavita, K. (2005) *Immigrants at the Margins. Law, Race, and Exclusion in Southern Europe*. Cambridge: Cambridge University Press.

Cornelisse, G. (2010) 'Immigration, Detention and the Territoriality of Universal Rights', in N. De Genova and N.M. Peutz (eds), *The Deportation Regime: Sovereignty, Space, and the Freedom of Movement*. Durham, NC: Duke University Press.

Dahl, H. (2008) 'De gode hjelperne: om skjuling i dagens Norge'. Master's thesis, University of Oslo.

De Genova, N. (2010) 'The Deportation Regime: Sovereignty, Space, and the Freedom of Movement', in N. De Genova and N.M. Peutz (eds), *The Deportation Regime: Sovereignty, Space, and the Freedom of Movement*. Durham, NC: Duke University Press.

De Genova, N.P. (2002) 'Migrant "Illegality" and Deportability in Everyday Life', *Annual Review of Anthropology* 31: 419.

Dean, M. (2010) *Governmentality: Power and Rule in Modern Society*. London: Sage.

Dembour, M.-B. and Kelly, T. (2011) 'Introduction', in M.-B. Dembour and T. Kelly (eds), *Are Human Rights for Migrants?: Critical Reflections on the Status of Irregular Migrants in Europe and the United States*. Abingdon: Routledge.

Department of Regional Administration (2005) Odelstinsproposisjon 112 (2004–2005) *Om lovomendringeriutlendingsloven (innkvarteringvedsøknadomasyl mv.)*. Kommunalogregionaldepartmentet: Oslo.

Diken, B. and Bagge Laustsen, C. (2005) *The Culture of Exception*. London: Routledge.

Fangen, K. and Kjærre, H.A. (2013) 'Ekskludert av staten, inkludert av hva', in K.F. Aas, N.B. Johansen and T. Ugelvik (eds), *Krimmigrasjon, Den Nye Kontrollen av de Fremmede*. Oslo: Universitetsforlaget.

Fassin, D. and Pandolfi, M. (2010) *Contemporary States of Emergency*. New York: Zone Books.

Folkeson, S. (2009) 'Ingenmannsland'. Master's thesis, University of Oslo.

Foucault, M. (1997) *Ethics: Subjectivity and Truth*. London: Allen Lane.

Foucault, M. et al (2010) *The Government of Self and Others*. Basingstoke: Palgrave Macmillan.

Foucault, M. et al (2007) *Security, Territory, Population: Lectures at the Collège de France, 1977–78*. Basingstoke: Palgrave Macmillan.

Hjelde, K.H. (2010) 'Irregular Migration, Health and Access to Health Services in Norway', in T.L. Thomsen, J.B. Jørgensen, S. Meret, K. Hviid, and H. Stenum (eds), *Irregular Migration in a Scandinavian Perspective*. Maastricht: Shaker.

Johansen, N.B. (2013) 'Noe med helse og irregulære migranter', in. K.F. Aas, N.B. Johansen and T. Ugelvik (eds), *Krimmigrasjon, Den Nye Kontrollen av de Fremmede*. Oslo: Universitetsforlaget.

Khosravi, S. (2009) 'Sweden: Detention and Deportation of Asylum Seekers', *Race and Class* 50(4) 38.

Kjærre, H.A. (2010) 'No Direction Home—The Margins of a Welfare State and Illegalized Body', in T.L. Thomsen, J.B. Jørgensen, S. Meret, K. Hviid and H. Stenum (eds), *Irregular Migration in a Scandinavian Perspective*. Maastricht: Shaker:

Kjellberg, J. and Rugeldal, C. (2011) *Illegal: papirløs i Norge*. Oslo: Spartacus.

Mohn, S.B. (2013) 'Passet påskrevet—Straff og kontroll av utlendinger i norsk offisiell statistikk', in K.F. Aas, N.B. Johansen, and T. Ugelvik (eds), *Kontroll på Grensen eller noe sånt*. Oslo: Universitetsforlaget.

Müller, J.-W. (2003) *A Dangerous Mind*. New Haven: Yale University Press.

Øien, C. and Sønsterudbråten, S. (2011) *No Way In, No Way Out?: A Study of Living Conditions of Irregular Migrants in Norway*. Oslo: Fafo.

Ojakangas, M. (2005) *Impossible Dialogue on Biopower: Agamben and Foucault*. Foucault Studies, No. 2, May: 5.

Phuong, C. (2006) 'The Removal of Failed Asylum Seekers', *Legal Studies* 25(1): 117.

Pinter, I. (2012) *I Don't Feel Human*. The Children's Society, London: UK.

Rajaram, P.K. and Grundy-Warr, C. (2004) 'The Irregular Migrant as Homo Sacer: Migration and Detention in Australia, Malaysia and Thailand', *International Migration* 42(1): 33.

Redfield, P. (2005) 'Doctors, Borders, and Life in Crisis', *Cultural Anthropology* 20(3): 328.

Rose, N. P. et al (2006) 'Governmentality', *Annual Review of Law and Sociology* 2: 22.

Sandberg, S. and Pedersen, W. (2011) *Street Capital: Black Cannabis Dealers in a White Welfare State*. Bristol: Policy Press.

Schinkel, W. (2010) 'From Zoêpolitics to Biopolitics: Citizenship and the Construction of "Society"', *European Journal of Social Theory* 13(2): 18.

Schmitt, C. (1996) *The Concept of the Political*. Chicago: University of Chicago Press.

Skilbrei, M.-L. (2013) 'Menneskehandelspolitikk i Brytningen Mellom Kriminalitets-bekjempelse, Innvandringskontroll og Rettigheter', in K.F. Aas, N.B. Johansen, and T. Ugelvik (eds), *Krimmigrasjon. Den Nye Kontrollen av de Fremmede*. Oslo: Universitetsforlaget.

Søvig, K.H. (2013) 'Straffansvar og straffeforfølging av humanitære hjelpere ved ulovlig opphold', in K.F. Aas, N.B. Johansen, and T. Ugelvik (eds), *Krimmigrasjon. Den Nye Kontrollen av de Fremmede*. Oslo: Universitetsforlaget.

Stenum, H. (2010) 'Workers and Vagrants: Governing the Foreign Poor in Denmark', in T.L. Thomsen, J.B. Jørgensen, S. Meret, K. Hviid, and H. Stenum (eds), *Irregular Migration in a Scandinavian Perspective*. Maastricht: Shaker.

Thomsen, R. (1972) *The Origin of Ostracism: A Synthesis*. Copenhagen: Gyldendal.

Utlendingsdirektoratet (2008) *Reglement for økonomiske ytelser til beboere i statlig mottak*. Utlendingsdirektoratet. Rundskriv: RS 2008–035.

Valenta, M. (2012) 'Avviste asylsøkere, kamp mot uttransportering og livet utenfor mottakssystemet', in M. Valenta and B. Berg (eds), *Asylsøker i velferdsstatens venterom*. Oslo: Universitetsforlaget.

Vevstad, V. and Brochmann, G. (2010) *Utlendingsloven: lov 15. mai 2008 nr. 35 om utlendingers adgang til riket og deres opphold her: kommentarutgave*. Oslo: Universitetsforlaget.

Vitus, K. (2010) 'Waiting Time: The De-subjectification of Children in Danish Asylum Centres', *Childhood* 17(1): 26.

Walters, W. (2010a) 'Deportation, Expulsion, and the International Police of Aliens', in N. De Genova and N.M. Peutz (eds), *The Deportation Regime: Sovereignty, Space, and the Freedom of Movement*. Durham, NC: Duke University Press.

Walters, W. (2010b) 'Foucault and Frontiers: Notes on the Birth of the Humanitarian Border', in U. Bröckling, S. Krasmann, and T. Lemke (eds), *Governmentality: Current Issues and Future Challenges*. Abingdon: Routledge.

Weber, L. and Pickering, S. (2011) *Globalization and Borders: Death at the Global Frontier*. Basingstoke: Palgrave Macmillan.

Welch, M. and Schuster, L. (2005) 'Detention of Asylum Seekers in the US, UK, France Germany, and Italy: A Critical View of the Globalising Culture of Control', *Criminal Justice* 5(4): 331.

15

People on the Move: From the Countryside to the Factory/Prison

Dario Melossi[1]

Many years ago, in *The Prison and the Factory*, I claimed that the origins of a 'modern' system of punishment, through the punitive use of detention, were connected to the emergence of a 'modern' system of production based in the factory. Their common roots could be found in the institution of a sort of 'penal manufacture'—the workhouse (Melossi and Pavarini 1977). In my analysis I drew on Marx's concept of 'original' or 'primitive' accumulation in Chapter 27 of the first volume of *Capital* (1960 [1867]). In those pages Marx referred to the (forced) transformation of peasants into proletarians, constituting a 'primitive accumulation' of the 'living' part of capital, ie labour. At that time, I was unable to see in those passages that Marx was referring also to migratory movements. Such blindness to the issue of migration, and to the relationship between production, penality, and *migration*, remains common in much contemporary theoretical and analytical work in criminology. Even those who write of a 'political economy' of punishment often do not take migration into account, subscribing to a national/citizenship framework characteristic of Marxism's birthplace in the century of the nation state—the nineteenth century.

In this chapter I revisit key assumptions about the political economy of punishment to explore what they might contribute to an understanding of contemporary practices of migration control. I outline a system of social change that can be tracked down by reconstructing the cyclical business processes and the data on imprisonment rates and migration flows. In so doing, I trace the long historic trajectory of relationships between capitalism, migratory movements, and processes of criminalization. The chapter highlights the centrality of migratory movements for the historic formations of the working class, and thus the relevance of Marxist theory for our understanding of historic and contemporary processes of migration control. Finally, by outlining the changing relationships of migration and penality,

[1] A previous version of this chapter was presented at a conference in Oxford on 19–20 April 2012, convened by Katja Franko Aas and Mary Bosworth. I thank Mary and Katja for the precious comments they offered even if of course the responsibility for the final result is only mine.

the chapter aims to challenge the lack of consideration given to such relationships in much of the theoretical and analytical writing within criminology.

1. A Cyclical Theory of Punishment and Social Structure

According to a 'long cycle' or 'long wave' perspective, what is most significant in international socio-economic development, considered in terms of technological innovation and/or class conflict, happens in long cycles of roughly 50 years, where the 'peak' and the 'trough' of the cycle are separated by periods of about 25 years (very close to the span of a generation) (for classic accounts see Kondratieff 1935; Schumpeter 1939; Kalecki 1972 [1943]; more recently, see Wallerstein 1974; Arrighi 1994; and Rennstich 2002). Scholars of this view see the movements in the cycle as induced by the efforts of the actors in the economic and political arena—essentially entrepreneurs and workers. 'The State' is considered a third party, playing somewhat of a 'relatively autonomous' role between the first two. Each one of these actors tries to overcome the limitations imposed on its development and 'freedom of action' by the adverse activities of the other.

Innovation—Schumpeter's 'process of creative destruction' (1943: 81–86)—constitutes a crucial tool by which entrepreneurs undercut and 'destroy' the power of labour when a prolonged spell of prosperity has placed workers in a privileged position. The result of such innovation—usually backed by political-legal power—is to disorganize the type of economy in which the former type of working class achieved its power. Likewise, adapting to the innovations implemented, the 'new' type of working class recruited under these conditions—often from 'lowly' 'immigrant' quarters—would eventually find the way to reorganize and bring increasingly effective action (at least as effective as the 'old' type of working class was able to bring) to the new setting of social relationships and power. At this point, the cycle starts anew, similar to the preceding one in pattern, but completely different, however, in detail.

The 'peaks' are of paramount importance in understanding the logic of the 'long cycle' argument in relation to changes in imprisonment. It is around the peak that a long spell of prosperity ends and turns into an 'economic crisis'. From the standpoint of the working class, prosperity enables increasing power, stronger organization, and a robust capacity for wage demands. On the opposite side, that of entrepreneurs, the strength of the working class translates into reduced profit margins and the necessity for change and innovation. Innovation is often the technological result of widespread feeling that the boundaries of the 'old' social system are too rigid and suffocating for the development the long period of prosperity has made possible. The most enterprising sectors of the elite are thereby able to sidestep the long-established competitors and the type of working class that grew together with prosperity—not to mention what is most important in terms of class conflict, ie to destroy the given organizational forms of that working class.

During prosperous periods leading to the peak years when the 'showdown' between labour and capital takes place, punishment is less of a 'necessity' for the social system as a whole. When most people who look for work can find it, the general social attitude is favourable even toward the lowest members of the working class. Prison conditions will be decent, and it will be possible to work within prisons, both because this is deemed to be a good tool for 'rehabilitation' and because the high wages outside make it worth it to produce at least certain goods at 'controlled' prices (something that often the unions outside object to). The basic stability of periods of prosperity means that no 'strangers' have to be called in to work, and even if they are, the general climate of tolerance and the good disposition of society extend also to them.

At the same time, however, periods of intense economic development are also times when, especially toward the end of the growth phase of the cycle, the system's hunger for labour stimulates a fast-increasing migratory movement, jealousies, and strong individualism. In the decade that would be seen as the most exemplary of this cultural temper, the American 'roaring twenties', the end to migration in 1926 following the introduction of a system of national quotas, *preceded* by three years, not *followed*, the Black Thursday of 24 October 1929! The new social phase generally has its roots in the preceding one. In the years of depression, for instance, the defeat of the 'old' working class as well as of the least competitive economic sectors translates into a progressive devaluation of human beings. Especially in the years before the 'peak', increasing recourse is made to a 'new' kind of working class—youth, women, immigrants—that does not share in the values and general 'ethos' of the old one, thereby creating resentments, conflicts, and, what is most important to entrepreneurs, divisions, within the working class. During times of depression, the number of the unemployed increases, 'crime' becomes more and more associated with the 'newcomers', tolerance disappears, prison work and 'alternative programs' are also shelved, and a generally mean feeling of envy and *revanche* takes hold in a society increasingly structured around lines of hierarchy, authoritarianism, and exclusion.

At the same time, however, as Ivan Jankovic pointed out when he realized that the relationship between unemployment and imprisonment did not hold during the Depression, 'the extent of unemployment during the Depression and the conciliatory policies of the New Deal prevented the positive correlation between imprisonment and unemployment' (Jankovic 1977: 27). In situations of economic crisis a kind of solidarity is established when the sharing of a common destiny among masses of people who once again come to see themselves as members of the working class[2] brings forth an attitude of tolerance that somehow mitigates the most envious tendencies. The importance of politics in this regard cannot be denied. After all, the American 1930s were the most left-leaning years in American history, and the deeds of such famous gangsters as John Dillinger or Bonnie Parker

---

[2] In Italy recently the number of those who describe themselves as members of the working class has increased remarkably inverting a decade-long tendency toward the subjective 'middle-classization' of class distribution. I refer here to research results by Ilvo Diamanti and the Demos Institute (see <http://www.demos.it>).

and Clyde Barrow assigned them true legendary status, almost the aura of rightful vindicators of a defeated and suffering working class (Gorn 2009).

More than a decade ago, Charlotte Vanneste identified the location of the 'peaks' and 'troughs' of such long cycles over the last century and a half (Vanneste 2001: 56). In relation to Vanneste's description of these cycles, it may represent a useful exercise to compare, if only in a merely suggestive way, the 'slope' prediction of the 'long cycle' model, which, according to Vanneste, is an 'ideal type' that applies to the generality of capitalist development in the most advanced countries, with the actual behaviour of imprisonment rates in two countries, Italy and the United States, for which we were able to collect the necessary information (see Figure 1). According to Vanneste's reconstruction, the peaks would be located *grosso modo* around 1870, 1920, and 1970 (and 2020), and the troughs around 1850, 1895, the end of the Second World War, and the end of the twentieth century. Because, according to the hypothesis, the imprisonment rate should 'behave' in countercyclical fashion, we would derive the prediction of an increase in imprisonment rates in the three cyclical 'downswings', 1870–1895, 1920–1945, and 1970–1995, and a decrease instead in the three 'upswings', 1850–1870, 1895–1920, and 1945–1970. Today we would find ourselves in the middle of a new decrease (1995–2020).

When we look at Figure 1, the vertical axes correspond to the mentioned 'peaks' and 'troughs'. The behaviour of imprisonment rates seems (roughly) to correspond to the predicted rate only for the twentieth century, ie the last two 'long cycles', but not for the previous rate in the nineteenth century. Furthermore, whereas we may be able to predict the general direction of the slope, the specificity of the size of incremental change year by year may vary greatly in different countries and under different circumstances. But, how does migration fit into all of this?

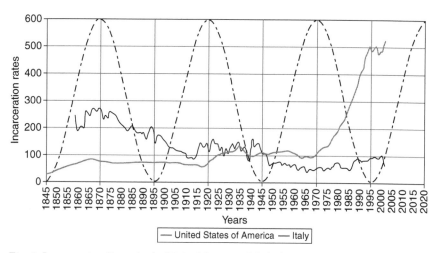

Fig. 1 Incarceration Rates in the United States and Italy (1850–2006) per 100,000

2. Between the Seventeenth and Eighteenth Centuries: A Pre-history

Between the end of the sixteenth and eighteenth centuries, Amsterdam merchants 'invented' what would then become the future 'form' of the prison (but also, at the same time, of the manufacture, the proto-factory)—the 'workhouse'—in order to punish and teach the poor to labour at the same time (Sellin 1944). 'Penality', in the English Bridewells as in Dutch seventeenth-century institutions, was at the very core of the constitution of a 'capitalist' mode of production; it was at the centre of the 'making' of a 'disciplined' 'working class'. At the same time, however, this very project was at the service of a certain kind of *rationality* that would reform and transform all aspects of social life, morality, and work. In this sense, a certain way of thinking about imprisonment is an indicator of the historical change that was taking place in those centuries as coherent and as telling as the introduction of the factory, the market, and all the other accoutrements of capitalism.

Processes of migration and 'modernization' in connection with some form of 'globalization' date at least to the late Middle Ages (Wallerstein 1974). Migratory movements constituted in a sense the womb within which all types of working class originated. At first there were 'people on the move' from a rural to an urban environment. At the same time, however, such 'move' was indissolubly linked with 'crime' and 'punishment' from the very beginning. Marx was among the first to note this process. Writing about 'enclosures of common land' in fifteenth-century England that were at the very roots of a 'primitive accumulation' constitutive of a 'capitalist mode of production', Marx stated:

The proletariat created by the breaking up of the bands of feudal retainers and by the forcible expropriation of the people from the soil, this 'free' proletariat could not possibly be absorbed by the nascent manufacturers as fast as it was thrown upon the world. On the other hand, these men, suddenly dragged from their wonted mode of life, could not as suddenly adapt themselves to the discipline of their new condition. They were turned *en masse* into beggars, robbers, vagabonds, partly from inclination, in most cases from stress of circumstances. Hence at the end of the 15th century and during the whole of the 16th century throughout Western Europe a bloody legislation against vagabondage. The fathers of the present working class were chastised for their enforced transformation into vagabonds and paupers. Legislation treated them as 'voluntary' criminals, and assumed that it depended on their own good will to go on working under the old conditions that no longer existed. (Marx 1960 [1867]: 734)[3]

Those 'dragged from their wonted mode of life'—the migrants—were labelled as 'criminals'. Migrants are the 'fathers [and mothers!] of the present working class'. This is not something that we are inclined to see during periods which are not characterized by huge mass migration, whereas they are somewhat obvious in

---

[3] This passage by Marx was the main foundation of my sections in Melossi and Pavarini (1977: 9–62).

periods like the current one. So, for instance, as I mentioned at the start of this chapter, when I moved from the just quoted passage by Marx in order to write my sections of *The Prison and the Factory* in the 1970s (Melossi and Pavarini 1977), I was unable to see that Marx was writing here also about migratory movements 'internal' to a country. His 'vagrants' were our contemporary 'migrants', as well as the American 'hoboes' of yesteryear (Anderson 1923). In this passage, Marx asserts that 'legislation treated them as "voluntary" criminals, and assumed that it depended on their own good will to go on working under the old conditions that no longer existed'. The processes that they have to undergo and that are brought down on them are considered as instances of the migrants'/vagrants' lack of adaptation or even of their predisposition to bad behaviour. The largely 'involuntary' products of development are at once the culprits of their new status.

In the same way in which migrants and workers are twin modern concepts, so the destiny which was waiting for them at the end of their travel, after that 'bloody legislation against vagabondage', was the 'factory form', which doubled up as a penal factory—the 'workhouse'—and which, 'invented' in the sixteenth and seventeenth centuries, was both a form of relief for unemployed workers and a punishment for criminalized despondent workers (Melossi and Pavarini 1977: 16–33). Prisons—as the successors to workhouses[4]—were and remain symbolic 'gateways' through which 'newcomers' are 'processed' in order to be admitted into the social contract, that is to say into the 'city'. In one of the central narratives of modernization, in fact—that most celebrated section of the *Manifesto of the Communist Party*—Marx portrays the trajectory of capitalism in history as one of destruction and rebuilding—'all that is solid melts into air' (Marx and Engels 1985 [1848]: 83; Berman 1982: 95). This 'destructive nihilism' (Berman 1982: 100) is embedded in the ordinary working of capitalism (Polanyi 1944).

In short, one of capitalism's most characteristic markers is migration and its connected coupling with a condition of 'anomie' or 'alienation'. At the same time, these human forces that have been somehow 'liberated' and set in motion by the movements of capitalism had to be transformed into controlled and disciplined production (Hirschman 1977: 14–20)—discipline being what the factory and the prison had in common—Foucault's Marxian point of departure. The particular role historically played by 'vagrancy', and vagrancy laws, in the very constitution of modern penal law, becomes then clearer (Chambliss 1964). Vagrancy, which had been called the 'chrysalis of every species of criminal' at the end of the nineteenth century (Duncan 1996: 172), was, together with the 'crime' of refusing to work at given conditions, the original crime for which imprisonment, the modern form of punishment, was to be administered (Melossi and Pavarini 1977: 16–33).

---

4 William Penn's penal reform in 1681, part of the broader Quaker 'holy experiment' of Pennsylvania, was the clearest and most explicit link between the workhouses and the modern penitentiaries. Penn decreed that 'all Prisons shall be workhouses for felons, Thiefs, vagrants, and Loose, abusive, and Idle persons, whereof one shall be in every county' (Dumm 1987: 79).

3. The Age of the Crowd in Europe

The nineteenth-century internal mass migrations in Europe created what were seen as the 'classes dangereuses', the *canaille sans phrase* of the nineteenth century (Chevalier 1958). This was the period of pioneering industrialization when even women and children were employed en masse in 'Satan's mills', and Karl Marx's good friend and comrade, Friedrick Engels (1975 [1845]), could write one of the very first sociological tracts of modernity describing the masses of workers huddled in the filthy, overcrowded, and unsanitary quarters of Manchester. Soon, as we know, the poor Irish men and women who were leaving their land after the potato famine started seeking solace from their condition not only going eastward but also across the Atlantic, in a process which, during the second half of the nineteenth century, would bring millions of Irish people to the United States.

In the last few decades of the nineteenth century and in the period just before the First World War, however, two different processes started unravelling in Europe, reinforcing each other. On the one hand, the enormous 'surplus population' caused by an 'industrial revolution' that swept, one after the other, all European countries, found an outflow in emigration toward Northern and Southern America (especially the largest countries of Southern America, such as Argentina and Brazil). On the other hand, the conditions of the working class started to improve markedly and, together with such conditions, eventually the working class's capacity for organizing and therefore attaining basic rights (about the length of the working day, the limitations to women's and children's work, and so on) grew. Throughout Europe, in country after country, first emigration, then the betterment in material and legal-political conditions led to an improved feeling of security and a reduction in the criminalization processes, developments that, in turn, reduced prison populations. The implications, for some, were clear. Italian criminologist Enrico Ferri (1979 [1884]: 93), for instance, noted that the decrease in the crime rates and imprisonment, first in Ireland and then, after 1881, also in Italy, was due to emigration, which should be listed among those tools of crime prevention that he called 'penal substitutes'—methods of indirect social defence from crime (Ferri 2009 [1884]: 334–335). His view seems to be borne out in Figure 2, where the data of Italian imprisonment admissions are inversely related to data on emigration from Italy, especially during the main emigration periods, at the beginning of the twentieth century and after the Second World War.

However, if a connection could be established between emigration, general betterment of social conditions especially among the poorest strata of the population, and the decrease in crime and imprisonment rates, an alternative conclusion could also be drawn in Cesare Lombroso's notation, according to which:

Recent statistics for the United States ... document high rates of crime in states with large number of immigrants, especially from Italy and Ireland. Out of 49,000 arrests in New York, 32,000 were immigrants ... Immigrants belong to the human category with the greatest incentives and fewest barriers to committing crime. Compared to the resident

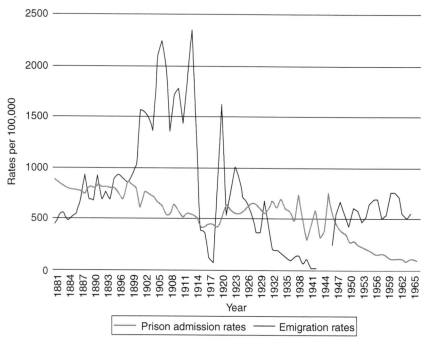

Fig. 2 Prison Admission Rates and Emigration Rates in Italy (1881–1965) per 100,000

population, newcomers have greater economic need, better developed jargon, and less shame; submitted to less surveillance, they more easily escape arrest. Thieves are almost always nomads. (Lombroso 2006 [1896]–[1897]: 316–317)

Was this indeed the case? Beyond Lombroso's volatile, temperamental, and absolutely non-politically correct attitude, his was not an isolated position. How was the network of relationships between migratory movements and processes of criminalization taking shape across the Atlantic, in the first country where, at the same time, large-scale migratory processes were taking place together with the early development of a social science deeply interested in 'explaining' crime and delinquency?

4. Chicago: Migrants, Fordism, and Gangsters

Between the 1880s and the First World War, the United States moved from being mostly a rural country to becoming the most powerful industrial society in the world. As part of its industrialization and urbanization, it witnessed large-scale migration first from Northern European countries, such as Germany and Ireland, and later from Eastern and Southern Europe, Asia, and Central America. Often the migratory process would take place in two steps. At first the 'supernumerary' peasants would move from the countryside to the big cities, especially the major ports. From there, they would migrate, and, with them, fear. Fear about crime in a sense followed these (former) peasants. No longer feared at home, they started to be feared on American shores, from the streets and alleys of New York to those of Buenos Aires (Salvatore and Aguirre 1996).

The factories, stockyards, and privileged logistic position of Chicago represented a big draw and, if the city was certainly not the first American urban conglomerate where the issue of crime and migration emerged as a major urban problem, neither were the specific national origins of the Chicago immigrants—Italian, Polish, Jewish, and later American Blacks from the South—the first to whom a label of crime and deviance was successfully attached. Throughout the nineteenth century the major urban centres of the East Coast had been sites of organized violence between the established groups and the newly arrived. At first, a deep preoccupation about the pathology of migrations was linked to nativism and racism, as well as fear of the competition of migrant workers on the labour market. These fears certainly played a role in promoting foreigners' criminalization in the United States during the 1920s and 1930s. Whether couched in terms of alcohol in the period of Prohibition or later with drugs, such fears were strictly related to deviant representations of 'non-American' peoples and habits (Rainerman and Levine 1997). Soon, however, the sociological progressivism of the time was quick to note, against the sensationalism of the press, that immigrants' involvement in crime was not significantly higher than the natives. Already the US Immigration Commission (1911) had pointed out that the 'foreign born' were less criminal than the native, a finding repeated in the Report of the Wickersam Commission (1931).

In an economy that had been dominated by the production of heavy mechanical goods at the time of the railways, the central working role had been that of the skilled worker. The craftsmen at that time were German and Irish. Decades of transition would then follow from this age to that of the assembly line and the automobile (Baran and Sweezy 1966), a process fed by the huge mass migration of (industrially) unskilled Southern and Eastern European peasants to America,[5] which made 'Fordism' (the 'scientific' management of work ('Taylorism') plus the rationalization of factory work ('Fordism' proper)) possible.

The legislative changes in immigration laws in the mid-1920s in the United States brought de facto to a restriction of 'undesirable' immigrants—undesirable on political and racial grounds, making it much more difficult to immigrate for Southern and Eastern Europeans, Asians, and, later, Mexicans—and was tantamount to redefining the issue of migration and crime also for North American sociologists and criminologists. In fact, criminologists began paying increasing attention to the crimes committed by the children of immigrants, so-called 'second generations', taken between the old world of their parents and their new world—a classic situation of *anomie* or 'culture conflict' in the words of the sociologist Thorsten Sellin (1938), himself a child of immigrants.

---

[5] Beside the great panic about their 'criminality' (Teti 1993; Salvatore and Aguirre 1996), there was also high public concern about deviance of the more 'native' internal migrants, the 'hoboes' (Anderson 1923).

Between the 1920s and Roosevelt's 'New Deal', public interest in crime developed and, together with it, the implementation of agencies and legislation devoted to fighting crime and the study of crime from a socio-criminological perspective. In a 1953 landmark piece, sociologist Daniel Bell reconstructed the development of organized crime in America as an aspect of the social climbing, and the increasing integration, of the various ethnic groups, in turn, into an 'American Way of Life'. Whether Italian, Irish, Jewish, or Polish, according to Bell the various gang organizations grew in increasing complicity with the urban power machines. This unconventional power structure was then used to enter the conventional power structure, and the old gangsters' children, now turned lawyers, engineers, and small entrepreneurs, could finally enter the American middle class. When Daniel Bell was writing, in the early 1950s, this had happened for Americans of European descent, while groups coming from other ethnic minorities, especially African Americans (who were also migrants, but *internal* migrants, coming from the South), were starting to replace ethnic Europeans in new gang formations.

In fact when American legislators had introduced a 'quota' system to contain 'undesirable' populations, the mass migration of African American rural workers from the South to the North, which had begun during the First World War, intensified. These workers were escaping the Jim Crow laws and the blatant racism of the post-bellum era in the South.[6] After the civil First World War the end of the regime of legal slavery and the acquisition of at least formal rights of citizenship by the African American minority had meant the end of the 'domestic' punishments inflicted by the slave master. There started that 'disproportion' in the experience of (public) penality that stayed on thereafter in the African American experience. In addition, following the Civil War the Southern states saw a sudden and massive increase in the African American population within prisons, similar to what had already happened in the North, where a small, free section of the Black population was already filling public prisons (Sabol 1989). There emerged at this point quite clearly what Thorsten Sellin (1976) called 'penal slavery'.[7] As Angela Davis explains (2003), slave labour was therefore replaced by forced prison labour—for example with the introduction of the lease system and chain gangs—bringing Blacks back to the plantation but this time as convicts, submitting them to the same 'domestic' punishments, but this time as disciplinary punishments within the penal realm. First as 'chattel', then as forced labour under contract, they were exposed to a condition of full fungibility.[8]

---

[6] An escape narrated most famously by the first great African-American writer, Richard Wright (2005 [1940] and 2008 [1944]).

[7] Developing an intuition by German theorist Gustav Radbruch (1938).

[8] Did they come close to being an example of what Giorgio Agamben has called 'bare life' (1998)? The mind goes to German concentration camps during the Second World War or Stalin's gulags—a concept of full fungibility of labour power that is hard to detach from what Foucault has called 'State racism' (1976). In 1939, in a letter to Horkheimer in New York, Georg Rusche stated that he was ready to write an article, for the journal of the institute, on 'the most recent development of the German penal policy'. These were 'the unbelievable scarcity of workers' that in Germany had caused 'truly interesting new phenomena' among which Rusche probably had in mind the emerging forced labour camps (Melossi 2003: xxix–xxx).

5. Post-Fordism, Globalization, and Crime in America

It was not until the recent 'age of globalization' that North American criminological and sociological interests turned again toward migration, and this time contemporaneously with what was happening in Europe and elsewhere. In between, the preoccupation of criminology was with the issue of the generations successive to the immigrant generations, their integration, and their possible contribution to phenomena of deviance and crime. It is not by chance that the discussion in the 1930s had shifted from Thorsten Sellin's *cultural* kind of conflict to Edwin Sutherland's *normative* view (Cressey 1968). When descendants of the Chicago School, such as Robert Sampson, began to pay attention to the results of globalization, they seemed to come up with outcomes not very remote from the classic Chicago School findings. In fact, even very recently, Robert Sampson (2012: 251–259) noted that first generations are in a sense 'protected' from crime by their relationships with their original families within tried and true 'ethnic niches', which separate the migrant youth from the more obviously crime-prone currents of the context in which they find themselves. Sampson could even maintain—to the chagrin of his many Conservative critics—that in the 1990s Mexican immigration to the United States was one of the factors contributing to declining crime rates (Sampson 2006). At first their cultures of origin are crime-adverse, and this is especially the case within so-called 'ethnic enclaves' (Martinez and Valenzuela 2006; Sampson 2006; Stowell 2007; Stowell et al 2009). However, when their offspring integrate within American society, one of the unfortunate consequences of the integration process is their participation within cultures that are characterized by a higher level of crime and violence. Rumbaut et al (2006: 71), for example, showed that the incarceration rates for foreign born males in *all* American ethnic groups are systematically lower than the incarceration rates for US born males in the same groups, as appears from the following table:

Table 1 Percentage of Males 18 to 39 Years Old Incarcerated in the United States, 2000, by Nativity, in Rank Order by Ethnicity[9]

| Ethnicity (Self-Reported) | Males, Ages 18–39 | | % Incarcerated, by Nativity | |
| | | | Nativity | |
	Total in US (N)	% Incarcerated	Foreign Born	US Born
Total	45,200,417	3.04	0.86	3.51
Latin American Ethnicities				
Salvadoran, Guatemalan	433,828	0.68	0.52	3.01
Colombian, Ecuadorian, Peruvian	283,599	1.07	0.80	2.37

(Continued)

---

[9] Table 1 is reproduced (adapted) with permission of Rumbaut et al (2006: 71).

Table 1 Continued

| Ethnicity (Self-Reported) | Males, Ages 18–39 | | % Incarcerated, by Nativity | |
| | | | Nativity | |
	Total in US (*N*)	% Incarcerated	Foreign Born	US Born
Mexican	5,017,431	2.71	0.70	5.90
Dominican	182,303	2.76	2.51	3.71
Cuban	213,302	3.01	2.22	4.20
Puerto Rican[a]	642,106	5.06	4.55	5.37
Asian Ethnicities				
Indian	393,621	0.22	0.11	0.99
Chinese, Taiwanese	439,086	0.28	0.18	0.65
Korean	184,238	0.38	0.26	0.93
Filipino	297,011	0.64	0.38	1.22
Vietnamese	229,735	0.89	0.46	5.60
Laotian, Cambodian	89,864	1.65	0.92	7.26
Other				
White, non-Hispanic	29,014,261	1.66	0.57	1.71
Black, non-Hispanic	5,453,546	10.87	2.47	11.61
Two or more race groups, other	1,272,742	3.09	0.72	3.85

Source: 2000 US Census, 5% PUMS. Data are estimates for adult males, ages 18 to 39, in correctional institutions at the time of the census.

[a] Island-born Puerto Ricans, who are US citizens by birth and not immigrants, are classified as 'foreign born' for the purposes of this table; mainland-born Puerto Ricans are here classified under 'US born'.

In the 1990s, there was a true rediscovery of the sociological and criminological interest in the nexuses between migration and crime and between migration and punishment (Marshall 1997; Tonry 1997; Martinez and Valenzuela 2006; McDonald 2009). This interest focused in part on the United States and in part on a comparison between what was going on in the United States and what was going on elsewhere, especially in Europe. Rumbaut owed much to the perspective of many important scholars, such as Alejandro Portes and others, according to whom second-generation children follow a path of downward mobility into a sort of 'underclass' where they join a section of the native born. They find themselves within urban environments haunted by labour market segmentation, class barriers, and racial discrimination. Contrary to the destiny of first generations, these groups of native-born youth find themselves in danger of joining, within excluded and marginalized sections of American society, in the same hopeless and negative social destiny. The results of Rumbaut's analysis of the connection between first generations, second generations, and risk of imprisonment seem to give credence to such predictions.

Rumbaut mobilized the traditional explanation of the Chicago School about so-called ethnic niches to explain the very low imprisonment rate of first generations. He drew attention to the fact that the various ethnic groups have very different incarceration rates from each other but, within each one of them, American born have higher rates than foreign born within the same group. Rumbaut explained that, in the shift from first to second generations, not only does one exit the somewhat conservative and protective warmth of his ethnic niche but one also enters a wider world that is characterized—as the old Chicago School vulgate would say—by heterogeneity, mobility, and anonymity, thereby crucially lowering social controls. There is, however, also a logic of 'racialization' at work, ie the construction of an inferior 'other'—as Calavita comments on the Southern European case (Calavita 2005: 144–156). Second-generation children face the prospect of down-ward assimilation within a labour market segmented according to class, gender, and national origins (see Brotherton and Barrios, Chapter 11 in this volume).

6. Global Post-Fordism

After the Second World War, in response to the consolidation of a Fordist develop-ment model in Northern and Central Europe, a mass movement of Southern Europeans toward those areas developed, which was also marked by fear of increasing crime (Ferracuti 1968; Kaiser 1974). This was when European criminological dis-course about migration took off, following a roughly similar pattern to that in America. The question of 'migration and crime' was again the centre of attention in the 1990s (Marshall 1997; Tonry 1997), this time also in Southern Europe which, after the halt to immigration in Western Europe of the early 1970s linked to the so-called 'oil crisis' and the transition from a 'Fordist' to a 'post-Fordist' type of economy, became attractive to migrants from other continents (De Giorgi 2002; Calavita 2005). In 1970, in Europe, mass migrations were of Northern African, Asian, and Eastern European workers, and here too the concern about 'criminal' invasion followed (Marshall 1997; Tonry 1997). It was in this latest economic cycle—apparently centred in the 'immaterial' economy of network society (Castells 1996)—that so-called 'post-Fordism' emerged (De Giorgi 2002; Welch 2002; Lacey 2008; Lee 2011). Kitty Calavita has cogently shown the nexus between the paradoxes of current migration, especially to Southern Europe, and the requirements of a 'post-Fordist' economy (Calavita 2005). In these very different examples, we witness a bifurcation in the 'moral economy' of the working class (Thompson 1971) between a respectable 'old' working class, expressing moral indignation at the mores of the newcomers, and a 'new' working class, the subject of extensive processes of criminalization. This social process is the phenomenon I have elsewhere called the 'cycle of production (and re-production) of *la canaille*' (the rabble) (Melossi 2008: 229–252).

In Italy and in Europe today it seems that we have followed a similar path to that of the United States, probably the only difference being the distinctly 'crimino-genic' effects of today's European immigration laws. Here too we hear the familiar complaint that 'our data undoubtedly show that foreigners in our country commit a disproportionate amount of crimes relative to their number' (Barbagli 2008:104), even if this statement is immediately qualified by the fact that the authors of these crimes are in the great majority *undocumented* foreigners. The Caritas (2009) organization has shown that, at least in Italy, foreigners' contribution to crime rates—measured by reports to the police—is very close to Italian crime rates, especially if one takes into consideration the demographic profile of the two groups. If, by immigrants, one therefore means *documented* immigrants, the preoccupation in Italy with their contribution to crime is certainly exaggerated. As to *undocumented* immigrants, one should remember that the connection to be established is between deviant behaviour and the *condition* of lack of documents, not some kind of 'personal quality'. Generally speaking, the latter are in fact people who entered legally (for instance on a tourist visa) or who acquired the proper documents for work, but subsequently lost the requirements to stay—a particularly critical problem in the current situation of economic crisis, given that work is one of the premises for maintaining a permit to stay legally in the country (and in the European Union). The problem is of course that the condition of being without documents places the foreign citizen within a set of conditions and constrictions that increase all the risk factors for criminal behaviour enormously (besides making him or her more visible to official agencies of control).

In other words, the problem of the relationship between documented status and the risk of deviant behaviour is first of all a legislative and more generally normative problem which concerns Italy, as well as many other members of the European Union, because of the cumbersome nature of entry procedures. Especially in the case of unskilled labour (which is the kind of labour de facto in demand), until the beginning of the economic crisis, those who aspired to come and work in Europe would try to enter by every means possible, thereafter to play a game of wait and see. The need for labour in European societies was so great that, sooner or later, some kind of individual or collective amnesty provision would be enacted—thereby recognizing the rational, albeit unlawful, strategy of migrants, not to mention the importance of their contribution to the welfare of the country. However, this situation creates a sort of 'gap' in the migrant's biography, when he or she has no chance to work legally, therefore making him or her more likely to become prey to a variety of illegal or downright criminal 'occupations'.

The nature of the problems has changed with the economic crisis that began in 2008 and which has increased migrants' unemployment dramatically. A report by the European Commission (2009) to the European Parliament showed that the rate of unemployment for third country documented nationals had risen from 13.6 per cent in 2008 to 18.9 per cent in 2009 (8.4 per cent for nationals) in the European Union. The consequence has been that:

overall immigration to developed countries has slowed sharply as a result of the economic crisis, bringing to a virtual halt the rapid growth in foreign-born populations over the past three decades. In the two years since the onset of the global economic crisis, temporary workers flows, business migration, and 'unregulated' flows such as illegal immigration and free movement within certain parts of the European Union have experienced the largest decreases. (Papademetriou et al 2010: 1)

In Italy, this is probably connected also to the hostility created by various governments in both its more and less official aspects. The percentage of foreigners in prison has also declined in Italy by 2.6 per cent between 2010 and 2012.[10]

Like the United States in the 1920s, the changed scenario may shift attention from first generations of migrants to the integration of their children. To the traditional North American distinction between 'first' and 'second' immigrant generations may be added, in Europe and especially Southern Europe, a tripartite distinction among 'undocumented' and first and second generation migrants. While many migrants are undocumented in the United States this category seems to have been less important than in Europe vis-à-vis the issue of criminalization (Melossi 2012), even if the recent legislative changes, spearheaded by Arizona laws, have centred on the conflation between illegal immigration and criminal behaviour. In contrast, throughout Europe, undocumented migrants (and their corresponding category 'unaccompanied minors') seem to suffer the bulk of the criminalization process, whereas the relationship between (documented) first and second generations is similar instead to that in the United States, as far as criminalization processes are concerned.

Conclusion

In the introduction I noted that many years ago, in *The Prison and the Factory*, I claimed that the origins of a 'modern' system of punishment, through the punitive use of detention, were connected to the emergence of a 'modern' system of production based in the factory and that their common roots could be found in the institution of a sort of 'penal manufacture'—the workhouse (Melossi and Pavarini 1977). The 'vagrancy' discussed in that connection, however, was not all that different from contemporary issues of 'migration' and I began to realize that a strong working class, as it was in the 1970s, belonged in a society characterized by small numbers of people in prison and low numbers of migrants. On the contrary, both social phenomena belonged instead in that period of capitalist 'revanche' in the 1970s which, in Italy, had yet to start (Melossi 2008: 229–249). We went on to see how it is possible to reconstruct at least the hypotheses of a connection between the type of economic development, the structure of labour required by such development, the existence and type of migrant movement, and finally the prevailing constructs of crime and penal response. The late nineteenth-century society of railwaymen and skilled Northern European workers was not the same as the Fordist project of a few decades later, built around the 'integration' of former peasants from Southern and Eastern Europe, and later of Southern African-Americans and Latin Americans. Each of these social formations calls for certain ideas of crime and penality, different in the 'sending' country and in the 'receiving' country, a complex social system that can be reconstructed also by

---

[10] ISMU, newsletter of 8 March 2012.

establishing the connections between long historical cycles, imprisonment rates, and migration flows. It then appears clear that the social focus on the criminality of newcomers—in periods of tumultuous development and unrestrained immigration—gives way subsequently to a preoccupation with the integration (and criminality) of the second (and following) generations, in periods when the combined strength of xenophobia and economic depression have halted migrant flows from abroad. These trends and developments have essentially kept pace with the uneven, problematic, conflictual, but apparently unstoppable process of globalization, which is at least as old as capitalism itself, as such different authors as Marx, Schumpeter, Wallerstein, and Arrighi have shown time and again in their work. A new *canaille* ('rabble') is cyclically produced and reproduced by capitalist development at every new phase, which, through its own struggle and capacity to strive for recognition and self-empowerment, turns into an ever new 'working class'. The connections between 'migration', 'crime', and 'punishment'—however sensationally they may appear on the surface of journalistic reports and short-sighted sociological analyses—are grounded within such deep-seated cyclical processes.

References

Agamben, G. (1998) *Homo Sacer: Sovereign Power and Bare Life.* Stanford: Stanford University Press.

Anderson, N. (1923) *The Hobo.* Chicago: University of Chicago Press.

Arrighi, G. (1994) *The Long Twentieth Century: Money, Power, and the Origins of Our Times.* London: Verso.

Baran, P.A. and Sweezy, P.M. (1966) *Monopoly Capital: An Essay on the American Economy and Social Order.* New York: Monthly Review Press.

Barbagli, M. (2008) *Immigrazione e sicurezza in Italia.* Bologna: il Mulino.

Bell, D. (1953) 'Crime as an American Way of Life', *Antioch Review* 13: 131–154 (reprinted in D. Bell (2000) [1960] *The End of Ideology: On the Exhaustion of Political Ideas in the Fifties.* Cambridge, MA: Harvard University Press.

Berman, M. (1988) *All that is Solid Melts into Air: The Experience of Modernity.* London: Penguin.

Calavita, K. (2005) *Immigrants at the Margins: Law, Race, and Exclusion in Southern Europe.* New York: Cambridge University Press.

CARITAS/Migrantes, Redattore Sociale (2009) 'La criminalità degli immigrati: dati, interpretazioni, pregiudizi', in Agenzia Redattore Sociale, *Guida per l'informazione sociale. Edizione 2010.* Capodarco di Fermo, Redattore Sociale.

Castells, M. (1996) *The Rise of the Network Society.* Oxford: Blackwell.

Chambliss, W. (1964) 'A Sociological Analysis of the Law of Vagrancy', *Social Problems* 12: 45.

Chevalier, L. (1958) *Classes laborieuses et classes dangereuses à Paris pendant la première moite du 19 siècle.* Paris: Plon.

Cressey, D.R. (1968) 'Culture Conflict, Differential Association, and Normative Conflict', in M. E. Wolfgang (ed), *Crime and Culture: Essays in Honor of Thorsten Sellin.* New York: Wiley.

Davis A.Y. (2003) *Are Prisons Obsolete?* New York: Seven Stories Press.

De Giorgi, A. (2002) *Re-Thinking the Political Economy of Punishment: Perspectives on Post-Fordism and Penal Politics.* Aldershot and Burlington, VT: Ashgate.

Dumm, T.L. (1987) *Democracy and Punishment: Disciplinary Origins of the United States.* Madison: University of Wisconsin Press.

Duncan, M.G. (1996) *Romantic Outlaws, Beloved Prisons.* New York: New York University Press.

Engels, F. (1975) [1845] *The Condition of the Working Class in England in 1844.* New York: International.

European Commission (2009) *Report from the Commission to the European Parliament and the Council: First Annual Report on Immigration and Asylum.*

Ferracuti, F. (1968) 'European Migration and Crime', in M.E. Wolfgang (ed), *Crime and Culture: Essays in Honor of Thorsten Sellin.* New York: Wiley.

Ferri, E. (1979) [1884] *Sociologia criminale.* Milano: Feltrinelli.

Ferri, E. (2009) [1884] 'The Data of Criminal Statistics, Continued', in N. Rafter (ed), *The Origins of Criminology: A Reader.* Abingdon: Routledge.

Foucault, M. (2003) [1976] *Society Must Be Defended.* New York: Picador.

Gorn E.J. (2009) *Dillinger's Wild Ride: The Year That Made America's Public Enemy Number One.* Oxford, Oxford University Press.

Hirschman, A.O. (1977) *The Passions and the Interests.* Princeton: Princeton University Press.

Immigration Commission of the United States (1911) *Immigration and Crime*, 61th Cong, 3d Session, Senate Document 750, Vol 36.

Jankovic, I. (1977) 'Labor Market and Imprisonment,' *Crime and Social Justice* 8: 17.

Kaiser, G. (1974) 'Gastarbeiterkriminalität und ihre Erklärung als Kulturkonflikt', in T. Ansay and V. Gessner (eds), *Gastarbeiter in Gesellschaft und Recht.* München: Beck.

Kalecki, M. (1972) [1943] 'Political Aspects of Full Employment', in M. Kalecki, *The Last Phase in the Transformation of Capitalism.* New York: Monthly Review Press.

Kondratieff, N.D. (1935) 'The Long Waves in Economic Life', *Review of Economic Statistics* 17: 105.

Lacey, N. (2008) *The Prisoners' Dilemma: Political Economy and Punishment in Contemporary Democracies.* Cambridge: Cambridge University Press.

Lee, M. (2011) *Trafficking and Global Crime Control.* London: Sage.

Lombroso, C. (2006) [1896–1897] *Criminal Man* (trans and intro M. Gibson and N. Hahn Rafter). Durham, NC: Duke University Press.

Marshall, I.H. (ed) (1997) *Minorities, Migrants, and Crime.* London: Sage.

Martinez, R. Jr and Valenzuela, A. (eds) (2006) *Immigration and Crime: Race, Ethnicity and Violence.* New York: New York University Press.

Marx, K. (1960) [1867] *Capital—Volume One.* London: Lawrence and Wishart.

Marx, K. and Engels, F. (1985) [1848] *The Communist Manifesto.* London: Penguin Books.

McDonald, W. (ed) (2009) *Immigration, Crime and Justice. Sociology of Crime, Law, and Deviance, Volume 13.* Bingley, UK: Emerald/JAI Press.

Melossi, D. (2012) 'Punishment and Migration between Europe and the USA: A Transnational "Less Eligibility"?', in J. Simon and R. Sparks (eds), *The SAGE Handbook of Punishment and Society.* London: Sage.

Melossi, D. (2008) *Controlling Crime, Controlling Society: Thinking About Crime in Europe and America.* Cambridge (UK): Polity Press.

Melossi, D. (2003) 'The Simple "Heuristic Maxim" of an 'Unusual Human Being. Introduction', in G. Rusche and O. Kirchheimer, *Punishment and Social Structure.* New Brunswick: Transaction Publishers.

Melossi, D. and Pavarini, M. (1981) [1977] *The Prison and the Factory: Origins of the Penitentiary System.* London: Macmillan.

Papademetriou, D.G., Sumption, M., Terrazas, A., Burkert, C., Loyal, S., and Ferrero-Turrión, R. (2010) *Migration and Immigrants Two Years after the Financial Collapse: Where Do We Stand?* Washington DC: Migration Policy Institute.

Polanyi, K. (1944) *The Great Transformation.* Boston: Beacon.

Radbruch, G. (1938) 'Der Ursprung des Strafrechts aus dem Stande der Unfreien', in *Elegantiae Juris Criminalis.* Basel: Verlag für Recht und Gesellschaft.

Rainerman, C. and Levine, H.G. (1997) *Crack in America: Demon Drugs and Social Justice.* Berkeley: University of California Press.

Rennstich, J.K. (2002) 'The New Economy, the Leadership Long Cycle and the Nineteenth K-wave', *Review of International Political Economy* 9: 150.

Rumbaut, R.G., Gonzales, R.G., Komaie, G., Morgan, C.V., and Tafoya-Estrada, R. (2006) 'Immigration and Incarceration. Patterns and Predictors of Imprisonment among First- and Second-Generation Young Adults', in R. Jr Martinez and A. Valenzuela (eds), *Immigration and Crime: Race, Ethnicity and Violence.* New York: New York University Press.

Sabol, W.J. (1989) 'Racially Disproportionate Prison Population in the United States', *Contemporary Crises* 13: 405.

Salvatore, R.D. and Aguirre, C. (eds) (1996) *The Birth of the Penitentiary in Latin America: Essays on Criminology, Prison Reform, and Social Control, 1830–1940.* Austin: University of Texas Press.

Sampson, R. (2006) 'Open Doors Don't Invite Criminals,' *New York Times*, 11 March.

Sampson, R.J. (2012) *Great American City: Chicago and the Enduring Neighborhood Effect.* Chicago: University of Chicago Press.

Schumpeter, J.A. (1943) *Capitalism, Socialism and Democracy.* London: Unwin.

Schumpeter, J.A. (1939) *Business Cycle.* New York: McGraw-Hill.

Sellin, T. (1976) *Slavery and the Penal System.* New York: Elsevier.

Sellin, T. (1944) *Pioneering in Penology.* Philadelphia: University of Pennsylvania Press.

Sellin, T. (1938) *Culture, Conflict and Crime.* New York: Social Science Research Council.

Stowell, J.I. (2007) *Immigration and Crime: Considering the Direct and Indirect Effects of Immigration on Violent Criminal Behavior.* New York: LFB Scholarly Press.

Stowell, J.I., Messner, S.F., Mcgeever, K.F., and Raffalovich, L.E. (2009) 'Immigration and the Recent Violent Crime Drop in the United States: A Pooled, Cross-sectional Time-series Analysis of Metropolitan Areas', *Criminology* 47: 889.

Teti, V. (1993) *La razza maledetta: origini del pregiudizio antimeridionale.* Roma: manifestolibri.

Thompson, E.P. (1971) 'The Moral Economy of the English Crowd in the Eighteenth Century', *Past and Present* 50: 76.

Tonry, M. (ed) (1997) *Ethnicity, Crime, and Immigration: Comparative and Cross-National Perspectives.* Chicago: University of Chicago Press.

Vanneste, C. (2001) *Les chiffres des prisons.* Paris: L'Harmattan.

Wallerstein, I. (1974) *The Modern World-System, vol. I: Capitalist Agriculture and the Origins of the European World-Economy in the Sixteenth Century.* New York/London: Academic Press.

Welch, M. (2002) *Detained: Immigration Laws and the Expanding I.N.S. Jail Complex.* Philadelphia: Temple University Press.

Wickersham Commission 1931 National Commission on Law Observance and Enforcement *Crime and the Foreign Born* Washington: US Government Printing Office. Report No 10 (republished in 1968 by Patterson Smith, Montclair, New Jersey).

Wright, R. (2008) [1944] *Black Boy.* New York: Harper Perennial Modern Classics.

Wright, R. (2005) [1940] *Native Son.* New York: Harper Perennial Modern Classics.

16

Epilogue: The Borders of Punishment: Towards a Criminology of Mobility

Ben Bowling

The predominantly 'White' and wealthy countries of North America, Europe, and Australasia endeavour to protect themselves from what they believe are imminent threats to their territorial integrity and privileged lifestyles. Wealthier enclaves in Asia and elsewhere follow suit. Global population pressures, economic crises, and shifts in political power generate profound insecurities in the old, new, third and fourth worlds alike. Typically dominant groups take defensive measures against external 'enemies' and threaten internal minorities. The result is further conflict and an even greater propensity to migrate. As economic interdependence encourages transnational movements of capital and tends towards a 'borderless world', political and social pressures pull in the opposite direction. (Richmond 1994: xv)

We must all learn to live with ethnocultural diversity, rapid social change, and mass migration. There is no peaceful alternative. (Richmond 1994: 217)

Anthony H. Richmond, whose pioneering studies of racism spanned more than four decades from *Colour Prejudice in Britain* (1954), and *The Colour Problem* (1955), to *Global Apartheid* (1994), concluded in the latter that international migration policies are akin to the formal systems of racial segregation that were brutally enforced in twentieth-century South Africa. Since that book was published 20 years ago, the effects of global apartheid have become even more clearly visible. The trend is towards a racialized world, segregated geographically between the haves and the have-nots, with worldwide systems of pass-laws, stronger and longer walls and fences, databases of suspected and unwanted persons, and prisons filled with 'foreign nationals' who have transgressed criminal or immigration law. As the chapters in this volume have illustrated, borders have become a key locus for discipline and punishment, and have grown ever higher, thicker, and tighter. As an epilogue to this outstanding collection of essays exploring aspects of this development, this chapter considers four questions. First, a conceptual question: to what extent can migration control be considered a criminological problem? Second, an empirical question: what harms flow from contemporary migration control practices and to what extent can these be construed as a form of punishment? Third, a theoretical question: how might we understand the infliction of border-harms in relation to a criminologically inflected theory of global apartheid? Fourth, a practical question threads throughout the essay: what is the role of academic scholarship in thinking about and responding to the harms produced by the punitive border? In other words, what can be made of a criminology of mobility?

Border Work, Criminology, and the Crimmigration Control Industry

The punning title of the book and the conference from which this collection emerged, *The Borders of Punishment*, points to the fuzzy edges and ambiguity inherent in approaching the control of border zones from a criminological perspective. It problematizes the boundaries of existing notions of state punishment, the forms that it takes, the places that it can be imposed, and the sources of its legitimacy. It implies that the border can be the *location of punishment*. This volume also inaugurates a new sub-field—a criminology of mobility—implying that a discipline defined by the study of crime and punishment can bring something to the study of border work.

Two immediate objections to claiming border work as a criminological topic might arise: (1) border crossing is not a crime; and (2) immigration law enforcement is not a form of punishment. Sceptics might claim that the former is a transgression akin to trespass, the latter merely an administrative process. They might also point to the axiom that for something to be called a crime it must cause some kind of injury or loss to a person or to the state. Consider the *Oxford English Dictionary* definition of crime: '[a]n evil or injurious act; an offence, a sin; esp. of a grave character' or 'an act or omission constituting an offence (usually a grave one) against an individual or the state and punishable by law'. Whether the subject is the dishonest taking of property or the use of violence, the culpable infliction of harm lies at the heart of the concept of criminal behaviour.

By contrast, border crossing, in itself, can hardly be construed as a crime. On the contrary, mass border crossing is an essential feature of the late modern world. The process has been accelerated by neo-liberal globalization, and the global capitalist economy, which requires people to be free to move with the flows of money. Literally millions of people cross international borders on foot or by train, plane, automobile, or boat every day for work or pleasure. Within the European Union alone, there are at least 780,000 cross-border commuters—people who live in one EU country and travel daily to work in another (European Commission 2009). The number of people moving permanently or semi-permanently is an accepted part of contemporary life. It is also very extensive. The number of international migrants was estimated to be around 214 million people in 2010 (International Organisation for Migration 2011), a figure with profound implications for the world economy. To take just one element, the value of cash sent by migrant workers back to their home countries was estimated by the World Bank at over US$440 billion in 2010. How, then, can a form of human behaviour that is not only intrinsically harmless, but essential to global economic success, especially for developing countries, be thought of as a criminological subject?

The criminologists' answer is straightforward and draws upon labelling theory and decades of research on other kinds of criminalized (and sometimes eventually decriminalized) groups such as homosexuals, drug takers, and the mentally ill. This work has demonstrated that no act is intrinsically criminal; a crime is an act against which a rule is enforced (Becker 1963). What is important is who feels harmed by the act and the power of those defining the act as criminal in comparison with those against whom the rule is enforced. The first task of the criminological enterprise is therefore to understand *the process of criminalization*: that is, to examine how acts become criminalized, in what ways, and with what effects. A second important task for criminologists is to understand the nature of punishment, the types of pain inflicted or rights withdrawn as a penalty for infraction, and the kinds of justifications that are advanced. The essays in this volume all point towards theory, method, and empirical evidence that begin to engage with these tasks.

A third task is to examine in detail the emergence and operation of systems designed to control behaviour that has been criminalized. One of the many reasons criminologists should care about migration control is that the attempt to control the movement of people across borders has created an industry that parallels the domestic crime control industry (Weber 2002; Weber and Bowling 2004). This migration-control industry is comprised of many, if not all, the elements that make up the (much more intensively studied) crime control industry. It includes mechanisms for intelligence gathering and surveillance; policing and law enforcement; a specialized legal process, courts, and tribunals; and detention centres, prisons, and other means of 'disposing' of cases. It is separate from domestic crime control and 'criminal justice' systems but runs parallel to them, links into them at important nodal points, and extends into transnational space. There are good reasons to think that the migration control industry will become an important and integral element of the emerging system of global social control. The implication is that criminology will be incomplete if it ignores these novel forms of discipline and punishment while the rich theoretical and methodological traditions established within criminology may well have something to offer a new generation of scholars attempting to make sense of these new developments.

Crimmigration law

Law is a suitable starting point for considering the emergence of a parallel system of control situated at the nexus of crime and migration (Dauvergne, Stumpf, and Zedner, Chapters 4, 3, and 2 respectively in this volume). Law defines physical boundaries between nation states and the boundaries between acceptable and unacceptable behaviour. It defines the character of wrongs: separating civil, administrative, and criminal offences. Although modern immigration law is considered administrative, from the very earliest times states have attempted to control border crossing through criminal law. Such laws have designated certain forms of presence—such as vagrancy—as behaviour liable to criminal sanctions as well as administrative sanctions such as deportation (Weber and Bowling 2008). In recent years, the convergence of immigration and criminal law has led to what Juliet Stumpf (2006) has termed 'crimmigration law'.

The convergence of immigration and criminal law has a number of distinctive features. First, border crossing infractions—such as unlawful entry or re-entry, overstaying, attempting to enter with false documents, failure to register, and unlawful employment—have become defined as specific criminal offences. Western politicians and government departments now refer almost universally to 'immigration crime' and emphasize arrest, prosecution, and removal at the forefront of the policy response (Aliverti 2012). People committing these transgressions, described as 'illegal immigrants' for many years, are now being re-cast as a new type of criminal: 'immigration offenders'. Such people are liable not merely to removal or visa or entry restrictions, but also to criminal prosecution and punishment prior to being deported (Stumpf, Chapter 3 in this volume). Second, the criminal grounds for deportation of non-citizens have expanded and the relief available to suspected offenders has been reduced. Thus, relatively minor criminal offences such as shoplifting and drug-possession offences can become grounds for deportation or denial of re-entry and, in some jurisdictions, can be applied retroactively. Third, a range of new criminal offences has been created that criminalizes concealing, harbouring, shielding, aiding, abetting, employing, carrying, and associating with criminalized migrants. Institutional targets such as international airlines can be fined for carrying unlawful migrants, as can government departments or corporations who employ them. Private citizens are also targets. For example, someone who rents a home to a person who has overstayed his or her visa or who drives an illegal entrant to a doctor is liable to criminal penalty. The goal of these policies is to prevent undocumented migrants from accessing public facilities. In Alabama, what the *New York Times* has described as the country's 'cruellest immigration law' is a 'sweeping attempt to terrorize undocumented immigrants … and to make potential criminals of anyone who may work or live with them or show them kindness'.

The convergence of immigration enforcement and criminal justice systems has been facilitated by fundamental shifts in governmental thinking that are common to both systems. Historically, both were essentially reactive. Criminal law and criminal justice were concerned with retribution and rehabilitation 'after the fact', and, while deterrence was integral to penology, it depended essentially on visible forms of punishment for detected offenders following due process of the law. The so-called 'new penology' draws on a pre-emptive approach drawing on notions of 'risk management' based on actuarial calculations (Feeley and Simon 1992). The logic is that through pre-emption, the disreputable, dangerous, and disorderly can be excluded or contained. The risk management approach also extends far beyond criminal justice to securitize other parts of the social system including health, education, housing, and employment, as well as border control. It requires that information is shared and techniques of control—including monitoring of entitlement, execution of warrants, enforcement, detention, removal actions, etc—are coordinated across the piece.

A second unifying trend is that variously described as 'populist punitiveness' or 'authoritarian populism'. In both spheres, there is a clear tendency towards tough talk on both law and order and migration control in pursuit of electoral advantage. Taken together with the shifts towards pre-emption, there are sharp increases in levels of coercion, punishment, and control. The changes in the substantive law described above have been accompanied by shifts in the governmental discourses seeking to legitimate migration enforcement. Like the substantive law, the rhetorical justifications for migration control have become more punitive. The moral case for immigration control has become highly focused on migrants as deviants and rule-breakers, people who have cheated their way into a country, 'cut in front of the line', or are 'bogus' in some other way. They are also portrayed as a source of danger in the form of the drug trafficker, violent criminal, or terrorist. New folk devils have been added to the pantheon. Among these, there are few people portrayed as more evil than people-traffickers (Lee, Chapter 7 in this volume). The border itself has also been re-cast as a protective membrane, a buffer against drugs, guns, and dangerous people. Deportation has also been re-cast specifically as a form of penalty and as criminal disposal rather than simply the consequence of an administrative process. This is particularly relevant for the long-term lawful permanent residents for whom deportation imposes by force a very significant deprivation of liberty (see Barker, Stumpf, Gibney, Chapters 13, 3, and 12 respectively in this volume).

Crimmigration control technologies

Just as crime control is a motor for technological innovation (Bowling, Marks, and Murphy 2008), the migration control industry is also driving the development of scientific endeavour, product design, and manufacturing. Technology in both spheres can be described as a 'force enabler' increasing the capacity for social control (Bowling, Marks, and Murphy 2008). Defensive technologies such as fences—sometimes extending for thousands of miles—fortified with razor wire and electricity define and defend borders and fortify border posts and detention centres. Border control increasingly draws upon military force including battlefield weapons and the full panoply of military forces on land and sea. New hybrid forces such as FRONTEX (the European Agency for the Management of Operational Cooperation at the External Borders of the Member States of the European Union) with militarized Rapid Border Intervention Teams (RABIT) operating at Europe's Southern border is just one example of a global trend.

Information communication technologies are also deployed here and include databases of visa applicants, lost and stolen travel documents, mobile fingerprint devices, and so on. Information is collected through human intelligence sources such as the deployment of secret intelligence agents overseas, the posting of immigration liaison officers in foreign embassies and airports, and the cultivation of informers in source and transit countries (Bowling 2010; Bowling and Sheptycki 2012). Information is increasingly shared transnationally. Contemporary border information systems, such as the UK's e-borders, collects arrivals and departure information, while carriers provide advance passenger records electronically. The names, dates of birth, nationality, and travel document details are then checked against multi-agency watch-lists before boarding. According to the UK government, the intention is to create a clearer picture of passenger movements in and out of countries: '[t]his wealth of information will help border control, law enforcement and intelligence agencies, and other Government departments to target their activity.'

One example of a strategic immigration and border security initiative can be found in 'The Five Country Conference', comprised of the United Kingdom, Canada, the United States, Australia, and New Zealand, which aims to prevent identity fraud, ensure economic prosperity and enhance border security, protect public safety, and provide protection against 'violent foreign criminals'. In 2009, the five governments signed a joint agreement to enable biometric data sharing for immigration purposes. This 'high value data sharing protocol' allows countries to share fingerprint records for matching against immigration databases in all of the other countries. Where matches are found, officers share biographical information on a bilateral basis. Databases of criminal records including fingerprints, DNA, travel documents, and details of deported aliens have been created across law enforcement agencies, immigration, and prisons (Aas, Chapter 1 in this volume). In this context, prisons have become 'a site of information gathering on what is otherwise a transient, fragmented population' (Bosworth 2008: 210).

Crimmigration policing

Domestic policing and border control are converging. In many places, what have previously been distinct law-enforcement agencies with different traditions, organizational cultures, lines of responsibility, and accountability are now becoming linked formally and informally (Pickering and Weber, Chapter 5 in this volume). It is now increasingly clear that there is continuity between traditional domestic territorial policing, the 'police like' activities of border control agencies, and transnational policing organizations (Bowling and Sheptycki 2012). Traditionally, the powers of border control agents were limited to checking travel documents at borders, with highly circumscribed powers to detain people for questioning and to refuse entry. During the mid-twentieth century, border agencies were expanded significantly and were shaped by domestic police through secondment from established forces alongside massive financial and technological investment and training (Weber and Bowling 2004). This also involved the development of a significant criminal investigation, prosecution, and detention capacity. Importantly, this was housed within a single agency; focusing first on breaches of immigration law it subsequently expanded into trafficking, forgery, and counterfeiting. In the United Kingdom, it has long been an ambition to create a single frontier force and, in the immediate future, the National Crime Agency will have a unified border policing command. In the United States, immigration officers are now the largest armed law-enforcement agency in the US Federal Government (Stumpf, Chapter 3 in this volume).

Pickering and Weber (Chapter 5 in this volume) argue that border policing has become transversal—cutting across the boundaries between organizations, internal and external, and public and private life. They note that immigration authorities are becoming more police-like and show how border control agents operate extensively within domestic space, having been granted powers of arrest, search, and seizure within the nation state (Weber and Bowling 2004). Police are also becoming much more involved in immigration enforcement, policing both external and internal borders (Pickering and Weber, Chapter 5 in this volume). The gathering of intelligence from various sources, targeted raids by armed immigration enforcers, mass arrests, and prosecution are now occurring frequently in many countries (Brotherton and Barrios, Stumpf, Chapters 11 and 3 respectively in this volume). The policing of migration also operates well beyond the borders of the nation state both virtually, through shared intelligence systems, and physically, in the form of immigration liaison officers posted overseas. In some cases, in the Caribbean islands for example, US immigration officers work out of foreign airports conducting 'pre-clearance' checks so that passengers can effectively be admitted to, or excluded from, US territory before even leaving the point of origin (Weber and Bowling 2004; Bowling 2010).

The academic discipline of police research, a sub-field of criminology, should now pay attention to the work of border police, a neglected cousin within the wider 'law-enforcement family'. Observational work on border agents—including immigration service, customs, airport security, and others—shows very clearly that their everyday work is very similar to that of their equivalent uniformed patrol officers and plain clothes detectives. They are engaged in surveillance of general and suspect populations, stopping individuals to carry out interviews or detaining them for extensive questioning, conducing searches of their bags, clothing, and possessions, filing intelligence reports, and maintaining databases. Whether this is at the border, within domestic space, or in the transnational realm, they work just like the police (Bowling 2010).

The shifting relationship between domestic police, border protection agencies, the military, and others in the security sector has profound implications for the provision of safety. It fundamentally unsettles the boundaries between interior and exterior, domestic and foreign, criminal justice and regulatory agencies, and military force and civilian governance (see Aas, Chapter 1 in this volume). The result is a much closer connection between all of these agencies, and the creation of new hybrid ones. Organizational boundaries are reconfigured as domestic agencies become more closely meshed with one another, but also with transnational entities (Bowling and Sheptycki 2012). All of these developments raise troubling and difficult questions about legitimacy, fairness and effectiveness, accountability, and control.

Immcarceration

The convergence of crime and migration control is also evident in what might be called *immcarceration* (Kalhan 2010). A 'secure estate', made up of immigration detention centres, holding cells, and prisons—which only came into existence in the 1970s and 1980s—is growing rapidly to contain people straddling the criminal-migrant boundary (Bosworth and Kaufman, Chapters 8 and 9 respectively in this volume). This 'secure estate' houses people who have committed crimes detected while attempting to cross borders such as drug couriers, those who have committed 'immigration crimes' such as illegal entry and overstaying, and foreign nationals convicted of crime within domestic space and who are scheduled to be deported at the end of their sentences. It also includes the so-called 'non-returnables', individuals who cannot be removed to their home country or anywhere else because they are stateless, cannot verify their identity, or are at risk of torture or victimization if they are deported. Immigration detention centres look and, in many cases, feel like prisons. They have a distinctly punitive and criminal character. The relationship between political and economic marginality and the fissures of race, ethnicity, and nationality have led to the emergence of what we might call the cosmopolitan or 'multicultural' prison (Bowling, Phillips, and Sheptycki 2012; Phillips 2012). Foreign nationals make up one in every five European prisoners and in some countries foreign nationals comprise a majority of all prisoners (see Aas, Kaufman, Ugelvik, and Bosworth, Chapters 1, 9, 10, and 8 respectively in this volume). The convergence of immigration and crime control has produced a system of inclusion and exclusion that simultaneously defines what is permissible within nation state borders by casting human beings as a problem belonging to another nation state. In such cases, the justification for imprisonment is merely exclusion. There is no pretence that the purpose of imcarceration is rehabilitation or reform; its manifest goals are incapacitation, deportation, and deterrence.

The Harms of Crimmigration Control

Crime control systems are intended to inflict harm on their objects (Bowling 2011). As Nils Christie (1982) points out, punishment is concerned first and foremost with the infliction of pain. The painful nature of punishment is far more obvious when it takes the form of whipping, branding, and hanging, but it is still abundantly clear in the case of imprisonment and other punishments of the soul (Foucault 1977). If it is to 'work' it has to hurt. The substantive intentions of this pain infliction are, of course, righteous. Punishment is intended to right wrongs, maintain order, provide safety, and deliver what the offender deserves in a deontological sense. Debates about criminal justice are, therefore, often discussed in terms of the proportionality between the seriousness of the offence committed by the individual and the severity of the punishment inflicted by the state. What then can be said about the pains inflicted by the newly emerging system of crimmigration control and how—if at all—can these be justified in terms of some notion of the good?

Consider the nature of the pain inflicted on the body or soul of the transgressor. One way to characterize this pain is as the withdrawal of rights, the most fundamental of which is the right to life. There is good evidence that the securitization and militarization of the border have led to injury and death at the hands of border guards who have shot people attempting to climb over fences, or have beaten them to death during capture or detention. Deaths have also been caused by electric fences and landmines at the border and in people taking extreme risks in border crossing, including dying from dehydration in the desert, drowning at sea, jumping out of windows to avoid police raids, or committing suicide in a desperate attempt to enable a family to be granted leave to remain. According to Weber and Pickering's (2011) detailed study, more than 16,000 people have died at the European border in the past 20 years, with countless more dying in the world's other border zones.

The non-lethal physical harms inflicted on irregular migrants are also wide-ranging. These include harm to the body through the infliction of injury, disease, malnourishment, hunger, infection, and unwanted pregnancies. Johansen (Chapter 14 this volume) shows how concerted efforts by various organizations effectively deny rejected asylum seekers (and other irregular migrants) access to the basic necessities of life: such as money, shelter, clothing, medicine, and food. Systematically deprived of *Lebensmittel*—the German word for food, but translated literally as the *means to live*—migrants are effectively manipulated out of the country. People who are detected, arrested, and detained by the authorities are deprived of fundamental rights to liberty, freedom of movement, association, family life, and privacy. Those who are deported are deprived of a range of social, political, and economic rights to work, health care, welfare, and state aid. This is particularly evident in the case of established long-term residents who may experience the loss of family, home, work, and savings built up over decades of residence (Gibney, Chapter 12 in this volume). Some deportees are returned to places they left as children or young adults where they may have no family or social contacts or even any knowledge of the country. As Chan (2005) argues, 'deportation is about the desire to control difference ... it is not just an administrative practice, but also a political practice, a disciplinary tactic and an instrument of population regulation'.

The harms of migration control policy are very clear. But does the infliction of these harms amount to punishment? Punishment in a penological sense involves the infliction of harm or pain, by the state, on an offender, for a crime. Are the burdens of migration control sufficiently similar to criminal penalties to justify calling them punishment? Perhaps they are better described merely as the unpleasant side effects of an otherwise benign attempt to regulate the movement of people across borders, as the unintended consequences of action, collateral damage, or obiter punishments. One way in which immigration penalties differ very significantly from criminal penalties is that they do not generally trigger due process protections. The criminal law, in this sense, is only for citizens (Zedner, Chapter 2 in this volume).

It could be argued that the justifications for migration control start from a different set of premises from those concerned with crime control. Criminal justice systems are typically justified either in backward-looking terms—that offenders deserve to be punished for the harm they have caused to others—or in forward-looking terms—that punishing offenders will create a safer society through deterrence, rehabilitation, or incapacitation. Critical perspectives add that in fact the un-spoken justifications for punishment are the management of surplus populations, dividing working-class populations, draining away revolutionary dissent amongst the 'dangerous classes', and generating a captive pool of low-paid industrial labour.

Formally, stop and search at airports or on the streets, the use of holding cells, street level stop and search, and detention in immigration centres pending removal is not geared towards punishment, but merely towards administrative control (Weber and Bowling 2012). And yet, these mechanisms are *experienced as punitive* as well as merely intrusive, coercive, and exclusionary. Moreover, contemporary migration control does seem to point to the emergence of penological justifications for the infliction of pain that are necessarily required. In the speeches of senior politicians in the overdeveloped world, 'immigration offenders' are portrayed as immoral beings who deserve to have certain burdens inflicted on them. Thus, those involved in organized immigration crime, facilitation, harbouring, carrying, and employing 'illegal immigrants' are said to deserve severe punishments. Particularly risky people—those who pose some kind of threat, even while this is only suspected rather than actual—are also said to deserve certain kinds of pre-emptive punitive intervention. Other kinds of immigration offenders—the bogus or 'failed' asylum seeker, the economic migrant, the person who tries to jump the queue—are liable to punishment at least to the extent that they should be prevented from taking up certain kinds of benefits—rights to remain in a wealthier country, to work there, or have the benefit of health care, etc. It is evident from empirical research on decisions to detain migrants that enforcement mechanisms are intended to serve an explicit deterrent function (Weber 2002). It is obvious that tough border control policies are intended to send a deterrent signal to would-be migrants who do not qualify as the 'brightest and best'.

The powers to coerce, monitor, and punish have migrated from the criminal justice system to inhabit border control agencies hitherto thought of as adminis-trative. It is now clear that the crimmigration control industry has very extensive surveillant, defensive, and carceral power. Whether or not these powers can or should be seen as punitive in a strictly penological sense is perhaps a moot point. It is may be more productive to think of these measures as '*punitive* rather than punish-ment' (Aas, Chapter 1 in this volume). As Stumpf shows in Chapter 3 of this collection, the effect of the *process* of crimmigration law enforcement is punitive. It is now clear that pain inflicted through coercion, incarceration, exclusion, and deportation of 'crimmigrants' is not merely incidental. It is used by the state for the purpose of punishment and is experienced as such by those against whom it is inflicted.

Theorizing a Criminology of Mobility: Thinking Beyond Global Apartheid

Apartheid—literally apartness—is the Afrikaans word for racial separateness or segregation that was used to define the policy of the government of South Africa in the second half of the twentieth century (Omond 1986). It built on principles and legislation going back several hundreds of years that inspired such policies as the partition of India and ancient practices of expulsion, banishment, and segregation the world over. The laws of apartheid required that all must be classified by race, and this provided the basis of the laws governing where people were allowed to live, work, and be educated, and under what conditions. It is worth pondering the fact that apartheid, which once provided the auspices to criminalize transgression of geographical and racial boundaries, is now itself defined as a crime against humanity by the 2002 Rome Statue.

Anthony Richmond, whose work was cited at the beginning of this chapter, argues that the legislation and regulatory systems designed to prevent migration to Western Europe, North America, and Australasia are remarkably similar to those adopted by South Africa to control the movement of people within and outside its borders (1994: 210). The basis of the world system, for Richmond, is one that discriminates against the poor in favour of the rich and places black and brown people in a subordinate position to whites. Contemporary immigration policies seek to encourage rich white people, who are seen as readily assimilable and pose no threat to the dominant language, culture, or religion. Nonetheless, rich countries require unskilled labour in such fields as manufacturing, agriculture, domestic service, and many of the dirtiest and more dangerous occupations. These require a large pool of internal and external labour which has to be regulated and managed, marginalized, casualized, rendered temporary, and granted only restricted rights.

Clearly, economic power is a driver of these forms of inclusion and exclusion. However, Susan Smith's (1989) work shows that ideological themes based upon 'race' pervade both high political discourse and common-sense racism in wider society. For Smith, racial ideology is the medium through which the popular legitimacy of iniquitous social and economic arrangements is secured. Racial segregation, whether de facto or de jure, is a politically constructed problem and a policy outcome. The question then becomes, how can such unjust practices be sustained in countries—such as those of Western Europe and North America—which pride themselves on notions of equality and fair play? For Smith, institutional racism—an implicit variant of apartheid—is a pervasive process sustained across many different social institutions whose procedures have the effect of producing a mutually reinforcing pattern of racial inequality. She argues that organizations allocating power and resources develop conventions that distinguish 'the deserving from the undeserving and the reputable from the debased' in ways that advantage or disadvantage people competing for goods and services (Smith 1989: 102). These conventions often invoke attributes of race or ethnicity either explicitly or implicitly as criteria for inclusion and exclusion in dispensing scarce resources.

Not only are the *practices* deployed in Western migration control remarkably similar to those of the apartheid system, but the *ideological justifications* articulated to defend these measures also echo those advanced by the dominant white minority in South Africa (Richmond 1994). In some quarters of the mainstream political class, and among right-wing commentators, the justifications for migration control are explicitly racist. References are made to the supposed need to preserve the 'white race' from being contaminated or over-run by others who are inferior in terms of high and low culture, intelligence, and beauty. In these extreme versions of racial justification, but also in the more moderate ones, arguments are put forward about the need to preserve ethnic identity, and to protect religion and language, as well as cultural and state institutions. Western migration policies, like apartheid, are justified based on the need to preserve state security and to defend the nation against threats to law and order. The desire to preserve economic privilege, and to exclude migrants from employment, housing, education, and health services, is also a central to this and coupled with the wish to regulate population movement. Policies of separation, containment, and exclusion and their justifications, which were argued forcefully in South Africa until the demise of the apartheid regime, are now being promulgated across Western Europe, North America, and Australasia and are being emulated in the more powerful of the emerging economies.

In developing an agenda for a criminology of mobility, it seems absolutely critical that researchers engage fully with theories of racism and ethnicity because it is clear from many of the essays in this collection that phenomena are racially coded and have racialized outcomes. People identified as black, brown, or yellow are cast as the 'usual suspects', become the targets of enforcement action because they seem to be out of place, and then become the 'property' of border protection agencies, the police, and the prison (Bowling, Phillips, and Sheptycki 2012). Border enforcement agencies, domestic street-policing, and the 'secure estate' of prisons and immigration detention facilities all invoke racial characteristics. The nexus between immigration and criminal law enforcement has the effect of immobilizing people in the 'global South' and entrenching their position among the over-policed and over-imprisoned in the 'global North'.

One of the key goals of a research agenda in this area should be to explore the intersection between 'race', political economy, and the coercive powers of the state in the new and hybrid forms that are growing up in the nexus between crime and immigration control. The task for future research in transnational and comparative criminology is to 'make visible new variations on racial and ethnic discourse and their effect on the everyday experience of the coercive powers of border protection, policing and imprisonment' (Bowling, Phillips, and Sheptycki 2012: 43). The tentative work in this field has shown that similar patterns of inclusion and exclusion are evident in immigration enforcement, street policing, and in the prisons.

Racial attributes are no longer as explicit as they once were in the era of the English colour bar, Jim Crown segregation in the United States, the 'White Australia' policy, or South African apartheid. The 'whites only' signs are consigned to history, but today's racial exclusion also has its explicit edges. The use of nationality, sometimes coded in racial terms, is still justified in most countries as a ground for targeting people for stop and search and interrogation at borders and domestically (Weber and Bowling 2012). Immigration police target migrant workers, using 'foreign appearance' as the ground for identity checks following other contact with police. As Vigneswaran (Chapter 6 in this volume) shows, mobility is often criminalized where migrants are victims of a criminal act. Migratory status and ethnicity are intertwined in many cases. Officials in many countries refer to their entire ethnic minority population as 'immigrants' or 'foreigners' irrespective of their nationality or place of birth. It is well documented that ethnic and racial difference are often used as the basis for suspicion and as grounds for coercive and intrusive practices (Bowling and Phillips 2007; Weber and Bowling 2012). Ironically, systems and structures created to combat discrimination against ethnic minority communities, promote equality, and help integrate communities are now used to identify, anticipate, and control the supposed threats of undocumented migration. It is unclear where exactly these policies are headed, but there are certainly signs that ethnic separation is back on the domestic agenda based on the idea of the inassimilability of migrants. Mainstream commentators and political leaders in many countries—Angela Merkel, David Cameron, and Nikolas Sarkozy among them—have condemned multiculturalism as a failure, seemingly oblivious to the social and cultural realities of mass migration, human difference, diversity, and mixedness in the contemporary global metropolis.

Conclusion

Domestic crime control systems are gradually being shaped by the transnational turn. Police, prosecutors, and prison officers are becoming increasingly 'globally aware' and talking more frequently to their counterparts in other countries. Practices such as transnational police cooperation; mutual legal assistance in the investigation of crime; prosecutorial and judicial cooperation; rendition and extradition of suspects; deportation of convicts; and the transfer of prisoners are now commonplace. Criminal law enforcement is increasingly considered a transnational business. Nonetheless, the domestic crime control industry remains largely moored to the nation state in which it was built. The migration control industry, by contrast, was never so securely anchored in domestic space. The tasks involved in controlling the flows of people (and goods) through land frontiers, seaports, and airports, and in linking across seas and international airspace are, and always have been, intrinsically transnational. This border work has germinated, taken root, and is now flourishing in the liminal spaces, the nowhere and no-man's-lands, between states. The crimmigration control infrastructure—customs and immigration facilities, airport holding cells, refugee camps, exclusion zones, and immigration detention centres—has become a new transnational space in its own right. The agents of crimmigration control inhabit a space of flows rather than a space of places. They are mobile and tend to be international in outlook. They have close links with their counterparts in other countries (in some places they are co-located) and they have good links with customs, airport security, and secret intelligence agencies involved in 'high policing'. It seems predictable that as the coercive and intrusive powers of the state grow beyond national boundaries, crimmigration control will become the keystone in the architecture of global governance and social control.

We live in a world society characterized by interdependence so deep that the future of the planet and its inhabitants are entirely bound by one shared destiny. There exists no supranational government, but it is clear that the rich and powerful states of the world are working individually and collectively to 'protect their privileged position in much the same way that Afrikaners and others of European descent sought to maintain their dominance in South Africa' (Richmond 1994: 216). The fear, harboured in the over-developed world, is that as the developing economies outside the West gain economic and political power, Western hegemony and territorial integrity will be undermined as global migration becomes normal. For Richmond, the attempt by a coalition of Western governments to impose a system of global apartheid 'is bound to fail' (Richmond 1994: 216). Like its South African variant, no system of segregation by class, gender, or race can ever be legitimate or consistent with democratic values and principles. No wall, however high, will ever contain the flow of human beings moving to find the basics of human life—food, water, shelter—and beyond this the pursuit of opportunities for work and the hope of a better life. Global apartheid, therefore, will eventually collapse 'as surely as the South African version has done' (Richmond 1994).

In the meantime, we live in a world polarized between a 'gilded but insecure elite and a threatening temporarily subjugated mass' (Reiner 2010: 258). Neo-liberal and authoritarian values lead states to build longer, stronger, and taller fences. Racist ideologies linger to create a major social division globally. Within local contexts, marginalization, criminalization, and 'prisonization' remain redolent with ethnic and racialized discourses. Economic and racial differences are en-trenched within and between societies. If a fairer and more cosmopolitan future is to be created, a radical shift in global political economy is required and the mechanisms of exclusion, segregation, and criminalization must be torn down. Responding to the global apartheid system created around the criminal-migrant control nexus requires us to move beyond 'post-imperial melancholia' saturated with 'race talk' and fixated on fears of cultural incompatibility (Gilroy 2006). An alternative 'multicultural conviviality' (Gilroy 2006) has the potential to engender a global 'capacity to live with difference' (Hall 1992: 359). Radical thinking about decriminalizing migration could build on a tolerant, humane, and pluralistic 'planetary humanism' which is global in outlook and cosmopolitan in ethos and values (Gilroy 2006). We need to promote economic equality through the creation of networks of 'connectedness and solidarity' that 'resonate across boundaries, reach across distances, and evade other cultural and economic obstacles' (Gilroy 2001: 5).

This collection of essays can be read in the spirit of this cosmopolitan vision, although it also shows that current policies are heading down the wrong road and illustrates some of the complexities that are inherent in halting and eventually reversing some dangerous trends. The volume provides ideas, information, and insights that can help us to understand the ways in which crime and migration control systems are converging in the powers of law, surveillance, policing, and detention. It helps us to understand the circuits of power that bind the crimmigration control industry together and make it so dangerous and damaging to human lives. It documents the legal convolutions and the surveillant and coercive mechanisms that are coming into being and the horrific damage that is being inflicted on the human beings at whom it is directed. The final word—for now—is that a critical criminology of mobility is an urgent and important theoretical, empirical, and practical project. It has the potential to provide tools with which to understand and resist the power of the coercive, punitive, and carceral arms of the emerging transnational state system.

References

Aliverti, A. (2012) 'Making People Criminal: The Role of the Criminal Law in Immigration Enforcement', *Theoretical Criminology* 16(4): 417.

Becker, H. (1963) *Outsiders*. New York: Free Press.

Bosworth, M. (2008) 'Border Control and the Limits of the Sovereign State', *Social and Legal Studies* 17: 199.

Bowling, B. (2011) 'Transnational Criminology and the Globalisation of Harm Production', in M. Bosworth and M. Hoyle (eds), *What is Criminology?* Oxford: Oxford University Press.

Bowling, B. (2010) *Policing the Caribbean: Transnational Security Cooperation in Practice*. Oxford: Oxford University Press.

Bowling, B. and Phillips, C. (2007) 'Disproportionate and Discriminatory: Reviewing the Evidence on Stop and Search', *Modern Law Review* 70(6): 936.

Bowling, B. and Sheptycki, S. (2012) *Global Policing*. London: Sage.

Bowling, B., Marks, A., and Murphy, C. (2008) 'Crime Control Technologies', in R. Brownsword and K. Yeung, *Regulating Technologies*, Oxford: Hart Publishing.

Bowling, B., Phillips, C., and Sheptycki, J. (2012) 'Race, Political Economy and the Coercive State', in J. Peay and T. Newburn (eds), *Policing, Politics and Control*. Oxford: Hart Publishing.

Chan, W. (2005) 'Crime, Deportation and the Regulation of Immigrants in Canada', *Crime, Law and Social Change* 44: 153.

Christie, N. (1982) *The Limits to Pain*. London: Wiley.

European Commission (2009) *Scientific Report on the Mobility of Cross-Border Workers within the EU-27/EEA/EFTA Countries*, European Commission DG Employment and Social Affairs.

Feeley, M. and Simon, J. (1992) 'The New Penology: Notes on the Emerging Strategy of Corrections and its Implications', *Criminology*, 30(4): 449.

Gilroy, P. (2006) *After Empire or Postcolonial Melancholia*. New York: Columbia University Press.

Gilroy, P. (2001) *Against Race: Imagining Political Culture Beyond the Color Line*. Boston: Harvard University Press.

Foucault, M. (1977) *Discipline and Punish: The Birth of the Prison*. London: Penguin.

Hall, S. (1992) 'New Ethnicities', in J. Donald and A. Rattansi (eds), *Race, Culture and Difference*. London: Sage and Open University Press.

International Organisation for Migration (2011) *World Migration Report 2011*. Geneva: IOM.

Kalhan, A. (2010) 'Rethinking Immigration Detention', *Columbia Law Review, Sidebar* 110: 24.

Omond, R. (1986) *The Apartheid Handbook: A Guide to South Africa's Everyday Racial Policies*. Harmondsworth: Penguin.

Phillips, C. (2012) *The Multicultural Prison*. Oxford: Clarendon Press.

Reiner, R. (2010) *The Politics of the Police*. (4th edn) Oxford: Oxford University Press.

Smith, S.J. (1989) *The Politics of 'Race' and Residence*. London: Polity.

Stumpf, J.P. (2006) 'The Crimmigration Crisis: Immigrants, Crime, and Sovereign Power', *American University Law Review* 56: 367.

Weber, L. (2002) 'The Detention of Asylum Seekers: 20 Reasons Why Criminologists Should Care', *Current Issues in Criminal Justice* 14(1): 9.

Weber, L. and Bowling, B. (eds) (2012) *Stop and Search: Police Power in a Global Context*. London: Routledge.

Weber, L. and Bowling, B. (2008) 'Valiant Beggars and Global Vagabonds: Select, Eject and Immobilize', *Theoretical Criminology* 12(3): 355.

Weber, L. and Bowling, B. (2004) 'Policing Migration: A Framework for Investigating the Regulation of Mobility', *Policing and Society* 14(3): 195.

Weber, L. and Pickering, S. (2011) *Globalization and Borders: Death at the Global Frontier*. London: Palgrave Macmillan.

Index

Printed and bound by CPI Group (UK) Ltd, Croydon, CR0 4YY